In honor of those who died in battle with the 191st Assault Helicopter Company (1967–1971)

Every person who fought for this nation has a story; all are important in their own realm, all should be told in their own light, and that gem hidden within can only be found by the true seeker.

—James Fischer
Kingsville, Texas

Contents

Foreword

Film footage of the Vietnam War almost always depicts iconic scenes of UH-1 "Huey" helicopters as they *slick* in American troops to hot landing zones under heavy enemy fire. The 191st Assault Helicopter Company (AHC), the "Boomerangs," knew the routine well. It led all other assault-helicopter companies in the Twelfth Combat Aviation Group in total combat flying in 1968. Each 191st chopper came with a bright-orange boomerang painted on its nose section to illustrate its motto: *Boomerangs always come back*. Tragically, not always.

Reminiscent of the author Ernest Hemingway, Major (MAJ) John D. Falcon (Ret.) delves deep into what is true about war and the human condition in his raw and gritty history of helicopter warfare at the height of the Vietnam conflict. Only a Vietnam vet and former member of the 191st could accurately recreate the sights and sounds of the Vietnam battlefields, or show us the fear and horror in witnessing close friends torn to pieces. MAJ Falcon gives the reader just that.

Even though America has been almost continuously at war since 1918—WWI, WWII, Korea, Vietnam, the War on Terror—only a minute percentage of its citizens have actually served in the military and gone to war. The collapse of the World Trade Center on 9/11, repeated attacks on the US and other Western nations, the ghastly spectacle of terrorist beheadings and massacres of Christians, and the nearly twenty years of American troops fighting terrorism in Iraq and Afghanistan have made remarkably little impact on the lives of most Americans. Other than for those who have lost loved ones to hostile action, we have a tendency to forget the past and move on.

The War on Terror will be known as America's longest war. WWI and WWII were wars to end all wars. Korea was the "Forgotten War." Vietnam was the war of the forgotten soldier. Those who fought in Vietnam—and were regarded by protesters at home as "baby killers"—slipped back in-country afterward, as though they should be ashamed. Many, if not most, locked their pain inside and have only reluctantly talked about their experiences, except to other veterans.

"We tried to tell you about this pain forty years ago," a generation of Vietnam vets say, "but no one wanted to listen."

MAJ Falcon penetrates the protective wall that surrounds many Vietnam veterans, a wall that in the past prevented them from telling their stories, in their personal perspective, about soldiers and airmen in combat who lived with violence and death. The grisly scenes he describes are accurate, raw, and unembellished—helicopter crews like sitting ducks on LZs under fire; medevacs risking their own lives to rescue the wounded; infantry soldiers landing into hell against an entrenched enemy; gunships providing cover fire against machine guns, RPGs, and antiaircraft fire—all seen through the eyes of grunts in the air and on the ground.

At the same time, he provides comprehensive insight through a range of action that shows the assault-helicopter company as a cohesive unit composed of many different individuals and positions, all working together toward a common goal and mission. Large-scale airmobile operations brought the different factions together into a functioning force. Slick pilots, gunship pilots, door gunners, crew chiefs, Air Force fast movers, artillery, infantry, command-and-control, company commanders, battalion commanders—all saw the same events unfold, but from different positions and perspectives.

The Freedom Shield's descriptive power moves from the intensely personal voice of an infantryman leaping out of a hovering Huey under fire to see his best buddy cut down, to the big picture of commanders controlling the action from the sky, or commanders at corps and theater level moving colored pins on a map. No two levels shared the same threat level or viewpoint, but each of the warriors telling his part of the story contribute to the rich tapestry of what it actually is like to face death in mortal combat.

The numerous veterans who contributed to this work feel obligated to speak for those who died gallantly as members of the 191st AHC, and to tell those stories that might otherwise have vanished into history and time. The names of those who gave their all appear here in honor of their service and sacrifice. The families of these men suffered, perhaps, the greatest loss of all.

—Charles W. Sasser, Army Special Forces (Ret.)
Author of *One Shot-One Kill, Hill 488, Night Fighter,*
The Walking Dead: A Marine's Story of Vietnam,
and other works about the Vietnam War

Acknowledgments

Special gratitude is owed to the several hundred men who served with the 191st Assault Helicopter Company and who furnished excerpts, materials, and photos, and assisted in locating missing links in their stories. With far too many to name without risk of leaving out key persons who contributed immeasurably in this effort, I render my sincerest gratitude to all concerned. In effect, it has been a monumental effort on the part of many, and their outcome is truly a gift to all who served with the 191st in Vietnam.

Special thanks are due to my wife, Irma, for her undying loyalty and support during my tours of duty, for the care of our children and household during my absence, and for her strong encouragement to create this book for the sake of all who served with the 191st. Equally enthusiastic were my son, Christopher, and daughter, Monica, who frequently screened my drafts. Greatest of all contributions go to my editor, Val M. Mathews of The Exit 271 Studio, who worked tirelessly with me on the craft of creative writing, story structure, and language; Colonel Clarence A. "Bud" Patnode Jr. (Ret.), who helped immeasurably with weapon technology and the overview of unit development and initial employment, as well as proofing the final manuscript; Chief Warrant Officer Five Roger B. Stickney (Ret.), who graciously provided the glossary and helped tremendously with proofing and technical writing assistance; Specialist Five (SP5) Roy Kekoa Ahuna, who graciously provided the cover photo and the photographs inside. Furthermore, gratitude and appreciation go to the staff of Mountain Arbor Press and Casemate Publishers.

CHAPTER I

Ben Tre—A Bloody Fight

But this was Vietnam; life here perched on the unpredictable, always about to take a turn.

In war, life has a way of turning on a dime. It is often a small choice that determines who lives and who sacrifices their young lives. The Vietnam War was no different than any other bloody war; however, for the young guys who lived it, breathed its vigorous stench of rot and mud, the Vietnam War was like no other.

In retrospect, life was simple here: turn left, you live; turn right, you die. The Boomerang, Bounty Hunter, and Green Delta aircrews of the 191st Assault Helicopter Company (AHC) had their share of both choices. Either way, these choices left lasting wounds.

By late morning on September 30, 1968, the combat operation of the 191st AHC forged ahead like any other day. The quiet Specialist Four (SP4) Glenn Lawfield, a striking youngster with clean-cut looks, always available with a pleasant demeanor and a warm smile, reported that morning as gunner for Boomerang One-Three, a lift ship that was a Huey configured for troop transport, or a *slick* for short.

"I'm Boomerang One-Three Golf, correct, sir?" Lawfield asked Warrant Officer One (WO1) Dave Perez, his aircraft commander (AC).

SP4 Andy Johnson came up from behind and smacked Lawfield on the back. "If he still *remembers* what to do."

Although Perez, Lawfield, and Johnson were Boomerang One-Three's regular assigned crew, Lawfield hadn't flown in weeks. On this day, he volunteered to substitute for someone else. The crew was together again, and Johnson and Lawfield were happy for it.

Lawfield cocked his head and flashed Johnson that pleasant smile. Lawfield hailed from near Detroit, Michigan, and bunked next to his buddy, Johnson. The two were barely out of high school and acted like high school buddies, inseparable and always joking around.

While Lawfield and Johnson prepared for their morning's mission, they chatted about home and what they would do when they returned to the States. They both had made a pact to visit each other once they were safely back on friendly soil.

"Hey, Johnson!" Lawfield called to his best buddy. "When you come up to visit me in Detroit, I'll introduce you to the finest women in America. That is, if you still *remember* what to do." They both laughed.

Lawfield mounted the aircraft's M60 machine guns on their pintles. He swung each to its fore and aft limit, ensuring that if needed, they could traverse their full range of motion. It would be unforgiving if a weapon hung up at the wrong moment. The thought of surviving this day hung foremost in Lawfield's mind, as it did in the minds of each crewmember.

With mission preparations completed, Boomerang One-Three's morning unfolded in an uneventful routine as the entire Boomerang flight took to the air.

The last wisps of fog drifted up from the jungle and evaporated as the morning sun heated the vast network of rice paddies. From above, the scene appeared tranquil. For a brief moment, its beauty could hold a man in its sway like a seductive woman. Nevertheless, behind the veil—deep in the dense green palms, tall green grasses, and underground mazes of intricate tunnels—lurked the enemy, trained and ready to kill. The American aircrews remained on edge.

With the cooler monsoon season now gone, humidity and tropical heat aggravated combat tensions. The pungent smell of mold and the sickening, almost-flowery aroma of decaying mud filled the crews' nostrils and permanently embedded in their gear. Helmet headbands, soaked with sweat, compressed their weight on aircrew skulls. Neck agony grew by the hour.

Tolerable, Crew Chief Johnson thought, *in comparison to battle stress*.

Lawfield pulled his helmet off and wiped sweat from his brow. Anticipating enemy gunfire from the tree line below, he cleared the moisture from his eyes to best view the field. He was well aware that mere seconds could make a life-or-death difference. If fired upon, Lawfield had to volley back without delay. The anxiety racked the nerves of everyone on board. With a nimble finger posed on the trigger of an M60 machine gun, Lawfield remained focused on the jungle below. His heart pounded while the slick ascended out of the landing zone (LZ) and climbed to a safe altitude.

All guns on the assault aircrafts remained silent, and their crews happy for it. Chief Warrant Officer Two (CW2) Bill Janes and CW2 Larry D. Miller flew the lead Boomerang ship. Janes took note of the enemy's absence. All was quiet so far. *This just might prove to be a good day*, he thought.

Nonetheless, every troop insertion and extraction proved to be a nail-biter. The flight descended through five hundred feet above ground level (AGL) to drop off troops into the LZ. Intercoms fell silent. Stomachs tightened and hearts shuddered as the crew braced for the gut-wrenching explosion of "Receiving fire! Receiving fire!" followed by the airframe tremor from M60 machine guns spitting out 7.62-millimeter bullets, 350 rounds per minute. But for now, the flight descended in peace.

Nestled in an ancient agrarian culture, the jungles, rivers, and rice paddies below seemed to move at a pastoral pace. But this was Vietnam; life here perched on the unpredictable, always about to take a turn. While on short final approach to insertion four, the 191st AHC flight was pommeled from cockpit to tailfin. The rapid smack and ping of metal on metal echoed through their fuselages.

The North Vietnamese Army (NVA) elements had anticipated the American attack and had prepared well, hiding in concealed enemy emplacements. The 191st birds were restricted from returning door gunfire for fear of hitting Americans nearest the enemy.

Flying the chock-three bird, Captain (CPT) Ray "Big Swede" Rugg (Boomerang One-Six) watched sparks leap off the skins of the first two aircraft as enemy tracers ripped through them. The radios were jammed with pilots alerting lead of warning lights flashing impending engine failure, leaving the 191st AHC tactical frequency nearly unusable. The enemy knew they had the flight in a vulnerable position. The tall trees in front of the formation required a slow ascent out of that hellhole, giving the enemy ample time to inflict maximum battle damage. Most alarming to Rugg, during the slow climb-out the tail boom of the chock-two bird jerked back and forth, an indication of severe pilot stress. Perez, its AC, was a seasoned combat-assault pilot, but Rugg suspected the worst—someone on the crew had been hit.

Feeling the heavy dose of enemy bullets slam into his aircraft, Perez carefully monitored the engine instruments. Uncertain if its power could complete the perilously slow ascent, the skillful AC lightly held the controls, demanding no more than minimum stress on the wounded bird.

Years later, the experienced Perez recalls that day's climb-out from the enemy-infested LZ: "I knew I had to remain cool. If I got hit, my copilot, barely a week in-country, might have to fly the bird out."

With full throttle and a windshield of blue sky, the bird reached only fifty feet AGL when a North Vietnamese soldier stepped out from the lush green coconut palms, aimed his AK-47 at the bird's nose, and cut loose.

"At that very instant," Perez recalls, "it seemed like the heart-throbbing pause in a nightmare, a time warp when escape seems futile."

The world's big motion picture paused in the middle of a live streaming, a common sensation in battle. Time seems to stand still except for the pinpoint moment of what's coming at you, inch by inch, in slow motion, sometimes with no hope of deflecting it, dodging it, or changing the pending outcome.

"I saw the fire from the muzzle of the enemy weapon," Perez continues, "and saw the Plexiglas shatter in small pieces as the bullets ripped through the aircraft chin bubble, smacking my right boot off the foot pedal. Without even thinking, I placed it back to maintain directional control as we continued the climb-out. As calmly as I could, I told my brand-new *peter pilot*, 'We're still receiving fire, but keep your cool. We'll be out of here in a minute.'"

Perez was hit in the foot, but hoped it wasn't anything serious. "Just keep your hands near the controls in the event you need to fly the bird out of here," he said to his frightened copilot. His peter pilot, like all greenhorns experiencing the pit of hell up close and personal, was spooked. "I wanted him close to the controls in case I took another, more serious hit," Perez recalls. Not wanting to add to the lad's already overladen fears, Perez kept his cool.

Perez cleared the trees and leveled off. He glanced down at a large hole in his boot. The bullet tore out a hunk of his right foot on the outer edge, close to the heel, and peeled back the boot's leather. At about this moment, things seemed to happen in rapid sequence for Perez. Wind from the open cargo bay rushed through the bird's interior. Specks of blood and small pieces of human tissue gathered in rapid succession across the cockpit windshield.

"I knew it was not *my* blood," Perez recalls, "and almost as soon as I saw it, Johnson keyed the intercom and announced that Lawfield was hit. Since I was still flying the aircraft, I told my copilot to climb over the console and help Johnson provide first aid to Lawfield. I was feeling pain, but not enough to prevent me from flying the bird."

The Huey had received a beating. The engine oil pressure dropped. The tension in the flight controls softened, growing sluggish and less responsive. Perez had to set it down soon. He called Janes and Miller in lead to report his battle damage and wounded crew. "Lead, this is One-Three. I just took several hits and have wounded on board. Request permission to break formation and return to the PZ [pickup zone] to await medevac."

"Roger, One-Three," Janes in the lead bird responded. Janes immediately contacted the first platoon leader, CPT Rugg. "One-Six, this is Lead. Did you copy that?"

"Lead, One-Six. I copy."

"One-Six, Lead. Break formation and take care of One-Three while we resolve our battle damage. We have a serious fuel problem." Lead's voice rang loud with concern.

Rugg knew, however, that he also needed to check his own bird for battle damage lest he risk adding to the emergency at hand. Without a second thought, he broke formation and headed to Ben Tre Airfield. Rushing wind noise from faster-than-normal airspeed alerted Rugg's crew that speed was key to their rescue mission. Lives were at stake. With seat belts fully tightened and headgear firmly snugged down, the aircrew sat with their stomachs tensed while the slick traveled at its maximum speed, 120 knots—a speed that, given the slick's unknown battle damage, could rip it apart. Some crewmembers prayed in silence.

Meanwhile, Perez's bullet-riddled helicopter lumbered toward the previous PZ. The young Gunner Lawfield gushed blood from a deep shrapnel wound on his upper cheek. Penetrating deep into his skull, the fiery piece of steel accomplished the enemy's intent: it delivered a death knell and left the crew helpless to save their crewmate. The heart-wrenched crew chief and newbie copilot held down their stomach contents and worked through the metallic stench of human blood to comfort the wounded youth.

"Glenn, can you hear me?" Johnson asked Lawfield. Consciousness slowly slipped away from his bunkmate and good buddy, and Johnson's voice trembled. "Glenn! Talk to me, buddy." But Lawfield did not respond, and Johnson grew more hysterical. "I want to hear you say something. Glenn, *taaalk* to me, brother."

Struggle as he did to stay alive, Lawfield's final gasps fell silent in minutes. His body relaxed, releasing all its earthly fluids, and lay quiet. Johnson wept, and the immense battle raged unfettered.

With nerves strained to their limits and emotions running rampant, Perez fought off the discomfort of his wounded foot that radiated pain up his leg. Lawfield's death had rattled Perez's mental composure, but getting the battle-damaged aircraft back to a friendly PZ was critical. Instruments, including the engine oil gauge, warned of looming engine failure.

"Fighting to keep my foot on the rudder pedal, I searched for a landing spot," Perez recalls. "The sloppy flight controls hammered my brain with the reality that landing the bird in enemy-held territory was death defying, yet imminent."

Making his final Mayday call, Perez had stressed the urgency to Rugg, his platoon leader. "Boomerang One-Six, this is Boomerang One-Three."

"One-Six, go ahead."

"One-Six, this is One-Three. I'm approximately two clicks west of the last PZ with wounded on board. I'm gonna try to make the PZ, but need medevac soonest."

"Roger, One-Three. I'm en route and have visual contact with your bird. Be there in six or seven mikes."

In battle, every second can alter fate. Nevertheless, Rugg had no choice but to land and check his bird for battle damage. In less than three minutes, the platoon leader was back in the pilot seat. He restarted the engine with an abbreviated fast start and lifted the slick into the thin air. He scanned the horizon to his south and caught a glimpse of Perez's damaged slick in the distance.

Pulling max power, Rugg followed the flight path of the battle-torn Huey until he landed within twenty meters. He thanked God the One-Three aircraft and crew made it back to the friendly PZ. Janes and his flight lead bird and crew were already there, shut down and with no visible burn damage, the crew safe. *Maybe a good omen.* But Rugg's mind darkened when he drew close to the heartbreaking sight of Perez's bird.

Human tissue, plastered on the bullet-riddled windshield and brilliant red under the Asian sun, alerted Rugg of the gravity of the situation. The concerned platoon leader knew all too well what awaited.

With the cargo door open, the foul smell of a life just expired—the blood and human fluids, like a rotted tooth extraction but worse—percolated through the air. Rugg stuck his head through the cargo hatch. Blood pooled wide under Lawfield's body, and Rugg's eyes sank deep into their sockets. He had looked at the young Lawfield as if he were his little brother. Rugg's lips pulled tight into a downward turn, and he reached for the boy's body. A glimmer of hope took hold, and he hauled the youngster from Perez's aircraft. The crew helped him load Lawfield onto his bird for a rapid flight to Dong Tam Hospital.

But it was too late. On September 30, 1968, SP4 Glenn Lawfield breathed his last breath aboard Perez's ship before it even touched down in the friendly PZ.

Johnson and Perez spent some time on the hospital pad trying to cope with this reality. Perez's wound required minor medical treatment, and he was awarded a Purple Heart. Lawfield earned a Purple Heart, too, posthumously. Nevertheless, the disparity of sacrifice was immense.

Lawfield's hospital run had done little to soften the blow for his fellow aircraft crewmembers. When a warrior with mortal wounds struggles to remain alive, images of his closing moments are permanently etched into the memories of those who witnessed his last breath and final heartbeat. It is *those* images that years later spring back to life on the living faces of the dead. They form a permanent mental scar. Ben Tre was a hellhole that both Rugg's and Perez's crews would never forget.

"The death of Lawfield worked on the minds of all of us," Perez recalls, "but I think Rugg took it worst of all. Battle stress was clearly carved into his face."

Decades later, the wounds of that day are still fresh. "He was just a *kid*, for Chrissakes," Rugg explains. "The most wholesome and decent kid you could ever meet. You would think that after seeing so many people die, it would get easier to let go. But it doesn't work that way. It burns a hole in you every time you see one of your crewmembers get killed." Rugg's facial expressions assume the same posture witnessed by his crew on that fateful day. "As the breeze blew through the locks of his hair, you would think he was sleeping," Rugg explains. "But in reality, his youthful expression just reached into your heart and tore at the very fabric that bonded us together."

The day Lawfield was killed, Rugg had been close to his date of rotation back to the US, and would soon be free from combat stress. He took little comfort, however, in this fact. His deep sense of loyalty to all those who served him intensified his deep pain. The loss of human life gripped him, leaving a lasting impression.

Rugg saw his share of battle death. One might expect that by then he would have grown calloused and accepted the consequences of war that were beyond his control. But even though decades have elapsed since this experience, his pent-up anger and pain are still evident when he recalls the young Lawfield's death.

"When I saw him lying there on the floor of that Huey, *lifeless*, it really tore into my soul. Eighteen years old, fighting in a stupid, damned war that nobody back home seemed to want, and now he was dead." Rugg's face collapses into a grimace like you might see on a person who just lost a family member. "To make matters worse," Rugg continues, "people in California spat at US soldiers returning from Vietnam. Of those who knew him and were close to him, all would tell you that

Glenn Lawfield was one of the finest youngsters our country had in uniform." Every loss has dug long roots into Rugg's memory, as well as every place where fatalities occurred.

Embedded in the minds of all warriors who survived the horrors of Vietnam are the names of places where their comrades bled and died—Van Tuong, Ia Drang, Khe Sanh, Ben Tre. Among those who fought, the very name of the battle site yields a certain reverence for the kindred souls whose lives ended in the rice paddies, thick jungles, and battle-torn assault helicopters of Vietnam. Among the numerous battle sites where the 191st pilots, crewmembers, and support personnel died in action, *this* is how the survivors remember Ben Tre.

***

As capital of Kien Hoa province in the military IV Corps region of South Vietnam, Ben Tre is remotely situated along a narrow canal that connects two major distributaries of the Mekong River. Located twenty miles northwest from the South China Sea, the community draws its subsistence from the waterway, which provides a fishery refreshed twice daily by the tide, and also serves as a transportation route for the substantial sampan river traffic. Because the enemy operated beneath the jungle canopy with substantial impunity and easily imported war material along the river in sampans, Ben Tre was an ideal location for an enemy stronghold. However, the town itself and its small airstrip were generally secure, at least during daylight hours.

By late August and into September of 1968, the Ninth Infantry Division prepared to send a strike force into the greater Ben Tre area. The 191st AHC, based at Bearcat, fifteen miles northeast of Saigon, was selected to provide the airmobile assets.

On the evening of September 29, 1968, the operations order (OPORD) was issued for Ben Tre. A nervous trio huddled around the second platoon's assignment board. The flight assignments officer and the two section leaders were going through a frustrating mad scramble trying to come up with the customary two ACs to fly lead the next day. They couldn't. It had escaped their attention that allowable flight-time restrictions grounded the extra second platoon's ACs, so they had to get help from the first platoon. CW2 Bill Janes, a loaner AC from the first platoon, would share the cockpit with CW2 Larry D. Miller of the second platoon. Miller, a crusty ol' combat-assault pilot who was cool under fire, was selected to lead the Boomerangs into battle. With that settled, the three headed for the bachelor officer quarters (BOQ) to retire for the day. By tomorrow evening, the young Lawfield would have lived his last day.

On the eve of his death, however, the barracks busted into a bristling scene of food, booze, and laughter. Some wrote letters home to their sweethearts or family. Most of the others joined the typical crew banter, recalling combat stories and ribbing each other as if nothing else mattered, and for the moment, nothing did. Yet as the crews celebrated, mortar and artillery rounds blasted in the distance with the occasional staccato rips of automatic weapons fire.

The celebration continued amid the barrage of war sounds, a grim reminder of what existed outside the confines of the 191st home base at Bearcat. As part of the Army's Bearcat complex, home of the Ninth Infantry Division, the 191st was privileged to have security by a battalion of grunts assigned to protect the bunkers surrounding their installation. In turn, the 191st supported the Ninth Infantry in battle.

A number of 191st vets who fought with the Ninth Infantry often spoke of the mass killings they had witnessed as the division first settled into the war. Launching from Bearcat, Boomerangs and Bounty Hunters also supported the Thai Army's operations in the corps area between Bien Hoa and Vung Tau. The Thais were vicious fighters who at times were seen carrying severed enemy heads. Bounty Hunter CPT Bruce Palmer once mentioned that upon visiting a Thai unit stationed at Bearcat, he and his crew chief were offered beer being passed around in a Viet Cong (VC) skull.

Fortunately, the Ninth Infantry Division influenced a measure of civility to the enemy beheadings by Thai forces, and the Ninth gave the 191st personnel a measured feeling of security. Save the bombardments by enemy mortar teams, the 191st area was safe. Hence, the relaxed mood of partygoers preceding the morning combat assaults became a ritual. The evening of September 29, 1968, was just the routine of war in an assault-helicopter company.

On the morning of September 30, it was announced at Boomerang operations that a full-scale combat assault was ordered into Ben Tre. When a *hot spot* happened to be on the operation's board for the day, the seriousness of the mission was written on the faces of battle-experienced pilots. Newly arrived aviators quickly learned to read the body language and reactions of these seasoned aviators. This morning, alert newbies—including Perez's copilot, the peter pilot—recognized the hint of concern as preparations were underway. And when the first platoon's three-quarter-ton truck, nicknamed the Tijuana Taxi (TJ Taxi), delivered machine guns and ammunition out to the flight line a shade earlier than normal, the new hands correctly sensed that something big was about to unfold. Tension filled the air.

With the flight lead pilots selected the previous evening at the crew assignment board, early dawn found Miller and Janes exchanging casual greetings.

"Larry, how about you take the lower preflight and I'll do the top?" Janes asked.

"Sounds good enough to me," Miller replied.

Operating under the call sign Boomerang, personnel who delivered troops into battle had their own aircraft parking area at Bearcat where they assembled in the morning. Gunship personnel with call sign Bounty Hunter occupied a different aircraft parking zone. This facilitated battle preparations for different weaponry. The Boomerang's slicks used M60 machine guns, while the gunships required high-explosive (HE) ordnance such as 2.75-inch rockets and 7.62-caliber miniguns. On the morning of September 30, both assembly areas bustled with soldiers performing their premission duties. It was a busy sight.

With the preflight accomplished, both lead pilots got their cockpit workspace squared away for the day's operation. Most importantly, they unfolded topographic maps used for ground navigation and placed them in a handy spot.

"Another day in the life of hunting these bastards," Janes said. "Ain't this fun?"

"Yeah, no shit!" Miller said and laughed. "Seems like these fuckers never stop coming, like fucking ants out of a hole in the ground."

Medium-framed and built like a football player, Miller spoke with a measured vocabulary that wasted no words, whereas the gregarious Janes—light of build, blond hair, with an easy personality—gave the crew a communication uplift. A friendly sort, Janes greeted all crewmembers with a smile and cheerful words. With both pilots strapped into their seats and helmets off, the two projected a classic, all-American, salt-and-pepper contrast for the crew.

In the back, Crew Chief SP4 Andy Burney, a sandy-haired, medium-weight, and feisty lad, focused on his crew-chief duties to ensure the bird was mechanically sound for the mission. Gunner Private First Class (PFC) Richard Fuller, a tall, gutsy African American with an athletic manner that exuded strength and confidence, made sure the crew-served weapons were in top working order and had plenty of ammo.

Simultaneously, each Boomerang crew completed the same process, including the Boomerang One-Three aircraft where Lawfield's fatal destiny awaited. Pilot start-up procedures initiated the final preparation for takeoff by rolling throttles to the start position, flipping on switches overhead and on the console, and engaging the start trigger on the collective stick control. The whine of seventeen turbines soon permeated the air, and the smell of JP-4 flooded each cargo compartment and cockpit as the 191st AHC completed its run-up procedures. In moments, seventeen main-rotor blades turned at idle speed. With routine instrument checks complete, each AC took control of his aircraft and increased engine rpm from 6,000 at idle to the full 6,600.

After each bird reported "flight ready," Miller hovered the lead ship onto the active runway where, one behind the other, the entire flight lined up for lift-off. With rotor blades now spinning at lift speed, kicking up clouds of rotor wash, the noise would be deafening without ear protection. Soon the trailing ship gave the "ready" signal, and the entire flight lifted into the air like a huge flock of aerial predators.

Departing Bearcat, they headed fifty miles southwest to Dong Tam, where they refueled. By replenishing their fuel that they had burned to this point, Miller could give the grunts maximum airlift time for when combat demanded extended support—often the difference between life and death for infantry troops on the ground.

Proceeding ten miles southeast to Ben Tre, the vegetation changed as the flight crossed the Mekong River. Large coconut trees that clustered like huge stands of mature pines in the southeastern United States replaced the short nipa palm, abundant north of the river. The coconut palms, which normally would offer beach memories of American summer holidays, sharply contrasted with the seriousness of the day. The dense jungle, with few large landing areas, made it easy for the NVA to anticipate potential LZs where American troops could be inserted. The NVA's lengthy and undisturbed occupation of this region gave them a decided combat advantage. Aware they had the edge, they remained unafraid and ready for battle when the 191st flight arrived over their well-prepared battle emplacements. Insertion after insertion brought the two forces closer and closer together. Tensions ran high as minds buckled down and focused on what was to come.

The first three insertions were performed with no enemy contact. The formation dropped into the LZ, and the grunts exited the birds. No shots were fired. With its coordination fine-tuned by numerous rehearsals, the 191st AHC flight hung together like a group of giant raptors descending upon a jungle clearing. The flight lead bird touched the ground first. The *toe* of the formation led, followed by the rest until the last bird, the *heel*, firmly planted. As seen by the air mission commander (AMC) in the command-and-control (C&C) ship, from a vantage point of 1,500 feet AGL, the lift-off was executed in the same order. This left ten evenly spaced groups of soldiers on the ground, resembling a giant footprint where the flight had just been.

During most insertions, exposure was measured in seconds, but when tracers streaked through the sky and bullets punched through fuselages, time in the LZ seemed eternal. Guns at the ready and eyes focused on the tree line nearest the flight, the Boomerang crew chiefs and gunners tensed up when their slicks descended to within three hundred meters above the touchdown point. They didn't relax until their birds safely regained airspeed and altitude. Time after time, this sequence had been duplicated by the 191st crews until it was second nature. Each time, everyone anticipated the sudden explosion of gunfire that often threatened the flight. Crew chiefs and gunners knew that fractions of a second in response could mean the difference between life and death. Fingers stayed poised over the M60 triggers with the safety switches off.

By late morning, and after three uneventful insertions, the birds drew low on fuel. Miller called C&C and requested permission to take the flight to Dong Tam for a load of JP-4. C&C acknowledged and followed suit.

The sun was now perched at the high point of the day. With the morning coolness burned off, the heavy heat caused lift conditions to deteriorate. After each bird was filled with JP-4, one by one Miller surveyed the ACs.

"Are you experiencing difficulty with the normal load of six troops?" Miller asked each AC. Hearing no concerns, he lifted the lead slick off the refueling ramp and proceeded to the active runway where the formation, once again, assembled for departure.

After lift-off, the flight crossed the Mekong River and headed for the heavy jungle surrounding Ben Tre. However, this time C&C vectored them to a different PZ from the one they had used that morning. There, the flight picked up a fresh bunch of troops and headed southwest from Ben Tre, deeper into suspected enemy territory.

As they approached the LZ, Miller gave the flight its usual prelanding instructions. "Boomerang Flight, this is Lead. We'll be landing south. Go staggered left." Moments later, the birds eased into the assigned formation.

Since the right side of the LZ was thick jungle, the staggered-left formation kept the trailing ships out of the trees. Miller relayed the instructions from the infantry commander and ordered the flight to land as far forward in the LZ as possible. This took lead to within thirty meters of the tall coconut trees that bordered the south end of the huge clearing.

"There must have been four hundred to five hundred meters of open ground in that clearing," Janes recalls. "No sooner had the flight settled on the ground than all hell erupted. The flight began taking fire from the entire length of the tree line on the right. Leaping out of the birds in seconds, the grunts hit the ground with their M16s blazing on full auto. In a heartbeat, the LZ turned into an inferno of hot lead striking the birds. Lead took several rounds, one of which punctured the aircraft fire extinguisher and splattered fragments on both of my legs below the knee hard enough to make me believe I was wounded. Sitting in the right seat, I could clearly see when the enemy tracers started zipping from right to left across the nose of the Huey and then working their way onto the bird. Above the battle noise, I hollered that I was hit and instinctively initiated a steep takeoff.

"By pulling in sufficient power to clear the high trees, with little forward airspeed and a full load of fuel, I strained the old D-model to its limits. But with hot lead flying through the cockpit, I didn't need any more incentive. It was either get the hell out of there now, or kiss my ass goodbye. With assholes puckered tighter than a snare drum and radios crackling with ACs screaming that their birds were taking fire, the flight departed the LZ with considerable battle damage, but thank God, no casualties."

As with any near-death experience, Janes had felt relief beyond expression as the flight gained airspeed and altitude. With adrenaline still pumping but his breath relaxing, he expressed gratefulness that no bird was left behind in the LZ. All ten aircraft had made it out.

"Larry, can you take the controls? Something spanked the shit out of me, and I feel something wet down there. I think I'd better take a look."

"Sure, Bill. Go ahead."

Luckily, no blood. The cold, wet substance flowed from the damaged fire extinguisher. In the meantime, the Bounty Hunter gunships blasted the tree line along the periphery of the LZ with a strong volume of rocket fire. They emptied half of their tubes with a single pass. Against the solid, dark-green background of jungle foliage, the bright-orange explosions and the puffs of white smoke painted a picturesque scene for the ground troops who were preparing for the fight of their lives.

Mud flew in all directions from the edge of the coconut trees, but the NVA continued to emerge, seemingly from foxholes and tunnels everywhere. The angle of fire from the aircraft machine guns to the enemy positions was too narrow above the heads of friendly forces for Boomerang slick crews to engage the enemy without the risk of killing Americans. Hence, the slick door gunners were prevented from firing. The Boomerang crews clearly witnessed the enemy killing Americans in the open LZ. They wanted their blood, but they couldn't chance hitting friendlies.

The Bounty Hunter gunships, on the other hand, flew right over the enemy positions and stared straight down through the coconut trees. As the NVA maneuvered into attack positions to fire at the departing Boomerang slicks, the Bounty Hunter gunships let loose on the enemy with a vengeance.

Gunship Crew Chief Specialist Five (SP5) Gordon Hahn recalls a typical scene: "When you flew slicks and were not allowed to suppress enemy fire with door guns, you were like a sitting duck. But with the Bounty Hunters, we could fire back with at least our M60 machine gun or rockets—some heavy gonads."

From aboard the lead Bounty Hunter gunship piloted by CPT Palmer, the gun crew had spotted the enemy in full battle-dress uniforms and helmets. It was easy to distinguish the NVA from the VC, since traditionally the VC wore black pajamas.

The voice of Bounty Hunter Gunner SP4 Gerald "Jerry" Kahn blared over the radio. "These are NVA, sir!"

The NVA swarmed out of spider holes and tunnels dug in the ground under coconut palms. Well experienced in this type of combat, Kahn, along with Crew Chief SP4 Robert Lynn "Heinie" Heinmiller, cut down the NVA force as they ran toward the LZ. There were simply too many, however, to stem the horde.

Flying the Bounty Hunter wing ship that covered Palmer, CW2 Robert Gilbert rolled in as Palmer's gunship cleared the LZ and unleashed a long blast of minigun fire that caught some of the enemy in the open. Blood splattered from NVA soldiers as multiple 7.62-millimeter bullets hurled through their bodies at almost 2,800 feet per second. But the NVA blistered the grunts with machine-gun fire, and American soldiers were dropping dead in the LZ. Tracers flew in both directions, to and from the coconut palm trees, with the heaviest volume from the NVA.

The Americans on the ground were far outnumbered. "As the last bird cleared the LZ, from the fourth insertion," Janes recalls, "the entire flight—Boomerang slicks and Bounty Hunter gunships—headed for Ben Tre Airfield, where they landed to inspect the damage. Two slicks were hit in vital areas, leaving only eight flyable ships to react to what was now a full-blown tactical emergency [tac-e] for the ground commander. C&C called and gave us a new PZ location. The troops just inserted were in a vicious firefight and needed rapid reinforcement. With the remaining eight flyable slicks, the flight headed east a few clicks and picked up another forty-eight grunts. Missing the usual smiles and conversation that preceded most PZ lifts, these grunts were stern-faced and quiet. Checking clips in their M16 rifles and combat pack straps for security, their demeanor demonstrated the will of the American soldier. They meant to make a difference. Pinned down by a large NVA force, their buddies needed help, and they prepared to engage the enemy with deadly force. A credit to their courage, their facial expressions were an image of sheer determination. They were prepared to get into the fight and balance the difference in the odds against the Americans."

This time, Miller, in lead, had landed the flight as far back in the LZ as space allowed, hoping he could avoid a repetition of what occurred in the previous insertion. Allowing for more takeoff room would also give the flight greater airspeed and altitude to clear the tall tropical forest. Catching the flight by surprise in the previous LZ forced the ships into a slow, nearly vertical ascent to escape. Miller sensed that the aging Hueys could not take the strain without overheating and blowing their engines in a hostile LZ. He hoped that by landing farther back in the LZ, the added stand-off distance might allow the birds to clear the trees early enough to break *away* from the enemy positions.

"It was certainly worth a try," Janes recalls, "in order to keep the flight from running the gauntlet of enemy fire again."

But the experienced NVA had anticipated the helicopter approach by wind direction. The enemy shifted troops to the approach end of every clearing where they anticipated combat air assaults. It appeared as if the enemy had gained intelligence information alerting them of the American attack into their stronghold that day.

Flying chock three, CPT Rugg called lead on downwind. "Lead, this is One-Six."

"This is Lead. Go ahead, One-Six."

"Lead, One-Six, recommend a trail formation to minimize dual targeting for enemy guns. Let's not make it easy for these bastards to align two of our birds in the same sight picture."

"Roger that, One-Six. Good thinking," Janes responded, and called the rest of the ACs. "Boomerang Flight, this is Lead. We'll be landing in trail formation . . . go trail."

In moments, the trail bird verified. "Lead, we have trail."

"Roger, understand we have trail."

The new approach denied the enemy a firing angle from the flank that could align two aircraft in the same gunsight picture. With only eight birds left, the LZ had sufficient space to accommodate the trail formation—a well-considered move. Again, the flight received fire one hundred meters before touching down, and again the grunts scrambled off in an instant with guns blazing. Most frustrating to the slick crews was the inability of the gunners and crew chiefs, such as Lawfield and Johnson, to return fire with their door guns. With friendly troops scattered throughout the

LZ, it was impossible to determine the whereabouts of each pocket of American soldiers. Controlling friendly fire proved to be a serious and practical matter. Under no circumstances would any AC risk killing Americans.

Knowing that the LZ was going to be hot, Palmer and his Bounty Hunter gunships prepared to protect the flight. As the slicks landed, the gunships unleashed a heavy dose of support fire on the right side of the LZ. Wingman Gilbert covered Palmer while CW2 Mike Holt and his copilot, WO1 John Perrin, in a lone gunship, covered the less-vulnerable left side of the flight. But again, the NVA poised with guns ready.

As the gunships descended to low altitudes for maximum impact on the enemy, the air over the LZ filled with bright tracers. The sky lit up with what looked like thousands of green fireflies sailing through the air in one steady stream and smacking against the birds' sides—but *these* deadly fireflies sent sparks flying where they ricocheted. Every fifth bullet in an enemy gun traced its direction of flight by powder burning from its aft end. To the aircrews, it posed a spectacular show of targeted death coming straight at them. All three gunships received hard blows as they overflew the enemy positions. The Bounty Hunter cockpits in both Palmer's and Gilbert's gunships lit up with warning lights indicating hydraulic damage. Both Bounty Hunter pilots knew their birds would not stay airborne for long.

Holt's gunship also took a round through the tail-rotor driveshaft, creating a condition that made the aircraft extremely dangerous to fly. A high-frequency vibration rattled Holt's foot pedals. Still, Holt flew one final pass over the enemy-infested jungle to ensure that all the Boomerang slicks had cleared the LZ. Releasing all his remaining ordnance, Holt's single gunship blasted the tree line, sending enemy body parts sailing through the air. Pleased with the gunship action, the ground commander called for more of the same. But with his rocket tubes empty, Holt had to break off from the fight to go back to Ben Tre Airfield to rearm and refuel. Back on the ground, Holt inspected the tail-rotor driveshaft.

The extensive damage stunned Holt, and he was forced to concede the fight. Although he had full knowledge that the grunts were catching hell in the LZ, Holt had no choice but to wait for a replacement part. "It's a helpless feeling," Holt recalls. "You know they need you bad, and you want to get back into the fight, but there isn't a damn thing you can do about it." Holt had remained at Ben Tre Airfield with hopeful anticipation that the 191st's maintenance crew would arrive soon and get him back in the air. The crews fought the enemy without him as the afternoon turned to dusk.

The rest of the flight made it in and out of the LZ without casualties, but the Hueys suffered a severe beating. By this time, it was routine to return to Ben Tre Airfield to check for damage. Three of the eight slicks that descended into the LZ on one lift took hits in critical areas and could not get back into the fight. To make matters worse, all three gunships remained grounded with battle damage. With air assets diminished by enemy fire and troops locked in mortal combat with the NVA, the ground commander asked for all that was left of the Boomerang flight. Only five slicks were flyable, including the fateful ship with Gunner Lawfield. So, a gunship fire team was requested from Dong Tam, and two Thunder Chicken gunships from the 195th AHC[1] that happened to be working nearby responded that they were en route.

Meanwhile, the slick flight picked up thirty troops and headed for the LZ. Miller and Janes slowed the slicks down to sixty knots to allow time for the Thunder Chickens to close the gap. In five minutes, the Thunder Chickens contacted lead and told Miller they were in position to cover the flight. At about the same time, C&C gave Miller and Janes a new vector to a different LZ. With only five flyable birds remaining, C&C had picked a smaller clearing farther to the east, several hundred meters away from the hot LZ. Again, because of the danger of killing Americans, the slicks were denied clearance to fire their door guns. The Boomerang door gunners, fingers on their triggers, stood down.

The new, tight LZ required a nearly vertical descent and departure; however, before the birds settled onto the ground, the relentless and clever enemy poured machine-gun fire into the Boomerang ships. Confused about the location of friendlies, the Thunder Chickens did not fire back. In seconds, a hail of enemy bullets engulfed the LZ. Perez called lead and announced his bird had taken heavy battle damage. He had wounded on board, but would try to make the last PZ. Unknown to the other crews, the young Lawfield had received his fatal blow.

Watching the flight from 1,500 feet above the battle, the C&C pilots above the scene witnessed the deluge of enemy fire that engulfed Janes and Miller and the rest of the birds as they dropped troops in the hot LZ.

"Larry, are they shooting the shit out of us, or what?" Janes in the lead cockpit asked Miller.

Miller, steady on the controls, was stoic as ever. "Yes, they are."

Coming out, lead was trailing a large cloud of what appeared to be smoke. C&C immediately hailed lead and advised that they were on fire.

"Roger, understand on fire," Miller responded, and initiated a descent to a small clearing near the LZ.

"I don't think we need to go down. Let's get the hell out of here," Janes said to Miller. "There're too damn many bad guys. I can smell fuel, but I don't feel any heat." Miller agreed. "I got it!" Janes said, and he added full power.

As it turned out, the bird was not on fire. Perforated fuel cells leaking JP-4 produced the cloud of smoke as the fuel flew up into the hot engine exhaust. The bird was flyable but losing fuel fast. Miller and Janes agreed that the bird would not

---

1 Shelby L. Stanton, *Vietnam Order of Battle: A Complete Illustrated Reference to U.S. Army Combat and Support Forces in Vietnam 1961–1973* (New York: Stackpole Books/Rowman & Littlefield, 2003).

make it back to Ben Tre Airfield. With a swift but wise decision, the two experienced ACs chose to return to the last friendly PZ location, which was considerably closer.

"We got to stretch this fuel as far as we can," Miller said.

"I know, but we have no one behind us who can pick us up. And until we know if we have any flyable birds left, we're flying lone wolf. Might be shit out of luck, buddy. I say we call Charlie-Charlie [C&C] and give him our sit rep [situation report]. He may be our only hope."

"Boomerang Six, this is Flight Lead."

"Lead, this is Six. Go ahead."

"Six, do you still have us in sight?"

"Roger, Lead. Still have your smoke column in sight. Evidently, you're not on fire, but the chance for you to explode in midair is causing some high stress on my nerves. Why don't you put the damn thing down? We'll get someone to pick you up."

"Roger that, Six," Miller replied, cool under dire circumstances. "We're hoping to make the previous PZ. Too many bad guys where we are. We'll keep you posted."

Forced to redirect their attention to the fight, the C&C pilots turned their focus to resolving the tac-e requiring more aviation assets. American lives hung in the balance.

With prayers from the sweaty crew, the minutes stretched into an agonizing experience. The bullets that ripped holes in the fuel tanks sprayed JP-4, soaking Crew Chief Gurney. He knew that any fire would scorch him to death. Gunner Fuller, also well sprayed with fuel mist, feared the same fate. Survival for the lead crew was at a critical juncture. It felt as if only a miracle could save the aircraft and crew.

Like any well-trained and seasoned pilot, Janes ran scenarios through his head. What reaction might the fuel hitting a hot exhaust have at slower speeds? Would less airspeed create a density accumulation with a greater amount of fuel mist igniting all at once? With maintenance knowledge surging to the forefront, Janes continued to assess the unknown.

These possibilities plagued not only Janes's mind, but also all souls on board. While still within sight of lead, the C&C crew watched the horrific drama play out. Each observer visualized himself in the lead bird. A bundle of nerves, the C&C crew waited for the massive explosion to rip the Huey to shreds. All stomachs turned over.

Keying the intercom, Janes shared his thoughts with Miller. "Larry, I recommend that we maintain airspeed on this approach until we get low level, and roll the throttle back on short final until we need power to cushion our touchdown. At least then if this thing flares up, we might be able to un-ass the bird before we all barbecue. What do you think?"

"Sounds like a plan to me. Let's go for it."

"Looks like the PZ is to our left at about two forty out. Give it a shot. It has enough clearing."

"Okay. Here we go."

Lowering collective pitch but maintaining eighty knots, Janes turned from an easterly direction to northwest. He encountered a tailwind that made little difference in the smoke as the bird descended. Janes called the crew chief. "Andy, you guys feeling any more heat?"

"No, sir. No change." Burney's voice raised to a high pitch. "But I'm soaked with fuel."

Janes gulped back his concern and pulled up his mental reserves. He made the final turn to line up for the 120-degree approach. A friendly voice came on the air.

"Lead, this is One-Six," Rugg said. "I have your direction of approach. I'm headed in there to pick up One-Three's wounded. Looks like you'll have enough security from the grunts. Hang in there, and I'll come back to get you after I run the wounded into Dong Tam Hospital."

"Roger that, One-Six. Please let us know if you see any fire when we get close to the ground."

"Roger that, Lead."

The rest of the flight headed back to Ben Tre Airfield. The three surviving battle-scarred slicks made their final approach. They barely cleared the trees to the old landing strip. Earlier that morning, the flight had left the Bearcat with eleven slicks and three gunships. Enemy fire had riddled seven aircraft, reducing their flyable birds to seven, a 50 percent combat loss for the 191st AHC—a rare, single day.

The Boomerangs and Bounty Hunters had established a well-deserved reputation for extraordinary airmobile support. With no reason to expect September 30, 1968, to be any different from any other day, their early-morning departure had been characterized by the poise and confidence of combat veterans en route to another stellar battlefield performance. But despite the tremendous technological advantage air mobility provided, it was no match that day for the enemy troops' strength and their element of surprise. Fate turned on a dime.

In a loose trail formation, the flight lumbered across Ben Tre's airfield with a beaten demeanor that one sees in heartbroken high school football players limping off the field after a brutal loss in the divisional state championship.

The first bird back made a loud whistling sound with each rotation of its rotor blades, a symptom of battle damage behind the spar, on the trailing edge of the rotor blade. Wind passed through the bullet holes and the missing chunks of blade material. It created an eerie sound, and the bird struggled to remain airborne. Bullet holes on both the second and third aircraft stitched a uniform pattern from the forward end of their tail booms all the way back to their vertical fins. At a glance, it was evident that the flight had been in one hellacious gunfight. Although stunned, the 191st aircrewmen were resolved to see better days ahead, knowing full well that today had not been their best day.

Even though the rigors of war made the loss of aircraft and crewmembers a frequent occurrence for this band of warriors, the emotional drain had a way of manifesting its weight into premature lines on young, grim faces. The sunken eye sockets of many bore an unmistakable hint of inner stress and battle fatigue. The seasoning and callousing that happens to soldiers at war had long since become an integral part of this unit's culture. These servicemen were oaks, to the last one.

The pilots settled the battle-weary ships onto the sod area next to the active runway and shut down. On each slick's nose in bright orange, a painted picture of a boomerang—a silent symbol of the will of its pilots and crew, for boomerangs always come back.

Meanwhile, Rugg raced to Dong Tam Hospital with the wounded Perez and the body of young Lawfield, killed in action (KIA).

An unsung hero of the day, Rugg returned from Dong Tam Hospital and picked up the downed Boomerang lead crew of Miller and Janes. He shot his final approach into the Bearcat just as twilight folded over base camp and the last residue of color faded from the sky. A quiet man, Rugg retired to his bunk without supper.

Some of the other weary soldiers retreated to their bunks, as well, while others, the sizzle of battle still in their veins, ate and drank with their comrades. Meanwhile, the crew chiefs prepared their ships for a future that was swiftly and surely preparing for them.

CHAPTER 2

Birth of the Assault
Helicopter Company

Helicopter soldiers, as they were called by the NVA, snuffed out the fire in the stubborn enemy's belly.

Battle-hardened by years of war, the NVA believed they could rid Vietnam of the *soft* Americans with one powerful, decisive blow. They had ousted the French in 1954 at the Battle of Dien Bien Phu, a brutal fifty-five-day siege, and they were positioned for a repeat performance. But the NVA soon discovered that brute force wouldn't defeat the tightly packaged American will and tactical might. This tight tactical package? The assault-helicopter company.

In the spring of 1962, at the urgency of Secretary of Defense Robert McNamara, the Army assembled a group of experts charged with researching, testing, and evaluating the battlefield employment of helicopters. The US Army Tactical Mobility Requirements Board, better known as the *Howze Board*, hustled to comply with the defense secretary's directive and, therefore, developed the Eleventh Air Assault Division (Test).[1] However, as was the case with wheeled vehicles that replaced the horse and with track vehicles that replaced the cavalry, rotary-wing aircraft drew their share of criticism.

J. A. Stockfisch, in his report *The 1962 Howze Board and Army Combat Developments*, explains in great detail the controversy the board experienced. "Since Army aviation was a continual source of tension between the Army and the Air Force (including the World War II Army Air Forces), attention is given to the disagreements of 'close air support.'" Central to this entire torrent of criticism was the timing of the board's convening. The board met while the bulk of the military hierarchy focused on the Soviet threat to western Europe. High-level military brass perceived the Soviet threat as requiring heavy conventional units, and they feared that the new technology of light airmobile units could only occur at the expense

---

1 Shelby L. Stanton, *Vietnam Order of Battle: A Complete Illustrated Reference to U.S. Army Combat and Support Forces in Vietnam 1961–1973* (New York: Stackpole Books/Rowman & Littlefield, 2003).

of heavy units. At the same time, the incoming Kennedy administration placed a much greater emphasis on the need to fight "small wars," or counterinsurgencies, and strongly supported the Howze Board and other officers who embraced new technologies. It was a giant shove in the right direction. For airmobile advocates, the emphasis from the Kennedy administration drew the desired change.

Eventually, Army strategists convinced high-level brass to fully develop the Eleventh Air Assault Division into a complete airmobile division. Its primary mission? To engage and destroy enemy units by *vertically* enveloping their ground forces. Highly mobile and able to land on terrain accessible by no other aircraft, the helicopter was the perfect delivery vehicle. Its proof of viability came soon after and would tip the scales in favor of American lives.

On a bright Sunday morning, November 14, 1965, the NVA met American airmobile forces in battle for the first time. In the Ia Drang Valley of Vietnam's Central Highlands,[2] the First Battalion, Seventh Cavalry (1st/7th) of the First Air Cavalry Division (Airmobile) shattered the NVA notions of a speedy Dien Bien Phu–type victory. At the base of the Chu Pong Massif, a 2,400-foot mountain chain with forests stretching five miles into Cambodia, approximately 450 troops of the 1st/7th made their stand against two full regiments of NVA with 2,500 enemy soldiers. Chu Pong gave the NVA an observation advantage and a high-ground battle superiority. Based on conventional battle wisdom, this combat scenario and overwhelming enemy-troop strength had the potential to produce a massacre of Americans.

The LZ for troop insertion lay in a clearing directly below Chu Pong with the North Vietnamese stronghold above. Tactically named *LZ X-ray*, the landing zone, with its large, clear area, could accept the largest number of troop-carrying helicopters at one time, a total of eight UH-1D Hueys, more affectionately known as *slicks*. There, for the first time in its existence, the airmobile concept arrived in Vietnam. In the shadow of Chu Pong, the Huey was destined to prove worthy or fail at the expense of hundreds of American lives. The suspense was colossal.

Facing a considerably larger force of the NVA's finest soldiers, the 1st/7th Cavalry Battalion dug in. With stubborn repetition, the NVA massed decisively larger numbers of its best troops against the smaller American unit. For three days and two nights, in some of the bloodiest fighting of the war, the NVA hammered the Americans with everything they could muster.

Day one exploded into a battle of attrition. Stacking enemy bodies without letup, 1st/7th soldiers poured fire into the attacking enemy ranks. Throughout the melee, UH-1 cav helicopters inserted troops from the 1st/7th and supported them with ammunition resupply or medevacs as needed.[3] Though skewed in favor of the US

---

2 LTG Harold G. Moore and Joseph L. Galloway, *We Were Soldiers Once and Young* (New York: Random House Inc., 1992), 59.
3 Moore and Galloway, *We Were Soldiers Once and Young*, 147.

force, death totals in both enemy and friendly forces were staggering. Relentless, the enemy's fire reached the American unit's command post (CP), striking fear among higher-ranking battle planners. Typically, this type of penetration is a tipping point in most ground assaults. The higher CPs stationed in Saigon felt the weight of a battle that was surely a loss for the Americans. Nonetheless, stubborn 1st/7th troops regrouped and fought off their attackers, regaining control. In Washington, DC, fear of losing this battle gripped responsible US brass well up into the hierarchy of President Lyndon B. Johnson's cabinet. Obliged to keep the president informed, Defense Secretary McNamara briefed the White House daily.

Not to be deterred, waves of NVA soldiers continued to charge the Americans with confidence built from years of combat experience and numerous victories against French occupation forces. But the greatest enemy oversight was the strength given the American ground force by an ever-constant flow of men, equipment, and supplies ferried by assault helicopters.

This airmobile resupply and reinforcement produced a decisive difference. Although enemy attacks continued, the assault helicopters were able to strategically insert American troops wielding modern US weapons. These troops decisively repelled NVA soldiers by well-placed ground fire. The assault helicopters' main resupply weapon for the troops was the Colt M16-A1, *the individual soldier's weapon*, with a firing capacity of 650 rounds per minute. Among combat veterans, the effectiveness of a circular perimeter of 450 American soldiers armed with this type of firepower is akin to an enormous circular saw of fiery lead. Through constant resupply, the assault helicopter allowed for this weapon to be foremost in this performance result.

For certain, combat effectiveness on the ground at LZ X-ray was stabilized by expedient air-assault reinforcements inserted into the LZ when needed. In the early afternoon of the first day of fighting, the 1st/7th commander, Lieutenant Colonel (LTC) Harold Gregory "Hal" Moore Jr., realized his worst-case scenario: "We were in heavy contact and did not have my entire battalion on the ground." But soon "Old Snake," Major (MAJ) Bruce Crandall, commanding the assault-helicopter company, "came up on the radio and announced he was inbound with the fourth lift of the day. He was carrying the last few men of CPT Tony Nadal's Alpha Company and the lead elements of CPT Bob Edwards's Charlie Company troops."[4] The American reinforcements were good news and changed the battle tide. Supported by gunship strikes and powerful artillery barrages that dismembered enemy bodies and sent human pieces tumbling into the air, the American soldiers held their perimeter and quickly laid the battleground awash in enemy blood. Wave after wave of enemy met the same fury.

---

4 Moore and Galloway, *We Were Soldiers Once and Young*, 78.

As darkness fell on the first day of fighting, the NVA were introduced to another American battle tactic they had not experienced during their French engagements. Well-organized and brilliantly planned indirect-fire support, combined with air and gunship strikes, shattered enemy morale. Knowing that low visibility obscured enemy movements during hours of darkness, LTC Moore ordered all his elements to register interdicting artillery fires on suspected enemy approach routes to his troops. He also directed the tactical interlocking of machine-gun fields of fire for added effectiveness. This also protected an American platoon trapped and surrounded by NVA, away from the battalion's position.

The shock effect on the unsuspecting enemy was devastating. Enemy shouts and screams lifted into the night air for all the battlefield to hear. The chilling desperation in the human cries of anguish, shouted in a foreign dialect as they passed their final living moments, confirmed the horrific effectiveness of the tactic. The cries of the dying penetrated even the calloused hearts and minds of the strongest American soldiers, inflicting a heart-wrenching impact. Yet, the Americans steadfastly held their perimeter through the night. On command, rounds continued to land on enemy positions in the dark.[5]

The nonstop airmobile support by MAJ Crandall's assault-helicopter unit drew a moment of conflict in the late hours of the first day of battle. The assault birds had pulled pitch at 0600 hours and didn't shutdown until after 2200 hours, thirty-seven miles to the northeast. Crandall recalls his experience of exiting the aircraft: "I was approached by the commander of the medevac helicopter company, who proceeded to chew my ass for having led his people into a hot LZ and warned me never to do that again. I couldn't understand how he had the balls to face me when he was so reluctant to face the enemy. If several of my pilots had not restrained me, that officer would have earned a righteous Purple Heart that night."[6]

Nighttime squelched the battle scene, but dawn brought even stronger enemy effort to break through the American perimeter. Though stubborn in their mission objectives, enemy brass was forced to pack and run when, on the second day of fighting, the Americans mounted a counterattack in the direction of the Chu Pong Massif to reunite with the surrounded American platoon. Quickly leaving their defensive positions and assembling into attack formation, 1st/7th troops levied their might against the enemy in a surprise move that caught the NVA unprepared. Supported by the very core of the airmobile principle, its powerful mass of air and gunship firepower accelerated the aggressive 1st/7th move toward the Chu Pong slope. In its path, the 1st/7th encountered a bloody turf of decimated enemy positions and soldiers. Hidden from observation by the Americans, enemy bodies were

---

5 Moore and Galloway, *We Were Soldiers Once and Young,* 153.
6 Ibid., 147.

piled high behind giant termite mounds. The NVA paid a high price in attacking the well-armed 1st/7th. A lesson paid in blood.

The third day of fighting brought a progressive reduction in enemy aggression, a sign of enemy defeat by heavy attrition. Its forces effectively decimated, NVA commanders ordered withdrawal. When the 1st/7th was extracted from LZ X-ray, not a shot was fired at the departing battalion. Dedicated helicopter gunship and artillery support tipped the scales in favor of the smaller airmobile force. The enemy was finished, and the airmobile concept sound and proven. Helicopter soldiers, as they were called by the NVA, snuffed out the fire in the stubborn enemy's belly.

From this resounding victory at Ia Drang, a whole new approach to battle became fascinating to military tacticians. From it would come improvements in aircraft lift capabilities and advanced attack potential. New rotary-wing weapon systems evolved, such as the powerful AH-1G (Cobra) attack helicopter that became a stalwart performer in close air support for ground troops. Cobras also provided excellent fire cover for assault birds of the 191st.

After the Battle of Ia Drang on the Chu Pong Massif, ground combat would never be the same. Helicopters could land in terrain so isolated and rugged that Army trucks could not negotiate nor access it. As a result, the enemy was left with no place to hide. Cover and concealment no longer offered the tactical advantage it had historically delivered. This changed the entire course of conventional warfare. The NVA witnessed the changing of the guard firsthand. Finding the First Air Cavalry's powerful punch much too expensive in body losses, the NVA melted into the jungle and retreated to the sanctuary of Cambodia and Laos.

Having repeatedly demonstrated their spectacular strength, the First Air Cavalry's performance forever laid to rest early skeptics' questions of airmobile effectiveness. The airmobile concept was now, officially, the next big thing of the Vietnam War. From this trend emerged the media poster child of the era: the UH-1 (Iroquois) helicopter, affectionately nicknamed the *Huey*. Not a day went by when American TV viewers were not treated to a heavy dose of the marvelous Huey: Hueys evacuating wounded, Hueys attacking enemy positions, Hueys carrying troops into battle.

With its five-hundred-pound L-11 gas-turbine engine that produced 1,100 shaft horsepower, the five-thousand-pound Huey could nearly lift its own weight, delivering a payload of three thousand pounds while carrying one thousand three hundred pounds of fuel. The D-model (slick) had a forty-eight-foot rotor span and was red-lined for maximum airspeed at 120 knots, but it cruised best at 80 knots. Stripped of offensive weapons, it had only two pintle-mounted M60 machine guns used for defense. This slick configuration allowed the Huey to work as troop carrier, transporting six—and at times seven—fully equipped combat troops. The Charlie-model gunship had the upgraded 540 rotor system and wider blades that enabled cruise speeds up to 140 knots. It carried an array of weapon systems. Its 2.75-inch folding-fin rockets, with either ten- or seventeen-pound warheads, delivered the primary punch. Its secondary systems included an electrically powered 7.62-millimeter minigun with six rotating barrels that could spit out six thousand rounds per minute, adjustable to two thousand, and a 40-millimeter grenade launcher with a rate of fire of thirty rounds per minute. Equally deadly, two bungee-mounted M60 machine guns, each in the hands of excellent marksmen: a crew chief and a gunner.

As a tactical package, an assault-helicopter company produced a formidable battlefield solution. It delivered combat-ready troops into action with remarkable efficiency. With the helicopter advantage, the infantry ground troops could be resupplied or reinforced far quicker than any enemy effort could match. In retrospect, it isn't any wonder that the Army found itself in one hell of a hurry to create more Huey outfits. Amid this post-haste fervor to increase airmobile assets for the new helicopter war, the 2029th Quartermaster Truck Company, Aviation, of WWII, came out of retirement on September 30, 1966, and transformed into the 191st Aviation Company, Airmobile Light.[7]

Whether by fluke or by design, when the Army's decision makers threw the 191st together, they had no inkling of the spirited beast it would become. The entire process was initiated from the Pentagon, where the table of organization and equipment (TOE) experts released the authority for assembly of the 191st AHC.

On December 1, 1966, an action officer prepared the order for equipping the 191st AHC. Clicking with the noise of typewriters, the Pentagon room pulsed with activity. In moments, the electronic directive reached a warehouse supply officer, whose staff scrambled to fill the order. Aircraft, weapon systems, munitions, communications gear, and an array of other combat gear convened from destinations worldwide.

The Army furnished used *major end items*, such as aircraft and vehicles, to newly formed combat organizations when new equipment was unavailable. The hardware authorization for the 191st AHC was akin to acquiring vehicles from a used car lot. While a used vehicle might deliver acceptable service, its longevity cannot compare to most new units. At the rate US forces were losing UH-1 helicopters in Vietnam, its producer, Bell Helicopter Company, could not replace the numbers fast enough. One can easily imagine the normal wear and tear of combat aircraft. Hence, a repair depot was created to refurbish those birds with reparable damage. That became the supplier of hand-me-down helicopters for the 191st AHC. Organizational timing was the reason for this equipment disposition. The 191st was born late in the birth order of assault-helicopter companies; therefore, like a kid brother, it would have to live with hand-me-downs and leftovers.

Headed for Vietnam, this conglomerate of equipment and supplies was transported expediently to marry up with its users in-country. Equally hurried, the administrative

7 191st AHC Unit History, 1968–69.

branch of the Pentagon assembled the personnel order to meet the equipment in Vietnam and form the 191st AHC.

The equipment and supply order was inanimate. It required minimal human interaction. But the personnel ordered to operate this equipment were another matter. This encompassed the human side of combat operations. And while military equipment has its design limitations and employment doctrine that orients its employment to users, soldiers add a totally different perspective to this combat equation. Each personality is its own world, so to speak.

Unbeknown to Army authorities, when the First Airmobile Cavalry Division was formed, most of its officers and men were selected from organized units en masse. This omitted many qualified soldiers who aspired to serve in the airmobile field. The 191st was fortunate to gain many volunteers previously passed over. And while the First Cavalry Airmobile received all-new aircraft, equipment, and supplies, the 191st made do with hand-me-downs and spare parts. To make up for this, the unit's personnel closed the gap with field expediency and the will to excel. This eventually led to outstanding performance from a unit assembled from a hodgepodge selection of used aircraft, spare equipment, and overlooked personnel who wanted to make a difference. And they did. The 191st story defines a new breed of soldier: the combat assault-helicopter crewman.

CHAPTER 3

Patnode Commanding

Patnode had seen the inner soul of the 191st AHC and understood the precious gem
hidden within its underdog appearance.

Buzzing with the loud banter of military personnel en route to their first combat
assignment, the passenger cabin of the Boeing 707 was packed with the officers and
men of the newly minted 191st AHC. To entertain themselves on the long trip to
Vietnam, the fresh-faced Boomerangs and Bounty Hunters shared aerial-combat
stories learned in flight school. Others sought spiritual reassurance and prayed in
quiet reverence. A few joked and ribbed each other like young men often do. Of
course, alcohol contributed to the frequently comical spectacle.

One hardcore rebel harassed his flight school friend who was blessed with a
beautiful wife. "Hey, William, put me in your will," he said. "Your wife will need
a real man to take care of her if you get your balls shot off."

Two others, whose flight school classmate married a gorgeous cheerleader from
their former high school, mocked the wedding in typical guy style. "Did you hear
about Bobby and Gina getting married? You remember? That sexy cheerleader with
the big boobs from high school?"

"No! You got to be kidding?"

"No, man! Not kidding. They got married last month. There is no way he can
handle that—that's too much woman for his puny ass."

"Naw, man! He ain't hitting that right. She's gonna need a lot more than he's got."

But their young antics hid the inevitable question plaguing the mind of each young
pilot and aircrewman: *Who among us is not coming back alive?* The foolish behavior
persisted among the hard drinkers until their bodies yielded to the alcohol. With
comical semblance, their bodies slumped and their heads bobbed uncontrollably.
Some passengers howled at the spectacle as inebriated asses gradually slid down the
seat cushions, their knees becoming trapped by the seat in front. The sound sleep
that followed would come at a stern price when the hungover bodies woke up in
Vietnam.

Sitting in the front row, MAJ Clarence "Bud" Patnode shared a seat with First Sergeant (1SG) Thomas D. Croley. Patnode quietly recalled the major events in his military training that had prepared him for war. Despite the hodgepodge assembly of spare parts and spare people, Patnode had spent enough time with the brand-new 191st at Fort Bragg, North Carolina, to know what the unit could deliver.

At Fort Bragg, the first to breathe life into the 191st AHC were the unit's command personnel, staff officers, and noncommissioned officers (NCOs). Of those, the administrative officer CW2 Benjamin Hauser was the heart of the unit, pumping lifeblood into the functional components of the 191st. Each stroke of his pen gave life to a working part—a human body ordered to deliver skill sets essential for airmobile support of infantry troops in Vietnam. But looming ahead with heavy impact were orders for unit deployment that mandated departure dates, which harbored irreversible consequences. Either you fill your authorized manning levels from available personnel, or go without. "Hell, we got more cooks than crew chiefs," Hauser had said to his NCO assistant. To make a tough situation even tougher, one individual coming in was a conscientious objector. This fact worried Hauser.

"When first assembled at Bragg," Hauser recalls, "it all sounded good on paper, but in reality, people just showed up from every conceivable source in insufficient numbers, skill levels, and attitudes. When we finally shipped out, unit components were scattered to various ports of debarkation to be united in Vietnam by who knows who, where, or how."

Patnode had managed to ready this hodgepodge outfit for battle, and had no doubt about their level of motivation and commitment. What was more, he was prepared to draw on his experience on the Field Test Committee of the Howze Board. He had organized and observed many of the tests and evaluations that had created the airmobile concept. Armed with this state-of-the-art tactical knowledge, Patnode would waste none of his command opportunity. Born of a French-Canadian father who inculcated a hard work ethic, and an English-Scots-Irish mother with strong principles, Patnode's time was at hand. Patnode would become the stabilizing force the unit needed to prove it worthy of its tough assignment. In fact, if it weren't for Patnode, the 191st would have been decapitated soon after stepping foot in Vietnam.

Some twenty hours earlier, the 191st warriors had departed the US West Coast to become an airmobile asset of the First Aviation Brigade in Vietnam. The anticipation of combat among the men was rampant, creating myriad thoughts of what their futures would hold. In just a few hours, the airliner would land at Bien Hoa Air Base in the Republic of Vietnam (RVN), and a very memorable part of Patnode's Army career would take on a new reality. The Howze Board had a pivotal effect on American battle tactics, and its findings had become the very instrument that laid the groundwork for the combat role in which Patnode would soon operate. Now, five years after the Howze Board and less than six months after joining the 191st AHC at Fort Bragg, Patnode was on his way to the RVN, where he would live or die implementing the airmobile tactics he had personally tested and evaluated as a member of the Howze Board.

Deployed to Vietnam on May 24, 1967, the main body of the 191st AHC arrived at Bien Hoa Air Base eager to join the fight. The First Aviation Brigade was the first of its kind, and without question the most powerful assembly of aviation assets ever conceived by the United States Army. This fact excited 191st members. It created aspirations for greatness among many of them. Their opportunity was finally at hand.

Once the door of the Boeing 707 opened, the 191st officers and men peered out into a world far removed from any semblance of the American ecology they had just left. Vietnam had a very distinct stench that raised the bar of bad air well beyond anything in America. It smelled rotten, like something equal to a giant fish kill that had overripened under a scorching sun.

MAJ Patnode and 1SG Croley looked at one another with raised eyebrows as if to say, "Well, here we are, and *man*—what a cesspool!"

At a glance, it was easy for the Americans GIs to see why the country needed help. The prevalence of ox carts may have been a sign of an older, pastoral culture; nonetheless, to the Americans, life in South Vietnam seemed to be in disarray, with the Communist threat to their democratic freedoms looming in their future.

Stepping onto the off-loading stairs, Patnode got his first clear view of Bien Hoa Air Base and scanned the scene. The young major's gaze locked with that of a two-star general, standing tall and erect at the bottom of the stairs, the embodiment of military hierarchy. Patnode trotted down the steps and stood at attention as the general approached. He read the general's nametag: Seneff. Patnode was about to meet the First Aviation Brigade commander. He stood a little stiffer. He knew that Major General (MG) George P. Seneff occupied a high-profile seat in the Vietnam theater of operations, and his presence signified the high priority bestowed upon arriving aviation units. Patnode had no doubt that the general viewed the deployment of the 191st as an important event in the overall war effort.

MG Seneff was accompanied by Colonel (COL) Nicholas G. Psaki, the Twelfth Aviation Group commander, and LTC James M. Leslie, the 214th Combat Aviation Battalion (CAB) commander. Well composed in a military manner, Patnode rendered a snappy hand salute. "Good afternoon, sir. I'm Major Patnode, commander of the 191st Gun Platoon. I'm reporting with the 191st Assault Helicopter Company main body, sir!"

General Seneff returned the salute. Concerned by the designated 191st company commander's (CO) absence, his eyes opened wide and his eyebrows raised in an inquisitive look. "Where is your company commander?"

"He stayed behind with the rear detachment, sir!"

The general's mouth pulled down into a frown, and his eyes narrowed. He appeared visibly disturbed. "Why?"

"I don't know, sir. I can't really answer that question."

Without another word, the general departed and left the 191st main body of troops standing alone on the Bien Hoa Air Base tarmac.

A transportation officer approached Patnode. "Sir, I'm Captain Evans [pseudonym]. I'm charged with the responsibility of transporting your troops to Bearcat." He pointed to a convoy of five-ton troop carriers. "If you'll have your troops move to the transport vehicles you see over there?"

"Roger that."

Patnode directed 1SG Croley to organize and load the troops. Not having heard Patnode's conversation with MG Seneff, the gaggle of fresh-faced Boomerangs and Bounty Hunters remained in high spirits, leaping onto open tractor trailers and continuing their youthful banter from the day before. The convoy took off, heading fifteen miles south of the city of Bien Hoa in Dong Nai province to a place called Bearcat.

On both sides of the road, dense jungle stretched out for forty miles. The Boomerangs and Bounty Hunters wished they were flying above the tangle of jungle instead of sitting in uncovered tractor trailers with no weapons and no protection. Those with previous combat experience felt naked without their sidearms.

"This place gives me the creeps!"

"We're not in Kansas anymore."

"Just get me in a bird!"

Nonetheless, they arrived safe and in one piece at Bearcat, home base of the US Ninth Infantry Division, just fourteen miles due east of Saigon. It was nothing much to look at—just a hot, steamy hole in the jungle. It lacked significant preparations, but that would change soon enough.

First, the fledgling AHC faced an immediate survival challenge. No sooner had they arrived at Bearcat when MAJ Patnode was summoned to the 214th CAB's command headquarters. After reporting without delay, Patnode stood once again before General Seneff and his two high-ranking officers, COL Psaki and LTC Leslie. Again dispensing with preliminary small talk, the general went right to the core of what was on his mind, opening the meeting with a direct and very disturbing question for Patnode.

"I am considering disbanding the 191st to use the equipment and personnel as fillers. What are your thoughts about that, Major?"

Having spent nearly six months with these men at Fort Bragg in preparation for deployment to Vietnam, MAJ Patnode knew their capacity and motivation. Patnode realized that cannibalizing the 191st to fill voids in other aviation units would be a grave mistake. *What a waste that would be*, he thought. Patnode had seen the inner soul of the 191st AHC and understood the precious gem hidden within its underdog appearance.

Arriving in Vietnam minus its CO was not out of the ordinary for the 191st, considering the sequence of events the unit had already undergone. Certainly, on the contrary, MG Seneff viewed the missing CO as equivalent to decapitation. To the informed staff officers watching the dismal arrival of the hodgepodge unit, they might have deduced that the First Aviation Brigade commander saw the 191st as a headless chicken with no directional control. The reactivation and retrofitting of the 191st with its mix of ingredients from leftover personnel and hand-me-down older birds with tired airframes and well-worn engines was enough to cripple most chances of success. It's no wonder the general's staff doubted the outfit would make the grade. In their minds, it was doomed to fail.

But Patnode knew better. "General, that is the *dumbest* decision you could make."

For a few seconds, the meeting room fell into a dead stillness. All were stunned by the audacity of MAJ Patnode's condescending words to the general. The startled LTC Leslie grimaced and stood by for the ram that the general would surely give Patnode. But it never came. Somehow, Patnode's words struck the right chord, and the general's expression softened slightly.

"Why do you say that?" This time the general's tone was almost congenial.

"Sir, this unit has something you can't order and you can't issue. It has an *outstanding* positive attitude!" Although Patnode truly believed in what he was saying to the general, he wished his earlier remark had been more tactful. He could tell from LTC Leslie's facial expressions that his foot-in-mouth response to MG Seneff had deeply disturbed his battalion commander. The last thing he needed was to end up jobless and become a staff officer under LTC Leslie.

"Major, do you really think you can make something out of this outfit?" The look in the general's eyes was sincere.

"Yes, sir. I can!"

"Okay, you got it. Colonel Leslie—assemble the 191st troops!"

Just that fast, the meeting at the 214th headquarters ended, every bit as bluntly as the meeting at Bien Hoa. The general and officers headed to the 191st Company area. In the short walk that followed, Patnode wondered how the troops would react to his assignment as their new CO. The answer was not long in coming.

In the 191st Company area, the entire population of the newly arrived 191st AHC mingled about, unaware of how their fate took a turn. Many of the pilots among the fresh lot had survived the rigors of flight school together. Norman R. Kidd, Jack L. Dodson, Sharel "Spike" Edward Bales, and David C. Hall all graduated from Officer's Rotary Wing Aviator Class of 66-20 before joining the 191st at Fort Bragg. As they waited, they joked around and ribbed each other, just as they had done in flight school back in Fort Rucker, Alabama, a far cry from the rice paddies of Vietnam.

MG Seneff addressed the 191st troops. His remarks were brief, introducing Patnode as their new CO and encouraging them to get combat-ready as soon as they could. Afterward, the general turned to face Patnode.

"Atten-tion!" Patnode called the company to attention and saluted the general. Patnode and his men remained at attention until MG Seneff and the senior officers left.

With the simplicity of that conclusion, the identity of the 191st was saved from becoming extinct in a war that was perfectly suited for the killing machine it would become. Unbeknown to the decision makers assembled there on that auspicious day, the 191st AHC was destined to deliver legendary combat performance and become an airmobile crown jewel of the Ninth Infantry Division. Time would soon bear out this fact.

Patnode ordered the platoon leaders to the orderly room tent for his first official command meeting. With his mind still reeling from his sudden command assignment, Patnode addressed his men. "Gentlemen, following this meeting I need to inspect the company area, and I need the officer in charge of the advanced party to accompany me. Who is that person?"

CPT Richard Jenkins [pseudonym] raised his hand. "Sir, that would be me, Captain Jenkins."

"Very well, Captain. Please stand by after the meeting."

"Yes, sir!"

"Gentlemen, I am pleased that the 191st Assault Helicopter Company has finally arrived at our combat base of operations, and I'm sure I don't have to emphasize the work that's ahead. I'm going to expect daily briefings from you concerning the readiness status of your section or platoon. These meetings will begin at 0600 hours, which means if you plan to eat breakfast, you need to be in the mess hall no later than 0500 hours. Any questions on that assignment?"

With not even a murmur from the troops, Patnode continued: "Very well! By tomorrow morning, I need to see a list of your assigned personnel and a confirmation that your list is numerically correct in accordance with the unit manning report submitted daily to higher headquarters by First Sergeant Croley. Any questions? No? Okay, this concludes our first command meeting. I'll see you again in the morning. Meantime, feel free to seek me out if you find a major problem in your assigned area of responsibility. Thank you."

Expecting to arrive in Vietnam and soon be joined by the CO from Fort Bragg, along with the rear detachment, Patnode had no earthly idea he would become its first CO. In fact, he had prepared the 191st troops with the contingency that someone with in-country experience would more than likely be assigned command of the company and would lead them into battle. Suddenly, the weight of that responsibility landed squarely on his shoulders. But if the burden was unsettling to Patnode, he never showed it.

Patnode's troops celebrated his new position. In fact, many were relieved. First Lieutenant (1LT) Dee Kennedy later explains: "The Stateside CO before Patnode had published a bizarre OPORD requiring all pilots to fly with an entrenching tool strapped to their web gear. Virtually each pilot who went over with the unit was planning to seek reassignment from the 191st for fear of having to fly under such a strange leader." That attitude quickly reversed when the general gave Patnode the company command.

MG Seneff's hunch about Patnode proved correct. The troops had trained with him and had developed a rapport with the young major, and now they would rally behind his leadership and produce optimal results. Patnode had certainly made an impression on MG Seneff. Seldom in the history of war is there a record wherein a subordinate addressed a commander three levels above him with the condescending words used by Patnode—and survived to tell about it. But to get promoted to a command position on the spot was an anointing of unprecedented proportion. Patnode won a big moral victory, and his troops were happy. The unknown potential of getting a CO they might not like was now resolved, and the unit could get underway with their battle preparations.

With Patnode's first command meeting concluded, he signaled for Jenkins to meet him outside the orderly room tent. "Captain Jenkins, let's start by you showing me around the company area so I'll know where everything is, and then we'll focus on overall status of the settlement process."

"Yes, sir! I recommend we start with the maintenance area and proceed from there, if that's all right with you, sir?"

Patnode nodded in agreement, but he was not happy with what he saw. There were no bunker facilities for the officers and men to take cover in during enemy attacks. There were no maintenance tents to cover the entire airframe of the UH-1 helicopters. In fact, mechanics assembled mere pup-tents over the tail-rotor assembly to deflect some of the rain while working. During the monsoon season this would be a constant problem when wind blew these pup-tent covers away, allowing hydraulic components or fluid to become water-contaminated. Appalled, Patnode mentally filed the images away to research a better resolution.

"Sir, the tents and equipment arrived piecemeal," Jenkins said. "And while the unit's advance party preceded the main body and unit combat equipment by several weeks, some of these components you see being installed now arrived very recently—like two or three days ago. Our job, of course, was to carve out a home for the 191st here at Bearcat. We've done the best we could under the circumstances, sir."

Patnode nodded his head in acknowledgment.

Decades later, Patnode recalls, "Our host unit, the Two Hundredth Assault Support Helicopter Company [ASHC], went way beyond what was expected of them to assist us. They helped the advance party set up our area, they shared the mess hall with us, and even volunteered to do the routine garrison duties while the 191st prepared for action. They were truly great hosts."

The early arrivals, although sometimes criticized, staked out a spot for the unit to settle, and prepared the area despite being hammered by monsoons. Although constructed crudely at times, the area had the installation essentials, including tents for maintenance, flight operations, sleeping quarters, showers, and open-pit latrines. The latrine was particularly unforgettable.

"Straddling a slit trench for a bowel movement was a sobering experience," recalls one pilot. "It took a while to get the hang of it without dropping your wallet or pocket articles down into the smelly pit."

Fortunately for early arrivals, not all life-sustaining essentials in Bearcat were that unsavory. Months later, compared to the unit's initial digs, the new wooden barracks seemed like upscale living.

Now responsible for the well-being of nearly three hundred troops, Patnode set out to solidify his unit and prepare it for battle. The enormous responsibility of the unit mission, which required the mixing and meshing of people, equipment, and material in combat scenarios, proved to be a hefty load. This job required a firm hand. Three days after the 191st arrival, that realization was put to the test.

In the maintenance area, compartmentalization efforts were underway. The 606th Maintenance Detachment, which provided helicopter maintenance support, and the Twenty-Sixth Signal Detachment, which serviced the aircraft avionics equipment, erected signs identifying their hours and areas of operation. They roped off their work spaces, specifically emitting a hands-off and stay-in-your-lane approach for "customers" requesting support. Further asserting their authoritative attitude, they listed certain paperwork and forms requiring completion and signature by proper authority before services would be rendered. In effect, the penetration and support of their "fiefdoms" would require a work order, or some other administrative impediment. But this was war in the middle of a bloody jungle, not a cushy job back in "the world."

Within a few short seconds, Patnode visualized the bottleneck effect it would have on his unit's productivity. Careful to hide his anger, Patnode summoned 1SG Croley. "Top, assemble the maintenance personnel and bring all these signs you see here to a pile in the middle of the maintenance area. I need to speak to this support group."

"Yes, sir!"

Maintenance personnel assembled around the pile of signs dumped in the middle of the area. Patnode looked into the faces of the maintenance crews, making sure he had their undivided attention. He stepped onto the pile of signs and stomped a couple into splinters.

"Understand this!" Patnode launched into a stern lecture on his philosophy of teamwork. "There will be no bureaucracy separating the various units that need to work together here to get this job done. I am not happy with the message these signs project."

He stomped on a few more. "We are one unit for all, and we have a tough mission to accomplish together. We cannot afford to build bureaucracy into our operation. If there is paperwork that needs to be done, then you make damn sure that it does not create a stumbling block for production. If the aircrews have problems completing any forms required for your support, then you do what is necessary to help them get it done. I do not want to hear that a bird is down because the paperwork has not been properly completed. We must all be willing to do whatever it takes to sustain the unit in combat and to ensure our pilots have the safest birds they can fly. It matters not what the military specialties are. We do whatever *the hell* it takes to get the job done—as one team!"

The maintenance crews knew their commander meant business, and nary a one wished to test the veracity of his words. Quietly, when dismissed, they returned to their work stations and began preparing for an all-out effort to comply with Patnode's directives. The stern ass chewing produced the right effect. The first sergeant was later heard telling the operations section, "Man, they started jumping through their asses!"

There was no doubt in Patnode's mind that the maintenance operation needed his personal attention. Making that need a high priority, the new CO laid out a maintenance schedule for the aircraft to begin their periodic inspections (PE) at the rate of one per day. He ordered crew chiefs to assist in the process and remain with their birds through the entire PE. This wise order properly sized the unit's maintenance load for its technical resources, identified maintenance trends created by combat stress, and struck a vein of goodwill between his crew chiefs and maintenance personnel. In turn, camaraderie developed between the flight crews and maintenance personnel, which facilitated one-on-one communication when the crew chiefs had routine questions. As a bonus, the crew chiefs became better technicians. Patnode's engineering background was right on target, and his operational planning allowed the 191st AHC maintenance system to generate a significantly higher ratio of flight hours than any other AHC in Vietnam.

As Patnode walked away from the maintenance area, he realized the magnitude of the responsibility he had accepted from MG Seneff. Reaching into his military experience, Patnode knew he had to lead by example and provide the necessary guidance and influence that would unite his troops. Collecting his thoughts after he visited each of the 191st platoons and sections, the young major rolled up his sleeves and went to work.

Patnode watched as his unit reassembled and regained the tactical strength it had achieved at Fort Bragg. The slick and gun platoons got busy equipping and preparing the aircraft for sustained war operations. They armed and checked weapons systems and distributed essential combat gear to the flight crews and ground personnel. Individuals staked their claims to bunks in tents that would be their home until permanent barracks could be completed. In a busy and efficient whirl, 1SG Croley and the orderly room staff set up a headquarters for the company. The training officer, 1LT Ollie "Dee" Kennedy, and the tactical operations center (TOC) personnel completed the communication links with higher headquarters, which included the necessary protocols for quickly acclimating to Bearcat flight operations. Patnode drew on all his faculties to reestablish essential order to the deployment as soon as possible. He was anxious to get on with the mission they came here to perform: largely, combat-assault operations in support of the Ninth Infantry Division.

A new product of its time, the 191st was a gift horse that the Ninth Infantry Division only vaguely knew how to handle. It had come along at the right place and at the right time to deliver immeasurable death and destruction upon the enemy. Patnode knew this. With an Eighty-Second Airborne company-command tour behind him, he could very clearly see both sides of the tactical equation, air and ground. He was satisfied that things were coming together as he had envisioned on the Howze Board. Soon he would coordinate some airmobile tactical solutions with the ground-force commanders that would forever change the course of American battle strategy. Specifically, his implementation of fire-support options never before tried on the battlefield evolved into battle doctrine and endured well beyond the Vietnam War.

Typically during airmobile assaults, supporting artillery fires were shifted away from the LZ periphery to avoid hitting friendly air traffic. Instead, Patnode urged infantry commanders to inform the C&C pilots of the max-ord (altitude of artillery trajectories) along with the azimuth (direct compass bearing) from the guns to the target and point of impact (exact map coordinates where the artillery fire would land). Under Patnode's command, the C&C pilots vectored the combat-assault flights under or around the artillery fire. This brilliant move, unconventional at the time, kept the heat on the enemy.[1] The pressure remained constant as troops were inserted into an LZ. This tactic not only saved American lives, but further intensified the vertical-envelopment impact on the enemy. The constant artillery pounding kept the Vietnamese forces pinned down while the assault force landed and deployed into attack formation.

A big boost for the 191st came in the way of infusion, a practice used by the US Army in Vietnam to cross-level experienced and inexperienced personnel from one organization to another. As entire units arrived in Vietnam, their date eligible for return from overseas (DEROS) for everyone in that unit was the same. Left unchecked, an organization would lose most of its original and battle-savvy personnel simultaneously. Infusion offered balance, assuring survival of more troops. Attrition for most combat units was about 5 percent per month, so that 60 percent would have left in a year anyway. Infusion was designed to get units started off well and decluster DEROSs as a by-product.[2] Here again, Patnode's engineer brain anticipated a potential problem. Consulting with his admin officer, CW2 Benjamin Hauser, Patnode developed a method for ranking the efficiency levels of people leaving the

---

1 Decades later, a retired Patnode, watching a televised national news program from a comfortable sofa, smiled to himself when he saw the same attack formation utilized in Iraq. American gunships flew low level, under an umbrella of protective artillery fire, and methodically destroyed an entire Iraqi tank division in a desert war.

2 Infusion practice and its functional ratios were furnished by COL Lee Dyment (Ret.), Ninth Infantry Division G1, 1968–1969.

191st so that he could confer with commanders of units furnishing replacements and ensure he got equally capable personnel.

From one of these trades came CPT Leonard J. Rodowick, who was one of the most outstanding maintenance officers in Vietnam at the time. With Rodowick at the maintenance helm, Patnode devoted himself to other pressing matters. Shortly thereafter, the 191st also acquired a combat-hardened gunship pilot, CPT Robert Stack, who requested assignment as gun-platoon leader. However, Patnode informed Stack that he would get that job at some point in the future; for the time being, there was a pressing need for an experienced operations officer. Sandy-haired, square-jawed, boisterous, with movie-star looks and arrogance, the swashbuckling Stack took the operations job. Later, he would make a hell of a splash as gun-platoon leader. Following these two early infusion successes came many more during the 191st AHC deployment in Vietnam. These achievements continued to bear out the wisdom of Patnode's precedent.

Despite its conglomeration of spare parts and spare people, the 191st AHC was awarded the Meritorious Unit Commendation for its extraordinary battlefield performance, and in its first year alone, the unit logged more combat-assault hours than any other aviation outfit in Vietnam. The individual acts of bravery from its flight crews, as documented in subsequent chapters, are innumerable. Patnode never had any doubt.

$$***$$

On one evening, Patnode, tired after a long day, retired to his bunk to indulge in much-needed rest. Next door, the rowdy Bounty Hunters partied at their crude bar in a tent they christened "The Long Branch Saloon." The saloon grew into a long-standing tradition with the unit's gun platoon. Loud and raucous, the young pilots were doing what comes natural for their age and gender—drinking beer and liquor, sharing lewd jokes, and viewing stag films. They were reeling in the moment, with little knowledge or appreciation for the toll it took on their CO's sleep. Wisely, Patnode had instructed the engineer sergeant to rig an off switch in his tent so that, at any given time, he could pull the plug on the saloon's festive activities. That night, Patnode hit the off switch.

The sudden blackout occurred as the stag film was reaching its climax. A blast of expletives exploded from the innermost bowels of the saloon. "What *dumb* moth-erfucker pulled the plug?"

An assortment of other phrases not commonly used in the English language broke through the dark. A quick inspection by the video hosts soon revealed the power cable entering MAJ Patnode's tent. The calamity died down soon after and a peaceful silence settled in. The young, frustrated Bounty Hunters slinked off to their bunks, unsatisfied. But for Patnode, it was a soothing reprieve from a long, hard day.

In the morning, Patnode, up bright and early, assembled his officers for business as usual. Noticing a few pairs of bloodshot eyes, Patnode enjoyed the moment. There's no better way for these troops to learn from their mistakes but to make them tug the line. *They'll learn!* Slowly but surely, the ingredients for a spectacular unit fell into place. With their new commander urging them on, whether they would be victorious or utterly quelled and defeated, they would do it together, as one unit.

CHAPTER 4

Combat Ready

The group would make this steamy, breath-stealing tangle of nipa palm and tropical growth their new home for one year—but the bond they forged would endure a lifetime.

Out on Bearcat's flight line, the crew chiefs, gunners, and support personnel engaged in an anthill of activity, checking and rechecking equipment and weapons systems with focused intensity. Butterfly stomachs were the order of the day. The excitement in the air was equivalent to what Roman gladiators must have felt as they entered the Colosseum for a fight to the death. This was the real thing.

In the maintenance area, aircraft mechanics conducted helicopter run-up checks. The exhaust from turbine engines wafted through the operations tent nearby, where newly arrived 191st pilots gathered. With the sharp smell of JP-4 in their nostrils, the more-seasoned pilots leaned back in their chairs while others scooted up to the edge of their seats. Some of the greenhorns exuded a naïve tranquility. Other, worldlier newbies clenched their jaws and leaned forward in anticipation of the mission at hand. Either way, the whole tent buzzed with a fizzing, pent up energy, and all eyes zeroed in on the man up front.

Standing six feet tall in spit-shined boots, starched fatigues, and a flat-top crew-cut, the wiry MAJ Patnode offered a striking command presence. He conducted the serious business of reviewing intelligence reports, aircraft assignments, and the battle plan for the next day, making sure his aviators had the mission details down pat. Tomorrow they would fly their first combat assault.

Foremost in Patnode's mind? The knowledge that the majority of his aviators, after thirty-two weeks of helicopter flight school, arrived in Vietnam with only eight short weeks of basic combat training and seven short weeks of airmobile combat training at Fort Bragg, North Carolina. Though rated "combat ready," Patnode knew the 191st aviators were still wet behind the ears.

While infusion provided some seasoned veterans, most of the lads had landed in Vietnam for the first time. Looking out over the fresh faces of the new aviators,

Patnode knew that the rigors of actual combat would rapidly harden these new bloods. The experience would come swiftly—and the seasoning would be sharp and biting.

Centered in the front row was the imposing, six-foot-two "Big Okie," a sandy-haired warrant officer from Oklahoma named Tommy G. Sandefur. Sandefur blocked the view of the smaller 1LT Sharel "Spike" Edward Bales. Hailing from Colorado, Bales had that clean-cut American look about him. Although more reserved than most of the boisterous bunch, there was no doubt that he had a heaping spoonful of American grit. Sensing Bales's need for eye contact, Patnode shifted his stance to the left and locked eyes with the young, round-faced lieutenant. Patnode witnessed a mélange of expressions in the American mix of mugs: the husky 1LT David C. Hall, raised on his family farm in Massachusetts, married and with one daughter; CPT Norman R. Kidd from Ohio, shared the same first name as his father, married with one daughter; 1LT Jack L. Dodson from Idaho, born on Valentine's Day, lucky in love with four children and a wife; and CPT Stan Cherrie, a young gunship pilot, square-jawed, blond, with eyes that exuded the look of a predator about to charge. Patnode's gaze settled for a while on Cherrie. *An excellent attribute for a gunship pilot.*

Others, whose personalities appeared more discernible to the commander, radiated soft, naïve calmness. Out of the bunch, many of these fine faces exuded the demeanor that is characteristic of young Americans raised in households deeply steeped in human values. Patnode read their sheltered natures—he knew killing humans would cause them considerable consternation and grief. What's more, flying out of this hellhole seven days a week, Patnode anticipated that in the mix of these young faces, some would not live to see American soil again.

Adding perspective to the pilot briefing, the distant thud of artillery and mortar fire reminded everyone present of their purpose in Vietnam. The harsh violence awaiting them would soon transform their lives in ways they could never imagine. Most painful of all, the death of an unlucky soul sitting in the chair either to their left or to their right would hurt them as deeply as losing an extended family member. With their twelve-month combat-duty assignment at Bearcat, the group would make this steamy, breath-stealing tangle of nipa palm and tropical growth their new home for one year—but the bond they forged would endure a lifetime.

With preparations completed, their anticipation of actual combat was running foremost in their minds. Starting from a new soldier's first day in uniform, the training cadre drummed in the importance of defeating the Communists. Films of actual war footage affirmed the expected conditions faced by the 191st pilots. Now, at the threshold of meeting the enemy, all this anticipation created apprehension over who among them might die in this friggin' war. Though unspoken, this thought ran through the minds of everyone in the operations tent.

"You've trained well. You're prepared to do this job," Patnode told them. He anticipated the unspoken apprehension and spoke with care, delivering reassuring words to his green pilots.

But on the minds of the fresh pilots, as well as the seasoned, were the stories of the early Ia Drang battles on the lush green Chu Pong Mountain, where American helicopter pilots of the First Air Cavalry made their mark. Like flashing beacons, these war stories warned of profound suffering and death. Despite the favorable battle outcomes, Ia Drang's 305 air cavalry soldiers killed in four days quickly made news in military circles. Surrounded by a much larger North Vietnamese force, it was common knowledge among chopper crews that total annihilation of an American battalion was only prevented by the employment of helicopters.

After a brief pause, Patnode concluded: "And you're equipped far better than the enemy. You'll do fine in combat."

In terrain so replete with jungle canopy, the conventional modes of moving personnel, supplies, and equipment proved useless. This realization forever ratified the worthiness of airmobile operations. Helicopters swiftly positioned artillery and troops into jungle clearings otherwise inaccessible, giving American commanders virtual control of any ground they chose. Henceforth, Army helicopter pilots were viewed as brokers of firepower and mobility. The fresh pilots of the 191st were about to step into this historic—but often harrowing—role.

Unfortunately, on May 26, 1967, just three nights after arriving in Vietnam, the 191st received its first major blow. While flying a night combat mission in bad weather with the 3rd/5th Cavalry, CPT Kidd, the 191st gun-platoon leader, and 1LT Dodson were killed in a weather-related midair collision. It had only been a couple of days since Kidd and Dodson had gathered in the operations tent before their new commander. There was no way for Patnode to predict which one of the brave pilots would be the first to go. The glumness that fell over the company was a harsh introduction to the first of many heartbreaks that would periodically strike the 191st during its war-zone service.

Unlike other casualties that occurred in flight school or in other Stateside environments, these losses hit deeper into the crews' hearts. These men were part of an everyday ritual of living and working in close quarters under tough circumstances; the experience bonded them together like family. A sudden loss caught those who had shared their immediate living space unprepared in dealing with their brother's empty bunk. The residual implications lingered even after the bunk became home to a new arrival. The first tragic events brought the reality of the 191st mission into focus for all to contemplate, and it served notice of the uncertain future that lay ahead.

To maintain unit strength and combat effectiveness, replacements arrived to fill the vacancies created by the recent tragedy. As the new individuals stowed their own personal effects into the recently emptied living spaces, life gradually returned to a semblance of normalcy. But those closest to the deceased never fully recovered.

As these sad events inevitably repeated, a coping mechanism, which veterans know well, often manifested itself. To cope, those touched by the loss of a close brother often acted standoffish with the newer folks. The new guys mistook this protective measure as an air of aloofness, when in reality the emotions behind the actions stabbed at the heart of seasoned soldiers. They were all too familiar with investing too much of an emotional stake in a new face. Bonding with the FNG (fuckin' new guy) simply meant greater pain later if that person were killed. So, with no specific discussion among established unit members, they often chose not to get too close with the newbies. It was simply their way of protecting themselves from tragedy.

Not understanding, the newcomers went about their business quietly in semi-isolation until, at some point, the brotherhood relented, accepting the FNG into the clique. Once the new arrivals experienced loss firsthand, exposing themselves to the heartbreak and vulnerability that the seasoned crews knew all too well, they understood the initial coolness. Each Boomerang and Bounty Hunter would eventually be stung by war and earn a broken heart. Ironically, collective grief seemed to strengthen mental purpose and create a seething desire for vengeance, resulting in stellar battlefield performance. The unit's fighting blood was aroused by their losses.

Soaring with a vibrant *esprit de corps*, the 191st lift platoons adopted the name Boomerangs after the Australian weapon designed to return to its launching point. CPT John V. Hedrick, second platoon leader, suggested the name, with the idea that "Boomerangs always come back" might be a fitting motto. In the midst of planning the 191st AHC's first combat-assault mission, in which the unit would be carrying the Aussies into battle, the name popped up in Hedrick's mind, and the name stuck. Battle-dressed by SP4 Richard Weske and SP5 Bill Faucett, two highly artistic painters, the 191st birds flew into combat with a prideful array of colorful murals and witty names, such as *Supership* and *Mother Goose*, painted on their sides, along with a picture of a boomerang in bright orange on their noses. Weske, hailing from California, would later lose his life to hostile fire on May 21, 1968.

"Boomerangs always come back" became a phrase that frequently echoed from within the loud and high-spirited gatherings of 191st pilots. Characteristic of aviator brotherhood, their libation functions were especially lively and became a post-mission bonding ritual to let off steam. Standing out among the more notorious "Barrelhouse Kings" were the men who sparked these raucous sessions: 1LT John Arnold, who could fade a fifth of George Dickel in one sitting; CW2 Larry Miller, who could swallow a twelve-ounce Bud in one gulp; the unforgettable big Swede from Montana, CPT Rugg, who could consume his share of spirits and walk away appearing steady as a rock. An outstanding assault platoon leader, Rugg kept a mental note of who was flying the next day and made sure his young aviators didn't overindulge. He needed them fit for battle in the early morning, and he led by example—a quality he maintained throughout his tour in Vietnam. From these rowdy assemblies emerged an emotional fabric that wove the young flight crews into a kinship that only death could part—and not even then. Ironically, their high-risk mission took its toll and too many Boomerangs did not fulfill their motto.

Every Bounty Hunter gunship of the 191st AHC had a red pentagon on the nose with the words "For a Few Dollars More." The 191st gun platoon borrowed their name—"Bounty Hunters"—from Clint Eastwood's 1965 Western film *For a Few Dollars More*. In keeping with Western film culture, they wore red bandanas, priced the heads of bad guys, and collected enemy battle flags, which they proudly displayed in their Long Branch Saloon. These Bounty Hunters knew their stuff and did it well. In one especially productive firefight, they were credited with 131 confirmed kills in a single day. After six months in-country, the Bounty Hunters' kill ratio would have made Clint Eastwood proud. No question about it, these lads earned their name.

By design, the 191st Boomerangs and Bounty Hunters worked as nonorganic assets under the operational control (OPCON) of the combat units they supported. This arrangement had been worked out by the Eleventh Air Assault Division (Test), a move that affirmed, over and over, the wisdom of the Howze Board. The grunts relied so heavily upon 191st combat support that it was not uncommon for 191st pilots to log double-digit flight hours in a 24-hour period. This quickly accelerated the 140-hour monthly maximum, requiring extended down time for the overcommitted ACs—a condition that wrecked OPORD assignments and infuriated authorities up and down the chain of command for the resultant aircraft shortages. Nevertheless, *regulations be damned!* When their infantry brothers called, the 191st flight crews answered with guns blazing. Regardless of how tough the fray or how long the fight, the 191st had the infantry's back. Decades later, the gruff old Boomerang survivor Bill Janes likened these working conditions to the "care and treatment of a borrowed mule."

Mule or not, platoon leaders and ACs relished the efficiency of their crews. The tighter the bond between crewmembers, the more the unit achieved. It highly pleased CPT Rugg to see and overhear interactions between his crew chiefs and gunners as they ragged one another over their individual aircraft achievements. Intraplatoon competition further bonded the pilots, aircrews, and personnel into one fierce unit.

Rugg recalled hearing about one such occasion that typified this friendly competition. The platoon's three-quarter-ton truck driven by SP4 Art Almaraz and dubbed the TJ Taxi moved about with pride, delivering ammunition and supplies to the flight line each morning. Filled to capacity with M60 machine guns, munitions, and a fussy bunch of crew chiefs and gunners, the harmless-looking TJ Taxi would have packed one hell of a wallop in a firefight. In a friendly rivalry between support personnel and flight crews, Almaraz occasionally boasted that his TJ Taxi packed more firepower than some of the assault ships, and he wished he could see his three-quarter-ton rig in combat. For most casual observers, Almaraz's TJ Taxi would be a sight to behold, but not for the cocky Bounty Hunter Crew Chief Heinmiller.

Proud as a peacock and wearing the red bandana around his neck that identified him as a Bounty Hunter, Heinmiller chidingly scoffed at Almaraz's boasting with his own wit. "Seeing your TJ Taxi in combat would be like watching a milk cow in a bull fight."

The peppery Almaraz quickly retorted, "Oh, yeah? Well, I'd like to see *you* wave that red snot-rag you wear around your neck in front of a two-thousand-pound Holstein bull."

Their friendly jousting and laughter heightened the excitement that preceded the morning lift-off of the combat-assault fleet. The 191st was quickly becoming one big warrior family—and happy to be one. Hearing of this exchange from one of his ACs, Rugg was pleased. Alvarez was his number-one three-quarter-ton driver.

Three months after arriving in Vietnam, the 191st grew into a reliable and well-trained fighting unit. With help from senior personnel, such as the 191st Intelligence NCO Sergeant First Class (SFC) Julius "Dewey" Emil Fambry, the unit assimilated the knowledge for measuring enemy strength in operational zones and assembled the necessary support for action. Like tough and durable fiber, the combat unit bolstered and fortified its pilots and crews through the numerous battles to come.

CHAPTER 5

Airmobile Schemes

Here in this metal bird, the only thing that mattered was their grit and dedication.

With M60s blasting tree lines and helicopter blades whopping, the Hueys climbed out of hellholes littered with entrails and body parts. In the skies above Vietnam, these young lads "remade" themselves. Their age, where they came from, who they were back home were of no consequence. Here in this metal bird, the only thing that mattered was their grit and dedication.

The 191st pilots, crews, and support personnel were tough and committed, no doubt. But what's more, they proved to be tactically creative, some even establishing precedent where others had dared not tread. Although the average crew chief and gunner aboard the 191st assault ships ranged in age from barely out of high school to barely old enough to drink, they adapted to adversity with unlimited resourcefulness.

Only months before, some were tinkering with how to get more gas flow from their hotrod carburetors. Now, SP4 Gerald "Jerry" Kahn from Long Island, New York, a dark-haired, leathery kid with a tungsten backbone, was remarkably adept at squeezing the most out of his death-delivering mechanisms. While tinkering with how to increase his M60 machine gun's rate of fire, he threaded together two mainsprings to augment a weaker factory part. The results were phenomenal. He and the curly-haired, blond Heinmiller, among others of the 191st, were the mini think tanks that devised some of the finer points of armed-helicopter employment used on the battlefield today.

Brilliantly transitioning from shoulder pads for executing football plays, Gunner Kahn and Crew Chief Heinmiller rigged monkey cords to their body harnesses so they could dangle out of the aircraft in flight. Stemming from frequent enemy fire aimed at their bird as the gunship broke from its gun run, the two bunkmates discussed ways to "hit back."

"Body harnesses with steel cables attached to the bird are the answer," Kahn said to Heinmiller. "This should allow us to lean out of the aircraft cargo door and place effective covering fire beneath the ship's underbelly when breaking off a gun run." Once rigged, Kahn suggested he be the first to try this "crazy act."

Kahn performed the first test on the ground. It worked! He figured he could lean out far enough that he could easily cover his side of the bird's underbelly—well into the Huey's climb to safety. Now to test it in action.

To the innovative lad's delight, the approval of the Bounty Hunter platoon leader came swiftly. "Try it," gunship pilot CPT Palmer said.

Months after adopting the practice of hanging out the door from steel cables, Palmer invited his drinking buddy, CPT John D. Falcon, who was the unit's executive officer (XO), to fly as peter pilot on a simple test-fire mission near Dong Tam, the Ninth Division base camp. Maintenance had just installed new weapon systems on a gunship that required test-firing. Unexpectedly, the mission turned into a vicious firefight. While overflying the nearby free-fire zone, a squad of enemy soldiers was observed transitioning through the area. Palmer engaged, and the fight was on.

Fighting as a lone gunship, the Bounty Hunter aircraft was most vulnerable when it broke off from a gun run. To their advantage, Kahn and Heinmiller were now experts at dangling out of the doors to shoot under the bird's vulnerable belly while the aircraft broke from its attack. With only a single strand of body-harness cable between them and certain death, they kept their M60s screaming with 350-plus rounds of 7.62-millimeter bullets ripping through the enemy. Amongst 191st crews, this act was called the *bigger-than-life testicle push*. Placing their combat boots on the sharp edge of the gunship's cargo hatch, Kahn and Heinmiller pushed outward into the free air to fire their machine guns. In addition to enemy bullets, death was only a cable-snap away. *Charlie*, a generic nickname for the enemy, had little choice but to keep his head down lest it be perforated. Still, Charlie fought with fury, knowing the single ship was vulnerable.

With enemy bullets zinging through the gunship like a hail storm, Palmer called for help. "Boomerang Ops, this is Bounty Hunter Three."

"Three, this is Boomerang Ops. Go ahead."

"Ops, Bounty Hunter Three. Please alert the standby gunship crew that we are single ship, in one hell of a firefight just across the Mekong River from Dong Tam, and need help."

"Roger, Three. The standby AC was here in ops—overheard your commo and is rushing to his bird now."

"Roger. Thanks, Ops. We're inbound to refuel and rearm now."

After refueling and rearming, Palmer and Falcon returned to the fight to find the enemy gone. The firefight ended as quickly as it started.

Returning to the 191st flight line with the new, well-tested weapon system, the crew set about assessing the bird's bullet damage and made an interesting discovery. An enemy bullet hit Falcon's armored seat on the bottom, square in the middle, and bounced off harmlessly. But not before it passed through a grease can left under the seat by the crew chief. The friendly ragging that ensued reached the entire population of 191st aviators, who appreciated the opportunity to rag the XO. The jest was, the enemy "greased up the bullet especially for the XO's ass-end."

The harnesses proved their worthiness. Enemies soon learned that shooting at gunships with a red pentagon on their noses was not wise at any time, even when the birds exposed their vulnerable bellies.

Gunner Kahn and Crew Chief Heinmiller regularly flocked together with SP4 Randy Edwards, SP4 Ron Lovellette, SP4 Roger Owens, SP4 Joe Kline, SP4 Bill Flores, and SP5 Ernest Lee "Ernie" Houdashell to hold "Barracks' Conventions." These get-togethers helped them to not only forge a brotherhood that evoked pride among their kindred, but also share technical advantages and innovative tactics.

Following the same management principle that makes a team far more effective than its individual members, these gunship crewmembers devised ways to refine their product. Among the many upgrades derived from their tinkering schemes, they increased the rate of fire of the M60 machine gun. It was Gunner Kahn who ingeniously thought of doubling the M60 machine gun's mainspring to throw significantly more lead at the enemy during the vulnerable gun-run breaks. This enhanced protection of the aircraft when its naked underbelly was exposed.

Also effective was the *snake in the grass* principle of suppression devised by California-born Gunner Flores. In California, hosing down grassfires was common-place. Flores extended the idea to hosing down a field of grass with M60 machine-gun bullets to neutralize the hidden enemy. Flores came upon this practice by learning to notice and mentally mark the spot where enemy soldiers crawled into the grass to hide from approaching gunships. When two VC dove for cover in the tall grass during a Bounty Hunter gun run, Flores, with his superb killer instinct, perfected the snake-in-the-grass kill drill. Keeping his eye on the spot where the VC slithered away, he simply sprayed the area on the next pass à la California fire-hose style. A few minutes later when the grunts finished combing the ground for bad guys, they dragged out two well-perforated enemy bodies and gave the smiling Flores a thumbs-up.

"Simply hose down the area, and *presto!* You have effectively suppressed the enemy who plink away at our slicks," Flores explains.

Thereafter, scores of enemy troops were killed using this tactic, and those who survived would not dare lift their heads for fear of incurring another California hosing. It worked. Flores shared this tactic with his brethren in arms. Soon, the practice grew to a standard application.

While the airmobile concept was conceived at a much higher military level, many of the tactics and operational fine points that gained a permanent role in our nation's defense were created by the pilots and crews of the 191st AHC. Apart from the creative know-how of gunners and crew chiefs like Kahn and Heinmiller, gunship pilots had a few innovative tactics up their sleeves, too. The pilots learned to use wind direction to affect rocket trajectories. This creative know-how translated into unit procedures that streamlined the entire flight into the wind to favor the most effective gunship protection. C&C pilots communicated this procedure to the ground-force commanders during the planning sequence of combat-assault missions, enhancing battlefield performance.

Much like the Flying Tigers of Burma or the Black Sheep Squadron of the Pacific, the Boomerangs and Bounty Hunters developed their very own unique character, differing from other helicopter outfits because of the decentralized mission. A striking example of self-actualized procedures were those of the maintenance test pilot (MTP) CW2 Perry Davis. When a ship went down for mechanical failure, he would often fly to the site and repair the bird on the spot. Rather than wait for a heavy-lift helicopter to retrieve the damaged aircraft, he would expedite repairs regardless of enemy threats in the vicinity. He faced the risk with expediency in mind. Far removed from their parent organization, 191st personnel had room to self-actualize with little interference from higher command. For all practical purposes, the battalion headquarters in their vicinity was a ceremonial patch between the First Aviation Brigade and the 191st AHC.

Derogatorily nicknamed *straphangers* by assault pilots, the majority of battalion aviators would not be caught dead flying combat assaults. What with happy hour at the officer's club starting at 1700 hours sharp, most straphangers would certainly not risk being late for these festivities or even worse, getting shot while flying with the Boomerangs and Bounty Hunters. They simply didn't have the gumption to fight. Missing, therefore, was the rigid military oversight that stifles creativity when performance occurs literally under the nose of superiors. This freedom allowed unrestricted practice and refinement of unconventional maneuvers that would prove extremely combat worthy. Gutsy engagement tactics emerged, such as low-level flying over canals and taunting the enemy to shoot first in what would become a firestorm of death and destruction upon the souls of the foolish enemy who dared. Many young and less-experienced enemy soldiers were suckered in to meet their maker by these unorthodox tactics. The 191st combat experience had no substitute. Connecting the dots from one battlefield scenario to another produced killer instincts and reflexes not possible through textbook training.

Gunners and crew chiefs produced innovative and unconventional thinking that surprised maintenance. CPT Falcon explains, "The 191st had professional civilian maintenance personnel hired by the US government to provide frontline support for units such as the 191st. They were specifically employed to solve technical problems with all aspects of the combat-assault mission. Aircraft maintenance (or armament) technicians were trained at American factories to fine-tune the systems for max performance in battle. I can recall several times when the professional technician would shake his head in a combination of admiration and surprise at the field expediency demonstrated by 191st gunners and crew chiefs. Two incidents in particular stick out in my mind.

"One had to do with the minigun system jamming when ammo belts twisted in voids that snagged the feed trays. The government-hired tech immediately communicated the problem back to the manufacturer for a solution and patiently waited for their response. After four days with no answer from the manufacturer, a Bounty Hunter crew chief, whose name I regret not remembering, used empty beer cans to fill the voids to streamline the feed system. Remarkably, the problem was solved and the miniguns were active again. Months later, the manufacturer furnished engineered parts to close the voids in the ammo-feed system, and the manufacturer's design defect was solved."

Herein again, the protection of the flight was improved significantly by the progressive thinking of these innovative and smart-as-a-whip 191st crewmembers. Brigade and battalion commanders of the Ninth Infantry Division delighted in the forward thinking and combat flexibility of the 191st. *Checkerboard squares, eagle flights,* and *jitterbug tactics* were tactical terms that became common vernacular between assets of the 191st AHC and infantry commanders, including COL John Hayes, commanding the First Brigade, LTC Don Schroeder, commanding the 2nd/39th, and LTC David Hackworth, commanding the 4th/39th.

A brilliant tactician and infantry commander, Hackworth was among the most detailed combat brains in the business. He took a topo map of his battalion area of operations (AO) and colored each square kilometer of territory to resemble a checkerboard square. Then he assigned a number to each click, and required his staff to post enemy sightings and movements under each respective number. Soon he had a clear picture of the most prevalent areas of enemy use and habitation. Thereafter, the routine was simple. He ordered an operation into the area and frequently caught Charlie asleep. Many enemy soldiers died from Hackworth's innovative thinking.

Even more effective, Hackworth ordered a full complement of infantry on choppers and sent them aloft in an *eagle flight* (a racetrack pattern in a holding area near an enemy stronghold). Carefully reconnoitering the enemy location and confirming enemy presence, he ordered a *jitterbug strike*. Eagle flight aircraft descended to a nearby LZ for a touch and go, and then again in another LZ nearby, until finally assaulting the enemy's stronghold with shocking results. The surprise damage was irreversible for the terror-stricken VC. Like a jitterbug hopping and skipping from one water puddle to another, the maneuver outwitted the enemy. With their overconfidence and complacency, they never expected the blow until the assault overtook them by storm. No time for salvation. Hackworth and his creativity stole the show when senior officers overflew Hackworth's battle sites. With his resultant promotion, he was soon to become the youngest full colonel in the Army.

The airmobile concept offered many combat options to savvy grunt officers like LTC Hackworth. He had a favorite cliché: *Out G the G,* meaning out-guerrilla the guerrilla, which he frequently used to emphasize beating the VC at their own game. The guerrilla war became the primary mode of fighting in Vietnam.

LTC Schroeder, on the other hand, with help from 191st slick pilots, devised a method for *body-snatching* live enemy soldiers for interrogation. The traditional way of gathering intelligence used reconnaissance aircraft and relied on photographs to track down enemy concentrations. But this old way involved a long procedure. The film had to be processed and the photographs analyzed. Meanwhile, the VC had long since dispersed, slipping away into the jungle.

Schroeder's body-snatching method was a far more effective method of acquiring real-time intelligence. On these body-snatching missions, the snatch team would fly over a known VC stronghold until they spotted a VC suspect. Like a giant raptor, the snatch-team bird would swoop down on the suspect. Hovering a foot above the ground, a crewmember would jump out and force the startled VC into the helicopter at gunpoint. The snatch team always consisted of several Bounty Hunter gunships that scoured the area thoroughly, making sure there were no enemy elements in position to attack. In effect, before each snatch, the immediate vicinity was cleared of enemy soldiers by the Bounty Hunters.

The live intelligence gathered from a freshly snatched VC often revealed enemy-troop concentrations at that moment and gave the Americans time to step in. After gathering intelligence from a snatched VC soldier, Schroeder immediately took action. He either ordered troops to quickly intercept the enemy, or he called in a firestorm of heavy artillery or napalm on the unsuspecting VC. Some of these chance opportunities produced hefty body counts.

Piece by piece, the 191st developed a tactical protocol that improved airmobile success, exactly as the Howze Board had deemed it should. The ingenuity of the crews, along with Patnode's engineer brain and Howze Board experience, mended gaps in tactical relationships that inhibited the synergy between aviation support services and infantry commanders for decades.

Flores, the innovative gunner, who after leaving Vietnam created a successful insurance firm, states: "Vietnam was an experience that I wouldn't trade for anything in the world. The people who served were great Americans, to the last one. I shall never forget them. And those who died, I remember each of them as if it was just yesterday. It is impossible for anyone who has not gone through that experience to understand the relationship one builds under those circumstances. It's a brotherhood bonded for life."

Producing resounding blows to the VC, 191st slick and gunship pilots who flew the missions were no doubt the bravest of the brave and reputed to sport brass balls—but above all, they were brothers banded together. This bond brought out the best of their innovative minds and mustered a creative grit beyond comparison.

CHAPTER 6

The Load Bearers

These 191st load bearers set the bar at a level beyond heroes.

Inspired by previous generations of their kind, young and vibrant volunteers meet America's need for strong warriors. These greenhorns, tenacious and intensely dedicated to our national defense, are truly the load bearers of the US's military might. To this day, they remain the greatest hope that this nation's freedoms will endure.

A number of these human jewels endowed the 191st AHC during the Vietnam War. They are among America's greatest heroes, and many volunteered to place themselves in harm's way for Old Glory, barely considering their own mortality. Indeed, some died with little or no account of their war effort. Given little fanfare for their enormous sacrifices, many served with honor and returned to their hometowns to resume a quiet life where no one would ever know of their extraordinary heroics under fire. Unfortunately, the eventual outcome of the Vietnam War is still viewed with shame by many. Indeed, a somber fact for a country so blessed to have these young souls bear the load for the entire nation. They committed their lives not only for America's military might, but also for our nation's values and higher ideals.

This chapter shares the stories of SP5 Roy Kekoa Ahuna, SP5 Perry E. "Skip" Waugh Jr., SP5 Ernest Lee "Ernie" Houdashell, and PFC Gerald David Aiton. Their stories bear witness to the commitment of the young men that heeded their nation's call.

***

SP5 Roy Kekoa Ahuna, a Hawaiian-born American, was drafted into service in August of 1966 during the enormous Vietnam War draft call. With his induction, the Army and the 191st AHC gained a remarkable asset. Trained in the 71H20 (clerical field) military occupational specialty (MOS), Ahuna's official title as company clerk represented only a small part of his actual duties. His official functions included so many essential tasks that he rapidly became indispensable to the operations section chief and the unit's first sergeant.

Born to a native Hawaiian father and to a mother of Japanese descent, Ahuna was endowed with the crosscultural strengths of races that met in beautiful Hawaii. There, Far Eastern customs meet Western influence, and the best characteristics of these human qualities were evident in Roy Ahuna. He inherited the delightfully polite nature and the ever-efficient industrial mind of his Japanese ancestry. Nurtured and bolstered by the American education system, by the time he was drafted, Ahuna had acquired the good old American mettle espoused by our free society. He knew the meaning of freedom and would fight for its cause.

As a young man, he was blessed with a wholesome environment in which he roamed free throughout the island of Hawaii, enjoying the nature of things and following his family's traditions. Spearfishing was among his favorites; it provided food for his family and gained him the appreciation of his mom, a strong-minded single parent raising three children. As a schoolteacher, his mother inspired him to develop his potential. Thus, in exemplary form, Ahuna joined the Boy Scouts of America and earned the coveted Eagle Scout badge.

Encouraged by his mother's connections to family members on the mainland, Ahuna and his siblings moved to San José, California, where his mother left her teaching profession and obtained a technical job with Sylvania. Settling into a comfortable lifestyle, Ahuna entered junior college, where he began studying general subjects on a part-time schedule while he continued to work. His academic load was unfortunately insufficient to satisfy his local draft board. He learned too late that he would not be given a deferment. The fact that he worked part time also meant nothing to the bureaucrats who administered the draft. His induction was rapid, and he was in the Army seemingly before he could fully comprehend its life-changing impact.

Ahuna's departure from his hometown's bus stop was a tearful scene as his family assembled to say goodbye. The oldest of three children, he was the first to leave home. No one had anticipated his sudden departure; it was a stressful experience for him and his family. The suddenness and shock was a very common occurrence felt by millions of American families during the Vietnam era. The thought of not seeing his family again brought on a heightened anxiety in Ahuna, and the reality sank in—he was going to war.

Never having left the sanctity of home, it was unsettling to head off into the unknown. Boot camp at Fort Lewis, Washington, was a shock, but there his polite nature and innate efficiency immediately set him apart from the pool of conscripts. Scoring high on the battery of tests administered to new inductees, Ahuna was given opportunity to attend Officer Candidate School (OCS); however, being uncertain about its commitment, he declined. Nonetheless, his responsible nature earned him favorable treatment from his trainers and fellow draftees, making his basic-training experience far less stressful than for some who resisted the regimented discipline. Clerical school at Fort Huachuca, Arizona, followed his basic training, after which he was ordered to Fort Bragg, North Carolina, where the 191st AHC would become the beneficiary of his services.

The appreciation was mutual. His section chief, WO1 Ben Hauser, and the section NCO, 1SG Thomas Croley, immediately recognized Private (PVT) Ahuna's skills and dedication. He quickly became a strong asset while in-processing personnel to fill the vacant slots of the newly formed assault-helicopter company. Reaching full strength was a predeployment requirement that preceded the combat training necessary to achieve an acceptable readiness level. Ahuna became an integral part of the steady, upward progression of the 191st AHC's personnel strength. Finally, in April of 1967, the 191st AHC reached its deployment goals and the loadout for Vietnam began.

"As the unit formed to board transportation," Ahuna recalls, "the first sergeant said, 'Look around you, troops! One in ten of you will not return.' In retrospect, I feel the first sergeant really didn't have to say that. It simply set our minds to thinking of who those unfortunate souls might be. For at least a few moments, I had a sinking feeling in the pit of my stomach.

"We then boarded buses and headed for the airfield, where we were packed into an airliner to head to the West Coast. After landing briefly in California for fuel, I next found myself breathing Hawaiian air when our Vietnam-bound flight made a refueling stop in Honolulu. My heart sank when I learned we would not be allowed to leave the airport. We then made one more fuel stop in Guam, followed by an immediate reboarding for the last leg to Vietnam. The familiar smell of the air in Hawaii made me yearn for the home ground where I grew up.

"I still had family [in Hawaii], and they dominated my thoughts from the moment I stepped off the plane. My call to my aunt's house was a great surprise to them, but the jubilation was short-lived when I announced that I could not leave the airport and would depart in ten minutes. Even though the short connection was heartwarming, my departure was wrought with homesickness. To come so close and not be able to see my birthplace was a huge disappointment. Just that fast, we were back in the Boeing 707 headed for another tropical climate, which would be nowhere near as hospitable."

When the airliner lifted off Hawaiian soil, its next stop was Vietnam. Reaching the war zone, Ahuna experienced a second cultural shock. If boot camp at Fort Lewis seemed foreign to him in terms of trainee treatment, Vietnam seemed obscene in terms of ecology. By comparison to Hawaii or California, the foul odor of Vietnam was particularly offensive to the Hawaiian.

"It smelled like rotten fish," Ahuna recalls, "a powerful odor one never forgets."

Deplaning with the rest of the unit, the young Hawaiian heard artillery and mortar rounds exploding in the distance. This was a certain signal that death lurked nearby and the reality of war was only moments away. *Wish I was home,* he mused. Again, Ahuna's thoughts cascaded back to home, his mom, and his younger siblings.

"Vietnam was nothing as placid as the home ground from which I had just departed," Ahuna recalls. "The first thing that caught one's attention was hearing artillery going off all over the place. That was sort of a 'welcome to the war zone' signal."

Within a few short weeks after arrival at Bearcat, Vietnam, home of the Ninth Infantry Division, the unit was flying combat assaults. Ahuna was at the center of activity in the company's orderly room creating the daily morning report, the instrument by which all personnel were accounted for each day. Worldwide, the Army had to know, or at least believe that it knew, exactly how many personnel it had and the whereabouts of each living soul. On each morning, nothing moved outside of that headquarters without the morning report being first delivered to the 214th CAB. Thereafter, Ahuna could perform sundry other admin chores. But as time permitted, he would visit operations, where the missions were planned.

Soon, Ahuna became familiar with the flight crews as they passed through the 191st operations center en route to the flight line for mission departure. During the day, he listened to the radio chatter as the flight engaged the enemy while supporting the infantry units. Intrigued by the action, his fighting blood was aroused, and he concocted a scheme to get into the fight. He asked 1SG Croley if he could go out with the flight as a gunner.

Taken aback, Croley looked at Ahuna as if to say, "Are you crazy? You want to go out there and get your *ass* shot off?" Seeing that Ahuna was serious, the first sergeant reluctantly approved his request, but only for a very limited exposure. "We need you in the orderly room," 1SG Croley said in a matter-of-fact tone.

It wasn't until Ahuna's brother, Stephen, joined the Marines and was scheduled for assignment to the Marine compound at Khe Sanh that Ahuna finally got an opportunity to fulfill his yearning for a combat-assault slot. He approached the CO, MAJ Patnode, and explained that he needed to extend his tour in Vietnam to keep his brother Stateside. The horror stories at Khe Sanh were weighing heavily on his mind. The mortality rate there was among the highest in the war zone. Ahuna was certain his younger sibling would die if stationed at Khe Sanh.

"Not on my watch!" Patnode said. Once again, Ahuna was turned down.

When the new commander took over, again Ahuna petitioned to keep his kid brother Stateside by extending his tour of duty. Fate changed for the Hawaiian, and the new commander agreed.

At this point, Ahuna knew that time was of the essence, so he hurriedly extended his enlistment in Vietnam for six more months and applied for a combat-assault position with the 191st AHC. The Marine Corps kept its word and Marine PVT Stephen K. Ahuna was allowed to remain at Camp Pendleton, California, while his big brother finished his Army tour of duty in Vietnam. Ahuna, forever the big brother, felt reassured that his little brother would remain safe.

Careful to avoid eye contact with 1SG Croley, Ahuna enthusiastically visited the arms room and drew a weapon and an armor breastplate from the supply room.

His first heliborne trip to the jungle outside the Bearcat perimeter was relatively uneventful, as were the second and third trips. In becoming a combat veteran, Ahuna looked forward to the combat assaults as the days passed. Being part of the action was fulfilling. In between he would perform ground duties with the flight platoon, and looked forward to flying again.

Each day was an adventure in the life of a combat-assault crewman. While some days were almost boring, other days rocked a soldier's nerves. Ahuna's M60 machine gun spoke with authority, employing suppressive fire during those nerve-racking insertions. Firefights were rapidly suppressed by the Bounty Hunter gunships. In minutes, enemy actions subsided and the VC melted once again into the jungle. For a few fleeting moments, the adrenaline rush fed Ahuna's fighting spirit. From near boredom to adrenaline rushes, life in the 191st AHC grew to be routine.

Nevertheless, the reality of war has a way of exploding a routine to bits. Toward the end of Ahuna's extended tour came a counterexample to the routine, and Ahuna was thrust into his first major exposure to enemy fire where the Americans lost the upper hand. The unit was inserting South Vietnamese troops when enemy fire engulfed his aircraft.

Bullets whizzed at the flight, striking the aircraft in much greater volume than the outgoing fire. In their efforts to cover the flight, Bounty Hunter gunships suffered more hits than they were scoring. Battles of this intensity are inevitable in the life of any assault-helicopter company, but this protracted exchange with the enemy was Ahuna's first of such a heated intensity. The opposition stood their ground and delivered a determined resistance that threatened to disperse the flight. The young Hawaiian recognized that the tactical advantage, however, can shift in a millisecond, and battle outcomes are always "up for grabs."

Determined to survive the exchange of gunfire, the young Ahuna returned the max rate his machine gun could muster. He maintained focus on enemy field positions that were firing on his ship. That day, with too many to effectively suppress at once, Ahuna's quick and nimble hand-eye coordination was pushed to its limits. In rapid succession, he shifted from one enemy gunner to the next as each opened fire on his bird and crew. After a harrowing descent into that hellhole, the flight finally broke ground, gained airspeed and altitude, and climbed to safety.

"Departing a hot LZ never felt so good," Ahuna recalls. "I thought we would never get out of there."

As was the case for many of the other 191st crewmembers, Ahuna felt this day just might be his last day on earth. After the hellish fight, the young Hawaiian breathed a sigh of relief. Only then did he realize he was getting *short* (approaching his DEROS). He figured now might be as good a time as ever to refocus his energy on his duties back at the unit's orderly room. A month later, he rotated back to the States, achieving a record of great service with the 191st AHC.

Ahuna contributed immeasurably to unit efficiency at its headquarters. Dictated by his MOS, he did not have to fly combat assaults. Nonetheless, he sought the taste of battle and made his contribution to the war effort in a fashion that satisfied his American spirit. More importantly, he bravely volunteered to go into harm's way to save not only the lives of his brothers-in-arms, but also the life of his little brother back home. In this unselfish act, he bore the load like other volunteers and gave very grateful regular crewmembers a breather from the stress of daily combat.

Ahuna truly is a quiet and unassuming hero, the likes of which are rare. His service remains a tribute to his ancestry and to the United States Army. The 191st AHC was fortunate to have him when the unit needed his dedicated service. From Fort Bragg to Vietnam, Ahuna left an indelible mark.

Leaving Vietnam in 1970, Ahuna returned to the San Diego, California, where he found employment in the semiconductor industry and has remained since. Ahuna now enjoys golf and traveling to tournaments to meet his younger brother, Stephen, who shares his joy for the game. Residing in Laguna Nigel, California, Stephen works for Charles-Abbott Associates, who provide planning services for the city. Remaining linked to their culture, the Ahuna brothers and their sister, Kapua, journey to Hawaii once a year to visit relatives and enjoy a stint of authentic Hawaiian customs.

***

SP5 Perry E. "Skip" Waugh Jr. stood with a wiry physique and sandy hair. Bestowed upon the 191st AHC by random assignment, he was an extraordinary gift. Somehow, from among the vast number of Army units that participated during the Vietnam War, he ended up assigned to the 191st, a destiny that became a perfect fit.

Waugh was born at Columbia Hospital in Washington, DC, on February 4, 1947, to parents of Scots-Irish and English blood. Having been fathered by an Illinois farmer and descended from considerable wealth on his mother's side, Waugh identified with a culture that cultivated the soil. Frequent table discussions between his parents underscored the wholesome benefits of farming. They both reminisced about the days of the agrarian culture their ancestors enjoyed and the happiness it brought to rural families. Waugh listened to this history and assumed these were foundation principles that made America strong and independent. Subsisting on fresh farm products and the region's local game and fish further reinforced his strong agrarian roots.

His Protestant upbringing instilled the exemplary human qualities that gave Waugh a sincere and trustworthy character. As a youngster, before graduating from high school in Oxon Hill, Maryland, he worked part time on an equestrian farm. Thus, at a very tender age, Waugh learned responsibility. All who worked with the young Marylander took a liking to him.

After enlisting in the Army in June of 1966, he was assigned to Fort Gordon, Georgia, for basic training, where he immediately distinguished himself as a superb marksman. He tied the installation record for the highest score achieved on the firing range. Clearly, his country upbringing contributed to his military training. After completing military police training at Fort Gordon, his next stop was the 191st AHC as the unit was being formed for deployment to Vietnam. His assignment turned out to be a plus, both for the unit and Waugh. He loved the mission, and he delivered exemplary work for the company. Waugh was stereotypical of most American soldiers of his era, but there was one looming difference between him and many of the other soldiers: affable and easily befriended, Waugh was congenial with everybody. He held no bias.

Having been raised in a spacious country house with his father, grandfather, uncle, and cousins, Waugh grew up surrounded by family. He carried on among his Vietnam buddies with the same type of kinship he enjoyed back at home. For him, everybody in the barracks was his brother, and he nurtured those relationships. He shared the goodies he received from home and whatever bootleg he acquired from the local Vietnamese land, such as when Waugh shot a large deer that turned into a venison roast for the entire company.

On that day, the mission took his crew over a jungle region rich in wild game. So, when Waugh spotted a worthy stag, his rural instincts automatically kicked in. Having just been released from a full day of combat-assault missions, Waugh asked his AC, "Sir, would you like to know how venison tastes?"

Waugh's question roused the AC's curiosity and taste buds. "Yeah, Skip—what you got in mind?"

"Well, if you'll turn right about ninety degrees, I'll show you."

As the gunship completed its turn, Waugh quickly dispatched the animal with the same skill that he tied the Fort Gordon marksmanship record. Cheers all around. The crew landed and carefully loaded the fresh kill into the aircraft for a speedy trip back to the company area for a well-deserved meal. After recruiting the unit forklift for skinning and butchering, he borrowed charcoal grills from the mess hall. In no time, Waugh demonstrated his country skills in preparing a feast from hoof to plate. The party lasted well into the night.

"My biggest concern," Waugh recalls, "was that I did not have the ingredients to prepare the sauce I was accustomed to making back home. I think it would have complemented the roast venison for the greater enjoyment of the crews. I love the stuff. The recipe came from my uncle, who occasionally grilled on weekends for our family."

Endowed with an adventurist penchant for action, Waugh considered transferring into a long-range reconnaissance patrol (LRRP) unit so he could experience the ground war as a grunt. But his platoon leader, CPT Cherrie, knew his worth, and so promoted him into a crew-chief slot to keep him in the unit. Waugh settled into his job and focused on keeping his assigned gunship, *Mother Goose*, in top shape. He matured into one of the 191st AHC's most valued crew chiefs.

Waugh took part in several major battles, but one particular battle in the fall of 1967 stands foremost in his mind. "On or about Thanksgiving, the base camp of an infantry battalion was attacked," Waugh recalls. "Wave after wave of determined NVA troops succeeded in penetrating the compound perimeter. In the night-long battle, many lives were lost, both American and Vietnamese. But by midmorning, the American flag still flew, waving in defiance while hundreds of NVA bodies decayed in the scorching sun."

A grateful artilleryman, SP4 Richard Garcia, recalls a similar memory: "The morning light showed hundreds of mangled enemy bodies tangled in the concertina wire surrounding the American camp. The vast carnage reeked of human decomposition. When the helicopters finally arrived to provide fire support and bring reinforcements and supplies, there was jubilation in the camp. We never thought we would make it through the night. The enemy was relentless in keeping up the attack all through the hours of darkness." Garcia, a native of Robstown, Texas, was assigned to the artillery unit protecting the camp.

The 191st had been called to support the beleaguered troops. Waugh's *Mother Goose* gunship was in the thick of the fray. After the nightlong battle nearly exhausted American munitions and medical supplies, the Boomerangs brought in fresh troops and logistics. Waugh's Bounty Hunter crew provided gunship cover for the Boomerangs as they evacuated wounded personnel to hospitals in Long Binh and other field headquarters with surgery facilities. The troops remaining on the ground repaired the damage and policed up the enemy bodies. They strung new wire along the perimeter and placed new claymores. Packed with hundreds of steel balls and HEs, there wasn't any doubt that the claymore mines were responsible for the shreds of enemy flesh hanging on the perimeter wire.

At first sight of the scene, Waugh felt a deep sorrow for the lost lives caught on the wire. His Christian upbringing tugged at his conscience. But Waugh's determination to fight against the Communist aggression, which he believed threatened his own existence, was foremost in his mind. Loyal to his country, he flew his mission and protected American soldiers. Body after body, Waugh watched his fellow soldiers carry American dead and wounded to the slicks for immediate evacuation. Waugh knew what needed to be done, and was dedicated to carrying out the 191st mission.

Flying for the first time with CPT Stack, the new gun-platoon leader, Waugh was in for a real eye-opener. Far more experienced in gunship combat than other 191st pilots, Stack put on a firepower demonstration with a flight-control touch like none Waugh had seen to date. Upon being released from covering the flight after the slick missions were complete, Stack was given instructions to follow up on the enemy's retreat to fix and destroy any remaining enemy troops they could locate. Maneuvering the Charlie-model Huey with remarkable skill, CPT Stack screened the area where the enemy set up machine-gun emplacements to cover their withdrawal. Stack methodically destroyed these enemy positions and made a lasting impression on Waugh.

"Man! CPT Stack could fly a gunship," Waugh recalls. "No ifs, ands, or buts about it. Stack was the best I ever saw."

From that day forward, the combo wreaked havoc on the enemy until the day Stack was wounded and evacuated back to the States. The relationship that emerged between the AC and the crew chief of the *Mother Goose* gunship, however, would last a lifetime.

As a crew chief on a Charlie-model gunship, Waugh participated in some of the most dangerous missions assigned to the 191st AHC. One of his specialties: incursions into Cambodia. Few enlisted personnel were recognized for achieving the criteria that awarded them the prestigious Distinguished Flying Cross. Waugh was one of only a handful. Furthermore, the Army decorated him seven times with Air Medals, each one with a V-device on its suspension ribbon, recognizing him for valor in combat. And for his wounds received in action, he was twice awarded the Purple Heart. No question about it, Waugh experienced more than his share of combat.

In June of 1969, like hundreds of thousands of other Vietnam War veterans, Waugh quietly left the service and rejoined American society. He worked in Utah's construction industry, where he currently resides with his wife, Roberta. The father of ten children, Waugh Jr. is a grandfather and a great-grandfather. No doubt his family for many generations will think of him with pride for his extraordinary record of military service and for his extraordinary dedication to his family. He is one of the heroic load bearers who not only survived the rigors of war as a combat-assault crewmember, but who also left a lasting mark on the 191st AHC.

"Flying with the 191st was, without question, the experience of my life," Waugh explains. "The people serving in the unit were great. The NCOs and officers were outstanding. The equipment was not the greatest—we were given used birds when we went over—but the maintenance personnel made do with what they had. I cannot think of another unit I ever served with that had people who worked as hard and were as dedicated to the mission. The 191st was tops in my book."

***

SP5 Ernest Lee "Ernie" Houdashell, one of America's volunteer load bearers, bravely helped fill the ranks of the 191st AHC in Vietnam. Houdashell, from a Protestant upbringing and German descent, frequently worked the flight line, often without a shirt but always with his red bandana, which marked him as a Bounty Hunter. Amidst a backdrop of olive-drab figures, this kid—hair brilliant blond, complexion a creamy white—stood out like an early cotton-ball sprout in a field of green. His presence on the flight line was bound to catch your attention if you eyed his section of the airfield. On occasion, the company XO would direct Houdashell to put on his T-shirt. The XO touted "uniform compliance" as his reason; however, his biggest concern was sniper fire. Although sniper action was infrequent, when it hit, Houdashell stood out like a brilliant-white beacon.

Gregarious to the hilt, Houdashell was a friend to all. In fact, at any gathering of his peers, he was one of the driving spark plugs of the function. Whatever it might be, whether drinking beer in the barracks after a long day on the battlefield or casually discussing tactics and technical jargon, Houdashell contributed his best. Team player extraordinaire, this youngster was mission-committed to the core. His enthusiasm lifted the crew; it was contagious.

When first arriving in Vietnam in 1968, Houdashell's enthusiasm was temporarily dampened by a baptism of fire. Medevacs extracted wounded from super-hot LZs. Enemy fire zinged by, lighting up the night, and machine-gun tracers flew everywhere. At each harrowing LZ, the overwhelming enemy action put the pilots and crew smack next to the brink of death.

"I arrived at Bearcat, Vietnam, right during the Tet Offensive," Houdashell recalls. "And, I was grabbed to fly cover for Dustoff ships. As the new kid on the block, I was flying on the gunner side of the ship. With my mouth dry as cotton, I was horrified by the wall of tracers that came up to meet us every time we attacked an enemy target. The pilot was screaming at me because I could not keep my M60 machine gun going fast enough to please him. My job was to provide covering fire for the ship as it broke off from each gun run. This required that I hang out of the aircraft on a monkey cord while aiming the M60 machine gun aft, beneath the bird's tail boom, to provide covering fire. This was somewhat unnerving for a newbie, and it took some getting used to."

But Houdashell made the grade with flying colors and was eventually given his own UH-1C Bounty Hunter gunship to maintain, tail number 66715. As crew chief, it was his responsibility to ensure that the bird was combat-ready each day. Beaming like a kid with a new toy, Houdashell thought that nothing was "more cool" than to have disposed to his care a combat aircraft with the strike capability of a Charlie-model gunship. He was ecstatic. With aircraft 715 under his charge, he joined the inner circle of this elite group of crusty warriors, the 191st AHC Bounty Hunters—Uncle Sam's hired guns.

Houdashell's learning curve quickly steepened. Killing tactics and skills were honed to a fine edge in the air—and at the Long Branch Saloon. Although the saloon was a crudely constructed, down-home-type bar built by the Bounty Hunters, it was treated as a members-only club. Outsiders were welcome *if invited*, and it was considered an honor to socialize with these keepers of the peace. As a full-fledged crew chief, Houdashell was truly one of them now, and it made him feel extraordinarily good. Bounty Hunter pilots and crewmembers would while away evenings, sharing details of their daily exploits. Newly assigned gunnies could informally cross-pollinate with the more experienced veterans over beer and loud music. True, these get-togethers could get rowdy, but the saloon bonded the unit, and the passed-on knowledge helped save lives.

The primary purpose in life for this aggressive clan of gunship crews was to protect the lightly armed Boomerang slicks during combat assaults. They did their job with a hot-blooded American style, rendering no mercy. "It's our guys out there we are sworn to protect" was the sentiment all around. Any enemy that threatened the flight received the Bounty Hunter's full measure of firepower until dead. The thought was, it was either our own troops or the enemy who would die on the LZ, and each crewmember knew it. Given powerful weaponry with which to conduct this peacekeeping mission, they were a force to be reckoned with, and they used it liberally. When enemy fire raked the 191st AHC slicks, Bounty Hunters rained death upon the enemy with a vengeance. Between troop lifts, when not covering the flight, they frequently supported the infantry troops in search-and-destroy operations for targets of opportunity.

The Long Branch Saloon offered an excellent training environment where combat experience and wisdom were exchanged. Destruction of enemy troops and their refuges was common bar discussion. However, Long Branch Saloon wasn't all work and tactic discussions. The rock music blared. The beer was always cold. And the talk often veered off toward girls, family, and hometowns back on American soil. The crews bonded in the heat of battle, but secured their fellowship in the saloon. This fellowship was tested daily.

"It wasn't all fun," Houdashell recalls. "Enemy fire varied from firefight to firefight, and it wasn't always our advantage. When the enemy had well-prepared positions and fought with conviction, they scared the hell out of you. Certain areas of our operational zone posed greater challenges than others. Ben Tre was always one of those.

"On one occasion, we were ordered to cover the slicks during combat-assault operations southwest of Dong Tam. We departed ahead of the slick formation to a destination I was not familiar with. Arriving at an abandoned airstrip well ahead of the Boomerangs, we shot our approach to the sod bordering the runway and shut down to wait for the flight. Unbeknown to me and to the rest of the crew, this was Ben Tre, an area known to harbor large concentrations of enemy. The AC WO1 Richard VanDusen and his copilot, WO1 Bill Grebe, casually stepped out of the aircraft and took a seat in the cargo compartment while Gunner SP4 Ron Lovelette and I tied down the blade and secured the ship. Off in the distance, we could see the flight headed our way. As they initiated their descent to land on the airstrip, enemy mortar rounds exploded on the far end of the strip, working their way to our location. Without a spoken word, we all quickly exited the gunship and sprinted to a nearby bunker. Seeing the explosions, the flight diverted to parts unknown, leaving us there to fend for ourselves with no help. Evidently, no one saw the Bounty Hunter ship tied down on the sod. Even worse, all of our individual weapons were on the aircraft. Except for the Smith & Wesson .38 pistols that the pilots carried in their side holsters, we were defenseless.

"The enemy stopped the mortars as soon as the flight left, and all was quiet for a few minutes. Assuming it was safe to venture back out to the aircraft, we ran back to the bird and began the run-up procedure, only to have the mortars start exploding again. We scrambled back to the bunker. Back and forth, this scenario went on for about a half an hour before we finally decided that it would be better to risk the mortar attack than to be taken prisoner and remain a guest of the enemy for the duration of the war. We finally made it out of there and rejoined the flight with glee.

"Never had I been so happy to join the rest of the outfit in the air. No doubt, the laundry workers incurred extra work after we got back to Dong Tam. Getting caught away from my weapon with the enemy bearing down on us and no place to go but the bunker on that abandoned airfield was a lesson I never forgot. I would imagine that the enemy watching us was getting a big charge out of making us run back and forth from the bird to the bunker. No doubt, if we had stayed there long enough, they would have either attacked with reinforcements and taken us prisoner, or would have zeroed in on our bird and destroyed it. I still have bad dreams about that day."

Stories like these were just one of many replayed back in the Bounty Hunters' Long Branch Saloon—stories that would forever replay in the hearts of the guys who were there.

Completing his second tour of duty in Vietnam, Houdashell returned to his Texas home, where he quietly reentered private life. However, he couldn't ignore growing social stigma affecting returning Vietnam veterans. The negative image often created by the anti-Vietnam War protests and the peace movement needed a change for the better. He vowed to correct it. Now possessing leadership skills that could influence people, Houdashell decided to devote his life to public service.

At the time of his interview for this book, Ernie Houdashell was serving as the elected county judge of Randall County, Texas. No greater compliment can be paid to any American than to be given such public trust. His election comes as no surprise to any of his Vietnam brothers.

***

PFC Gerald David Aiton, a gunner on a 191st assault ship, performed his duties with bravery and distinction. An affable youngster, Aiton awoke on the morning of April 29, 1968, to begin a now-familiar routine. Although not long in the unit, he had already earned a reputation for returning enemy fire with superb accuracy. Aiton could handle an M60 machine gun like an old pro—swift and lethal.

As a member of the 191st AHC, Aiton was an important part of the airmobile assault fleet that daily met the enemy in the South Vietnam jungles. As gunner, his job was to protect the ship and crew. The primary tool of his trade was the aircraft's pintle-mounted M60 machine gun. Daily, he mounted the gun at the start of operations in the morning and removed it for cleaning and storage when the flight returned to home base at the end of the day.

Gifted with extraordinary mechanical ability, Aiton could assemble and disassemble the gun blindfolded. He knew every part by feel and could likewise identify mechanical problems as they occurred on the battlefield. Like most gunners and crew chiefs, he carried his own array of spare parts in a bag, and did not hesitate to perform field-expedient repairs on the piece when needed. The outcome of his dedicated support was excellent suppressive fire when the crew needed protection.

"We were flying missions out of Dong Tam, generally in the region to the west of the installation," SP5 Dennis Stits, crew chief of the aircraft on which Aiton served as gunner, recalls. "The LZs were hot, and this operation went on for several days. On the morning of April 28, 1968, our bird caught quite a few rounds, one striking the aircraft just above Gerald's head. Upset with such a close call, on the following day, Gerald drew his M16 from the arms room, in event we were shot down. He wanted extra firepower to defend our ground position. I can only assume that he envisioned the pilots as poorly armed since they only carried .38-caliber revolvers.

"Over the course of several combat assaults, the enemy fire intensified. Gerald was doing a great job returning hot lead. He suppressed the enemy threats with extraordinary accurate bullet placement, and the pilots appreciated his efficiency under duress. It wasn't until his aircraft was banking away from the enemy shooters that he was struck by a stray enemy bullet and killed instantly. The pilot immediately requested permission to divert to Dong Tam to deliver Gerald to medical facilities, but regrettably he was dead on arrival. I spoke to the physicians who indicated that his wound was instantly fatal. He suffered little.

"I cannot begin to tell you how truly difficult it is to lose someone with whom you work and bond with every day. He hadn't been there long, but in the short time he was, Gerald made a significant contribution to the 191st AHC. I feel confident in saying that his effective fire suppression saved lives that would have been lost if the enemy fire he snuffed out managed to strafe the flight. Gerald Aiton was a great loss to the unit."

When Aiton fought the enemy to save the lives of his comrades in arms, he gave his whole heart and soul to a cause in which he truly believed. On the day he was killed in action, Aiton was properly dressed in all combat gear issued to him, including his body armor. Tragically, the round found a vulnerable, unprotected spot, a reality of the horrible sacrifices that occur in battle. And, while debates abound concerning the necessity of war, our nation continues to be blessed with youngsters like Aiton who volunteer for the sake of America's ideals and their willingness to give the gift of democracy and freedom to parts of the globe who cry out for our help.

How many times had Aiton saved his ship and crew, no one can possibly know, but many of the lives he saved went on to return to the United States, get married, and raise families. On April 29, 1968, in the Dinh Tuong province of Vietnam, PFC Gerald David Aiton gave them that gift and died a hero.

***

Among the greatest contributions made by military men and women who served in Vietnam, the 191st load bearers produced an advanced culture of their own. Irrespective of the conflicts against the war that appeared on American television each evening, they never lost focus on their responsibilities as warriors and technicians. With amazing expediency, they queried one another for solutions in tactical or logistical challenges and collectively resolved problems with clever field-expedient solutions.

Most remarkable, bullets and the constant threat of dying didn't deter their loyalty to the cause or break their spirit. Truly, the term "great American heroes" is insufficient to describe their valor and loyalty. These 191st load bearers set the bar at a level beyond heroes.

CHAPTER 7

A Combat Assault from Lead's Cockpit

It was just another wet morning in the freakin' Vietnam War.

During those intense days of multiple trips into hot LZs, a fleeting question often zipped through CPT John V. Hedrick's consciousness: "What the hell did I do to get *here*?"

Shipped to Vietnam with the 191st AHC during the initial deployment in 1967, CPT Hedrick was among the first few of the unit's officers to lead a combat-helicopter assault into the heart of enemy territory. Upon arrival in Vietnam, the 191st AHC was assigned to support the Ninth Infantry Division in the Mekong Delta and its surrounding areas. The locals refer to this delta region as Chu Long, meaning Nine Dragons, because nine waterways dovetail across the floodplains into the mighty Mekong River.

Here, Hedrick and his crew flew over egrets perched on the back of buffalo wallowing in rice paddies, over mangrove forests teeming with the calls of openbill storks and cormorants, over wooden boats floating down the mud-rich waters and loaded with coconuts and fruit, over the ruined remains of ornate Khmer pagodas and Buddhist temples stretching to the skies—and, of course, over the underground bunkers bristling with VC soldiers.

In the dry season from December to May, much of the delta lies flat, dry, and open—a vast airmobile LZ, allowing the 191st far greater selection of LZs than combat-assault units working central and northern zones. The numbers of 191st insertions and flight hours soared. But upon deployment, the 191st landed in the Mekong Delta in late spring, still early in the wet season. After being at Bearcat for just over a month, "We were still pretty green at this combat-assault stuff," Hedrick recalls. "We all realized that over here, if we didn't learn quickly, we could go home in a body bag. That nagging, terribly unpleasant thought definitely sharpened our mission focus."

The 191st AHC aircraft fleet included twenty-three UH-1Ds (slicks) and eight UH-1Cs (Charlie-model gunships). On a typical combat-assault day, the unit employed ten slicks to carry troops, one slick for C&C, and four gunships flying cover. The remaining birds were in PE or serving other tactical needs. Of highest priority was having replacement aircraft for those sustaining combat damage in the field or needing quick-turn, routine maintenance. Tactically, a light fire team covered each flight platoon, and the C&C bird would direct air-mission tasks on the battlefield. As a backup, each day, a designated standby crew would crank a spare slick in event any other bird failed its preflight check. This routine assured fulfillment of the 191st AHC's mission commitment—to support the infantry units assigned for that day.

On June 20, 1967, the 191st woke to carry out that mission commitment. It was just another wet morning in the "freakin' Vietnam War," and like all combat-assault mornings, it left Hedrick counting down the days until he could get out of this hellhole.

"Knowing that I was assigned to be flight lead with much of the responsibility for the day's mission," Hedrick recalls, "I got up at 0400 hours, grabbed a cup of coffee, and wolfed down a quick breakfast. I picked up my signal operating instructions [SOI] and received a briefing from ops. I was thus able to assign tail numbers to the ACs, help with the preflight of my ship, and be ready to initiate the crank for our planned lift-off at 0500 hrs.

"Our mission was to lift elements of the Third Brigade, Ninth Infantry Division, from a PZ at Tan An into what was very likely to be a hot LZ south-southwest of Rach Kien, a district town in Long An province at grid X-ray Sierra 740697. It was seventeen nautical miles south-southwest of Saigon. Each LZ had a name assigned to it, but this name only meant something to the grunts. To me, it was just a coordinate on the map. Once I got close, all I would need to do was ask the Bounty Hunter lead to mark the precise LZ with a rocket or smoke and give me a quick 'heads-up' on the enemy situation."

The day's objective LZ was The Bowling Alley—a very large rice-paddy area between two bends in the Sông Vam Co Tay. *Sông* means river in Vietnamese. Map readers variously nicknamed these distinctive river bends the Testicles, the Nuts, or sometimes, in more delicate company, the Mouse Ears. As briefed, this mission would be a major operation because two other assault-helicopter companies, the Tomahawks and the Greyhounds, were also tasked to participate with their ten slicks each for a total of three initial lifts.

Hedrick received a radio call immediately after the flight's on-time takeoff.

"Lead, Trail. You're off with ten."

Hedrick acknowledged the good news and released the spare aircraft and crew. The flight executed a gentle climb to 1,500 feet AGL—above small-arms range—turned southwest over the greater Mekong Delta, and headed to the PZ at Tan An, forty nautical miles from Bearcat. A slight hint of daylight spilled out behind the flight, while in front the western sky lay dark.

"I was the second flight-platoon leader of the 191st AHC, with the Boomerangs," Hedrick recalls, "call sign Boomerang Two-Six. That day I was leading our flight of ten Huey D-model slicks. Each carried six grunts, as infantrymen have long been called, and a flight crew of four: aircraft commander, copilot, crew chief, and gunner."

After the passage of several decades, many of the names of Hedrick's compadres have escaped him, but he will always recall *this* crew—CW2 Gary "Slick" Slanga, SP4 Cecil Stamper, and PFC Joey Bishop. "My life then was in their hands, and I'll never forget them."

The Boomerang Two-Six and the rest of the flight approached the PZ at Tan An. "The troops lined up in *sticks* of six, just the right distance apart so they could very quickly load onto the helicopters as soon as we landed," Hedrick explains. "We would seldom have to shut down, and we appreciated their disciplined and experienced leadership."

In a few short minutes, with troops safely aboard, the Boomerang flight lifted back into the air and headed southeast to the LZ a few minutes away. Hedrick radioed C&C. "Charlie-Charlie, this is Boomerang Two-Six. Eight minutes out."

"Roger, Two-Six. Hold clear, five clicks to the west at fifteen hundred feet and stand by."

"Charlie-Charlie, this is Boomerang Two-Six. Roger, understand hold five clicks west at fifteen hundred."

Too busy to respond, the C&C radio operator hit the squelch button twice—*click click*—the universal signal for transmission heard.

The 191st AHC's organic gun platoon, the Bounty Hunters, escorted the flight. They formed two gunship fire teams, and each team consisted of two Charlie-model Hueys, or "guns" for short. A rocket pod on each side of the gunship carried seven 2.75-inch folding-fin rockets. Some of these birds also packed a 40-millimeter grenade launcher mounted in the nose. The gunship's real teeth, however, came in two six-barrel, 7.62-millimeter, electrically fired miniguns and laid down bursts up to six thousand rounds per minute (although they were generally adjusted to fire at only two thousand rounds per minute to make their ammo last longer and keep the barrels from overheating). Equally deadly were the "M60s suspended in the cargo doors on bungee cords," Hedrick recalls. "The crew chief and gunner would normally carry two thousand straight tracer rounds and could shoot the eyes out of a snake."

The C&C bird loitered well above the range of small-arms fire. The infantry commander rode in the back, which gave him a bird's-eye view of the battlefield. From this vantage point, he coordinated in real time with the AMC to identify the optimal landing spots with the best tactical advantage. Normally, the gunships flew a racetrack pattern beside the LZ, laying down continuous protective cover for the slicks and the grunts on the ground. On this day, they expected the enemy to hit from the left. In preparation, both gunship teams worked the left side of the flight.

The flight approached the area where C&C had just directed it to initiate a racetrack holding pattern. Hedrick spotted a lot of smoke up ahead coming from, what he assumed from glancing at the map, their LZ. Air Force F-4 Phantoms and the Ninth Division Artillery aggressively prepped the LZ. The resulting thick smoke rose nearly straight up into the still morning air.

"The 128th AHC [Tomahawks] and the 240th AHC [Greyhounds] were the lead companies," Hedrick recalls. "They would be going in ahead of us, but as we listened to the radio, we realized they hadn't dropped their troops yet. We didn't know why. According to the briefed plan, the Tomahawks would go in first. Then we would wait for the Greyhounds to follow them. Once the Greyhounds called clear of the LZ, it would then be *our* turn.

"I knew from the mission briefing that morning that this one was not going to be a cakewalk. It was likely to be, as we called them then, a real clusterfuck. The intelligence that Division had shared with us, which was probably two to three days old at best, showed Charlie being deployed along the river. The approach to the LZ that Division chose for us appeared to be a U-shaped trap. Seeing reality on the ground is often much different from what one can glean from a sterile map sheet. Sometimes, during an early premission briefing, the AHC liaison would have to convince the supported unit's leaders that landing parallel to a tree line was much smarter than nose-on. That gave us shallower and faster takeoff options, and enabled our door gunners to deliver much more effective covering fire both during landing and takeoff. Being oriented parallel to tree lines generally gave our gunships a better advantage, too. Since the airmobile concept was pretty new, a lot of on-the-job learning was taking place on both sides. With unavoidable turnover due to attrition and combat losses, this education took time, and we were just now getting our feet wet."

It didn't take long for C&C to realize that a landing heading parallel to the tree line was the smarter choice.

"Boomerang Two-Six, this is Charlie-Charlie. You're cleared to descend."

"Roger, Charlie-Charlie. Two-Six is out of fifteen hundred."

Hedrick and his crew knew what that meant. "Things were about to happen," Hedrick recalls. "Just then, we heard the Tomahawks being cleared from the release point [RP] inbound for their approach to the LZ. As the Tomahawks closed on their touchdown point, the radios really came alive."

During each radio transmission, a loud staccato of M60 machine-gun fire blasted Hedrick's eardrums.

"Receiving fire! Two's hit!"

"Four's hit!"

"Six is hit!"

"Eight's hit!"

"Lead, Trail. Flight's down! Two and Seven are down and burning, but it looks like everybody's out okay. Three is picking up Two. Trail will pick up Seven's crew."

The Tomahawks under fire were only four to six minutes ahead of Hedrick's and the 191st flight. Meanwhile, the "Gunslingers" and the Bounty Hunters were "doing their thing," blasting the woods on the left.

With the Tomahawks now clear of the LZ, it was the Greyhounds' turn in Hell. Hedrick's Boomerang lead ship banked left, making a slow left turn back toward the LZ. CW2 Slanga gently let Boomerang Two-Six down from the racetrack pattern it was maintaining at 1,500 feet AGL and slowed from the *loiter* airspeed of ninety knots to the initial approach speed of sixty knots.

"This helped with our spacing behind the Greyhounds," Hedrick recalls. "Judging from the intensity of enemy fire that the Tomahawks took, we anticipated there would be plenty more of the same for the next two lifts."

"Greyhound One-Six, this is Charlie-Charlie. You're cleared inbound to the LZ."

"Charlie-Charlie, Greyhound One-Six. Roger, RP inbound—break, break, Flight Lead. Go staggered left. LZ is hot, left side."

"Lead, Trail. You're up staggered left."

"Roger."

Then, thirty seconds later: "Flight, commence firing."

"Three's hit—holy shit!"

"Two's hit!"

"Five's hit!"

A flurry of snaps and bursts boomed through the radio behind the shouting voices.

"Lead, Trail. Flight's down!"

A few seconds later, the grunts leaped from the helicopters and onto the ground.

"Lead's on the go. Breaking right!"

"Lead, Trail. You're off with nine. We left chock eight."

"Roger that."

The *Dogs*, supported by their gun platoon, the Mad Dogs, were in the clear. Boomerangs were up next.

"Boomerang Two-Six, this is Charlie-Charlie. You're cleared into the LZ."

At this point, fear is up close and personal. Years later, Hedrick recalls, "You are scared shitless, but there's nothing you can do about it. Your adrenaline's pumping. You put your fear aside, say a quick prayer, and into the grinder you go."

The fight continued. "Boomerang Two-Six is RP inbound." Hedrick's lips brushed against the microphone of his ballistic helmet.

A second call from C&C: "Flight Lead, go staggered right and close it up, guys. The LZ's hot. Full suppression, left side only."

Then a third call: "Bounty Hunter Lead, Two-Six, the fire seems to be coming from the trees on the left."

"Roger, Two-Six, left tree line."

From the chock-ten trail ship came the status call: "Lead, Trail. You have ten, up staggered right."

"Roger that!" Hedrick replied. He looked over at Slanga, his peter pilot in the right seat. "Well, Slick, you ready for another one?"

"Shit, why not, sir? That's why we make the big bucks, ain't it?" Slanga locked his shoulder harness, eased back on the cyclic, and engaged the force trim, which locked the cyclic a bit aft. The thinking was if both pilots take hits, the ship should pull into a climb and get them out of there.

Hedrick turned and glanced back over his right shoulder at Crew Chief Stamper and Gunner Bishop, and he asked them if they were ready. He got a quick "roger" from each of them. Both Stamper and Bishop wore a ballistic helmet, a flak jacket, and a ceramic chest-protector better known as a *chicken plate*. And both sat on extra chicken plates to protect their privates from fire below. Their duty station was in the well beside the hellhole. They leaned over their M60 machine guns mounted on fixed pintles. They were perched at the ready with nimble fingers.

"I briefly glanced to my right rear at a couple of the grunts," Hedrick recalls, "and I'll never forget the look of fear in those kids' eyes. Then I reached up and pulled down my helmet visor to protect my eyes from any flying plastic in case we were to get a bullet through the windshield. One round could turn the cockpit into a blizzard of flying plastic that could easily put out an eye. I pulled the armor plate on the left side of my seat to the front, locking it in place to block small-arms fire coming from the left. Then I slid down as low in the seat as I could.

"With one final glance down, I made sure my holstered pistol was pulled around and stuffed up between my legs, protecting my balls. This really didn't do any good, but it made some of us feel like it might. I locked my shoulder harness and again tried to slide even farther down. Sitting in the left seat, the metal plate by the door window gave some ballistic protection. The armored seat covered my backside and part of my right side from small-arms fire. But my lower legs and face were completely unprotected. I, too, wore a ceramic chicken plate over my chest, a flak jacket over it, and a ballistic helmet. If we could get them, we would even lay an extra chicken plate in the chin bubble for additional protection. With all this, we still felt like sitting ducks, and I now know what a pheasant feels like in hunting season when being fired at during takeoff. I haven't hunted them since I left Vietnam.

"I got lightly on the controls with Slanga. In case one of us were hit, the other would have seamless control of the aircraft. This was a company policy any time we expected a hot LZ. In the rare event that a pilot would become incapacitated, the front seats were pinned and hinged so they could be tipped backward onto the floor. The injured or dead pilot could be extracted, and the crew chief could take his vacated seat. We'd trained all of our crew chiefs, and even most of the gunners, in the basics of how to fly and make a landing. Luckily, none of my crews ever had to do this, thank God.

"The radio console in the Huey is between the front seats for easy access to either pilot. We operated on three different types of radios. FM [Fox Mike] for communication with ground units and artillery advisories. We could also monitor what the infantry commander was saying to his ground units on that frequency. VHF [Victor] for air-to-air transmissions and for our intraflight chatter, and UHF [Uniform] for communications with the C&C ship, company operations, airfield towers, etc. One channel of the UHF, called the 'Guard' frequency, would override all others on the UHF band and was used only for emergencies or urgent need. The survival radio we carried would *only* operate on that UHF Guard frequency. My additional duty, when not flying myself, required that I keep all these radios on the right frequencies at the right times. During the heat of an operation, I was fully challenged with trying to talk with my copilot, my crew chief, the gunships, and C&C, who, for some reason or other, seemed to want to talk to me all at the same time. With the entire flight behind me, my situational awareness was thoroughly tested, often.

"My primary tasks were navigation, monitoring artillery activity, deciding which would be the best formation to get all ten ships effectively landed amongst obstacles on the ground, to best counter the threat, and to provide for the safest offloading of troops. While doing all of this, I planned the optimal departure route. For instances such as this one, we could do what the preceding lift did, but that could quickly change if they took heavy fire on climb-out."

The flight continued. Hedrick was hailed by a Greyhound.

"Boomerang Lead, Greyhound One-Six. We left a crew in the LZ. Can you get them out?"

"Roger that, Greyhound One-Six. Boomerang Two-Six, out." Hedrick quickly hailed the Boomerang flight: "Boomerang Flight, Lead. The Greyhounds have a crew down in the LZ. I'll put down as close to those burning ships as possible. Loose, staggered right. Let's make it quick. Trail, you pick up the downed crew."

These fluid situations in combat required commanders, pilots, and crews with nimble minds.

"Normally, I would barely touch down, drag my skids, count to five, and call 'Lead's on the go' to start the takeoff," Hedrick recalls. "But if it was a hot LZ, then the approach terminated in a slow, forward hover, never touching the ground. The grunts rode the skids and jumped when the door gunners started firing."

This day, the LZ was red hot.

"I didn't want to stay there any longer than absolutely necessary," Hedrick explains. "We were big targets on the ground, and I didn't have to explain to my crew what was expected of them. We knew that downed crew would be looking for a quick escape, for sure. Being on the ground in a hot LZ is not real fun, especially for pilots who went to flight school to stay *off* the ground.

"To initiate door-gun suppression, I gave the command on short final: 'Flight, commence fire!' Ten machine guns and a pair of Huey gunships can put out a devastating amount of lead. The prepping fire by the F-4s and the artillery from Division was intense, but now, our gunships were pouring even more fire into the jungle to the left of the LZ. But I knew even this would not be enough to keep us from being shot at. Right then, the 'fun' started for us."

"Three's hit!"

"Five's hit!"

"Two's hit!"

Hedrick and his crew heard a loud *bam bam bam* and then his whole aircraft shuddered. "About this time," Hedrick recalls, "our asses puckered so much that they almost sucked the nylon webbing off our seats."

"We're hit, sir!"

"Where, Chief?"

"Tail boom, I think."

"No warning lights and no master caution, so we must be okay."

Surprisingly, "Most of the time when the aircraft took a hit, you didn't feel or hear anything. Sometimes the only sound was a *tick tick* or a *zip zip*," Hedrick explains. "These were generally small-caliber bullets that hit the blades or just zipped through the thin skin of the tail boom, vertical fin, or synchronized elevator. Sometimes you hear a *zzzip* or *whizzz*. These were rounds going through the cockpit or right behind your seat—or in this case, a *bam*! This bigger sound was a larger caliber round or one hitting a more solid part of the ship."

The crews felt this *bam* in the seats of their pants. "Bad sign!" And Copilot Slanga surely felt the shudder in the stick and the vibration coming up through the foot pedals.

As the Boomerang ships, still in loose formation, flared to decelerate for the landing, they held their noses high with their tail stingers just off the ground.

"Then we each leveled and slowed more, our skids a foot or so over the dried-up rice paddy," Hedrick recalls. "The smoke was so thick you could hardly see the other ships or the tree line. Before we'd even stopped, the grunts leaped off the skids, going prone, with those on the protected right side firing under the ship into the jungle on our left. SP4 Cecil Stamper laid down covering fire from the left door with his M60 machine gun. The Bounty Hunter gunships raced by at treetop level with their miniguns blazing out a *brrr-brrr-brrr* sound and rockets exploding ahead of them."

Even after decades, Hedrick still remembers the intense racket of that day. As he and his crew sat uncomfortably exposed, he finally got the welcome call.

"Lead, Trail. I've got the Dogs' crew aboard. After takeoff, permission to break off to Can Tho Hospital. One of these guys is shot up pretty bad."

"Roger, but get your ass over to Tan An ASAP. I've got a bad feeling I'm going to need you guys."

"Lead, Trail. That's a rog, out!"

"We're clear, sir!" Crew Chief Stamper yelled.

"Lead's on the go, breaking right," Hedrick replied.

Shortly after that transmission, Hedrick heard what he describes as the sweetest transmission yet.

"Lead, Trail. You're up with ten."

There wasn't a happier and luckier crew in all Vietnam.

"Roger that, Flight! Go trail. I want a complete checkout back at Tan An."

Rolling out on a heading toward Tan An, Hedrick initiated an artillery check: "Tan An Control, Boomerang Two-Six. Say Arty from grid X-ray Sierra 650688 to Tan An, direct, fifteen hundred feet."

"Boomerang Two-Six, Tan An Control. We have Arty from grid X-ray Sierra 551650 to X-ray Sierra 624764 and from grid X-ray Sierra 650688 to X-ray Sierra 494450. Max ordinate twenty-five thousand feet."

Hedrick repeated the advisory back for confirmation and received a "roger" while he plotted it on his map. He drew out the two gun-target (G-T) lines and plotted how high they were firing. "I could tell by the maximum ordinate given to me that we could safely fly under the arc of the northernmost fire mission," he explains.

Slanga kept a listening ear to all this while still controlling the aircraft. "All I had to do was just point in the direction I wanted him to fly," Hedrick recalls, "and tell him the altitude to maintain in order to get us back to Tan An without getting us blown out of the sky by our own artillery. I passed this information to the Bounty Hunters, figuring they may not yet have caught up with the flight, as was frequently the case. I suspected they were either back at the refueling/rearming point or continuing to cover the LZ. As the mission progressed and the gunships needed to refuel or rearm, the escorting fire team might be from any of the other lift companies, which is why they had call signs different from the lift companies. Keeping all this straight during the day required a high level of constant situational awareness."

The flight landed just outside the compound at Tan An, where troops for their second lift were ready to load up.

"It was prudent that we take time to shut down and carefully check the helicopters for battle damage," Hedrick explains. "Nothing major could be done to them at this time, but if airworthy, they would be back in the fight."

The slicks had been peppered with many small bullet holes. The crews covered the more significant ones with duct tape, or "two-hundred-mile-an-hour tape," as it was affectionately called.

"We were looking for major issues—any critical damage to the radios or anything that would make a ship unsafe for flight," Hedrick explains. "If a blade had holes, a strip of tape wrapped around it could keep the skin from peeling off and restore smoothness to the airfoil. You could normally tell when you received a hit in a blade because it would start making a buzzing sound. If the hole affected the leading-edge spar, however, the aircraft would be grounded. The blade had to be replaced on the spot or a maintenance officer would fly it back to Bearcat for repair. If this happened, we would trade aircraft with him to keep our flyable complement up to ten ships if possible.

"At times such as this, with a few moments of relaxed tension, the thought might occur that you had escaped death, yet again. A sudden, but brief onset of the shakes would hit you. As the saying goes, you just experienced a pucker factor of twenty on a scale of one to ten. But while you were in the air during a troop insertion, you didn't have time to entertain such distractions."

Like always, Hedrick walked the line and talked to the crews. He noticed WO1 Bill Smith, call sign Two-Zero, in the chock-two ship, slumped forward in his seat. There was a bullet hole in the ship at the same level as Smith's head, when seated upright. Hedrick ran back and jerked open the door. There was Smith, leaning over, attempting to pick up a cigarette from the ones scattered all over the cockpit floor. Hedrick thought he had been hit. Luckily, the bullet struck his helmet and glanced off.

"He was shaking so bad he couldn't pick up the cigarette," Hedrick recalls. "He just gave me a sick smile and shook his head. I patted him on the shoulder and continued walking down the line, checking on the others."

Two of the ships were grounded, which put Hedrick in a bind. "With one over at the hospital, this left me with seven ships, meaning that we would be making two more trips into the LZ instead of one. Stamper found thirteen holes in ours, but it was still flyable. Most of these were in the tail boom and none had hit the driveshaft, control cables, or a gearbox.

"Thank God Charlie wasn't properly trained to lead a moving aircraft when shooting at us. By aiming at the pilot in the lead ship, the rounds would hit aft along the tail boom. Or, they would hit the number-two ship or even number-three aircraft, depending on his separation from the adjacent birds. The third ship in the flight seemed to receive more hits than most of the others, so I took turns assigning the position of chock three to different pilots so that no one aircrew would be disproportionately exposed over and over again.

"I made a call to Boomerang Six, our CO, MAJ Clarence Patnode, in the C&C ship. I gave him our damage report and requested that two more aircraft be sent down. He would pass it on to the maintenance detachment so they would know which parts they would need to bring to repair the aircraft. Or, if they needed to, they would call one of the heavy-lift companies for a Chinook to sling it back to Bearcat. The CH-47 Chinook was a tandem-rotor helicopter that could easily carry a Huey beneath it.

"I made a quick radio call to the grunt LT [lieutenant], who was in charge of the troops, and he advised that we were ready to go, so they started loading as we cranked. I checked with Tan An Control for relevant artillery activity, and we were off again—total time fueling and checking our ships on the ground, maybe ten minutes.

"We met up with our gunship escort, got in line, and made another run into the LZ. It was much, much quieter by this time—still hot, but not nearly as exciting as last time. This was followed by a third run, and then we were released to go refuel. We shut down and grabbed a box of C rations for a late breakfast. It was pretty close to 0800 hours, and our day was just getting started."

During Hedrick's tour, this story details a typical airmobile mission for most, if not all, of the assault-helicopter companies in Vietnam. Often the crews woke up and roared through morning after morning, just like this one. *Good morning, Vietnam!*

These scenarios repeated themselves several times a day, every day, with few exceptions. Often, the crews landed back at Bearcat after the sun disappeared for the night. Most of the time Division requested that the 191st crews stay on station and conduct single-ship resupply missions, sometimes until well past midnight. "It was not unusual to fly twelve to sixteen hours a day," Hedrick recalls.

The mornings turned into afternoons, and the afternoons folded into the dark. Hedrick and his crew knew that this day in June 1967 was going to be one of those days. "As time wore on, fatigue became an ongoing concern, and during ground time between insertions, naps were a premium. Such quiet time was not to be wasted."

On that day, the 191st flew a dozen or so flights. "Leapfrogging units from one position to another and then maybe six to eight resupply missions in the dark with the aircraft completely blacked out," Hedrick explains. "These sorties were hairy as hell. Flying a bird heavy with supplies and descending below the trees into total darkness to a flashlight with only a red filter puckered the asshole beyond description. Sweat poured from every fold of the body before you lifted off to see a horizon again. Doing that several times a night burned off a few calories. With those missions completed way after dark, the crews were released to go home, but home was still forty nautical miles away. We would set the clock, head 055 degrees, fly a half hour, and call Bearcat Tower for a flight of ten inbound for refuel/landing."

During the 191st flight home to Bearcat, exhausted pilots often took turns flying to catch a *combat nap*. "After a few weeks," Hedrick explains, "we felt we could do these combat assaults in our sleep."

Once back at Bearcat, hungry and tired, pilots flew the damaged ships directly to the maintenance area. The other ships hovered into the sandbagged, perforated-steel planking (PSP) revetments. The day, however, wasn't over for the weary crews. After the pilots shut down, they filled out their logbooks and prepared their ships for the following morning's mission. The gunners took the machine guns back to the hootch to be cleaned, and the crew chiefs started on the postflight maintenance. On some nights, the crew chiefs didn't make it back to their own bunks. The pilots pitched in as much as possible to wrap up the day's duties, but still, the crew chiefs often slept in their ships.

"For me," Hedrick explains, "I would go to flight operations to turn in the tightly controlled SOI, join the debriefing, and see what kind of 'fun' was in store for us the next day. I would stop by the orderly room if it were still open, and then I would go to maintenance to see how many ships I could expect to be flyable the next day."

To Hedrick, it seemed that by the time he lay down in his bunk, his head just touching the pillow, someone grabbed his shoulders and said, "Wake up, Captain Hedrick. You have a mission to fly."

Another 329 days, Hedrick thought, *and I'll be out of this hellhole*. Almost everyone in Vietnam kept a short-timers calendar and could tell you, to the hour, when they were going to catch the Freedom Bird home.

CHAPTER 8

Lethal Climate

The enemy traversed the jungle landscape like ma đói, *hungry ghosts.*

Dedicated to flying grunt support, 191st pilots and crews faced death for the benefit of the foot soldier. With strong mental dispositions, many 191st aviators remained cognizant that only they stood between life and death for the brave soldiers sloshing through the swampy earth of Vietnam jungles. They were a godsend to these foot soldiers—and rain or shine, the 191st was there.

On August 29, 1967, the 191st received orders to support the Eleventh Armored Cavalry Regiment (ACR), also known as the Blackhorse Regiment, which was located thirty kilometers east-southeast of Bearcat. On this day, the rain and clouds were delaying lift-off. Special instructions and precautionary measures were needed to prepare the flight for departure to Blackhorse Regiment Fire Base.

"Boomerang Flight, this is Flight Lead. We have a weather problem at the moment. Prepare to form in trail formation on the active and shut down until the weather clears. Trail, please give me an *up* when the entire flight is formed and parked on the active."

"Lead, Trail. Roger that." Moments later: "Lead, Trail, your flight is formed and parked on the active."

Click click. Lead signaled his acknowledgment of Trail's communication.

Lead waited patiently for C&C to report adequate weather conditions over the objective. Ready and eager to go, he knew the flight would need to crank and depart in quick succession in order to slip through a hole in the clouds. This hole in the clouds could form and close back up quickly; therefore, the entire flight had to be ready to go at a moment's notice.

"Departing Bearcat, weather conditions couldn't have been much worse," CPT Stack recalls. "Low ceilings and rain created dangerously limited visibility for the better part of the day. The nagging memory of the terrible accident that killed CPT Kidd and 1LT Dodson less than three months earlier was still vivid in each aircrewman's mind and left them with a general uneasiness."

Kidd and Dodson had been in the same Officer's Rotary Wing Aviator Course (ORWAC) graduating class as 1LT Hall and 1LT Bales, who were flying Aircraft 715 for the day's mission. As Hall and Bales waited for C&C to give the flight a go, they eased the tension as most pilots often do by joking and ribbing each other, just as they did in flight school back at Fort Rucker. Hall had a loving wife and little daughter waiting at home, but like many pilots and crewmembers before a flight, he wisely put those pleasant thoughts of home and hearth aside.

The awaited call from C&C came in and energized the Boomerang fleet. The Hueys ascended in a loose trail formation through a large hole in the cloud layer over Bearcat. Once the trail aircraft climbed above the scud, the group reformed and turned toward their assigned destination.

When the Boomerang flight arrived at the Blackhorse Regiment's Fire Base, no better description of existing weather conditions could be said than what was uttered by a grunt.

"Man! Why didn't you guys just stay the fuck home? If you had, we'd still be dry. Now we gotta slosh through this shit all day."

The troubled soldier had remained hopeful that no aviation support would arrive. During rainy conditions, low-lying terrain and rice paddies, typically utilized as LZs when dry, filled with water, leaving narrow roads as the only landing option. Without the paddy dikes for use as temporary cover, the disembarking troops were left exposed much longer to potential enemy fire. The wishful grunt understood the potential future that was preparing for him and his brothers-in-arms.

For the pilots and aircrews, operating in sustained bad weather may have been the most lethal noncombat threat of the war, especially in areas of significant topographic relief. While getting a current weather briefing was always part of the premission planning sequence, forecasting tools available at the time were often defeated by rapidly changing conditions, which made navigation difficult at best.

To make matters worse, on this particular day, the low-hanging clouds could shift or fog could roll in to mask the elevated areas, causing terrain to suddenly appear dangerously close to a flight of slicks inbound. Furthermore, the slick pilots knew that storm cells could quickly grow without much warning. In the afternoons, especially, as thermal contrasts developed within air masses, it was not unusual for severe discrete rain cells to coalesce into a weather front extending for several miles. If one of these walls of intense rain hit an area where the Boomerangs had inserted troops, these foot soldiers could be effectively cut off and isolated. The enemy counted on it and cultivated this knowledge to their advantage. The Boomerang aircrews knew that extracting ground troops under these dangerous conditions risked their own lives. Nevertheless, when there was good reason to believe that friendly troops might be exposed to a superior force before the weather was likely to improve, particularly if nightfall was imminent, it became necessary to accept the weather risk and either try to get the grunts out, or fly reinforcements into their location. The flight leads were well aware of the risks and took precautions as best they could.

To inadvertently fly into one of these intense storm cells was treacherous at best. Heavy rain beating on the windscreen would easily overpower the wipers' ability to keep up, causing forward visibility to be virtually eliminated. The flying pilot would have to maintain visual reference and separation from the remainder of the formation by looking out the nearest cockpit-door window. Furthermore, the density of the rain reduced ambient light significantly to produce a surreal twilight appearance in the middle of the day. Flying in the usual staggered landing formation, it was all too easy to drift perilously close to another helicopter to the immediate front as it decelerated. A dangerous rate of closure is very difficult to recognize through a rain-blurred windshield. With very few exceptions, meshing rotor blades would be fatal to all participants, so the aircrews exerted every effort to maximize vigilance and separation. On this day, the threatening weather potential put the entire crew on edge.

The wishful grunt knew that bad weather kept most combat-assault units on the ground. But what he didn't know was that these brave and tough-grit aircrews of the 191st seldom stayed home. Their prime mission was to get the foot soldiers in and then get them back out again.

With the troops of Blackhorse Regiment loaded on the slicks, the flight headed to its designated LZ. The 191st was assigned combat-assault missions in the vicinity of the Blackhorse Regiment on and off for a number of weeks in the summer of 1967. The pilots were familiar with the area. The Blackhorse region was scenic and lightly populated. Dense, triple-canopy jungle covered the hills and valleys. Vibrant green, the larger trees covered the lower growth until the base of the forest disappeared into a deep, dark, almost-black hole. When enemy concentrations struck out, the dense canopy concealed them. They traversed the jungle landscape like *ma đói*, hungry ghosts. Hence, the area remained hotly contested between enemy forces and the Blackhorse Regiment.

The Blackhorse troops protected the area, securing the main supply routes (MSRs) of the southern extremity of the Central Highlands. The North Vietnamese knew that these MSRs were the lifelines that fed American forces operating in the Central Highlands and also distributed the marrow of feedstock from the giant logistic center at Bien Hoa. Thus, the enemy accorded the area a high priority. In the midst of planning the upcoming Tet Offensive, the largest of its existence, the NVA tactical plan included cutting South Vietnam in half at the Central Highlands. Gaining control of this vital region had always been a critical part of their battle plan and their overall war effort.[1] Therefore, most high-level enemy commanders did not entrust this crucial mission to the VC, so the North dedicated some of its finest troops to

---

1 COL Harry G. Summers Jr., *The Vietnam War Almanac* (New York: Facts on File/Infobase Publishing, 1985), 115.

battle the Blackhorse Regiment. But, whether the Americans engaged NVA or VC mattered little to the Blackhorse Regiment. Rain or shine, these guys hit the jungle with conviction and fought like the true warriors they were. It was the 191st AHC's job to get them there—and back out.

However, on this day, it was a challenge for the 191st pilots to navigate into the LZ. With clouds covering the earth beneath them, ground topography remained obscured. Trees, hills, familiar pagodas, and other key ground references were hidden from view. Mental pressure in these types of dicey weather situations builds with each kilometer flown. Under such hazardous weather conditions, typical thoughts plague the minds of the lead pilots: Are we headed in the right direction? Have we passed a turning point in our route? Are we clear of artillery? Why hasn't C&C called to tell us he has our formation in sight? *Blast it!*

Amid the pressure, flight lead maintained constant reference to the horizon so as not to lead the entire formation into a cloud bank. If the birds lost visual contact with one another, perils of a horrific midair collision were little more than a breath away. And no one wanted to experience another midair collision due to weather, as Kidd and Dodson did a few months ago.

Under poor visibility and low clouds, dropping the Blackhorse troops into the LZ required tactical adjustments. Normally, combat assault–troop insertions required the slicks to maintain a relatively tight formation for gunship protection. However, weather hazards forced the Boomerang landing formations to spread out well beyond the limits of adequate gunship cover and, at times, beyond the visual reference of the C&C ship. Radio communications were constant in order to maintain accountability. Sloppy but functional, the Boomerang flight continued to deliver airmobile support to the Blackhorse troops as the Eleventh ACR lived up to its reputation, combing the target areas for NVA and VC. The day ended with no enemy contact, and the troops from both the Blackhorse Regiment and the 191st AHC were happy it was over.

With the mission drawing to a close, there remained only one slight wrinkle: a gunship was down with mechanical problems. AC 1LT Hall (Bounty Hunter One-Four) and Copilot 1LT Bales (Bounty Hunter Two-Four) waited at Blackhorse Fire Base for maintenance.

As was customary, an MTP, WO1 Alton W. Pevey, his crew, and two mechanics were dispatched from Bearcat aboard Aircraft 018 with an emergency array of parts to repair the downed gunship. Typically, these efforts were limited to the bare essentials, just enough to get the Huey sufficiently airworthy to be limped home or to a maintenance depot where rear-echelon work could be performed. In accordance with the unit's standard operating procedure (SOP), the MTP would fly the problem aircraft back to home base after the mechanics performed a careful inspection of any necessary field repair. The flight crew of the grounded aircraft would take the healthy bird back home.

After Pevey's bird arrived at Blackhorse Fire Base, the two mechanics, Staff Sergeant (SSG) Richard L. Scaduto and Sergeant (SGT) Louis C. Muser II, determined that the downed bird did indeed require depot-level maintenance and needed be flown to Vung Tau by MTP Pevey and his crew.

They assembled for departure from Blackhorse. Due to the marginal weather conditions, they decided to depart with a few minutes separation for safety spacing. Departing for Bearcat, the good aircraft (Aircraft 018) lifted off first with six souls aboard: 1LT David C. Hall (AC), 1LT Sharel "Spike" Edward Bales (CP), SP4 Peter S. Martinez (CE), SP4 Joseph L. Whitaker Jr. (G), and the two mechanics, SSG Richard L. Scaduto and SGT Louis C. Muser II. Pevey and his crew departed second in the troubled gunship (Aircraft 715) and headed for Vung Tau for repairs. Weather conditions remained unchanged—lousy. Flight visibility was marginal at best, so the flight crews were forced to rely on the barest of visual ground references for navigation.

During rotary-wing flight school, trainees received fleeting exposure to instrument flying (flying by reference to instruments rather than visual ground references). Most helicopter pilots graduating during that era were awarded the pink tactical instrument card, nicknamed *tac ticket*. Training to this minimal skill level, it was hoped, would be sufficient to enable pilots to immediately and safely exit inadvertent instrument meteorological conditions (IMC) if bad weather reduced visibility below the required safety margin for visual meteorological conditions (VMC). The tac ticket was intended only to be a quick fix to allow aircrews to live to fight another day. Normally, chopper pilots did not upgrade their instrument flying skills and qualify for the Army Standard Instrument Rating until they completed their initial combat tour and returned to an environment where they could maintain instrument flying proficiency. Unfortunately, even pilots with an instrument rating are not immune from the disorienting impact of poor visibility. Weather can often be unforgiving, and adding a limping aircraft to the mix makes a dicey day at the office.

Within minutes after departure, MTP Pevey lost contact with CPT Hall's ship on its way back to Bearcat. "Bounty Hunter One-Four, do you read?" Pevey hailed Hall and his crew for nearly an hour, but with no response. Concerned that the aircraft may have gotten into some trouble with the weather, he radioed ops. At 2015 hours, the CO, MAJ Patnode, in the 191st AHC operations center, took the call from Pevey.

"Boomerang Ops, this is Boomerang Seven-One-Five."

"Seven-One-Five, this is Ops. Go ahead."

"This is Seven-One-Five. We departed Blackhorse approximately an hour ago, and I have not been able to establish contact with Bounty Hunter Two-Four. Did he make it back to home base?"

"Seven-One-Five, this is Ops. Roger understand, you've been unable to establish contact with Bounty Hunter Two-Four after you both departed Blackhorse. He has *not* arrived at Bearcat yet."

Concerned with Bounty Hunter Two-Four's communication void, Pevey's voice shuddered with emotion. "Roger, Ops. The weather is bad—we departed after Two-Four. With five minutes' separation, and due to extremely few breaks in the clouds, we never caught sight of them. We're about to land at Vung Tau and request your support to continue attempting to establish contact with Two-Four."

"Seven-One-Five, roger understand. We'll take it from here, thanks for the alert. Ops out."

Pevey knew Boomerang operations would react with strong measures, yet the human side of Pevey needed reassurance. He yielded, but with remorse over the troubling situation.

Upon hearing the call from Pevey, MAJ Patnode quickly moved to assemble a night search effort. Organizing a search team of two aircraft, he alerted the 214th CAB headquarters of his intent to immediately depart to take up the search. Unfortunately, the weather refused to cooperate.

Wisely, LTC James M. Leslie, the 214th CAB commander, issued orders to hold the search birds on the ground until the weather cleared sufficiently to offer a reasonable measure of safety. Patnode followed the orders and relayed them to his company. He certainly didn't need to lose any more birds or crews. Facing death each day, Patnode's men faithfully carried out his orders, and he cherished their loyalty. What's more, Patnode's willingness to face the same battlefield threat experienced by his men, day in and day out, inspired them. Tragically, this lethal climate was a threat beyond his control.

The anxiety within Patnode generated a myriad of death scenarios. Situations of this nature tend to conjure the worst in the imaginations of concerned commanders' minds. Patnode suffered from each passing minute, and the minutes turned into hours. Finally, at nearly midnight, three hours later, the search team was released. With MAJ Patnode and CPT Rodowick aboard Aircraft 945, and with CPT Stack and CPT Myers in Aircraft 820, the birds lifted into the air and continued the search for the missing crew.

After reaching the general search area, intermittent weather intensified the arduous task of terrain scanning, making the midnight search infinitely more difficult. Frequently, the team's visibility was severely restricted by heavy rain. Desperate to hear a response from the crew of the lost bird or find anything that might hint at their fate or status, the team searched and listened intently for a live signal. Nothing.

After long periods of fuel-burning orbits by both search birds in the suspected vicinity of the lost crew, the results drew a blank. Then, suddenly, southwest of Blackhorse, both search crews picked up a weak UHF signal on Guard frequency 243.0. Excitement suddenly surged through the search crews and hopes soared.

Visual focus intensified, and all eyes strained for any hint of light from the ground that might be a sign of life from the lost crew. But the signal disappeared, and there was nothing to hang their hopes on. Trying hard not to yield to the inevitable, Patnode refused to let go of the hope he gleaned from the brief UHF signal. Nonetheless, some irrefutable truths were nagging at the CO. Striving to utilize rational thoughts to sort them out, he reconsidered that the encouraging sign of life wasn't a coded signal, nor was it characterized by any familiar pattern. Slowly, the search team faced reality, terminated the midnight effort, and reluctantly returned to Bearcat.

A lost aircrew within the boundaries of South Vietnam called for extraordinary recovery measures. By daybreak, Patnode had, at his disposal, search assets from the Air Force together with a significant allowance of 191st AHC aircraft, which were released from combat duty to help with the search. The Blackhorse Regiment also had a contingent of troops prepared to insert at a moment's notice if any sign of the aircraft were spotted. A sophisticated search system was employed and controlled by Patnode, who assigned each aircraft certain grid squares and distances in between. Hours turned into days, and days into weeks with search assets dwindling as other combat urgencies claimed resources.

Finally, Patnode, with a heavy heart, suspended the search. Every possible lead had been carefully examined. Every person who could have known something about the fate or whereabouts of Bounty Hunter Two-Four and the crew aboard Aircraft 018 was interviewed. Air-traffic controllers from every possible communication station were canvassed, but still nothing about the lost crew was uncovered. Ground vectors to helicopter parts such as tail rotors and main rotors spotted on the ground by search crews were checked out for serial numbers that could tie the component to Aircraft 018. No link was made. Ground sweeps by the Blackhorse Regiment found nothing. Bounty Hunter Two-Four, sheltering Hall, Bales, Martinez, Whitaker, and the two mechanics, Scaduto and Muser, seemingly disappeared under Vietnam's thick blanket of night.

The weight of the loss darkened the spirit of the 191st AHC, as did the initial losses of CPT Kidd and 1LT Dodson three months earlier. Another threshold of pain was now reached and assimilated by the survivors who had bonded daily with the lost souls. The price of freedom was rapidly staking its eternal claim in the memories of the survivors. Patnode had already painstakingly written the letters to the next of kin, and now simply had to arrive at closure within his own heart and mind. CPT Rodowick and CPT Stack had also already performed the essential but heart-wrenching gathering of personal belongings of the missing under their platoon leadership, packaging them for shipment to the next of kin waiting back home.

Command reality seems unforgiving. It took some time for the heavy feeling inside Patnode to subside. Notwithstanding, the unending responsibilities demanded by the unit's continuous airmobile support mission kept his mind occupied, helping to relieve some of the mental anguish.

For quite some time, it was easy to visualize the faces and characters of the missing: 1LT David C. Hall was from Hanson, Massachusetts. He was a husky, athletic type, taller than average, and married. He received his undergraduate degree from Cornell

University before signing up for the service. 1LT Sharel "Spike" Edward Bales was originally selected at Fort Bragg for gunship work. Hailing from Berthoud, Colorado, he was slight of build with a friendly and engaging smile. Bales was reserved and much less boisterous than other Bounty Hunters. Both Crew Chief SP4 Peter S. Martinez and Gunner SP4 Joseph L. Whitaker Jr. were outstanding crewmen who worked diligently to ensure their bird was in top working order and fit to fight. Martinez was twenty-five years old and hailed from Illinois. Whitaker, from Oregon, was a mere nineteen years old and had a wife back home. Of the two mechanics aboard, one was SSG Richard L. Scaduto from New Castle, Pennsylvania, and the other was SGT Louis C. Muser II from Hoboken, New Jersey. Both were only twenty years old, but they shouldered the serious responsibility of making certain the 191st AHC birds were the safest any combat pilot could fly. Why their destiny turned on that fateful afternoon, only their maker can know. Without choice, the unit was forced to accept the unknown and reluctantly move on.

On September 17, 1967, a report filtered through channels and reached the 191st AHC with the news that the Blackhorse Regiment had found the logbook and UHF radio belonging to Aircraft 018 in a VC base camp. But nothing was said of the crewmembers or passengers.

As time slipped forward, the 191st AHC brotherhood suffered additional losses from combinations of wartime challenges and bad luck to further case-harden the Boomerangs' and Bounty Hunters' fighting spirit. The loss of 018 and its crew slowly faded into memory as daily combat took precedence and survival overrode all else, as it must. Soldiers need to live in the present, but nonetheless honor the past.

Knowing their important need for closure, Patnode kept the families of the missing foremost in his mind and never gave up the search until his rotation. With each opportunity, he would overfly the area and pore over every piece of information that could possibly yield a clue to the fate of these brave souls who rode to their final resting place in Vietnam.

The 018 aircraft and the bodies of the men were later recovered, returned to their families, and their status changed from missing to dead on November 20, 1967. According to the Vietnam Helicopter Pilots Association (vhpa.org), the ashes of 1LT Sharel "Spike" Edward Bales were scattered over Berthoud Pass, Colorado.

CHAPTER 9

Night Sampan Ambush

The black hole took on the appearance of a huge mouth ready to swallow the bird and crew.

One of the most harrowing missions ever assigned to the 191st aircrews occurred in the autumn of 1967, during a period when the enemy was building up forces and supplies in preparation for launching its Tet Offensive. The NVA moved supplies overland to secluded locations deep in Cambodia's jungles. Although Cambodia was supposed to be a neutral country, they allowed the NVA to have more protected movement of troops and supplies. The supplies were then transferred onto sampans for the final move into the South via the Mekong River. Using waterways for transporting its war goods, the NVA had long since learned not to attempt these movements during the day, when the US Air Force could strafe and bomb their river supply trains. Instead, the enemy ferried their military cargo into South Vietnam under cover of night.

To gather intelligence on the enemy's movements, US Special Forces (SF) teams were surreptitiously inserted into Cambodia. Quietly living among the jungle flora and fauna, the Green Berets survived alone in the wild amid dense enemy infestation. A communication link for their activities was carved into the side of a mountain, where a tiny compound with a postage stamp–sized landing pad served as the only contact the SF had with the outside world. The 191st gun crews christened the compound with the nickname *Pucker Six* because, in the words of the laughing Waugh Jr., it was a "harrowing experience." One of the first crew chiefs assigned to this mission, Waugh became a regular on the assignment board for Pucker Six. When the Army's Green Berets called, Waugh answered.

On the other hand, CPT Stack, flying the Charlie-model as AC, was unfamiliar with Pucker Six. That fact was set to change. Stack called for landing instructions and descended into what Waugh described as an "asshole-puckering approach path through a maze of higher peaks." Sweat beads formed on the old veteran pilot's forehead and rolled down his face as he maneuvered to land a fully loaded gunship on the tiny pad. The landing pad was shrouded in darkness, and Stack strained to acquire a visual reference. Finally, a strobe light flashed the landing signal: four flashes with a short pause between each series of flashes. He locked his eyes on the inverted-Y landing reference and eased the heavy, fully armed gunship onto the postage-sized pad.

The bird touched down, and Stack and his copilot, CW2 Ed McKee, breathed a sigh of relief. "Amen," they both said.

The two unstrapped their safety harnesses and made the short walk to the TOC for their briefing. Both Crew Chief Waugh and Gunner SP4 Rich Fleming tied down the blade and secured the ship before joining them in the operations tent. An SF sergeant stood in the front of the tent, waiting for Waugh and Fleming to get settled before starting his briefing.

"Good evening, gentlemen. My name is Sergeant Guess [pseudonym]. I will be briefing you on the mission for tonight. Before we get started, please take all items out of your pockets and place them in the baskets that Specialist Four Williams is passing out to you at this time. When I say everything, I mean even your wallets. Where you are going, you will not have any need for identification or anything that can serve as a reference to your national origin."

Not liking what he was hearing, Waugh didn't hesitate to speak up. "Why are we giving up our wallets, Sarge?"

"You won't need them." SGT Guess gave no further explanation. "Now then, gentlemen, you have been sent here to interdict enemy-supply movements from Cambodia. The North Vietnamese, as you may already know, move large quantities of munitions and supplies down the Ho Chi Minh Trail and preposition them in Cambodia."

Guess pointed to a large map on an easel. "Just across the border. Our SF teams have been observing these movements for quite some time and, judging from their pattern of activity, we believe tonight will be perfect for a helicopter ambush."

All during the briefing, Stack carefully wrote down the information necessary to communicate with the SF teams on the ground while McKee plotted their locations on his map. Stack would fly while McKee would navigate.

SGT Guess tapped a specific section on the map. "In *this* area is a canyon that has steep walls on both sides and follows the river for approximately three kilometers. Once the enemy enters this part of the river, there is no way out. They can't climb out because the canyon walls are approximately seven hundred feet high at the lowest point and steep enough to kill a mountain goat. Also, the river runs fast enough through this gorge that once committed, the enemy must run the gauntlet or drown—there's no turning back. We want you to catch these bastards right in the middle of this trap and blast the shit out of them. Our ground teams will vector you into position by sound, and you must descend into the canyon here." Guess jabbed his finger at the exact spot.

By this time, Waugh and Fleming were somewhere between peeing with excitement and soiling their britches, especially the bloodthirsty Waugh. Waugh kept a book on each enemy he *aced*. Putting Waugh on the door gun was like turning a 250-pound sheepdog loose on a pack of marauding coyotes. His instincts took over when it meant protecting US soldiers against a slinking enemy that killed Americans by ambush and then ran.

Waugh relished this opportunity to ambush the ambushers. *For once, the bastards will receive a taste of their own medicine*, he thought. But when Guess described the seven-hundred-foot canyon walls, Waugh immediately recalled their scary approach into the postage stamp–sized compound. *Now these crazy bastards are sending us into a canyon—at night!* Waugh visualized the worst scenarios of negotiating the canyon walls in the dark.

"These dudes are sick!"

Yet Waugh's killer instinct soon took over and he quit worrying; he knew that Stack was a damn good pilot. His job was to kill, and the thought of catching the enemy with no way out of a canyon brought on a huge surge of adrenaline. Like a fighting cock, he smelled blood. He was ready to fight, and protect his brothers.

As the briefing ended, the Bounty Hunter crew grabbed coffee and drinks. Waugh and Fleming played cards with the SF troops and waited for the SF team to report. The SF team was maintaining vigil upstream from the canyon, watching for NVA sampans to get underway. Stack and McKee moved to the corner of the TOC. There, they monitored the radio traffic and conducted their map reconnaissance of the canyon, plotting anticipated mission hazards.

"You realize there's a hellacious drop-off at the end of the helipad," McKee warned Stack.

"Yeah, tell me about it! Why do you think I was sweating my balls off coming into this fucking place? There's no go-around—you either make it or you're fucked." Stack's face showed concern. "These fuckin' Charlie-models are great once they're in the air, but getting the clumsy bastards airborne, with a full load of fuel and ammo, is not the kind of challenge we need in the middle of the night, especially in a place like this nasty hellhole."

The call came in the wee hours of the morning. Barely a whisper could be heard over the radio as the SF troopers on the ground were careful not to give their position away. Stack and McKee were nearly dozing off in their chairs, but Skip and Fleming were still deeply committed to their poker game. In mere moments, the crew strapped themselves into the gunship, and Stack wound up the engine to takeoff rpm. Gently, he eased pitch into the blades. Once he got the ship light on the skids, he asked Waugh to keep his eye on the rock wall behind the tail rotor.

"I'm going to slide this fucking bird as far back on this pissant pad as I can, Skip. I need all the takeoff room I can get. Be sure I don't run the fuckin' tail rotor into the rock wall, or we'll all be history."

"Roger that, sir. Come on back—you got about another twenty to thirty feet."

Meticulous on the cyclic controls, Stack applied aft pressure on the stick until the bird lightly slid backward. Unable to lift the bird cleanly from the ground, he continued to slide the Huey backward in short spurts until he heard from Waugh.

"That's good, sir! Any closer and the folks back home will get a telegram."

With McKee's words ringing loud in his head, Stack knew he could not possibly bring the gunship to a hover. It was simply too heavy. The only option: bounce the bird into the night sky. He pulled in all the collective pitch he dared without bleeding off rpm. Again, sweat beads worked their way down Stack's forehead, and he hoped like hell he could keep the tail rotor from hitting the far end of the pad. Applying soft forward pressure on the cyclic, Stack forced the bird to slide forward. The lumbering Huey bounced once and then bounced again about ten feet closer to the cliff. The telltale shudder of translational lift fed back through the flight controls to Stack's sweaty hand. The black hole over the cliff's edge loomed only a few feet away. Finally, the shuddering stopped, and the bird lifted off. Stack breathed a huge sigh of relief while the other three crewmembers relaxed, releasing the rigid tension in their bodies.

In ten minutes, they reached the point where they were vectored into the canyon by the SF team. Stack knew that the gunship was clumsy with its full load and would be slow to react in an emergency. He descended into what looked like a bottomless abyss—a black hole into who knows where. Though necessary for safety, reducing airspeed increased risk of enemy acquisition and fire. Worse, this being a single-ship mission, there would be no one there to assist or even report if the Huey went down. The black hole took on the appearance of a huge mouth ready to swallow the bird and crew.

Stack turned on the landing light. "Not a hell of a lot of room for maneuvering." The canyon offered a mere one hundred meters between its rock walls.

Waugh eyed the deadly terrain. "Holy cow," he said. He prayed silently. *Please Lord, don't let us run into one of these stone walls.* Sweat beads poured from all aboard.

McKee called out navigation advisories to Stack as they moved forward in the canyon, anticipating the narrow right and left turns. Stack turned sharply to follow the riverbed. Unexpectedly, a huge rock overhang filled the windscreen. Stack abruptly pulled aft cyclic to avoid what nearly ended their mission. Not plotted on topo maps, the jutting boulder narrowly missed their rotors. Stack delivered their lifesaving move, but not before they experienced a steep rise in crew pucker factor.

Twice more, with superior piloting skills, Stack saved the day with his smooth-as-grease pilot touch and avoided the deadly hazards. One strike, and they would have become victims instead of attackers. Hair stood on end as shivers ran up and down both pilots' backbones. Soon the gap widened, and McKee advised Stack they had left the narrowest part of the canyon behind. Stack and McKee breathed a little easier.

Abruptly, NVA came into view. There they were too many to count. The heavily laden enemy sampans floated down the river, twisting back and forth with the fast-moving current. The sampans were so numerous that they nearly touched one another as they made their way to South Vietnam in the protection of darkness.

The gunship's rockets exploded upon them. Caught completely by surprise, the NVA had little time to react. Their return fire was weak and ended quickly. Clearly, they were not ready for this attack. Immediately, secondary explosions lit up the canyon like a humongous fireworks display. McKee aimed the ship's forty-millimeter grenade launcher and ripped into the sampans with HEs. The grenades generated a staccato series of explosions which acted like strobe lights. In just small fractions of a second, the lights froze images of humans being blown off the boats or diving into the churning waters.

Waugh and Fleming boiled the river around the sampans with machine-gun fire. Turning their barrels red hot with a steady stream of bullets, both Waugh and Fleming changed them out almost as fast as they could acquire a new batch of targets. What must have seemed like an eternity to the enemy was over in fifteen minutes of vicious firepower—too soon for Waugh's liking. The bloodthirsty crew chief would just as soon have fought through the whole night against an enemy who laid his brothers to waste and then slipped back into the jungle.

The VC and NVA seldom stood their ground. Most of the time, they would hit and run, but this time they had no choice but to fight. For once, the tables were turned. They were the ones being ambushed, beaten at their own game by a savvy SF team who sacrificed and suffered immeasurable hardships living in the jungle for months. And now, finally, their hardships paid off as they watched the command performance delivered by the 191st Bounty Hunters. It was made sweeter by the fact that it happened in the enemy's own backyard, where Charlie felt warm and cozy with nothing to fear.

Like the Doolittle Raid over Japan, this successful mission had an enormous effect on the morale of the American troops. For the first time, the NVA were vulnerable. Political walls had created a safe haven for the enemy in Cambodia. From there, the enemy frequently launched attacks against American bases in South Vietnam and then retreated to their sanctuary to muse over their night's sorties. This time, Charlie was unable to escape to Cambodia.

The gunship cleared the canyon walls after expending its heavy ordnance. "Dirty bastards!" Waugh said. "I wish we could catch their asses like that *every* night. This war would be over in no time if the sons of bitches had the balls to fight."

With the aircraft much lighter, landing back at Pucker Six seemed like a snap compared to negotiating those steep canyon walls. Stack and McKee breathed easy as they refueled the gunship for their trip home to Bearcat. They agreed to take turns flying to keep themselves from falling asleep. In the early morning darkness, they lifted off.

After climbing to three thousand feet on a heading direct to Bearcat, McKee keyed the intercom and shared his thoughts with Stack. "Lucky we caught their asses by surprise. We could have gotten cooked in that fuckin' canyon if they'd been ready for us."

"Yeah," Stack said with a sigh of relief. "There was absolutely no maneuver room in that fucking hole."

CHAPTER 10

Human Wave VC Attack

"Leopard Two-Six, this is Bounty Hunter Six. Rockets are exploding on the bad guys now!"

First light revealed a collage of colors that promised the dawn of a gorgeous day. Wisps of fog drifted up from jungle streambeds as the night dampness evaporated with the rising temperature. Choking humidity would predictably intensify throughout the heat of the day; however, for now, the sky was clear, winds were calm, and the density altitude was forecast to remain tolerable for rotary-wing operations.

The 191st was now well versed in close-air support of American ground troops, mostly those of the Ninth Infantry Division. But on December 13, 1967, they would fly combat assaults with the South Vietnamese Regional Force/Popular Force (RF/PF), often referred to as the RuffPuffs—a friendly gibe aimed at their limited experience and timid behavior as they prepared to confront the enemy on the battlefield. The RF/PF were attached to the Eighteenth Army of the Republic of Vietnam (ARVN) Division.

For CPT Stack, the fiery gun-platoon leader, supporting the ARVN was another opportunity to do what he did best: fly an attack helicopter in support of friendly ground forces. Having acquired considerable experience in gunship tactics while assigned with the 334th Aerial Weapons Company, nicknamed the Sabers, he was ready to get back in the saddle. The stint he did as the 191st operations officer was now over, and he could refocus on leading the Bounty Hunters into combat. He loved flying guns.

As Stack approached his aircraft, he noticed that CPT Cherrie, his second in command, was already strapped in the AC's seat. Both had earned AC status, which was reserved for pilots who were judged to have attained a certain skill level and actual combat experience. But Stack, an exceptionally gifted pilot, possessed the edge in experience and could finesse a Charlie-model far better than most.

"Stan," Stack said, his voice mild and friendly. "I haven't flown much in the past several days. Do you mind if I fly the right seat today?"

Both Stack and Cherrie understood the seniority inference in Stack's request. The right seat of a UH-1C was equipped with instrumentation, and its weapon selection had the greatest firepower impact on enemy targets. Thus, the right seat was normally reserved for the most experienced pilot in the cockpit, the pilot in command. Both Stack and Cherrie recognized this responsibility and knew that Stack was the most experienced and skillful gunship pilot.

"Sure, Bob! You're the gun-platoon leader. By all means, take the right seat."

The two carefully strapped into their seat belts and shoulder harnesses and began the run-up procedures for their Charlie-model *frog*. The frog nickname stemmed from the wartlike bubble on the nose of the aircraft. The nose housed the devastating forty-millimeter M5 grenade launcher capable of firing up to 220 rounds per minute. On the gunship's sides perched two nineteen-shot pods capable of firing thirty-eight 2.75-inch folding-fin rockets. A forward center of gravity (CG) with the M5 grenade launcher installed caused the frog to fly with an exaggerated, nose-down attitude. This gave the bird an ungainly appearance. However, its armament system, combined with a skilled crew chief on the left and gunner on the right, made it an awesome weapons platform that Charlie never wanted to see.

Working in small groups of two or three guerrilla fighters, the VC knew this bird possessed too much firepower and moved too fast for them to oppose from the ground with their current caliber of weapons. Previous losses in major conventional battles, where both US and enemy forces faced one another as equals, instilled a seething respect among enemy commanders for American firepower. Therefore, the VC were forced to break down into small bands of guerrillas to reduce force depletion, which diluted the enemy's decisiveness. Death among their comrades opposing the American Charlie-model gunships brought hard-earned wisdom. Fleeing rather than fighting gunships became the norm among the VC.

The 191st AHC crew chiefs diligently performed their battle preparation and maintenance of these killing machines. Their MOS, coupled with their dedicated sweat of brow, fed a large portion of the air war over Vietnam. An excellent Bounty Hunter example of the caliber of grit found among the gunship crews was Gunner SP4 Daniel T. Leonardo.

On August 18, 1968, while in the heat of battle, Leonardo's M60 machine gun ran out of ammo, and the ship expended its load of rockets. With miniguns jammed, the gunship was powerless to provide cover for the flight amid heavy enemy fire. With a death-defying act of bravery, Leonardo stepped out onto the gun platform while the bird was in flight. He pulled ammo from the minigun canister, fed his M60, and continued suppressive fire for the slicks. Exhibiting guts galore, Leonardo singlehandedly performed a selfless act of heroism to save slick crewmembers' lives. Later, Leonardo was awarded the Distinguished Flying Cross for his heroism that day.

No question, the 191st AHC was fortunate to have exceptionally well-trained crew chiefs—products of MAJ Patnode's engineer mind and command policies. On this day, with SGT Floyd Davis as the crew chief, Stack would be the beneficiary.

Meticulously, to make sure all systems were functional aboard CPT Stack's ship, SGT Davis checked his gunship from head to toe. Battle savvy, Davis knew that high-intensity combat required hasty rearming. Inadvertently, crews could fail to slide a rocket all the way back to the rear of the pod, leaving a gap between the electrode and the rocket motor. If uncorrected, this would prevent ignition, or worse, delay it. Davis preempted this condition by first verifying the ARM switch was turned off. Then he carefully tapped the butt end of his Ka-Bar survival knife on the back of the firing electrode connected to each of the thirty-eight folding-fin rockets. This extra safety touch minimized delayed fires by insuring that the electrode could actually make contact with the rocket motor. Otherwise, these warheads would *hang* in the pod when the pilot-triggered electrical impulse failed to ignite the rocket motor. Hangfires created a hairy, suspense-filled clearing exercise—not something any crewmember wanted to be around once the aircraft got back on the ground.

In the only known case of accidental rocket ignition near Bearcat's 191st aircraft revetments, the rocket became the liability of a sister company. Exploding out of the tube with a loud *whoosh*, the rocket hit the edge of a revetment before traveling the thirty or so meters required for the detonator to arm. Bouncing up into the air, the now live warhead stabilized and zinged past several startled crews, narrowly missing a Pachyderm CH-47 Chinook helicopter on short final to Bearcat with a sling load of fuel bladders. Like a streak of lightning, the rocket headed out into the nipa palms and exploded beyond the perimeter fence.

An infantry soldier manning a bunker on the berm watched with amusement as baboons, feeding in a nearby marshy area along the perimeter fence, hightailed it into the jungle, where they proceeded to screech and howl as if the sky were falling. The hangfire calamity was enough to spook not only the baboons but also each soul working on the flight line. In the confusion, the airfield duty officer thought Bearcat had been hit by an enemy mortar and naturally felt duty bound "to alert the world" by setting off the loud, wailing siren that signaled an enemy attack.

To avoid a similar incident and the accompanying embarrassment, Davis continued to cautiously tap the back of the firing electrodes one by one, demonstrating this safety tip to his gunner.

"Not only does this add a measure of safety," Davis said to his gunner, "it also gives you a much more reliable weapon system." Alongside Davis, the gunner watched the safety demonstration with focused concentration. Today, they were flying with the gun-platoon leader, CPT Stack, so Davis performed the task with utmost care.

Stack's job, which included barely clearing treetops while receiving and laying down fire, was extremely dangerous. When fired upon by a determined enemy, escape without serious battle damage or crew casualties held little hope. Two gunship fire teams would fly cover for Stack and his crew while they reconnoitered low level for the enemy. CW2 Tommy Sandefur was the second fire team leader, with CW2 Ed McKee flying as copilot. Sandefur and McKee held the survival of Stack's ship and crew in their hands.

The slicks were all flocked behind CPT Dee Kennedy, a good ol' Alabama country boy, who was flying flight lead in Boomerang One-Six. The savvy Kennedy waited patiently for the standard up report from the trail ship, signaling that all aircraft had reached full rpm before gently easing his lead Huey airborne. From a hover, the Boomerang slicks took to the air. Fully armed and fueled, the two Bounty Hunter light fire teams followed the slicks as they departed Bearcat in route to Xuan Loc, a picturesque region of South Vietnam.

The flight to Xuan Loc proceeded with no enemy contact en route. Most agreeable, the clear sky lent a spectacular view of the triple-canopy jungle rushing by below. Nourished by the tropical Southeast Asian climate, the primeval forest was a solid mass of green hues. Majestic teak trees towered 150 feet above the jungle floor with several layers of undergrowth protecting their foundation soil. They provided natural camouflage for the abundant wildlife flourishing beneath it. Asian tigers and elephants, although rare, always offered chopper pilots a photo op. The big sandbar deer with enormous antlers and the abundant jungle fowl with their striking plumage provided equally valued mementos for keepsake photo seekers. Amid nature's serenity, all aboard each slick and gunship knew that the hard reality of the mission at hand was always just a shot away.

It was scenes like these that made the early-morning getups worthwhile—a few minutes of heavenly reverie before war entered and ransacked the peaceful picture. Crew Chief Davis enjoyed the view and quietly delighted at the scenery. Dotted with rubber-tree plantations and palatial villas built during the French colonial period, this southern region of Vietnam offered a stark contrast to the nation's population centers. As viewed from Davis's seat, most admirers of beautiful landscapes would love to own a piece of this visually arresting environment. Regrettably, war blotted its appeal. Davis's mind quickly returned to the task at hand: scanning for enemy signs.

The thick foliage appeared impenetrable. While many of the pilots relaxed and enjoyed the picturesque landscape with awe, Kennedy, like Davis, viewed the terrain from an entirely different perspective. As Boomerang flight lead, he remained tense with suspicion directed at every valley, every large clump of trees, every mountain peak. Any of these terrain features could mean disaster for the flight if he took the formation too close to a hidden enemy stronghold. Scrutinizing every possible location that could yield danger, Kennedy avoided even the potentially distracting small talk from his copilot in order to remain focused. Every airspeed or angle-of-bank adjustment made by the Boomerang lead became progressively exaggerated for aircraft farther back in the formation. Thus, gentle maneuvering borne of constant anticipation and superior map-reading skills comprised the major prerequisites for a successful flight leader.

Perspiration soaked Kennedy's flight suit by the time he reached Xuan Loc. He was glad for the break needed to meet the American advisor, CPT Leo Greenly (pseudonym), conducting this operation. The short rest provided recoupment for Kennedy's mental faculties. He breathed more easily as he and Greenly discussed the battle plan.

With grim faces, the RuffPuffs assembled in groups of seven in trail formation and waited to load onto the 191st birds. Quiet, unsmiling, and eyes wide open, they displayed acute concentration to every movement around them. War is friend to no one, and they knew it brought death. This day would test their fighting will. Fright was well reflected in their eyes. Clearly, like all fresh recruits, they were afraid to die.

In minutes the RF/PF unit was loaded onto 191st slicks by their American advisor, CPT Greenly. In less than an hour, the South Vietnamese RuffPuffs landed in their designated LZ and expeditiously formed a defense perimeter. Watching from C&C, the tactical command group relished a job well done by the American advisor. Evident from their smooth ground movements, the RuffPuffs' tactical education was sound. Their morning passed without enemy contact, and the rest of the day seemed destined for more of the same. The late afternoon, however, would inflict battle pressure that would scare the hell out of the RuffPuffs.

To expand the propensity for enemy kills, the Bounty Hunters were ordered to conduct a search-and-destroy mission to create a screening force north of the RF/PF operation. Flying low level over the thick jungle growth was tedious work, but it finally paid off. Just as Stack's gunship topped a nearby ridge, he spotted two enemy soldiers dashing for cover. But not fast enough. In a split second, Stack banked the frog gunship into attack position. With rocket sights aligned, he prepared to engage the fleeing VC, while Cherrie reported the enemy contact to C&C.

"Boomerang Six, this is Bounty Hunter Six."

"Bounty Hunter Six, go ahead."

"Boomerang Six, we have two enemy soldiers in our sights and are about to engage."

"Roger, Bounty Hunter Six. We have you and the enemy in sight. Engage at will."

"Bounty Hunter Six, roger!

The first rocket exploded harmlessly about thirty meters behind the runners. Before reaching the tree line, one VC halted, spun around, and aimed his AK-47 at the attacking gunship. Hardly had the first muzzle blast escaped his AK-47, when the second rocket blew him into a somersault of flailing arms and legs. He crumpled into a black pajama–clad pile of smoking flesh. As the second VC neared the thick jungle foliage, Crew Chief Davis engaged with his M60. Finding its mark, the burst slammed the enemy's body, leaving him faceup on the grass.

Immediately climbing to altitude, the cunning Stack scanned the surrounding countryside in a half-moon arc north of the kill and sent his second fire team to do the same with the area to the south. Nothing else moved.

After careful scrutiny of the ground surrounding the kills, Stack called Sandefur flying his wing ship. "Bounty Hunter Two-One, this is Bounty Hunter Six. Cover my approach as I land on the clearing. I think we should search those VC bodies to see what G-2 we might find on 'em."

"Bounty Hunter Six, this is Two-One. Roger that. Gotcha covered!"

Carefully approaching the first dead VC, Stack positioned the aircraft just short of the body, with Crew Chief Heinmiller facing the jungle, his M60 at ready, safety off.

"Okay, Sergeant Davis, be quick about it," Stack said.

"Roger that, sir!" Davis leaped out of the bird. Shaking down the first body, he collected a weapon and then moved quickly to the second. He retrieved another weapon and a tin container of unknown contents from the second dead body. Davis cradled this tin jewel under his arm like a football and bolted back to the bird.

Stack wasted no time getting airborne and calling C&C to report the collected weapons and the mysterious tin canister, similar to tin containers enjoyed by American fruitcake lovers during Christmas season—an unusual find so far from home.

Cherrie confiscated the prized tin from Davis and did his best to open it. His face turned several shades of red as he wrestled with the confounded thing. The tight-fitting lid was not going to yield without a fight. Cherrie clamped his fingers along the edge and pulled with gusto, but no results. The mystery inside remained sealed.

Stack called C&C. "Boomerang Six, this is Bounty Hunter Six. I'm low on fuel and request permission to break off to go refuel and rearm."

"Bounty Hunter Six, roger that. We'll be right behind you."

Departing the area, the gun team left in high spirits. As with any successful hunt when a trophy is bagged, success is rejoiced. Cherrie relished the mysterious tin he was vigorously trying to work open. Refusing to give in, Cherrie placed the tin faceup between his legs and pulled with both hands. At first, he tried to remove the lid while wearing his flight gloves, which made for slow progress. The slippery metal remained stubbornly unyielding. Finally, just as Stack was on short final into Xuan Loc, Cherrie pulled off his gloves and clamped down on the tin with all the gusto his Irish temper could muster. Determined to pull the lid off the container, he tugged, red-faced, his whole body shaking. The tin popped open with a loud snap and showered the cockpit with fermented shrimp and *nuoc mam*, a favorite Vietnamese delicacy with powerful odors that rival the worst in a mining-camp brothel.

Instinctively, Stack slammed the left pedal to the floor to get a crosswind flowing from his side of the bird to Cherrie's side. The trailing aircraft were alarmed, fearing something had gone wrong with the lead bird's flight controls. Stack intentionally shot the remainder of his approach with the chopper's tail canted awkwardly to the left until he felt the cushion of air build underneath the bird as it settled into *ground effect*, approximately three to five feet AGL. He continued to hover sideways until reaching the refueling point. Allowing for the engine to idle and cool, Stack shut down the aircraft. Without delay, the entire crew exploded out of the bird.

Cherrie slapped at his flight clothing, knocking off bits of shrimp and goo. His lips moved rapidly with facial expressions that only a barrage of expletives can produce. The other three crewmembers bent over laughing with a contagious racket that spread to the rest of helicopter crews as each landed and joined in at Cherrie's expense.

Sympathetic, the crew chief retrieved a can of Gojo, a grease-cutting compound, from the cargo compartment. "This will help get the stink off your hands, sir, but I don't know if there's anything we can do about your britches."

After refueling and rearming, the Bounty Hunters hovered to the parking area on a road adjacent to the compound. There they shut down to wait for further instructions from C&C. CPT Kennedy and the slicks had been waiting there since the last insertion, having already received instructions from C&C to proceed to a certain location for another RuffPuff combat assault.

Choosing to personally brief Stack and Cherrie, as opposed to relaying the map coordinates over the air, Kennedy strolled the short distance to the parked gunships. Stack waited for him outside the bird.

Kennedy pointed to map coordinates, and in the middle of repeating C&C's message, he suddenly stopped, wrinkled his nose, and looked at Cherrie. "Maaan!" he said in his good ol' Southern drawl. "What stanks so baaad?"

The gun crew burst into unrestrained laughter.

The red-faced Cherrie attempted an explanation, but Kennedy remained quite unmoved. With the philosophical essence of a true Southern gentleman, Kennedy downplayed the entire episode to leave Cherrie a graceful way out. "Well, Stan, whatever you say," Kennedy said. "At least you're not Stateside where you'd have to go home stinking like that."

With an amused grin, Kennedy returned to his bird. Arriving back at his aircraft, he pointed his index finger skyward and rotated his wrist—the signal for the flight to crank up. This set off a chain reaction up and down the single line of aircraft. Flight crews untied rotor blades, turned them ninety degrees to the fuselage, and stowed tie-down straps. With fire extinguishers in hand, the crew chiefs peered into their engine-cowling inspection ports, ready to react in the event a fuel fire erupted during start-up. One by one, all rotor blades turned as each aircraft initiated start and run-up procedures. Their engines soon reached flight idle—six thousand rpm.

With a few quick flicks of a thumb on the collective-stick's *beep switch*, each engine advanced to 6,600 rpm, the normal lift-off power for the UH-1. Kennedy called the flight: "Boomerang Flight, this is Lead. I'll be moving to the active runway for takeoff. Trail, give me an up as soon as we're all formed!"

"Lead, Trail. Roger that!"

Shortly, trail sent the *up* message: "Lead, Trail. You have a formation ready for takeoff."

"Roger, Trail. Boomerang Flight, Lead's on the go!"

With the slicks' guns at the ready and the gunships' armed-switches off to prevent inadvertent rocket discharge, the entire assembly of helicopters lifted from the tarmac. To enemy soldiers, they appeared as huge, airborne killing machines in search-and-destroy mode. The attack formation commanded attention. During abrupt overflights, enemy soldiers bolted for cover when assault-helicopter formations suddenly appeared overhead. So complete was the 191st air-assault package, an enemy force would seldom challenge their tactical capability in a conventional engagement. Instead, enemy tactics shifted to guerrilla operations that could best counter the US technical advantage.

Attacks from a wide front with enemy soldiers attempting to rush American positions were known to sacrifice living resources into withering gunfire from superior weapons. As if processing human lives and equipment through a gigantic grinding machine, the enemy yielded. To more effectively respond, they broke down into small guerrilla bands. Attacking in measured ambush, they inflicted what damage they could and retreated with minimal losses. This prolonged their fighting capability. Seldom attaining decisive results, they nonetheless interdicted regional communications and resupplies. Another outcome of this tactical shift came as no surprise to friendly forces. For the most part, day operations belonged to American initiatives while the night belonged to the enemy. This made operations like the RuffPuffs' mission seem to drag on and on to the point of boredom. The enemy simply didn't want to be found.

Skillfully, Kennedy planned each approach to PZs and LZs alike. He made sure that all advantages remained on the side of the Boomerangs. Over and over again, the RuffPuff soldiers were airlifted and inserted for one- or two-hour ground sweeps, while the flight returned to Xuan Loc to wait patiently for the next call.

As the RuffPuffs needed resupply, slicks delivered. Artillery and air support remained on call through the C&C command system. Reinforcements stood by ready for short-notice insertion. The RuffPuffs, although inexperienced, possessed all the killing power they needed. The enemy knew this and retreated into spider holes and tunnels while the RuffPuffs swept the area. Boring to the 191st Boomerangs and Bounty Hunters who preferred body counts, the operation dragged at times during the wait periods between insertions. Boredom seemed to be the order of the day, but not for much longer.

As the afternoon sun cast longer shadows, the end of an uneventful day with the RuffPuffs seemed imminent. At that point, C&C advised Kennedy and the RF/PF advisor, CPT Greenly, that they were breaking off for the day to coordinate tomorrow's operation with the scheduled ground-force commander. Greenly acknowledged C&C and immediately shifted his coordination directly to Kennedy and the Bounty

Hunters. His call for the final lift of the day came as the Bounty Hunters were still refueling and rearming. Therefore, the slicks took off and headed for the PZ without the Bounty Hunters' gun cover. Kennedy flew at sixty knots instead of the usual eighty knots to allow the gunships time to get airborne and catch up.

Approximately fifteen kilometers south of Xuan Loc, the long axis of the final PZ ran generally northwest to southeast, perfect for the prevailing southeast winds. Copilot McKee of the lead gunship on the second fire team could easily tell from his vantage point covering the left side of the PZ that the jungle clearing was of ample size. "Hardly a place for an ambush," McKee said. Its width spanned approximately four hundred meters, and its length extended approximately six hundred meters.

The flight would shoot a trail-formation approach to the south and land on a road that bisected the jungle clearing from north to south. The RuffPuffs were there waiting, with a relieved look. The day's operation was nearly over, and they were hopeful that they escaped the dreaded enemy contact. The last sweep brought them across an area from the west of the PZ to the road. There CPT Greenly assembled them in groups of seven for the final extraction.

On short final approach to the PZ, Kennedy in Boomerang One-Six called Bounty Hunter lead, CPT Stack and CPT Cherrie, to check on their position. "Bounty Hunter Six, this is Boomerang One-Six," Kennedy said. "How far behind are you? We can hold the landing if you need to catch up."

Cherrie answered for Stack: "Boomerang One-Six, this is Bounty Hunter Five. Go ahead and shoot your approach. We haven't quite caught up, but we have you in sight. We are only about one and a half minutes behind you and will be in position to cover you by the time you touch down."

"Roger that!" However, Kennedy remained concerned of the distance stated by Cherrie. A minute and a half is a lot of time under fire with no gunship protection. Despite Kennedy's concerns, the final approach and touchdown progressed without incident. The RuffPuffs were anxious to board, and some jumped in the birds with no delay.

Suddenly, in one big, coordinated movement, camouflaged covers over the emplacements slung open and out poured 150 combat-hardened VCs. Screaming at the top of their lungs and their weapons blazing, they charged across the open field toward the Boomerang ships. The unexpected human wave attack by a company-sized element came from the right side of the LZ in an area where the RuffPuffs had only recently swept. The cagey enemy had dug squad-sized holes in the earth along the western edge of the jungle clearing and artfully camouflaged the openings so that even when the RuffPuffs and their American advisors walked right over them, they remained undetected until the surprise attack.

Loading the RuffPuffs for the final extraction, Greenly was first to react. From his ground-level view, he was certain the charging horde of enemy was about to decimate his small force of RuffPuffs and him as well.

The attacking force moved rapidly, crossing a third of the 250-meter distance between the jungle and the 191st birds in less than a minute. Greenly foresaw a hand-to-hand combat encounter about to happen in mere moments. Knowing the weakness of his inexperienced RuffPuffs, the situation was dire. His high-pitched, frantic voice came over the air on the FM flight frequency as he hailed Stack and Cherrie in the lead Bounty Hunter ship: "Bounty Hunter Six, this is Leopard Two-Six. We have an attacking horde of VC from the west, need *immediate* gunship support." Greenly could easily see that the enemy numbers were overwhelming.

At that moment, with cool composure, Kennedy made his own urgent call. "Boomerang Flight, you're clear for takeoff! Order your gunners to suppress the enemy attack to the right with max rate of fire."

In less than five seconds, the entire line of Boomerang ships opened fire into the enemy line of attack with full suppression. The Boomerangs needed altitude and airspeed quickly. They lifted off with only the partial load of RuffPuffs.

Hardly had Greenly finished his call to Stack and Cherrie in Bounty Hunter Six, before rockets began exploding among the attacking horde. Coupled with the door gunfire from the slicks, the enemy was forced to hit the ground and take cover. At that moment, Greenly got his response from Stack and Cherrie.

"Leopard Two-Six, this is Bounty Hunter Six. Rockets are exploding on the bad guys now!"

Spaced out in trail formation, approximately thirty meters apart, the Boomerangs had an excellent view of the attacking VC. Almost simultaneously, as the entire line of slicks let loose, spraying M60 machine-gun bullets into the charging wave of enemy soldiers, the attack stopped. With thousands of rounds flying east and west across the battlefield, a horizontal slice of airspace, five feet wide and several hundred meters long, formed a vicious bandsaw penetrating the enemy at 2,800 feet per second. Human limbs and body parts flew through the air. The only thing on each crew member's mind: protect the RuffPuffs and each other at all cost.

By waiting for the slicks to begin loading the RuffPuffs before initiating their attack, the enemy unknowingly sealed their own fate. They gave Stack and Cherrie just enough time to catch up with the flight and position the lead gunship in exactly the right place at precisely the right moment to engage with maximum effect. Aligning his sights on the enemy's leading elements, Stack depressed his rocket buttons, and salvo after salvo of rockets exploded on the battlefield among the attacking VC. In seconds, the ferocity of the enemy attack diminished. To take advantage of the frog's high rate of fire, Stack directed Cherrie to engage with the grenade launcher.

"Stan, I'm getting low on rockets. Forty mike-mike the hell out of them!"

"Roger that!" Cherrie plunked down a string of forty-millimeter explosions along the entire leading axis of the VC charge.

Stack slowed the Charlie-model as much as possible to prolong Cherrie's attack with the frog system. Finally, running out of airspace over the field, Stack flew past the attacking mass and let his wingman continue the carnage. He turned downwind in the daisy-chain pattern, which kept the ships in rotation and firing one after another on the hot LZ. Stack knew he had one more pass in the daisy chain with his rocket tubes before he would be out of ammo. Completing his turn to final approach, Stack positioned his gunship in a perfect attack angle for his remaining rocket ordnance. Again, with perfect sight alignment, he proceeded to send barrage after barrage of devastating rocket salvos into the weakening enemy ranks. Fiery explosions sent shock waves through the enemy ranks. With the sun low on the horizon, the effect of rapid fireball flashes formed temporary dark spots on flight crews' visions. In minutes, enemy bodies littered the entire western portion of the LZ. Some were torn beyond recognition or human semblance while others simply lay lifeless. All were covered with fresh, still-oozing blood, and many had body parts missing. Smoke hung over the entire battle area, creating a stark contrast to the once picturesque scene of a lush green and majestic landscape.

Greenly's high-pitched screams of desperation turned to cheers for the Bounty Hunters as they continued to unleash their enormous firepower. "Bounty Hunter Six, this is Leopard Two-Six. Keep pouring the fire to 'em, man! You guys are doing a hell of a job—keep busting their asses. You're keeping us *alive*!"

True to his responsibilities for the RuffPuffs, Greenly chose to remain on the ground with the small contingency that did not board the departing 191st birds. Instead, with excellent battle savvy, he ordered the small group of RuffPuffs to take cover on the east side of the road and take the charging horde under fire. With just enough defilade offered by the crown of the road, his small band of inexperienced RuffPuffs got their first taste of real combat.

Stymied by gunship firepower, the organized thrust of the enemy attack was completely broken. The enemy soldiers milled about in total confusion, perhaps a sign of dead leadership in their ranks. Panicked, some ran for the jungle. Most VC chose to take cover underground, and the RuffPuffs were spared the horror of hand-to-hand combat.

However, a few other VC held their positions and continued firing at their greatest threat, the gunships. Seemingly oblivious to the deluge of bullets flying at his ship, Stack, now out of rockets, hovered over the tall grass in the field, rooting out enemies who were praying they could maintain concealment. Inside the gunship, adrenaline flowed by the bucketful.

The voice of Stack's crew chief, SGT Davis, crackled over the radio. "Sir! Turn right a hair. Turn right! I have a gook with an RPG coming toward us."

"Roger that!" Stack kicked in the right pedal, causing the aircraft tail to swing left abruptly. A sudden burst of M60 machine-gun rounds folded the approaching RPG attacker.

Heinmiller spotted another enemy suddenly standing up and leveling his AK-47 at the hovering gunship. "Left front, sir! Left front!" Instantly, hot tracers from

Heinmiller's machine gun ripped through the would-be shooter and sailed off into the distance behind the collapsing enemy body.

With the precision of a graceful matador, Stack expertly pedal-turned the gunship right and left to get his door gunners into position to kill. Davis and Heinmiller were having a field day, mopping up the scattered VC with their M60 machine guns. One by one, like birds being flushed, the VC rose out of the grass and made for the nearest tree line, only to be cut down by the crews' lethal machine-gun fire. Finally, Stack ascended for departure just as one crafty VC jumped up out of the grass and darted for the jungle tree line.

"Whoa, Bob! Whoa!" Cherrie's voice was full of excitement. "Let me get a bead on his ass. I'll frog the fucker!"

"Roger that!" Stack aligned the nose of the Huey with the black-pajama image scampering away.

Cherrie had three grenades left in the frog. The first explosion hit twenty-five meters behind the VC. The second, fifteen meters behind. The third slammed into him. He kept running for a split second as the upper portion of his body separated from his bottom half. The frog system was now empty.

Calling his higher headquarters to report the tac-e, Greenly was busy vectoring Air Force assets into the area to take over when Stack and Cherrie expended their ordnance.

After escorting the Boomerangs to safety, the second fire team, Sandefur and McKee in Bounty Hunter Two-One, returned to the scene. The few VC still alive on the battlefield low-crawled through the grass to the tree line. Unrelenting, Sandefur's rockets and McKee's minigun cut through them like a mill saw, sending showers of blood skyward as humans exploded. With their rocket pods and minigun canisters empty, they turned to their crew chief's and gunner's weapons until they also expended their M60 rounds. This left the second Bounty Hunter team working feverishly to eliminate the remaining enemy.

After clearing with Greenly and Kennedy, both Bounty Hunter fire teams departed for Xuan Loc to refuel and rearm. Waiting for the Bounty Hunters to finish their attack was Black Pony One-Five, the Air Force forward air controller (FAC), with a flight of F-4 Phantoms in a holding pattern five miles east of the battle area. Hearing the conversation end between the Bounty Hunters and Greenly, Black Pony One-Five immediately initiated contact with Greenly. Radios crackled as the Air Force pilot's sharp, cool voice came over the airways.

"Leopard Two-Six, this is Black Pony One-Five with F-4s in tow. We have five-hundred-pounders and napalm at your disposal, sir."

"Black Pony, this is Leopard Two-Six. Roger, drop your loads immediately to the west of the clearing with all the low-lying smoke. We'd like to block any retreating enemy until our gunships return."

"Understand, immediately to the west of the smoke. Will do!"

In seconds, the area to the west of the battlefield exploded in smoke and concussion. The five-hundred-pound bombs cut huge trees like matchsticks and slung them sideways for thirty meters. The lead jet dropped HE ordnance. Highly flammable jelly, dropped by the second jet, ignited and engulfed the green forest. In a wink, any remaining enemy burned. By the time the Bounty Hunters returned, the entire area was blackened with smoke and fire. The remaining RuffPuffs had been evacuated and the ecstatic CPT Greenly could not say enough about the Bounty Hunters. His gratitude for saving the lives of the men under his care would reach his higher headquarters in the form of recommendations for valor awards honoring the brave aircrewmen who saved his life and those of the RuffPuffs, who, after being surprised by a hoard of charging VC, hugged the earth and fired sporadically through the whole melee.

Arriving at Bearcat, the proud Boomerangs and Bounty Hunters requested a flyby that evening, which the tower approved. Overflying the airfield in crisp formation, accompanied by deafening rotor noise, the 191st AHC declared a day of victory for all to see. One by one, at a precisely timed interval, each aircraft peeled off from the formation, landed on the home pad, and then hovered to its respective revetment.

On the ground, the crews, tired and hungry, made their way to the mess hall for a well-earned hot meal. Rest would come later once the postflight maintenance was complete. Over dinner, speculation about kill estimates was the buzz.

"Man, there was a shitload of dead gooks on the field," Heinmiller said.

"Yeah man!" Davis nodded his head. "Must have been close to a hundred, I reckon. It's a wonder they didn't overrun the RuffPuffs. I would have hated to have been their American advisor. I'll bet that poor sucker shit his pants when that horde broke loose from the tree line. I don't see how in the hell we stopped them. Lots of lead flying through the air!"

"If we hadn't been exactly where we were when they sprung that attack," Miller said, jumping into the conversation, "I'd hate to think how many of our slicks wouldn't have made it out of there."

"I know." Davis's tone seemed solemn.

After helping the crew chief rearm and refuel the gunship in preparation for the next day's mission, the tired Stack grabbed a few bites of supper and quietly headed for the officer's billets. Knowing the officer's club would be lively after the events of the day and probably attended by Ninth Infantry Division staff officers, Stack passed on the temptation. Older than most 191st pilots, he valued his rest and the clear mind it brought the next morning. Though lacking some of the comforts of home, the Bearcat facilities were equipped with showers and adequate bunks. With a battalion of grunts guarding the berm around Bearcat, a secure rest was relatively certain. Stack appreciated that.

Strolling to his quarters, Stack rehashed some events of the day. It was almost unbelievable to him that they were able to pull off that kill. A shiver ran through

Stack as he visualized the worst. *Thank God, we made it.* Had they been a minute later, they might have lost some slicks and crews.

Stack rested easy knowing that he was finally doing what he came to Vietnam to do: fly guns. "Man, after having flown fixed wing my first tour and after fighting like hell to keep from repeating the fixed-wing tour," Stack explains, "I owe General Seneff one hell of a lot for helping me get the 191st assignment. There is no comparison to the satisfaction you feel when you have the firepower at your hands to do something decisive in battle. In an assault-helicopter company, guns were the only way for me."

The next day, the RuffPuffs went out to count enemy bodies. They confirmed 130 enemy dead. The 191st was now a hot item among the Ninth Infantry Division's tactical planning sequence. MG Robert R. Williams, commander of the First Aviation Brigade, was happy. His aviation brigade was making Army-wide news.

The swashbuckling Stack chalked up December 13, 1967, as just another good day in the US Army's war effort. But his best performance with the 191st was yet to come. Later in his career, he would contribute invaluable combat knowledge to generations of pilots who came behind him. As destiny would have it, he would eventually wear colonel eagles, and represent the Army at the US Air Force Academy with distinction.

CHAPTER 11

Tet Offensive: The Communist Buildup

They were prepared for any fight and relished the opportunity to "lock horns with the devil."

Through the hushed canopy came the air-splitting *whop-whop-whop* of the 191st AHC slicks and gunships. One fight at a time, the Boomerangs and Bounty Hunters honed their combat skills until they became a smooth and lethal machine. Maintaining tight formations, the slicks touched down on hot LZs and took off in a flash, as the gunships suppressed enemy fire with deadly accuracy. Hardened by months of high crew-mortality ratios inherent with helicopter warfare, the 191st pilots and crews had endured the full range of combat stress. From squad-sized skirmishes, where the slicks received light small-arms fire, to full-blown regimental-sized battles, the 191st AHC lost its share of life, limb, and blood.

The war now moved westward toward the Cambodian border. Leaving the pacification and security of urban areas to the South Vietnamese Army, American forces pressed deeper into the heart of enemy strongholds. In battle after battle, American forces rolled up enemy flanks at will. At the onset, US technology and firepower blasted huge holes in enemy lines and overwhelmed VC and NVA troops. Robust US search-and-destroy operations captured huge caches of enemy weapons and munitions. The 191st aircraft supporting the Ninth Infantry frequently ferried these enormous stores of enemy war material to US depots for destruction. Yet enemy generals remained undeterred.

Megatons of war material inundated Hanoi's rail yards and Haiphong Harbor and headed straight for enemy hands. Cambodia became the NVA's primary supply line, fed by China, Russia, and other Communist countries. Meanwhile, the Cambodian government simply looked the other way. With Cambodian soil placed off limits to American forces, the Washington politicians made it easy for the enemy to resupply and reequip their troops in the South. American generals pleaded with Washington political sources to interdict the enemy supply line in Cambodia. Unfortunately, the fear of escalating the war erected a political barrier, an invisible wall impregnable and unscalable, which restrained American forces to the confines of South Vietnam.

Americans continued dying in what was now a *political* war of attrition—exactly what the enemy hoped for. The continued buildup of enemy war supplies allowed North Vietnam to prevail until a day when they could attack with decisive force. That day would come months later during the Tet Offensive.

With supplies and reinforcements close at hand, the NVA now frequently stood their ground and fought in a conventional mode that contrasted vastly from the quick, hit-and-run skirmishes used earlier in the war. With the South Vietnamese Army now defending urban areas, the American forces shifted their primary focus to removing major enemy resistance from South Vietnam. As they pushed deeper into the heart of enemy strongholds, the hotter the LZs became and the more emboldened the enemy grew. When airmobile operations moved to the fringes of the Cambodian border, or outlying areas that lay far between the major cities, the Boomerangs and Bounty Hunters found themselves facing an entirely different enemy. This new reality exposed the 191st AHC to a steady increase in battle pressure. In this realm, airmobile advantages lost some superiority. Along the border, enemy forces freely moved and employed large, thirty-millimeter antiaircraft guns that immediately suppressed helicopter armaments. Unfortunately for the American soldiers who fought and died here, American politicians in Washington would not authorize the AHC units to *return* fire into Cambodia.

To the Boomerangs and the Bounty Hunters, every day began with an unpredictable outcome. On one day, blisteringly hot enemy fire would erupt from virtually every LZ; on the next day, sheer boredom would engulf the men. The pilots and crews, therefore, learned to take the war day by day. At times, this unpredictability proved frustrating. The most aggravating days entailed higher headquarters restricting the crews from exerting maximum combat pressure despite the fact that they were flying into heavy enemy-occupied areas. One of these hotly contested areas was the Parrot's Beak, a portion of southeast Cambodia that juts into South Vietnam. It gained its name by crudely resembling the outline of a parrot's head on the map. Vicious firefights flared up with North Vietnamese forces in the Parrot's Beak. These fights quickly escalated as the troops approached the fortified Cambodian border.

The 191st AHC frequently worked this hot area around Parrot's Beak. Usually, as the ever-vigilant enemy saw American choppers insert troops into this border region, they immediately dispatched a reactionary force to engage the Americans and attempt to draw them across the border into their strongholds. At times, in the heat of battle, American ground forces lost their geographic reference and inadvertently crossed into Cambodia. Yet, even in hot pursuit, Americans were forbidden from engaging the enemy once they entered Cambodia. Those who did were severely reprimanded. Like a bully who could reach across the table and punch someone on the nose and then retreat back into his chair and remain free from reprisal, the enemy relished this tactic and used it extensively. Sad but true, American politicians from their distant armchairs unwittingly created a sanctuary for the enemy. From Cambodia to Laos, the NVA launched attacks into South Vietnam and slipped back across those borders to safety—a heated point of contention in the US Congress.

In Washington, an ongoing power struggle existed between the political figures of the Johnson administration, who dictated the conduct of the war, and the military establishment, which resented the administration's tactical interference. President Lyndon B. Johnson and Defense Secretary Robert McNamara personally selected the targets to be hit by American airpower. Unfortunately for the soldiers risking their lives, Johnson and McNamara often ignored the advice of the US military leaders in theater, who clearly saw that the air strikes were not militarily significant.[1] Based on this ineffectiveness, General Westmoreland was forced into a war of attrition, which was under heavy fire from the media. The mounting number of American lives being lost daily for an effort that seemed to be going badly was quickly fueling the antiwar and peace movement.

Nonetheless, President Johnson, Defense Secretary McNamara, and other high-level administration officials refused to relinquish the reins to the military. President Johnson could not bring himself to trust his generals to contain engagements within the boundaries of South Vietnam. Favoring some of his civilian advisors, the president believed that applying gently increasing pressure on the enemy, the policy of *gradualism*, would bring President Ho Chi Minh of North Vietnam to the negotiating table. He was flat out wrong. Equally misleading was the fear of inviting Chinese intervention and even World War III if America escalated the Vietnam War into Laos and Cambodia. Although General Westmoreland and Admiral Ulysses S. Grant Sharp strongly urged the president to release the restrictions, President Johnson's advisors opposed the move. The resultant outcomes were well-equipped and well-supplied enemy troops that were far more lethal. The consequences of the president not listening to his generals were deadly for many American soldiers, a fact that seemed moot to the Washington politicians.

Stopping the flow of enemy troops and equipment, which were steadily pouring into South Vietnam through Laos and Cambodia, was an essential step to winning and bringing our troops home. Unfortunately, a huge difference existed between the military thinkers who wanted to apply enough force to win the war and the politicians who preferred to negotiate a settlement. The Pentagon lost the argument for taking out Hanoi's rail yards, which were steadily receiving massive amounts of war material through China. Similarly, Haiphong Harbor was, for most of the war, declared off limits to military action and, therefore, available for the enemy to use for receiving war material. Generals Westmoreland and Sharp understood that military strikes on Hanoi's rail yards and the Haiphong Harbor would have slowed

---

1 LTG Phillip B. Davidson, USA (Ret.), *Vietnam at War: The History: 1946–1975* (Novato, CA: Presidio Press, 1988), 31.

enemy supplies onto the Ho Chi Minh Trail to a mere trickle. Unfortunately, the political decision resulted in irreparable heartbreak for countless American families who buried their young sons killed in action.

With so many American lives at stake, Generals Westmoreland and Sharp strongly urged a full-scale incursion into Laos and Cambodia, the enemy strongholds that were reinforcing the VC and NVA in the South.

Because of the difficult terrain, it was not militarily possible to achieve victory with an aerial campaign alone. General Westmoreland needed sufficient men on the ground to get the job done decisively, once and for all. Although frustrated that the administration's policy of gradualism was not aimed at winning the war, General Westmoreland had no choice but to press on with this war of attrition. He was determined to lay waste to as many of the enemy as the confines of his authority would allow.

On the other side of the demilitarized zone (DMZ), another struggle, not unlike the political turmoil in Washington, took place between the hierarchy of the North Vietnamese generals and the country's politburo. General Vo Nguyen Giap, the NVA mastermind who defeated the French at Dien Bien Phu, argued for restraint. Adamantly, he advised against committing NVA units to large-scale conventional engagements with US forces. Learning well from the enormous NVA losses in the Ia Drang Valley, General Giap urged prolonging of the guerrilla war to effectively erode American patience. He was fully aware of the raucous antiwar and peace demonstrations taking place in America. And although no sources ever confirmed that he placed stock in any outcome from this unrest, he must have felt that somehow this would inevitably work in North Vietnam's favor. Time was on his side.

On the other hand, NVA General Nguyen Chi Thanh, who had been given command of Communist forces in the South, argued that it was time to step up the Communist strategy to Phase III of their tactical plan and press on with an all-out attack throughout the entire length of South Vietnam. If victorious, this phase of the war would purge the Americans from Indochina, and unite North and South Vietnam into one nation under Communist rule.

Influential with Ho Chi Minh, Thanh won his argument. July of 1967 found him deeply engrossed in preparations for the *Tong Cong Kich, Tong Khoi Nghia,* meaning "General Offensive, General Uprising." Safely tucked in Cambodia's jungles, amid his feverish preparation, fate struck Thanh a lethal blow. According to high-level North Vietnamese defectors, on or about July 4, 1967, a B-52 strike hit Thanh's headquarters and mortally wounded him. He died two days later in Hanoi. Thanh never saw the reality of *Tong Cong Kich, Tong Khoi Nghia,* the precursor of what would become known as the Tet Offensive.[2]

---

2 Davidson, *Vietnam at War: The History: 1946–1975.*

In the days preceding the Tet Offensive, most of the 191st AHC remained oblivious to all of the political dynamics occurring in Washington and Hanoi. News didn't travel fast on the battlefront. The pilots, crews, and support personnel focused on staying alive and getting the job done. Too far removed from all the media hoopla to be concerned with what might be happening in Washington, the Boomerangs and Bounty Hunters maintained a business-as-usual routine. The slicks and gunships continued flying the infantry into battle each day, growing more calloused with each fight. Slick pilots, led by the likes of 1LT Dee Kennedy, CPT Steve Petty, CPT John Crossman, CPT John V. Hedrick, 1LT Duke Essary, CW2 Harold Stitt, CW2 Don Sandrock, CW2 Clyde Wilkerson, CW2 Richard Inskeep, 1LT Edson "Skip" Parker, and 1LT Albert Duffield, among others, met frequently and exchanged ideas on how to improve the company's tactical strategies. Assisted by dedicated crew chiefs and gunners, who maintained a decisive edge with the fine-tuning of equipment and armament, the Boomerangs flew into battle with confidence.

The gun jockeys, led by CPT Robert Stack (wounded on the sixth day of Tet), included CW2 Randy York and CW2 Jonathan Haigh (both wounded on the first day of Tet), WO1 Tommy Sandefur (killed the second day of Tet), CW2 Robert "Perod" Schega, CW2 Larry G. Miller, 1LT Larry Sands, CW2 Roger Holford, WO1 Cecil Andrews, WO1 Merle Hawkins, 1LT David C. Burch, WO1 Bill Smith, and a host of gritty crewmembers who lived each day to challenge the enemy to a gunfight. All the *gunnies* were ready for the yet-to-be-launched Tet Offensive. Though unaware of what was coming, they were prepared for any fight and relished the opportunity to "lock horns with the devil."

These gunship pilots and crews remained convinced that's what they got paid to do. They were serving their president and their countrymen—and above all, they were protecting their brothers-In-arms. In the minds of slick pilots, these gunnies were a special lot, mentally twisted perhaps, but revered for the protection they offered the flight. When receiving fire in an LZ, a slick pilot's feelings of gratitude came at no holds barred when, in a flash, enemy fire was suppressed by the concussion from exploding gunship rockets. At moments like these, the price of living amongst the arrogance of the gunship pilots was worth every insult and every gibe the lift platoons endured from the Bounty Hunters.

"The crazy bastards earn their keep" became a common term of endearment uttered by slick pilots.

For the 191st AHC, the Tet Offensive, into which they were thrown unexpectedly, would bring this comradery and fighting spirit to a crescendo.

CHAPTER 12

The Tet Offensive Begins

In the Vietnam War, gratitude occupied small time slots.

On January 31, 1968, approximately three clicks north of Quang Tri in the DMZ dividing North and South Vietnam, a group of US Marines (Leathernecks) held a tiny outpost that they nicknamed the Alamo. The Leathernecks' orders: hold at all cost.

Not unlike the old Spanish mission in San Antonio, Texas, this Alamo was located at the leading edge of American resistance. The Communist forces dug in within mortar range on the opposite side. The Marines positioned an artillery battery adjacent to Gio Linh, a small coastal village. This battery was specifically detailed to cover Marines who were operating inside an area called the *Leatherneck Square*, a section of the DMZ deemed essential for occupation by US forces. Nearly surrounded by large concentrations of NVA, it was bordered on the east by the South China Sea. This DMZ area surrounding Leatherneck Square was reputed to be a major logistics center. It was here that the NVA received supplies via the South China Sea and then stockpiled them until they could be moved onto the Ho Chi Minh Trail—the main artery for enemy war materials headed for Communist forces in the South. Neither the inhabitants of the Alamo outpost in the North, nor the 191st personnel in the South, were aware of the enormous battle about to erupt. Time and surprise favored the enemy.

In the South, unaware that the Tet Offensive was only weeks away, the Boomerangs and Bounty Hunters continued their usual support role day in and day out. Familiar with South Vietnam's central and southern regions, 191st aircrews plotted map locations of all combat organizations they supported since arriving in the war zone. Friendly points of contact at each location combined to represent a network of allies prepared to move promptly in tactical emergencies. On occasion, when a 191st bird was shot down away from friendly troops, allies from one of these nearby friendly camps would come to the rescue. Providing security until the 191st could extract their equipment and crews, these friendly contacts were highly regarded by the 191st aircrews. At times, during down days, 191st pilots and crewmembers expressed their gratitude by delivering goodies to the austere families and allied camps who saved their skins. In turn, the ground units serving in the South offered their gratitude for the Boomerangs and Bounty Hunters that saved *their* skins. Gratitude is a deep but well-earned emotion that war nourishes—even though it often comes in transient moments.

Well versed with the areas served by friendly units in their operations zone, 191st combat readiness yielded maximum impact on the enemy. Bullet by bullet, man by man, including combat support services, the 191st maintained a decisive advantage over the enemy in the South. There was little the VC and NVA could do to overcome the airmobile edge provided by the Boomerangs and Bounty Hunters. Plus, most other AHCs stationed in the southern portion of Vietnam could closely replicate 191st AHC's performance. So, as a whole, American forces in the South hogtied the enemy and contained their forward aggression.

During the weeks before the Tet Offensive, firefights in the South committed the 191st into action with greater frequency. One would think that enemy actions plotted on the higher-command wall maps would provide an obvious alert to the increasing prevalence of enemy probes throughout South Vietnam. But no word of the impending enemy action was transmitted nor briefed at American command centers.

In the North, frequent skirmishes around the Alamo outpost were not unusual that close to the North Vietnamese border; however, daily probes by the enemy accompanied by heavy NVA artillery fire were growing more and more persistent. Intraservice arrangements complicated matters. Marines seeking communication channels across service lines had to go to the top of their commands. From there the channels of authority had to act expeditiously to get the message down to the Army level sought by the Marine tactical unit. This delay not only frustrated friendlies on the battlefront but posed a danger in separating friend from foe. Mistakenly, on occasion, friendlies would fire on each other. What effect this would have on the upcoming Tet Offensive was yet to be known. Some Marines operating in the DMZ offered a realistic perspective.

Having newly arrived on December 21, 1967, PFC Richard Valent, Fourth Battalion, Twelfth Marine Regiment, Third Marine Division, had to come to grips with what most fresh troops with no combat experience felt: fright, confusion, and a nervousness about the palpable air of death that seemed to engulf the outpost. Most disconcerting, the NVA situation seemed overwhelming. The enemy's daily artillery pounding and frequent harassment were delivered to Valent in a Welcome to Vietnam gift basket. Unbeknown to him and his fellow Americans at the Alamo, his arrival marked the high point of the Communist preparation for what would be their major offensive of the entire Vietnam War.

Valent was a youngster raised in a placid, South Texan, Christian home where all comers were welcome. It seemed like only yesterday he and his brothers convened their large group of friends for a wholesome baseball game in the neighborhood sandlot. To Valent, the hostile feel of this new and foreign environment was far worse than a fast ball to the gut.

As a gunner on a 155-millimeter self-propelled howitzer, Valent's job was to adjust elevation on the gun's fire-control mechanism, check the fuse and powder charge, as ordered by the fire direction center (FDC), and then pull the firing lanyard on command. Angered by the constant enemy pounding that threatened his life and his fellow Americans' lives, Valent felt instant gratification when he heard the howitzer blast out its own dose of death for the Communist enemy.

"My platoon sergeant, SFC Robert Markey," Valent recalls, "was a calloused Leatherneck experienced in battle. He barked orders to me and another newly arrived Marine, PFC Larry Joe Williamson, a Missouri farm boy. Short, stocky, and tough as rawhide wrapped in a flak vest, Larry Joe remained constantly on the alert. He kind of reminded me of one of those wide-eyed armadillos from back home that could run through a pile of cactus and come out unscathed. Like me, he was yearning for direction and comforting words that never came. There were no words of wisdom from the upper echelon of leadership that reassured our survival or instilled any measure of confidence. Instead we were left to our own devices to figure out what was in store and what we should expect from our introduction to combat. Without any encouragement, Larry Joe and I bonded like two magnets.

"We shared a youthful innocence in knowing very little about what we were doing and what to expect. Like two deer caught in headlights, we didn't know which way to zig or zag out of harm's way. Most memorable was a night just before the Tet Offensive, when SFC Markey ordered us to fix bayonets, and then he issued incendiary grenades with instructions for us to place them in the gun breech in event we were overrun by Communist forces. Larry Joe gave me that 'What the fuck is going on?' look. Markey's instructions raised alarming thoughts. I felt sure that the pucker factor at *this* Alamo was very similar to what must have been felt by Davy Crockett and his Tennessee volunteers at the real Alamo in Texas when they faced overwhelming Mexican odds. Being from Texas and knowing the history of that Alamo didn't help my nerves at all. You couldn't help but wonder if the asshole who nicknamed this Marine outpost the Alamo may have doomed us to the same fate.

"Enemy activity on January 31, 1968, started with a routine sapper attack on the northeast side of the compound at approximately two in the morning. [Surprise attacks by elite Communist units known as *sappers* were one of the most serious—and feared—threats to Americans in Vietnam.] But this time, the enemy thrust quickly changed tempo from what had been the norm. While before, sappers would probe and leave, this attack was followed by a heavy artillery barrage that incessantly rained 122-millimeter shells onto our positions. Relentlessly, the enemy shells kept blasting the compound as the sapper attack grew in scale to the point that we could no longer provide support with 155-millimeter indirect fire. The enemy ground attack rapidly closed with the Marine positions on the wire and fighting became hand to hand. SFC Markey ordered us out of the gun pits and into positions where we could defend the guns. Larry Joe and I scrambled forward to the trench line and began firing our M14s at anything that moved outside the perimeter fence. Light from the flares illuminated shadowy figures as they broke out of the darkness and were delayed by the concertina wire just long enough for an M14 burst to stop their movement. The smell of fresh earth and smoke from the shell bursts was all around us.

"Sporadically, RPGs would arc into the compound and explode behind us showering debris and hot shrapnel on our position. The battle persisted for what must have been two or three hours in predawn obscurity until finally, a faint tinge of light traced the horizon above the South China Sea. As the darkness gradually dissipated, NVA bodies could be seen tangled in the wire and lying silent on the ground stretching all the way to the brush lines, which bordered the north and west sides of the Alamo. The morning light also brought some uplifting tactical air support [tac air]. F-4s, from who knows where, rolled in on the enemy positions. Releasing their napalm, the jets scorched the ground with a blanket of fire that roasted the remaining enemy troops. We could hear their screams. The air currents brought the smell of their burning flesh. Although several hundred feet distant, the heat could be felt all the way to where we were dug in. One pilot, whom we knew only by his call sign, American Beauty One, was a real ham. He would release his ordnance and then put on one hell of an air show. Every time he got a secondary explosion, he would repeat the low-level pass and break over the enemy with a victory roll that brought cheers from all of us. It seemed like the guy knew he was hamming it up for us to enjoy—and we did.

"By midmorning the attack subsided and we were ordered to police the area while helicopters came to evacuate our dead and wounded. We later learned that the attack on the Alamo was only a diversionary move to keep us occupied and unable to support Khe Sanh with our 155s. Khe Sanh was evidently marked by the enemy as one of their primary objectives. That's what I remember of the morning of January 31, 1968."

Unaware at the time, PFC Valent and his fellow Marines were fighting off the northernmost thrusts of what would become known as the Communist Tet Offensive. Meanwhile, in the wee hours of the morning, 450 miles to the south, the tactical areas served by the 191st AHC came under heavy ground attack by the Communist forces. Before daybreak, the presidential palace, Military Assistance Command Vietnam (MACV) headquarters, and US embassy in Saigon became primary targets.

Although the Marine guards were caught by surprise and wounded by AK-47 fire and RPGs hitting the chancery doors, they recovered quickly and began striking their own counterblows to repel attackers. Confronting the enemy one on one in the embassy building and its grounds, the Leathernecks and military police (MP) turned the fray into a free-for-all. Every Marine together with military police reinforcements, and each able-bodied person acting on behalf of US interests, began shooting attackers on sight. Throughout Saigon, diplomats and high-ranking officials, awakened by the battle raging outside their bedroom windows, suddenly found themselves completely out of their element. They scrambled into flak vests and their thoughts shifted from a desk-jockey frame of mind to a save-your-own-ass urgency.

At the 191st AHC operations center, the staff, under CPT John Arnold, was getting inundated with urgent calls. Emergency messages jammed the airways faster than the staff duty NCO could process them. One message in particular grabbed the staff duty NCO's attention: "The US embassy is under heavy ground attack and needs emergency ammo resupply and medevac support." The ops officer rushed to wake MAJ Carlvin Griggs, the 191st XO at the time, and asked for guidance. Having been with the unit longer than any of the senior officers in the 191st, Griggs was respected for institutional knowledge in extraordinary situations. CPT Arnold knew this condition called for drastic measures, and Griggs was his go-to man.

Ops summoned WO1 Richard Inskeep and briefed him on the new mission. Running back to the pilot hootch, he woke his copilot, 1LT Edson "Skip" Parker.

"It was dark," Parker recalls. "It was not time to wake up, and I was not expecting to fly that day—but what did *I* know? I had been in-country less than thirty days, twenty-eight to be exact. WO1 Richard Inskeep told me to get up and get dressed. He then gave me an aircraft number and told me to meet him at the *White Flight* bird at 0445 hours."

Inskeep's and Parker's mission: resupply the US embassy in downtown Saigon with ammunition and medevac the wounded.

"A piece of cake," Parker said. "We'll be back in time for breakfast." He couldn't have been more wrong.

Inskeep and Parker took off at o-dark-thirty and headed for the "unmistakable lights of the big city, Saigon." Their bird crossed the Saigon River and approached the southeast edge of the city. The predawn darkness lit up with tracers, "red tracers from the good guys and green ones from the bad guys."

"Do you know where the US embassy is?" Parker asked.

"No, do you?" Inskeep replied.

The two pilots exchanged quick glances, their eyebrows raised in mild shock. Both geographically challenged, they had to make a tactical decision.

"We called ATC [air traffic control] and asked for radar vectors," Parker recalls. "Ask and ye shall receive—and we did. We headed south as advised by ATC and there it was, a six-story building with a helipad on top, just north of the Saigon River. Initially, I felt it would be a no-sweat, fast approach, offload ammo, take on the wounded, and off we'd go. Wrong again!"

With the lighted helipad insight, the pilots set up for a short approach. But as they drew closer, the helipad appeared empty—not a soul in sight.

"I wondered what was up," Parker recalls. "Did the VC, who'd stormed the embassy earlier, now have control? Were we flying into a deadly trap? Or were the embassy staff and its military contingent holding on by their skin and in desperate need of our help—like right now? We decided not to land but instead made a low pass over the building at high speed to conduct a quick recon. As we flew over the approach edge of the building, we took green tracer fire seemingly as big as basketballs—well, that's how big they looked to *us*. I could distinctly hear the *ping-ping-ping* as a swarm of bullets punched holes in our slick's formidable-looking but actually quite fragile sheet metal.

"My crew chief yelled over the intercom, 'I see a GI in the stairwell by the helipad!' But in a split second, we passed beyond the landing pad and were flying over the other side of the embassy roof, accelerating as fast as we could. Again, we took a few more hits from those big green tracers fired by the VC in the embassy courtyard seven stories below. Wow! We escaped *that* hornet's nest, but not really. We had to go *back* and finish what we came to do."

The pilots set up another downwind approach. Again, green tracers ripped through the air. The bird suffered a few more hits.

"We touched down firmly on the helipad, but the guys in the stairwell wouldn't come out to get their ammo," Parker continues. "The crew chief shoved the ammo boxes out the door, jumped down on the pad, and he and the gunner pushed them toward the stairwell. Two soldiers crawled out of the stairwell, an Army soldier who looked okay and a Marine who was pretty bloody. Both were helped into the aircraft by the crew chief and gunner. Once everyone climbed aboard, Richard and I both got on the controls and took off, knowing full well that we were going to get the shit shot out of us. This time, we were right. As we accelerated over the far edge of the embassy rooftop, we got the shit shot out of us. What a light show! Vertical and green, with all the sound effects. *Ping-ping-ping!*"

The crew chief took a hit. Luckily, the bullet was blocked by a chicken plate that was shoved under his backside. Parker would later recall that the chicken plate both literally and figuratively "saved his crew chief's ass." The bird continued its climbout, uneventfully for a mere six seconds.

"Hey, Rich!" Parker said. "The transmission-oil pressure gauge just went to zero. Maybe the gauge got hit."

Parker focused on the transmission-oil temperature gauge starting to rise. "Nope!" he said. "It's not the gauge. They hit the transmission! We have about sixty seconds to land before the transmission seizes and this baby lands *us*."

The entire crew scanned below for the best place to put the bird down.

"The best bet was south, across the Saigon River, only a short distance away," Parker recalls. "We started an immediate left turn and a descent toward the rice paddies just across the river. I made a Mayday call to ATC and to our operations section alerting them that we were going down just south of the Saigon River and would like some help real soon. Daylight was just breaking and that big, dry, empty rice paddy never looked so good."

However, once on the ground, the pilots and crew were in unfamiliar territory. As Parker recalls, they were "aviators without our aircraft, immediately transformed into ground troops, all alone, with no friendlies or air support anywhere in sight." At first, high fives and elated small talk filled the bird as the pilots and crew felt the surge of gratitude for being alive and unharmed. But as they knew all too well, in the Vietnam War, gratitude occupied small time slots. The pilots and crew, as Parker recalls, were "fully cognizant that the situation could change for the worst real fast."

With the engine now shut down, the wee hours of the morning were dark and still. The red and green tracers still lit up Saigon's skyline. "It was quiet and we were alone," Parker remembers. "No one was anywhere nearby. We made a plan. We would exit the aircraft, take all the weapons, ammo, and radios to keep them out of Charlie's hands, should he get the helicopter, and we would make our way to some groundcover. We gathered up all the necessary gear and headed for the jungle's edge, which was about a hundred meters to our immediate front. At about fifty meters, we noticed there was a big bunker right where we were heading. Not knowing who that bunker belonged to, but guessing it wasn't *our* team, we did an about-face and headed back to the broken bird. The four crewmembers set up a perimeter around the aircraft and the two soldiers we rescued from the embassy stayed in the helicopter.

"Just then, we heard the sweet sound of rotor blades, the big wide rotor blades of the 540-rotor system, driving two Charlie-model Huey gunships of our own Bounty Hunters. What a welcome sight those two awesome-looking war birds were, flying low over the tree line headed straight for us. Talk about a Band of Brothers! *Our* brothers were there for us, and we were so happy to see them. Shortly after the Bounty Hunter fire team set up their protective, racetrack pattern over our position, ready to immediately inflict great harm and destruction on any foe foolish enough to threaten us, we saw another welcome sight—one of our own slicks coming to rescue us from this undesirable situation. Within minutes, we were on our way back to Bearcat, dirty and tired but happy and thankful."

The entire mission that morning lasted for two hours, but to Parker, it happened in such a rapid succession that the time frame seemed as if it shrank down to a mere twenty minutes. Later that day, a Chinook airlifted Inskeep's and Parker's slick back to Bearcat to fly another day.

Back at camp, a close inspection revealed twenty-six bullet holes—one in the transmission and twenty-five in the fuselage. The maintenance crews went to work patching up the bird for another mission, or as Parker describes it, "another day in the office." And this day at the office was just beginning.

Inskeep and Parker along with the crew chief and gunner were among the first 191st responders to the battle of Tet in the wee morning hours of January 31, 1968. By midmorning, the Boomerang operations center was a beehive of activity. The

Communist onslaught rendered the original mission schedule, posted the day prior, obsolete. Before it hit the ops officer's desk in the wee hours of Tet, the entire aircraft fleet schedule had to be scrapped as all birds and crews were diverted to other locations. Previous-day missions sought to search and destroy enemy forces. The present tactical situation demanded urgent measures to defend against full-scale enemy attack. Finding the enemy was no longer a problem. Mustering sufficient force to regain control presented monumental challenges with enemy forces fully staged, supplied, and equipped. The initial onslaught of enemy action raged beyond control. Emergency messages poured in from numerous sources needing helicopter support. The armed Hueys were a high-ticket item, and if the Vietnam War had been a private commercial venture, the price of Bounty Hunter gunship support would have bought a king's ransom. Everybody was screaming for gunships. Having been carefully assigned the day prior to support a country-wide strategic plan, the 191st Boomerang operations now had the difficult task of documenting and controlling all the mission changes.

"It was a nightmare," MAJ Carlvin J. Griggs recalls. "The mission sequence that the unit exercised each day to control our aircraft was thrown completely out of kilter and, as our own emergencies began taking place, it became worse."

When the embassy resupply ship was shot down, followed closely by two gunships with wounded crewmembers downed over Long Binh, it was nerve-racking to get them recovered. The worst came to mind as battle exacted its price. With the entire country under attack, consequences of command decisions grew immeasurably. Despite the fury of enemy action, Griggs's mind remained cool. He always handled combat emergencies with a calm demeanor. But getting the combat situation under control, amid all the battle noise and confusion, took a steady brain and heart. Griggs moved decisively. Voluminous artillery fire outgoing from Bearcat signaled tactical emergencies close to home base. The enemy was coming for Bearcat. Many wondered if its defenses would hold.

The hairy situation also meant that outgoing rescue birds must dodge infinite HE ordnance flying to who knows where. Griggs's orders for standby crews to depart immediately for locations of downed Boomerangs and Bounty Hunters were resolute and clear. Departures were immediate and crews were well briefed. In short order, airlifts of the downed aviators and crews gave room for a sigh of relief from all concerned at 191st AHC headquarters. Through it all, Griggs remained calm. Confident in his pilots and operations officer, he prepared for resolving the innumerable unknowns. Straining his deductive reasoning for command reaction, Griggs methodically drafted his input for the OPORD of the following day. Battle was something the 191st was well tuned for. Griggs prepared to deliver the greatest blow his assets could deliver. Hell would be on the agenda. Time for short measures—gone. Griggs placed himself on the list to fly C&C the next day.

CHAPTER 13

New Bounty Hunter Six Enters the Fight

The ship was barely flying, and it skidded through the air sideways.

The greatest Bounty Hunter sting against the 1968 Tet enemy attack evolved through assignment of a determined gunship warrior with iron for a backbone. CPT Robert Stack arrived at the replacement depot in Long Binh with his heart set on flying guns for a combat assault-helicopter outfit. But Stack's hopes of flying Huey gunships shattered when he learned that he had been selected to fly U-21s, the Army's multiengine fixed-wing used primarily for VIP passenger transport. Stack was beside himself. Pleading with the assignments team yielded nothing. To them he was a number that needed slotting, and his previous Caribou experience was perfect for transition to the VIP bird that needed filling. No ifs, ands, or buts—it was a done deal.

Stack hurried out of the assignments section. *What a crock of shit.* With his blood boiling, he called General Seneff, commander of the First Aviation Brigade, whom he had met during his Eleventh Air Assault days at Fort Benning. Remembering the shining second lieutenant, the general arranged for Stack to get assigned to the 334th Aerial Weapons Company, the Sabers, at Bien Hoa, thereby planting the seed that would grow to become a remarkable attack-helicopter performance. After serving with the Sabers, Stack was later infused into the 191st AHC. Help from high places continued to bless his dream of flying guns. His father, no less, had a favorable impact.

Stack's father, an extraordinary Army officer, had served with MAJ Patnode, the first in-country commanding officer of the 191st AHC. Each day, Patnode applied every faculty of his gifted mind to the combat preparation and employment of the 191st. In one of his finer moments, he handpicked Stack from among the officers and men of the 334th Aerial Weapons Company at Bien Hoa for infusion into the 191st. Taking advantage of the Army's policy to maintain continuity of combat experience by infusing personnel from within the Vietnam theater of operations, Patnode conferred with the commander of the 334th and requested CPT Stack by name. He had a hunch about the kind of performance he could expect from Stack. His premonition proved to be correct.

Born into a military family, Stack cut his teeth and matured into his own character amidst Army culture and influence. It was no accident that he grew up inspired to join the Army and serve as his father did before him. There ended the similarity between their careers. Commissioned in the Ordnance Corps, Stack's father was a superb logistician who delivered vital combat support to battlefront units. He possessed a driven commitment for sustaining the cutting edge of the Army's mission. His entire scope of responsibility was designed to deliver technical services to frontline troops. His son, Robert, emerged as a horse of an entirely different color, however.

CPT Stack grew up amid the pomp and circumstance that abounds military installations. Having witnessed the gamut of awards and decorations bestowed upon warriors who placed duty, honor, and country before their own lives, young Stack became the product of those behaviors. They had grown to impress his young mind. From birth through maturity, his life prepared him for the role he would play in the 191st AHC. His mind, rich in Army purpose from the time he was a young boy, energized and charged his inclination to *join the fight*.

High school baseball and football were not enough to keep his action-loving heart content. At fifteen years old, he was riding horses through the wilds of Colorado and hunting mountain lion, elk, and deer. Hence, from the very beginnings of his desire to serve the Army, he knew he wanted to be at the war front. At eighteen, he enlisted in the Army to go to Airborne training and become a parachutist. During his enlisted service, he seized an opportunity to attend OCS, where he was commissioned as a second lieutenant of infantry. Stack joined the Vietnam War as a pilot of Caribou cargo planes after earning his wings in 1962.

Arriving back in the US after logging many hours as a fixed-wing jockey during his first Vietnam tour, Stack's warrior blood was unfulfilled. Again, pulled by his childhood Army roots, he maneuvered his career into rotary-wing aircraft by volunteering to transition to helicopters, thereby beginning a matched-pair relationship with the Army's venerable Huey. Driven by his strong desire to get into the fight, he set his sights on flying gunships. The growing number of American war casualties simply strengthened Stack's thirst for making a difference in combat. Seeing his fellow countrymen dying in frontline action reported by journalists, he felt compelled to join the ranks of patriots. He was moved by the emotion felt by Army families. With his father's image strong in his memory, he graciously accepted a second tour in Vietnam with full intent to serve at the *tip of the spear*.

Recharged with resolve to make a difference in the war, Stack soaked up every iota of information he could find about the UH-1C attack helicopter. The ongoing war captivated his fighting spirit. His flying was equally possessed with a drive to gain the edge. Gifted with a smooth pilot touch that wrung the best from any machine he commanded, Stack could finesse a UH-1 like no one else. Following his heli-copter transition, Stack knew, from day one, that he wanted to fly gunships. They captured his entire heart and soul. So, his stay with the 334th yielded a cornucopia of attack-helicopter experience. Knowledge of this experience enhanced Patnode's offer to Stack. At their first meeting, Patnode's words lit a flame in Stack's soul that remained for a lifetime.

"I'll never forget my first meeting with Patnode," Stack explains. "Everything he said struck a chord in my soul. First, he offered me the operations position and assured me that it would be only until a new officer arrived that he could appoint to that slot. Thereafter, I would get my wish and command the gun platoon. Man—my heart skipped a beat when I heard that. It didn't take but a millisecond to say, 'Yes!'"

Thus, when Patnode's offer came for Stack to infuse into the 191st and provide the unit an experienced edge, Stack jumped at the chance to make a difference. Within days, Stack demonstrated superb management acumen by organizing the unit's operations center, and establishing order to a flight-operations section, which up until his arrival, was still in the development stage. With ops in good order, his just reward came. Stack was elevated to the coveted leadership position, Bounty Hunter Six, commanding the 191st AHC gunship armada. Stack's time to excel came on the last day of January 1968. On that day, he would give the enemy their due and help turn the tide of battle in numerous Communist Tet Offensive engagements.

"The morning of January 31, 1968, started as a routine mission to Nha Be," Stack recalls. "After a thorough preflight inspection of my aircraft and its weapons systems, I lit my cigar, called my wingman to make sure his bird was okay, and then called Bearcat Tower for takeoff."

Lifting off from Bearcat, Stack assumed a heading for the Nha Be Tank Farm, so called because of the cluster of large petroleum storage tanks located there by the Navy. Strategically placed on the banks of the Nha Be River, the fuel station serviced the Riverine Force. An armada of Navy vessels that patrolled the river and carried troops into battle refueled there. Helicopter-landing pads also provided fuel support for combat-assault units. Pilots and crews enjoyed refueling at Nha Be to take advantage of the outstanding food service at the Navy dining facility. Overall, the Nha Be Tank Farm served as a strategic fuel depot on the southeastern outskirts of Saigon.

Stack and his crew lifted off, climbed to their cruise altitude of 1,500 feet, and checked their weapons systems to ensure they would arm.

"That done," Stack recalls, "I relaxed to enjoy my cigar."

Stack took a strong draw on his cigar to get it burning. The first exhale filled his nostrils with the soothing smell of good American tobacco. No sooner was Stack and his crew settled in for the flight when they received an urgent radio call.

"Any gunships in the Long Binh area, this is Paris Control on Guard. Proceed to Long Binh! Airfield under heavy ground attack—several hundred Viet Cong in the area. Contact Long Binh Tower on 241.0." The guard's rushed tone alerted Stack to the urgency.

Bounty Hunter Six was a mere ten minutes away from Long Binh. Stack contacted Nha Be Tank Farm to report their change of plans and then made a radio call to Long Binh Tower. There was no answer, so Stack assumed the tower had been evacuated. Bounty Hunter Six continued its flight.

"When we arrived over Long Binh, everything looked normal," Stack recalls, "and I felt someone must've panicked over nothing. We made a thorough high recon, and as we went down for a good close look, both my copilot and wingman reported that all armament systems were hot. After fifteen minutes of fruitless searching, I was ready to call it quits when my wingman called, 'Receiving fire!' Instinctively, I racked my ship around to put suppressive fire under him, but because he was still over the town, I had to hold my fire. He reported all gauges in the green, and we initiated a climb to one thousand feet."

Bounty Hunter Six flew back over the town. Women and children were fleeing—running in all directions. Stack had no doubt that the VC were responsible. He radioed ground locations in the immediate area to assess the situation.

"No one really knew what was happening," Stack recalls, "except that they were receiving fire from all directions and believed Long Binh was surrounded by VC. I relayed what I observed and asked permission to fire on known enemy positions in the city, but it was denied, as I expected it would be. No one had ever put an intentional air strike on a friendly village. A mechanized battalion from the Ninth US Infantry Division was approaching Long Binh from the west on Highway One. I attempted to contact them, but there was too much traffic to break in on their net. As the first three APCs [armed personnel carriers] entered the town, they exploded when hit by VC antitank rounds. I was able to locate the source of the enemy fire. It was coming from a large Buddhist temple just south of the road."

Stack made a crucial decision to take action because, in his words, "it was past the time for action." He called his wing to relay his plan.

"Wing, this is Lead. Fire mission."

"This is Wing, go ahead."

"Okay, on the large Buddhist temple, fifty percent of your armament—one pass, right break, and orient your right gunner to the friendly troops."

"This is Wing. Understand the Buddhist temple, fifty percent of my armament. Roger that."

Stack committed to his decision, knowing full well that he could be court-martialed if he was wrong.

"I took a hearty drag off my cigar, bit down on it hard, and rolled in on the temple," Stack recalls. "The next few seconds seemed like a lifetime and a half. The ground appeared to erupt in flashes, and red and green tracers whizzed by us. Some of the bullets found their mark, and the ship began to buck. Pieces of the Plexiglas windshield flew off. I squeezed off the rockets, counting them as they went: 'One, two, three . . .' Then a loud crash and a rush of air filled the cockpit."

Bounty Hunter Six's windshield shattered around Stack. Still, he continued to squeeze the rocket trigger. "Ten, eleven, twelve . . ." He counted with each squeeze. Blood trickled into Stack's mouth from his sliced lip.

The temple burst into flames.

"An agonizing scream pierced the hot air," Stack recalls. "My copilot had just got shot through the legs, and blood was spurting all over the cockpit."

Bounty Hunter Six drew dangerously close to the Buddhist temple.

"Sixteen, seventeen, eighteen . . ." Stack continued to count off the squeezes on the trigger. "It's time to get out of here!" he yelled.

The Huey took a hard right break. Stack pulled in every ounce of power.

"I could hear my wing ship's miniguns roar as they spat out their four thousand pieces of death a minute," Stack recalls. "It must have been awful to be on the receiving end of that gun, but it was sweet music to my ears. As we arrived in position to cover the wingman's break, I glanced over at my copilot and saw he was about to pass out from loss of blood."

In cool pilot fashion, Stack slapped his copilot on the shoulder. "Don't quit on me now! We may need that forty-millimeter cannon to bail wing out."

Stack's copilot, although weak, managed a faint smile and pulled down the hinged sight. They braced for the attack.

The wing ship just started his break when the ground again erupted in fire. The ground fire wounded the wing's AC, causing him to lose control of the ship.

"It looked as if he was going to crash," Stack recalls, "so we began another firing run to give him some cover. Things began to look up a little as the ground fire decreased and my wingman's copilot was able to get their aircraft under control. When the wing ship was clear of the target area, we started our break. Because we were alone, I started my break high and fast. Just when I thought we made it, I felt the bullets hit and simultaneously heard a loud bang at the rear of the aircraft. Charlie had just shot off my tail rotor! Because of main-rotor torque, the tail was trying to swap ends with the nose. It looked as if we were going to spin in when I bottomed the collective-pitch control and lowered the nose straight toward the ground.

"I needed to gain plenty of airspeed to streamline the aircraft aerodynamically if we were going to make it home, so I kept her in the dive until the last moment, pulling out just in time to clear the trees. When I leveled off I was indicating eighty-five knots, which is supposed to be sufficient to provide aerodynamic streamlining, according to Mr. Bell. I pulled in minimum cruise power and found he was correct. The ship was barely flying, and it skidded through the air sideways—its nose down and to the right with its tail high and to the left."

Stack surveyed the situation. His crew chief took a hit in his left shoulder and was lying on the floor trying to bandage himself with one arm. Meanwhile, Stack's copilot was losing more blood.

"I instructed the gunner to get the copilot out of his seat, stop the bleeding from his legs, and to help the crew chief," Stack recalls. "I then called the wing ship copilot and found he was on final approach to the Ninety-Third Evacuation Hospital strip. He thought the AC would be all right. But our unit SOP called for a landing at Saigon or Bien Hoa."

Although Saigon and Bien Hoa were farther away than the hospital strip, they both had improved runways designed for fixed-wing aircraft. The wide, smooth strip would give a chopper pilot with a tail-rotor failure an almost even chance of getting it on the ground in one piece. Plus, the extended runway would allow Stack to make a shallow approach with sufficient airspeed to keep the aircraft oriented in the direction of landing. On the smooth surface, the skids would slide with only minimal resistance. The hospital airstrip, on the other hand, was a different story. A running landing on its uneven terrain would likely snag a skid and cause the aircraft to topple end over end. A troubling fact. However, one look back at his copilot and crew chief and Stack knew the wide, level runways of Saigon and Bien Hoa were out of the question—they were just too far away.

"My copilot should have been in the hospital five minutes ago," Stack recalls, "so I decided it would have to be the Ninety-Third Evacuation Hospital for us, too. I called the hospital, declared an emergency, and requested a crash crew on standby. Within five minutes, we were on final approach for the hospital strip. My plan was to bring the ship in low and fast, cut the engine just short, and then execute a no-pitch-pull, low-level autorotation. I wasn't sure if it really could be done, but there wasn't any other choice."

Stack ordered his gunner to strap the copilot and crew chief into the back seat and throw everything overboard that couldn't be tied down.

"When he threw the heavy ammo box out the right side," Stack recalls, "I thought we were going to roll over. But after a brief fight, I got the aircraft under control again. I glanced back and saw the gunner strap himself between the two wounded men so he could better support them during the crash. Who says this younger generation doesn't have guts? As I got in a little closer, I could see the fire truck and ambulance by the runway. It was all I could do to avoid instinctively slowing down. Still flying sideways, we approached the strip. Damn! That ground was coming up fast.

"About sixty meters from the strip, I cut off the engine and pulled up the nose. Because that eliminated transmission torque, the ship began streamlining into the wind and almost lined up straight with the runway. Crossing the approach-end landing threshold, we were about ten feet off the ground and still going seventy knots. I eased the stick back and felt the stinger make contact with the ground.

Much to my surprise, this created an anchor effect on the tail of the aircraft that helped maintain directional control, so we aligned perfectly with the runway. Just then, I put it on the ground. We were still going sixty knots and started skidding wildly down the runway, dirt and rocks flying in all directions. The ship began veering to the right, almost rolled over but righted itself, and slid to a halt a few feet from the end of the runway."

With dust still swirling, the crash crew rallied around the chopper and rushed the copilot and crew chief to the hospital. Stack sat in his captain seat, trying to shake off the flight and collect himself. He wanted to appear as a calm and fearless combat leader. Acting as if nothing out of the ordinary happened is typical pilot behavior, especially a combat pilot.

Better light my cigar, Stack said to himself. A cigar between the teeth is a surefire way of shouldering the life-and-death decisions made with every roll, pitch, and yaw—and gives the appearance of fearlessness.

"Hmmm, I wonder where it is. I know it was in my mouth just a minute ago." Stack twisted around in his seat and leaned back to face his gunner. "Have you seen my cigar?"

The gunner grinned. "Sir, I didn't want to say anything, but I think you ate it while you were putting this beast on the ground."

Stack completed his aircraft shutdown and headed for the hospital to check on his crew.

"The scene was a madhouse," Stack recalls. "Wounded were lying everywhere on the grounds surrounding the hospital doors. Medical personnel were scrambling about, attempting to triage and group all the wounded. They sorted the most critical for immediate aid, segregated terminal cases to the side, and sent those who appeared to be low risk to a waiting area. I was relieved to see my copilot and crew chief among the low-risk crowd. But seeing my copilot still bleeding profusely and suffering excruciating pain, I took some morphine from the crew aid kit and injected him. With a barely visible smile and a faint nod of his head, he expressed his gratitude."

Still, Stack remained apprehensive about his crew's condition, especially his copilot, who appeared near death at times. Emotions run deep in relationships fused by war's daily life-and-death challenges. It's a brotherhood tone unknown to most, even blood kin. But soon enough, the hospital staff whisked the wounded Bounty Hunters into treatment. Satisfied that he did all he could for his wounded men, Stack headed for the helipad where his wing ship crew had parked their shot-up bird. Flyable but missing the wounded, AC Stack quickly energized the remainder of the crew who were standing by, ready for action, ready to protect their brothers getting hammered by enemy fire. A quick preflight revealed a few bullet holes in various parts of the aircraft, but none were debilitating. The bird was still airworthy.

After a quick run-up, and with rocket pods full and the 7.62-millimeter minigun rearmed and rerigged, Stack broke ground with a fire in his belly. Nothing could have lit Stack's resolve against the enemy more than getting some of his men wounded. Now, it was personal.

Climbing to cruise altitude, Stack called Paris Control and asked for vectors to whichever hot spot they felt he could be the most useful.

"Bounty Hunter Six, your timing is perfect. Proceed to the racetrack and contact elements of the 199th Infantry on their ground frequency. They're in *heavy* contact."

"Roger that, Paris. Thanks, out!"

Soon, Stack was approaching the area from the south and could see other aircraft engaging targets on the ground adjacent to the Phu Tho Racetrack. AH-1G Cobras were rolling in and blasting away at enemy troops occupying buildings along the western periphery of the racetrack complex. As he got closer, Stack recognized gunships from the unit he recently left, the Sabers. Knowing their frequency, he made contact and was immediately welcomed into the daisy-chain pattern of aircraft attacking the enemy emplacements.

Determined to defeat the allied effort, the enemy fought back with an intensity that Stack had never seen before. Each attacking bird received a groundswell of machine-gun fire when overflying the entrenched Communists. Neither side seemed able to dislodge the other or gain the upper hand. The 199th light infantry troops, who had been sent to secure the racetrack, were stalled approximately one click to the southwest. They had run headlong into two battalions of enemy, both with the mission to secure the same complex.[1] The Phu Tho Racetrack was the only nearby area large enough to use as a helicopter LZ. Furthermore, if the Communists controlled the racetrack, they could easily hit the nearby Tan Son Nhut Air Base with their eighty-two-millimeter mortars. Debilitating the air base was a major tactical objective for the Communists. In other words, the Phu Tho Racetrack was a prime piece of real estate—pricey enough to die for. A fight to the death was exactly what the enemy had in mind.

For the allies, losing this piece of ground would require a much longer approach path for relief columns to reach the inner city. This would certainly affect any rescue or reinforcement of high-value targets such as the US embassy or the presidential palace. Both the NVA and the Americans knew that control of the racetrack would dictate the outcome of the battle for Saigon. It had to be a fight to the finish.

Following Cobras into the strike zone, Stack lined up on buildings from where the enemy fire was the most intense and delivered his rocket salvos with devastating accuracy. After three passes by the long daisy chain of aerial gun platforms, enemy fire began to wane. On his fourth pass, Stack spotted a group of enemy troops out in the open, attempting to break away from the fight. Catching the enemy in the open was unusual. Traditionally, the NVA fought from behind barricades and

---

1 Keith William Nolan, *The Battle for Saigon: Tet 1968* (New York: Pocket Books/Simon & Schuster Inc., 1996).

bunkered emplacements. Not likely to be caught out in the open, they were masters of ambush tactics, taking American lives with ruthless tactics.

Stack knew these tactics. The enemy forces concealed *punji pits* containing foot-long, sharpened bamboo spikes sticking upward and coated with human feces. They were designed to impale the unwary American. The enemy forces were notorious for attacking at night when they launched mortars at US forces and then melted into the darkness. Seldom would they expose themselves and fight with conviction. But now these Communists were in a group out in the open, offering Stack a rare, sweet target of opportunity for justice—a chance to avenge his wounded and fallen comrades who grew to be his brothers.

With a flick of a switch, Stack laid down 7.62-millimeter rounds at the rate of nearly four thousand per minute, knocking down running enemy soldiers like dominos. One minigun pass and six enemy troops were slammed to the ground, each body contorting with pain and gasping for a final breath.

While in pursuit of the group, Stack descended very low and found himself broadside to enemy fire from the opposite side of a building where more enemy soldiers were holed up. But out of ammo and short on fuel, Stack couldn't engage. He marked the building in his memory bank and headed back to Bien Hoa to refuel and rearm.

Joining a line of Cobras at the petroleum, oils, and lubricants (POL) ramp, the thirsty Huey was hot-refueled and quickly repositioned to one of the many rearming points being used by the 334th Aerial Weapons Company birds. Crew Chief Heinmiller and Gunner Kahn, working in tandem, rearmed the gunship in record time. This resupply facility offered a great advantage over those of a typical assault-helicopter company because it was designed for simultaneous use by several gun platoons at one time. Aerial weapons companies comprised more than one gun platoon. These extra pads sped up the rearming sequence considerably. Again, ready for battle and rearmed far quicker than the ordnance-heavy Cobras, Stack was off the ground and heading back toward the racetrack. He flew as a single ship, but he felt comfortable knowing substantial reinforcement was right behind him.

Remembering the multistory building from where the blast of enemy fire had challenged his ego, Stack set up for a steep approach and rolled in using battle logic acquired from many previous engagements. Rather than attack the side of the building, he knew the enemy would most likely choose the upper floor to have a firing point with an elevation advantage. Attacking with a steep angle, he placed his rockets on the roof just above the spot where the enemy fire originated. This tactic detonated a huge ball of fire, an enormous secondary explosion that totally collapsed the entire roof span into a heap of smoke, flame, and debris. With intent to finish the job, Stack broke right to avoid the flying chunks of building and slowed the bird down enough to make a short right orbit for another low-and-slow pass over the structure. Anticipating that the raging fire might flush out some enemy, he overflew the building, staying slightly to the right in order to avoid the flames. The adjacent building had a huge, gaping hole blasted through its roof. Peering down inside, the crew chief spotted a group of VC working feverishly, trying to clear debris from the exit. Blast force from the secondary explosion blew debris into their stairwell, blocking their escape route.

"Sir, the gooks are trapped on the floor!" Heinmiller yelled. "The stairwell's blocked. There's no one behind us on downwind. Do another short orbit and let me stitch the bastards!"

"Roger that!"

Barely fifty feet above the building, the instant the gunship completed the turn with its nose attitude tilted left, the bungee-mounted M60 sprayed the trapped enemy. Human flesh flew through the room and painted the walls with blood. As the gunship passed over the building, one enemy, no doubt motivated by the flames now engulfing his fighting position, climbed up through the hole in the roof and jumped three stories to the street below. Unable to maintain his balance, he landed on his side and bounced several feet in the air. Crippled by the fall, he attempted to crawl away as Heinmiller's gun stopped his progress. Blood oozed from beneath his body and quickly spread beyond him on the street. He managed two or three more feeble crawl strokes before his body lost all motion.

Stack's blow devastated the enemy. Following the secondary explosion, the ensuing fire forced the Communist soldiers out of their positions, changing the enemy's posture significantly. The 199th Infantry force regained its momentum and pressed forward again. This small victory came with a price of blood extracted from the 191st.[2] Stack's gunship was stitched from nose to tail. And his second copilot caught a round through the leg. Ascending to altitude, Stack's bird came under fire from a .51-caliber machine gun that pulverized the tail rotor–control bell crank. The bell crank allows the pilot to change tail-rotor pitch and compensate for main-rotor torque. But at least *this* time the tail rotor was still turning and maintained some thrust. Nonetheless, faced with yet another tail-rotor emergency, Stack knew the drill well and handled it with even greater finesse than the last time.

Repeating his earlier routine, he resolved to see his men in the hands of medical personnel. He managed to land the bird smoothly at the hospital strip where medical crews again waited to evacuate the wounded copilot. Bedeviled by the enemy's growing carnage, Stack's guts twisted at the sight of the dead and dying American soldiers. In the two or three hours since his previous visit, the number of bloody bodies around the hospital grounds had doubled. Seemingly, the medical personnel were overwhelmed with casualties, and their treatment capability was pitifully diluted by the sheer volume. The wait for medical care for the wounded Bounty Hunters seemed eternal, and Stack felt helpless amid the hundreds of voices and sounds of the mass confusion. Fortunately, his wounded crewmembers were not critical and

---

2 Nolan, *The Battle for Saigon: Tet 1968.*

were handling their own pain as warriors who had watched many others die. They were grateful for their divine blessing in being alive. Suddenly, above the din of all the noise, a feminine voice called out.

"Robert—*Robert*. Bob!" She finally got Stack's attention.

Scanning across the body-covered grounds, Stack saw a familiar face and his expression changed to a look of pleasure.

"Hey, Joyce [pseudonym]! What are *you* doing here?"

Stack was renowned among the 191st AHC officers for his exploits with the American Red Cross *Donut Dollies* and other beauties who populated hospitals and Special Services in Vietnam. As the gorgeous young woman approached, the wounded Bounty Hunters smiled with envy. Her rich auburn hair, crystal-clear green eyes, and creamy, smooth complexion posed a striking contrast to war. The Donut Dolly embraced Stack warmly. As she extended her arms around his neck, her short skirt rose revealing a little leg to the wounded and battle-scarred soldiers behind her. Regardless of their wounds, many of the men lifted their heads to watch.

Her beauty radiated among the wounded with a mind-soothing warmth that momentarily silenced the relentless war sounds. Many of the men hadn't experienced such a warm and secure feeling since leaving the States months before. Surely, many wished they stood in Stack's lucky spot. As Joyce separated her embrace from Stack's, her breasts firmly wiggled back in place. He took her by the arm and moved off a few feet to speak to her in private. With a concerned expression, Joyce looked at the platoon leader as he spoke and then her face softened into a smile as she departed, leaving Stack to rejoin the wounded crew. In less than five minutes, Joyce returned with a nurse who flashed a warm smile at Stack before the two caretakers began tending to his wounded Bounty Hunters.

With that mission accomplished, Stack returned to the hospital landing pad to look for another flyable Bounty Hunter Charlie-model. He found two. Again, the lead ship was missing the wounded AC, so Stack quickly volunteered himself to fill the slot.

Approaching 1700 hours, the shadows were getting longer, but the staunch enemy resistance was truly galling the gun-platoon leader. In true American tradition, Stack's internal makeup was challenged with the thought that his departure from the battle-field was forced by enemy action. With ego stoking his fighting blood, he decided to rearm and refuel the last two remaining gunships and go look for another fight. The Communist forces were everywhere; shutting down now seemed like wasted effort. No sooner were the two gunships cranked when a Jeep with a blood-soaked NCO stopped at the edge of the refueling ramp from where the wounded individual motioned for Stack to hold in position. Stack motioned for the NCO to approach the AC side of the bird and then waited patiently. Hobbling in obvious pain, the bloody sergeant asked Stack if he could take his gunships to the northwest side of Long Binh, across from II FFV headquarters (Second Field Force Vietnam), where the NVA were threatening to overrun American defenses. Stack's eyes brightened.

"Roger that, Sarge! we're on our way."

To keep from blowing debris at the wounded man, Stack held his takeoff until the limping figure got back into the Jeep and drove off in the direction of the hospital. Without wasting another minute, the Bounty Hunter fire team lifted off and headed for the II FFV headquarters.

With the sun low on the horizon, Stack approached the battle site from the southeast. Again, the airspace seemed filled with tracers; this time, over a place called "Widow's Village," so named for the population of widows of South Vietnamese military killed in action. The widows sheltered there were given a small pension by the South Vietnamese government.[3] Situated directly across from II FFV, Stack couldn't believe the tenacity of the NVA. They appeared to be at least as determined as the NVA forces he had faced earlier at the racetrack. With that fight locked in place, the Communist forces were laying siege to the II FFV complex. A truly brave group of Americans engaged them, holding some ground just outside the compound fence in Widow's Village. As Stack overflew the Americans, he noticed an officer looking up and talking into a radio. Assuming the grunt was trying to reach the gunships, Stack dialed through several ground frequencies and finally made contact. Vectored to the north, the man on the ground asked that they orient their attack on a church with a heading of approximately 180 degrees and hit a yellow house across the street. With little room for error and the sun dipping below the horizon, Stack instructed his wingman to expend half his load on the first pass.

"Roger that, understand expend half the load. Wing, out!"

Ensuring that his target was safely acquired in his rocket sights with no chance of hitting the friendlies, Stack skimmed the rooftops and slammed rocket after rocket into the yellow house. Looking back, as his wingman followed suit, Stack watched the yellow house collapse in a heap of burning rubble. Bolting from various fighting positions among the surrounding houses in Widow's Village, a small batch of enemy soldiers disengaged and ran for a small patch of woods nearby. Friendly tracers pointed out the evading enemy and triggered Stack's predatory instincts. He dove his gunship at the retreating enemy like a giant raptor. Their bodies soon littered the path from Widow's Village to the patch of woods. Of the entire group, only two made it into the green foliage, with one limping painfully and bleeding from his lower extremities.

Both Bounty Hunter aircraft took numerous hits. Caution-panel warning lights lit up on the consoles. Stack knew that more than likely they sustained serious battle damage. With the fear of having no one to retrieve his crews, Stack gutted out the risk and flew all the way back to the 191st home pad at Bearcat. The fire team arrived at Bearcat with less than a minute to spare. Bullet holes in his fuel cells depleted Stack's fuel reserves down to vapor upon landing. Officially shot down for

---

3 Nolan, *The Battle for Saigon: Tet 1968.*

the third time that day, Stack's aircraft had to be towed from the POL point to the maintenance hangar.

January 31, 1968, officially ended for the Bounty Hunters. The list of 191st AHC's wounded and battle-damaged aircraft would not be known until late that night. Downing a quick supper, Stack immediately set out to assess his platoon's damage and plan for the following day. No doubt, it had been a hellish day. Although extraordinary, the day was not yet recognized for what it represented among the enemy. It would be months later, when intelligence sources had time to interrogate high-ranking enemy prisoners, that the Tet Offensive would be recognized as extraordinary by American forces.

By midnight, all wounded were accounted for and the airworthy birds were rigged for the next day's mission. Some of the remaining pilots and crews were still reeling from the intensity of the day's action, but most were settled in for a much-needed rest. Maintenance crews worked feverishly through the night to patch the aircraft that could be made airworthy with the least invasive repairs, leaving the major challenges for the following day. With only a short night's rest, February 1 arrived in a flash for the Boomerangs and Bounty Hunters. To Stack and other pilots and crewmembers, it was just another hot day at the office for the 191st AHC. With more to come for certain.

By 0500 hours, ten slicks, four gunships, and a C&C ship made up the order of battle for the 191st AHC, and the flight operations assignment board showed the Australian allies as the spearhead element for the day. With tactical emergencies contained in Saigon, Long Binh, and other major cities within the 191st AHC AO, the action shifted to outlying regions and communities where sizeable enemy forces were still entrenched. The Boomerangs and Bounty Hunters would be working the Vietnam sector assigned to the Australian allies. All of the slicks, escorted by a light fire team, were ordered to a location east of Bearcat. CPT Stack took the second fire team to a remote location just north of Vung Tau, thirty miles southeast. By midmorning, both fire teams were decisively engaging enemy forces across the entire AO, with actions mirroring the previous day's battles. Enemy forces that infiltrated certain towns and villages were fixed by the Aussies and the fight was on.

Historically, one of America's strongest allies, the Australians, fought with conviction and spared no opportunity to close with the enemy. On February 1, 1968, the Aussies were extremely effective, and the enemy body count quickly escalated with each airmobile assault. Inserted by the Boomerangs, the Aussies moved toward the suspected enemy target until contact was made, and with the coordination of a well-oiled machine, they set about using the firepower at their disposal to destroy the enemy in place. Once done, they moved on to their next objective. Suddenly, the one message that angered Stack more than any other came through the command frequency. One of his pilots had been killed in action.

Quickly Stack inquired, "Who?"

"Chief Warrant Officer Two Tommy Sandefur."

Stack remained focused on the work he was doing with his contingent of Aussies, but his heart was heavy with the depressing news. Meeting with stiff enemy resistance, the Bounty Hunter fire team supporting the Boomerang insertions took on a well-prepared enemy force. The gunships were repeatedly hit as they attacked the stubborn enemy, and Sandefur died immediately from a wound to his head. He died heroically fighting a determined enemy, and CPT Stack knew he had lost a superb gunship pilot and a dear friend.

"Only God knows" was a common saying frequently uttered by battle survivors who experienced the loss of a crewmember. The phrase expressed the sentiment of how a bullet just happens to find the exact spot at the exact moment to take one life of a soldier flying above at over one hundred miles per hour. It remains a mystery for mortals to ponder. Such was the case with Sandefur. Big Okie hailed from Tulsa, Oklahoma, and he and his wife, Carole, had two children, Lisa and Marc. Loved by all who knew him, his death came hard to the Boomerangs and Bounty Hunters.

The first day of February ended with no more casualties, and a gloom fell over the 191st AHC, the normal aftermath of losing a brother. Nevertheless, Stack continued to lead his Bounty Hunters into battle with a vengeance—as justice for Sandefur. In command of enormous firepower, he felt obliged to even the score. Having such destructive capability at his disposal, he almost felt as if it was incumbent upon *him* to avenge the death of Sandefur and all the wounded who could no longer account for themselves on the battlefield. It was his duty to his fallen brothers.

Three days after receiving the news about Sandefur, Stack started his day like any other, with his crew searching for any sign of enemy activity. Flying in the Ben Tre area, in support of Ninth Infantry Division troops, Stack was alerted by Crew Chief Davis that a group of young Vietnamese men was walking nonchalantly along a rice dike and pretending to be civilians.

"What makes you think they are enemy?" Stack asked.

"Because, sir, see that sack each is carrying?" Crew Chief Davis asked. "They have AK-47s in them!"

"I don't see how you can make an AK-47s out of those bags. They just look like bags of vegetables or something."

"No, sir! Look at the bottom of the bag, and you can see the barrels of the weapons. If you want, get down lower for a better look, and you'll see them."

CPT Stack had long since learned to respect Crew Chief Davis's superior vision with many incidents that demonstrated his extraordinary ability to see things that others couldn't. With good faith in Davis's assessment, Stack slowed the bird for a low-level pass over the suspects. Everything seemed normal. Stack maneuvered almost directly over the Vietnamese men. The men quickly went for their guns. But not quick enough—Davis was faster. His M60 stitched all five with one long burst.

Before dying, two of the five were able to get their AKs out of the bag but never got a magazine into their weapons. Again, Davis's eyesight proved invaluable to the crew.

While still orbiting the area around the dead enemy, Stack received an urgent call from C&C requesting his presence in the AO, a few clicks to the west. The grunts ran into a hornet's nest of enemy activity and his firepower was needed. As he caught sight of C&C, Stack called for vectors.

"Boomerang Five, this is Bounty Hunter Six."

"Roger, Bounty Hunter Six. The ground elements have encountered heavy enemy resistance from the bunkers along the canal directly to my front as I am flying now. I'm going to ask the grunts to pop smoke so you can ID their positions. Then you need to roll in on the bunkers. Blocking forces are already in place up and down the canal about one thousand meters in both directions, and another group of friendlies is positioned to the rear of the enemy bunkers approximately six hundred meters. We're not going to ask them to pop smoke because we don't want to alert the VC. Good copy?"

"Boomerang Five, Six, understand. Attack the enemy bunkers along the canal and maintain tight fire control to avoid the other friendlies. Good copy on the blocking forces. I'm going down for a quick recon. Out!"

At that point, Stack called his wingman. "Wing, Bounty Hunter Six, did you copy?"

"Roger that, Six. I'm on your left wing—I gotcha covered."

Dropping to about 1,200 feet AGL, Stack started receiving fire while still a considerable distance from the enemy, giving him cause to break off the approach and climb to attack altitude as the crew chief and gunner took the bunkers under fire for only a brief moment. The proximity of friendly troops prevented the two from laying down a blanket of fire over the area.

As Stack's aircraft climbed to attack altitude, the wingman called with an urgent voice. "Six, there's a sampan *di di mau*-ing. It looks like it has some guys with AKs on board." Di di mau-ing was their way of saying "leaving with great haste."

"Roger. Got them, Wing. Let me clear with C&C."

"Bounty Hunter Six, this is Boomerang Five. I copied that. They are confirmed bad guys. Take 'em out!"

Knowing that overflying the bunkers was the highest risk, Stack set up an attack pattern that would intersect the canal at an angle and allowed the sampan to travel some distance away from the hot spot. Stack placed a rocket centered on the vessel's long axis and watched as its contents exploded in a ball of fire. As Stack rolled in on the old junk, Davis could see VC diving off the sides into the water. Pinpointing where the enemy disappeared over the side, Crew Chief Davis boiled the water with M60 rounds. Deadly accurate. In the break, Stack began receiving fire from the canal, evidence that there were more enemy than what the ground forces estimated. Stack reported this to C&C and prepared to engage the bunkers. After two complete passes by the fire team, the enemy fire still had not subsided. Persistent as a honey badger, Stack continued the attack.

In the middle of the barrage, an enemy bullet zipped through the bottom of Stack's foot and exited above his ankle. The hot lead reentered above his knee and exited very close to his family jewels, finally bouncing off his chicken plate. Reporting his wound to C&C, Stack then called the next senior Bounty Hunter and announced he would be heading for the hospital. Nearly frightened out of his wits, the new copilot flew in the direction of the nearest US installation at Dong Tam. Stack took the controls, corrected his heading, and ordered the young pilot to Bearcat.

"This is above my pay grade," the young flight surgeon said when Stack arrived at Bearcat. The young doctor ordered him on to Long Binh.

Meanwhile, someone brought Stack a bottle of Jim Beam, and Stack anesthetized himself all the way to Long Binh. Once at Long Binh, the physician caring for Stack called Bearcat and chastised the duty officer for Stack's inebriated condition. Apparently, in addition to the surgery, the doctors had to pump his stomach.

On February 5, 1968, a contingent of Bounty Hunters accompanied the 191st XO to the hospital to visit the wounded Stack. CW2 Ed McKee recalls the occasion:

"A bunch of us went to bid him farewell, since we knew that his wound was serious enough that he would be evacuated back the States. We gathered around his bed as MAJ Griggs presented him with the Silver Star for his heroic performance during the Tet Offensive. We poked fun at his constant guidance for us to break off from gun runs with sufficient standoff range to avoid ground fire. All the celebrity he took in good stead, but we all howled when he sheepishly admitted that his biggest concern was whether his manhood was going to function correctly after he healed. That brought on a loud response that even the nurses wondered what the commotion was about with their favorite patient."

Stack was sent to Japan for recovery and then to the States. The 191st AHC had a series of gun-platoon leaders who performed admirably, but Stack's record of confirmed kills and engagements remained unmatched. As for the lovely Nurse Joyce, well, that's another story.

Hitting the landing zone (LZ), February 1968.

The 191st AHC sign with MSG Thomas D. Croley, SP4 Andy Kalicak, and SP4 Douglas Fricke Jr., October 1967.

Burning shit. Fifty-five-gallon drums, cut in half, were used as crapper receptacles. "Somebody's got to do it!" December 1967.

M60 machine-gun view from a Huey, February 1968.

Door-gunner duty, SP4 Roy Ahuna. February 1968.

Boomerangs heading home.

Chicken and beer BBQ with SP4 John Tumbri, SP4 Carl Scott Douglas (KIA), WO Dave Perez, SP4 Biersbach, SP4 Roy Ahuna, SP4 Evan Wilson, SP4 Chuck Floyd, CPT Lambert "Duke" Essary and others, October 1968.

Local mother and daughter visit during downtime.

Local kids pose for a picture in a village outside of Camp Bearcat, December 1967.

Local barber and laundry crew (Mamasan, Phi, Truong, and one other local) with SP4 Roy Ahuna, October 1967.

Boomerang needing extraction, November 1968.

Downed Bounty Hunter, September 1968.

Maintenance crew at night, February 1968.

The 191st bunkers ... on some nights, December 1967.

Night flares lighting up the skies at Camp Bearcat. January 1968.

Fuel-supply lines hit by an enemy rocket; scramble to move Hueys to safety.

Chinook and Huey. Bringing a Boomerang home, February 1968.

Field Day, SP4 Roy Ahuna, February 1968.

COL Clarence A. "Bud" Patnode Jr. and family after returning from Vietnam. Promotion to LTC.

Securing the LZ when dropping troops off on a mission, January 1968.

CHAPTER 14

Griggs Commanding

Death lurks in the trees. Stay away from tree lines.

A survivor of Tet and its bloodbaths, both friendly and foe, MAJ Griggs had sea-soned as a combat-assault pilot under a myriad of American blood sacrifices. A heart-wrenching number of his own pilots and crewmembers died fighting under his watch. The pain of writing to their next of kin was infused in his brain as an encumbrance to carry to his own death. During this war and into his old age, he would mask these memories in quiet solitude. Griggs was among the few who weathered the smell of blood and death without changing focus on his mission. His men saw him as an oak and followed his leadership with enthusiasm and faith.

Griggs served as a Boomerang for thirteen long, hard months. He was intro-duced to airmobile operations as a flight-platoon leader (Boomerang Two-Six). At the time, the 191st AHC was under the command of MAJ Patnode. After one month as a platoon leader, Griggs served a short stint as an operations officer; upon Patnode's departure, he served for seven months as the XO. Griggs's assign-ment as XO began under MAJ William Spurlock, who assumed command of the unit near the end of his second tour in Vietnam. Spurlock leaned on Griggs for professional recommendations, and the troops relied on Griggs as the go-to man for command decisions. This arrangement ratified Griggs's leadership influence and generated enormous appreciation among the unit's officers and men. Under Spurlock, Griggs more or less ran the company, and the men were happy with that arrangement.

MAJ Spurlock turned over his command of the 191st to MAJ Colbert L. Dilday, who came to the company after having commanded an aviation section of a separate brigade. Although Dilday had little combat-assault experience, he quickly learned C&C operations from his operations officer and from XO Griggs. MAJ Dilday, a take-charge commander, changed the XO's role. Instead of making the decisions and ensuring completion, the XO would now support the commander's decisions. As such, Griggs became the interface between company officers and the commander.

During this period, Griggs reinforced the strong following he built with the troops. With his suave style, Griggs would smooth out the ripples in issues between the troops and the commander without leaving any apparent discord. Working his diplomacy in a low-key fashion, the problems seamlessly disappeared.

The troops watched Griggs carefully negotiate his way through the reigns of three previous commanders (Patnode, Spurlock, and Dilday), and they identified with his role in these transitions. His diversity of assignments, at one time or another, brought him in contact with virtually all of the unit's personnel, and they were comfortable with his management and direction. The men saw themselves as part of Griggs's entourage. To the troops, he was one of them.

In combat, the troops watched Griggs fearlessly execute airmobile assaults, and like a pack of wolves, they willingly jumped into the fray with him. Leading by example, Griggs never demanded anything from his men that he himself would not do. In so doing, he earned their respect. A perfect example of Griggs's command presence and influence occurred on January 25, 1968, when the 191st supported an ARVN unit in the vicinity of Tan Tru, South Vietnam.

"We inserted two companies of South Vietnamese RF/PF Troops, who were ordered to conduct a search-and-destroy operation," WO1 Don Williams recalls. "Yielding no enemy contact, the RF/PF units formed extraction-sized loads in an area of thick, low-lying brush, where blade damage was probable. This forced landing to a hover exposed the 191st birds in silhouette fashion above the foliage—a lucrative target acquisition for the enemy, who took full advantage. Machine-gun bullets plastered the first lift requiring field maintenance for three birds, thus delaying the second lift. My ship was one of few remaining airworthy, fortunate to escape the extraction with no combat damage. Repairs for other birds held the second lift until after dark.

"Meanwhile, friendlies in the PZ were pinned down by an aggressive enemy unit that was well prepared and gained total control of the tactical ground. Going back into the LZ was murder. The VC tracers were literally covering the ground with a glow, making extraction a perilous matter. Like an army of fireflies shooting across the battleground, the sight of heavy enemy fire alone made the stomach tighten and raised the pucker factor. The thought of landing in that rain of fire was mental torture."

Despite the lethal wall of enemy fire, Williams volunteered to return to the PZ. And of course, he would. With Griggs leading the way as an exemplary figure, the 191st troops often committed themselves where others dared not tread. On the second lift, a Boomerang ship was shot down on the enemy-infested ground. Williams landed beside the disabled Huey and unloaded the ARVN infantry to guard the aircraft until additional help arrived. As rescue crews approached, Williams turned his aircraft lights so the pilots could vector on his location. Risking exposure of his own life and crew, he left the lights on and communicated instructions for the rescue birds and gunships. The enemy fire subsided considerably when the Bounty Hunters oriented their heavy barrages on the enemy positions.

Often exposed to enemy contact, the 191st gunships were lethal in their pursuit of enemy kills. More so, when the Boomerang flight was threatened, the Bounty Hunters attacked with a vengeance. With lifesaving effect, the actions of Williams were the instrumental component of that defensive move. Together with resupply of the decisively engaged ARVN, including medevac of wounded, WO1 Williams was the enduring workhorse that saved many friendly lives that day. Perhaps most redeeming for Williams, as he flew back to Bearcat at mission's end, he was called by 191st operations to inform him that his wife had just given birth to his second son, who was named after him, Donald L. Williams. Williams was ecstatic. No greater reward could have been given to the combat pilot at that moment than the birth of his child. The uplift of such news instantly recomposed his mind, transporting him from the tense moment of battle to the tender moment of knowing he had brought life to the world.

For his actions on January 25, 1968, WO1 Williams was awarded the Distinguished Flying Cross, an honor bestowed upon those who heroically risk their lives in combat. Williams earned this commendation with extraordinary valor—an exemplary product of Griggs's influence among his pilots and crews.

SP5 Roger Barkley recalls: "From the standpoint of my enlisted assignment, the 191st operated like no other unit I had served with. Flying as crew chief aboard WO1 Don Williams's aircraft, we flew missions into the heat of battle without reservation. Once during Tet, we carried an ARVN general into the heart of Saigon and made several gun runs as a single ship under fire from enemy positions. Attacking the enemy with a slick, armed with only door guns, was not the norm. Yet Williams did not hesitate to proceed without gunship cover. En route we saw the Bien Hoa ammo dump explode in a huge mushroom cloud that rocked our bird approximately five miles away. This served as warning that this enemy activity was not the usual attack-and-run tactics we usually saw from the enemy.

"Although my work remained at enlisted levels where I didn't communicate much with MAJ Griggs, I was pleased when he was selected to command the 191st. He would often fly into this type of enemy action. He made an excellent example for the unit."

It's no wonder that on June 20, 1968, MAJ Griggs assumed the reins of CO. Being selected to command the 191st did not just fall into Griggs's lap. Rather, the path to CO was forged by his brave actions and unrelenting commitment to his troops. After MAJ Dilday was scheduled to depart, the more likely scenario would have been to move Griggs into a battalion or group staff officer position and assign the company a new commander who did not have prior experience with the 191st. With only three months left on his tour, Griggs did not have enough time to take a command position. However, Griggs knew that bringing in a commander from the outside would make the company less effective during the transitional period—and this could mean a loss in lives. With this knowledge, he requested a conference with the group commander. By the close of their meeting, Griggs was given a thirty-day extension to his tour of duty and was handed the reins as the next commander of the 191st AHC. Because Griggs knew all the personnel, understood the unit's operational procedures, and had amassed a wealth of combat-assault experience, there was no loss of continuity. Indeed, the move saved lives.

Griggs took care to preserve the unit's momentum and continue its development into a stronger and more successful combat-assault company. Griggs's greatest asset: his honest and open ability to deal with people. He possessed all the qualities of a natural-born leader. Blessed with personality, intelligence, and a professional demeanor that inspired a high achievement level from his troops, the man was a giant among leaders. Born and raised in Hartsville, South Carolina, and graduating from The Citadel, the Military College of South Carolina, he exuded the image of a Southern gentleman. He received people with a genteel Southern style that engendered immediate friendship. He knew no strangers. Everyone who met Griggs would agree that the man they saw was the man they got. Putting on a facade for specific occasions was not in his character. With a warm smile, Griggs drew the best from his troops, and they willingly gave him their dedicated loyalty and support.

Among his first orders of business, Griggs replaced the mess sergeant with a truly talented individual who boosted the unit's morale—several-fold. For instance, Griggs heard numerous complaints from pilots who, after flying long, combat-assault days, returned to home base to find cold food or picked-over scraps. Meeting with SFC Robert Pagel, the incoming mess sergeant, Griggs laid out his new rules:

"I want plenty of hot food when the flight returns from the day's mission, regardless of the hour. And no substitutions from the menu! I don't want to hear from the flight crews that while the ground staff eat steak, the assault troops returning from their missions are fed cold cuts because the mess hall ran out of beef. What the rest of the company eats, so will the pilots and crews returning from the battlefield."

Pagel, a senior food-service career man, stood in silence and carefully listened to his new commanding officer. When Griggs finished, Pagel responded with the same resolute tone he had just heard from Griggs. The old NCO gave Griggs what he wanted to hear, but with a small caveat.

"Sir, I'll give you what you want," Pagel said, "and I assure you the troops will be happy with my performance. But I would like to ask for something in return. In my MOS, we are frequently overlooked and taken for granted when it comes to the career-building awards and decorations that most other troops receive. If I deliver on your demands and meet your high standards, I would really appreciate it if you would recommend me for a meritorious award of the Bronze Star. The Army is my home, and like all other *lifers*, I would like to advance as far as my ability takes me."

Initially Griggs was taken aback by Pagel's response but quickly recognized an achiever in Pagel—exactly what he hoped to have in all those who served under him. "Sergeant Pagel, I can assure you that you will be given every consideration that your performance deserves."

Pagel saluted Griggs and left the commander's office satisfied that he would get his due. Now, it was up to Pagel to upgrade the dining facility; however, Pagel only *shared* control. The dining facility at Bearcat was an ad hoc arrangement between several aviation companies. In accordance with Army protocol, combined missions were overseen by the senior person. Although Pagel was the senior person on-site, he knew that with the needs of more than one company on his shoulders, he had to be sure of his plan of improvement. After a few days of observing the dining-facility operation, Pagel figured out the problem and developed his plan.

"Too many spoons in the pot spoil the soup!" Pagel said.

He requested and was given authority to personally select the menu and handle most of the tasking. Using his own recipes, within weeks, significant improvement was evident. Throughout his tour, the food quality remained exceptional. When Griggs rotated, he recommended Pagel for a meritorious Bronze Star. The award was eventually presented to Pagel by MAJ Petric, the commander who followed Griggs. Decades later, in 1999, SFC Pagel called Griggs and thanked him for the award recommendation. At that time, Pagel was retired from the military and was working as the food-service supervisor for the Saint John's Hospital in Springfield, Missouri.

Hot food for the helicopter assault troops is just one example of Griggs's diplomacy, ability to deal with people, and focus on maintaining the unit's momentum and morale. No doubt, hot food and high morale helped to bolster the unit's mission and perhaps, indirectly at least, also helped save American lives.

Griggs had an extraordinary grasp of the unit's airmobile mission. He knew the importance of passing on his knowledge, garnered from many months of combat-assault experience in the 191st, to his subordinates. Where other unit commanders struggled to inculcate in their troops their reason for being in Vietnam, the combat-assault tactics used, and the safety rules essential for survivability, Griggs excelled. In fact, he shared this information with passion. Sitting with a group of new arrivals, the CO patiently explained the mission of the 191st and their role in the unit.

"You see," Griggs began his speech to new 191st pilots, "events that led to our present tactical operations started several years ago here in Vietnam, in the Ia Drang Valley, when the North Vietnamese Army and US forces first met in combat."

Griggs had firsthand operational experience in the Ia Drang Valley as an assistant operations officer of the First Airborne Brigade, First Cavalry Division. It was there that the airmobile concept, rehearsed at Fort Benning by the Eleventh Air Assault Division, was first put to the test in combat. Helicopters were used to insert, resupply, and mobilize the 1st/7th Cavalry in their battle to defeat a much larger enemy unit and proved to be the most effective way of fighting this war. In that battle, through the employment of airmobile infantry, an entire NVA division was nearly destroyed—even NVA's finest troops could not compete. Helicopters proved invaluable.

From these early engagements came a change in the enemy's tactics that had prevailed on the battlefield for centuries before in Vietnam. In a conventional war, opposing forces generally assemble their attack or defense formations along parallel lines, each facing each other, with the so-called offense seeking commanding terrain overlooking the enemy troop concentrations. During World War II, and again during the Korean War, these battle lines could stretch for over a hundred miles. These parallel lines were called the FEBA, an acronym for forward edge of the battle area.

In between these opposing FEBA lines lies the battle area, known as the *killing fields*. This killing field is where the shredding of human flesh is processed by the war machinery invented explicitly for that purpose. For eons, this type of combat-force deployment has received a high priority in the tactical-planning sequence of military operations. War history is rich with battle outcomes that were determined by the effective use of key terrain along the FEBA. Vietnam, however, was different. In this terrain of thick jungles that seemed to cradle enemy troops, there was no FEBA.

"As soon as you fly out of Bearcat, you are over unsecure territory," Griggs said to his troops. The newly assigned pilots leaned in and listened intently.

"As a proving ground for American weapons and munitions produced during the arms race of the Cold War, Vietnam has revealed to the world that American battlefield technology reigns supreme in conventional warfare. After only a handful of major engagements, the NVA and the VC quickly learned that there is little wisdom in facing American forces in a line formation. To do so would squander these precious human resources. After only a few major battles where the enemy got their asses decisively kicked, they quickly learned that it was better to melt into the jungle and attack our rear echelons, where America's least-mobile support elements are situated, such as field hospitals, general support maintenance facilities, and supply depots. But we can't sell them short either, especially the NVA."

Griggs paused, making eye contact with his men. "They can be fierce warriors," he said. "And they come with a long history of war in this region. When circumstances are decisively in their favor, they will not hesitate to face us in a conventional clash. We learned as much during Tet this year. During the Tet Offensive, the enemy attacked across the entire region of South Vietnam. But following their resounding defeat, the enemy action has now shifted to a guerrilla campaign. So, most of the tactics we will be employing are designed to support the infantry units in a guerrilla war. But don't feel any disappointment over the downscaled violence. You can rest assured that sometime during your tour with the 191st, you will participate in several conventional battles where the action will be intense and your mental faculties will be challenged to the max. These will happen with little or no warning. For that reason, it would be wise to avoid letting complacency relax your guard. You may go in and out of several insertions where no shots are fired; however, in the next LZ, the world suddenly explodes all around you."

Discerning the aircrews' reactions, Griggs knew he captured the newbies' attention. Among the new pilots were two commissioned officers, 1LT Richard Coates and 1LT John Falcon, who had arrived together the day before. Falcon was an infantry officer, and his career development depended on what Griggs had to say. Falcon leaned forward in his chair and soaked up every word.

"This radical change in their fighting strategy was forced upon the NVA by the introduction of American airmobile tactics, which is where *we* come into the picture," Griggs explained. "Air mobility has given US commanders the firepower and maneuverability to cover much larger geographic areas with fewer troops. This eliminated the need to physically occupy all the ground taken from the enemy. Any terrain, forward areas or rear echelons, can be assaulted from the air. Vertical envelopment can be achieved from any direction. Thus, holding captured ground has become less important than the ability to outmaneuver and outgun the enemy wherever they make a stand. Our birds give the infantry that capability. Assigned much larger areas to secure than what had been the case for their predecessors in previous wars, the expense of holding and improving all the territory seized in battle has become less attractive to American field commanders. With helicopters, it is believed that a battalion-sized unit can secure an area that, by proportion in World War II, would have required an entire Army division. Thus, the age-old practice of measuring war progress by the amount of enemy territory captured has been replaced by tactical attrition of enemy forces through vertical envelopment."

Griggs paused. "This is the strength and purpose of the airmobile concept." He tapped his desk for emphasis. As Griggs spoke, the *whop-whop-whop* of Hueys approaching seemed to rumble the air in Falcon's lungs. The smell of jet exhaust drifted into the orderly room and accented Griggs's voice. A formation of slicks lifted off, and the noise was loud and distinct as the ten sets of rotor blades displaced air and rose to face another battle. The smell of JP-4 fumes wafted in more pungent than before. The entire aura of the commander's briefing coupled with the flight activity occurring outside generated excitement among the newly assigned aviators. Heretofore, anticipation of real combat was just that, an idea. Now the threshold to battle was at hand. Griggs's words were firing up the warrior in Falcon. The newly assigned combat-assault pilot was ready for action, and he patiently waited to hear more from Griggs.

"And this shift in strategy has become the preferred tactical solution when deciding what to do with captured territory," Griggs continued. "The whole idea is to deplete the enemy's strength with superior firepower and maneuverability, without the American expense of occupying every square foot of captured ground. The liberated South Vietnamese are thereafter supposed to secure and occupy their own country. Our job is to help the US combat forces, and our allies, neutralize the enemy threat in South Vietnam. Thus, here in Vietnam, there are no established lines that represent a battlefront of any permanence. The downside to this strategy is that there is no measure of security beyond the ground physically occupied by friendly forces. There is no distinct measure of success or failure based on ground gained by offensive action. It has everything to do with the attrition of enemy forces by our tactical efficiency."

Griggs's emphasis on destruction of enemy forces versus captured ground was strategically planned at the highest command level and well before the 191st entered the war.

"In effect," Griggs continued, "by the time the 191st Assault Helicopter Company entered the Vietnam War, the layout of hostile and friendly soil had clearly been established. Unable to forcibly deny the enemy any terrain between friendly installations, death can come from any quarter outside of friendly compounds. Remember that!" Griggs again tapped his desk for emphasis. "Allied forces, including the 191st, must quickly adapt to that threat. Again, let me repeat that United States soldiers must know that once they depart a friendly compound, everyone is at risk."

At this point, Griggs relaxed his posture and leaned back in his chair before continuing. "That is the big picture," he said. His audience breathed a sigh and relaxed their postures as well. Reality quickly became ingrained in the mind of each newly arrived 191st pilot. Griggs saw to that. Scanning the newbies eye to eye, Griggs looked for signs of boredom among his pilots and became satisfied he held their undivided attention. He *liked* what he saw.

"Now let us get down to the core components of how we operate. The mission of the 191st is to provide airmobile support for the Ninth Infantry Division and other units identified. In clearer terms, on a daily basis we execute combat-assault operations in support of the Ninth Division. Command-and-control operations are always under the control of the unit CO, the XO, or the operations officer. So, a typical day occurs as follows: The C&C aircraft and crew depart Bearcat in early morning ahead of the flight, to establish initial contact with the infantry unit. Some thirty minutes or so later, the company flight of ten lift ships and four gunships departs. Recognize, at this point, that the *daily* company requirement is for fifteen helicopters. Up to now in our history, this requirement has never been missed.

"Combat assaults do not just happen; they are planned in detail, coordinated as necessary, briefed to all, and executed on time. The C&C commander arrives at the headquarters of the first unit to be supported and is briefed on the mission. He then provides guidance to flight lead and the Bounty Hunters. The flight may report to a preselected secure area to await mission instructions or fly directly to an extraction point to transport an infantry element from their overnight site. They might be transported to a base camp or to assault another area of suspected enemy activity. Most days begin this same way."

Griggs scanned the new pilots for hints of any procedural confusion before continuing. Satisfied, he moved on.

"A very important aspect of a combat assault is to select a touchdown point that allows gunship fire-support to both flanks. In other words, do not land close to a tree line. This is where the enemy will be hidden and where the gunships need to place covering fire."

At this point in the briefing Falcon and Coates recalled their ground school instructors during flight school. Most of them were ex–Vietnam War pilots, and they had revealed the same experiences as Griggs described in his briefing. Not only did the newbies lock their attention on what their new commander was saying, but they vividly envisioned what they learned in flight school. Its lethality came clearly into focus: *Death lurks in the trees. Stay away from tree lines.* The message was loud and clear. Falcon and Coates, neither knowing of their classmate's feeling, felt a surge of blood tingle on the back of their necks.

"Of course, this is not always possible," Griggs said. "Many times, the troops being supported will have a mission of searching the stream or palm line and will want to land as close as possible to these hostile areas. The intended touchdown point will usually be selected by the C&C commander and relayed to the lead gunship commander. The gunships in most assaults will pop smoke to signify the touchdown point. You will learn this and all the other small but important aspects of combat assaults during your first weeks when you will be flying as a copilot under supervision of an experienced AC.

"You will also learn that safety is a way of life with a Boomerang. Early in the Vietnam history of the 191st, there was a rash of helicopter crashes and the company came under close scrutiny from all higher commanders. Many of these accidents were caused by aviators exceeding safety limits to better support the infantrymen. Never forget you will be flying a D-model Huey, which is not a powerful lift helicopter. Normally our ships will carry six American infantrymen in addition to the flight crew. Always be concerned with your weight and balance. If your fuel tank is less than full, of course your payload can increase. There may be those occasions when you need to extract more than six infantrymen from a hot LZ. In such a situation, there is very little time for decision-making. Remember, *six* men saved is better than *eight* men killed or injured in a helicopter crash. In such a situation, you may be the AC—the one making this difficult decision.

"There are also my pet-peeve safety measures. Never let me catch you flying with your sleeves rolled up. Hover slowly in the revetment area and take extreme care. Consider this area like a school zone. When you are flying, your weapon must always be on your body. Do not hang it over your seat. During my first week back in Vietnam, I was flying as a copilot with a young, aggressive aviator who was the AC and we were involved in an accident. The helicopter was submerged in a river. Guess where my weapon was the last time I saw it?"

Griggs looked at the fresh faces of his new men. Falcon, having been a hunter since he was twelve, knew to keep his gun holstered and on his body.

"Correct," Griggs said, acknowledging the pilots' answers. "It was in the holster hanging on the back of my seat."

The audience snickered but knew the seriousness of the commander's advice.

"I don't remember how much I paid the Army for the loss of that pistol," Griggs said. "The monetary loss was not as bad as the lecture from my commander. Formation flying is also an important safety concern. There seems to be a belief that tight formation flying takes courage. This is not true. It really takes a dumb person to overlap a tail rotor with a rotor blade. The 191st does not fly a dangerous formation. We do, however, keep our ships tight enough that our gunships can cover the flight. Fly like a professional Army aviator, the way you were taught in flight school.

"Responsibility as an officer and a leader is important to you and to the unit. Normally, each aviator is assigned to one helicopter, and each platoon normally has ten helicopters. Providing guidance and assistance to your crew chief helps to ensure the helicopter is available for the next mission. Remember the crew chief pulls double duty. Maintenance of the helicopter is his responsibility, and he is also the second-door gunner on the aircraft. When the mission is over and the bird returns at the end of the day, the work for the crew chief is not over. He has to prepare the helicopter and his machine gun for the next day's mission. You as an officer assigned to that aircraft are expected to provide assistance to the crew chief. Let him know you understand his position and, when necessary, provide guidance. Check on him during the evening and make sure he is getting support from the maintenance shop. Be a part of the maintenance on your ship. There is more to your duty than flying."

Griggs paused for a moment and gave all the men a good, hard look. At first meeting, it's hard to judge what a group of warriors has in them. Soon enough, they would all show their worth and grit.

"My last point is to ensure you understand everything about the command-and-control of our combat-assault operations. The C&C aircraft is the tactical operations center for all combat operations. The aviators flying this aircraft coordinate every operation with the infantry commander and then direct every aspect of the mission. This aircraft is a *special* ship in that it is rigged with a console of radios separate from the aircraft radios. This provides the infantry commander the capability to communicate with his units and with supporting artillery.

"In this unit, the C&C mission commander will be the CO, the XO, or the operations officer. Those individuals would typically fly every third day. However, important staff duties on the ground frequently take one of these key officers out of the rotation. So, judging from the entries in my own flight record, there may be periods of time when they fly every other day. The 191st has an outstanding reputation with the Ninth Division battalion commanders. I believe there are two reasons for this. First, there is the attitude of everyone in the company. To the best of our ability, we support the infantry with an airmobile lift capability and with immediate air-to-ground fire support. Second, all the Ninth Division battalion commanders know the C&C commanders and have learned to trust them."

Leaving the briefing, Falcon looked at Coates and said, "Well, Dick, are you ready for this?"

"I reckon so," Coates said. "But only time will tell if we survive to tell about it."

"No shit!"

Both newbies made their way to the mess hall for a cup of coffee and to digest all that Griggs had laid out for them.

Because Griggs had spent far more time with the unit than other commanders, who stayed less than six months, he had been stung with the bitterness of losing men in combat in far greater numbers. He was deeply sensitive over the loss of each Boomerang or Bounty Hunter, and he agonized over the depressing tasks that followed. Griggs's worst moments in Vietnam were attending memorial services and writing letters to the next of kin.

"In my opinion, the exposure to hostile fire required of assault-helicopter pilots and crews made our job one of the most hazardous on the battlefield," Griggs explains. "Volumes have been written about the exploits of the cav and about medevac pilots. But in reality, *we* routinely performed the same missions for which those units are revered in history, except that our efforts occurred in relative obscurity. We were attached to the Ninth Infantry Division, OPCON to their airmobile demands, but seldom identified as factors in *their* battle outcomes. Most documented headlines referred to the units of the Ninth Division as victorious in battle while *supported* by helicopters. Why hell—*we* were those helicopters! But seldom would the 191st AHC be mentioned in those accounts. It was almost as if we were inanimate objects. Yet our troops bled and died just like the rest, if not more. That was hard to swallow, and now in retrospect, it still burns a bit."

***

On October 10, 1968, MAJ Griggs sent CPT Falcon to Long Binh on a supply run for aircraft parts. Although assigned as platoon leader of a flight platoon, Falcon had a background in logistics, which gave the unit an advantage in scrounging equipment and supplies. Before reverting back to Infantry Branch so he could fly helicopters, Falcon was initially commissioned in ordnance at Aberdeen Proving Ground, Maryland. Many of his APG classmates were now assigned to the huge supply depot at Long Binh. Griggs knew that Falcon could shorten the downtime of grounded aircraft awaiting parts when he called him to his office.

Summoned personally by the commander from among the newbies, all who heard the runner's message wondered what Falcon had done to deserve the commander's attention. Falcon proceeded to the orderly room posthaste. Mentally, the first lieutenant was also wondering what the hell he might have done. Worse, the admin officer was waiting Falcon's arrival and went into the CO's office ahead of Falcon to announce his presence. *Oh shit!* Falcon thought.

Ushered into Griggs's office, the admin officer motioned for Falcon to enter and closed the door behind him. Rigidly, Falcon approached the commander's desk and rendered a snappy salute. "Sir! Lieutenant Falcon reports as directed." Griggs returned the salute and motioned for Falcon to sit down.

"Lieutenant Falcon, we are short on parts, which is keeping some of our birds grounded. I noticed that you were commissioned in ordnance. With your background, do you think you could navigate your way through the depot at Long Binh and expedite our parts' orders?"

Falcon breathed a big sigh of relief. At that moment, he could have jumped with joy. Relieved that his summons was an opportunity to excel and not an ass-chewing session for whatever one of his troops might have done, Falcon quickly accepted the challenge.

"Yes, sir. I'll give it a shot. I haven't been there and don't know what I might run into, but I understand the procurement process well enough; so, if the parts are there, I should be able to get them."

"Great. Get the admin officer, First Lieutenant Radtke, to give you the keys to my Jeep and also the room assignment of Warrant Officer One Ross, who is in the hospital recovering from crash injuries. Please check on him while you're there."

"Yes, sir."

Decades later, Falcon reminiscences on that conversation and his assignment. "I had no idea how far Long Binh was from Bearcat by road nor how to find the depot, but I had a map and felt certain I could get there. There was no driver assigned to the vehicle, so it was recommended by the admin officer that I go by the supply room and check out an M16 with a few magazines of ammo.

"Before departing Bearcat," Falcon recalls. "I tracked down SP4 Alan G. Maw, one of my platoon's outstanding door gunners, and asked about a reliable M16AR. His immediate answer was, 'Sir, take the one assigned to me. I'll check it out for you. I know it works well, and it's maintained as it should be.' It was not a warm and fuzzy feeling knowing that I might have to engage any enemy force alone. As an infantry officer, ground assignments were part of my job, but at least in an infantry unit I would have company. Driving across thirty miles of jungle road alone, through enemy territory, was not my idea of playing infantry. But Griggs knew that other unit vehicles used the road frequently, and those trips went off without a hitch. The hard part came when I checked on WO1 Jerome Ross and learned he had died that morning."

WO1 Morris Jerome Ross hailed from Seattle, Washington, where he had been employed by the Boeing Company before he was called up for military service. He was twenty-six years old and married to Marcia.

"I'll never forget the look on Griggs's face," Falcon continues, "when I returned to Bearcat and gave him the bad news. It was the next day, during the memorial ceremony, when it finally sank in. I hadn't been there long enough to know Ross, but I could see the hurt in those who did. Later, I would have my own turn losing people with whom I'd bonded daily, and I got to feel the pain in losing brothers-in-arms."

Griggs genuinely demonstrated concern for the men he commanded, and it was clear to Falcon why the pilots appreciated his presence and leadership. Often flying with CW2 Eric James Rebstock, an outstanding second platoon AC with considerable combat experience, Falcon appreciated the superb tactical proficiency the AC had acquired under Griggs. This proficiency Rebstock passed on to Falcon. As a warning to Falcon, Rebstock cited the crash of August 12, 1968, with CPT Arnold Wayne Luke, which killed all aboard including Copilot Terry Roy Jens Jr., Crew Chief SP5 Gerald A. Wilson, and Gunner SP4 Arturo D. Montion.

Rebstock shared how the accident could have been avoided. "CPT Luke lacked experience, and during an engine failure, he pulled pitch instead of lowering the collective. He ended up with insufficient rpm to autorotate. All aboard were killed."

CPT Arnold Wayne Luke was twenty-seven years old, from Los Angeles, California, and received the Air Medal, among others. He was known as Buddy to his family. Copilot Terry Roy Jens Jr. was twenty-one years old and from Seattle, Washington. He received a Bronze Star, among other awards. Crew Chief SP5 Gerald A. Wilson was twenty-three years old and from Hilton, New York. He received a Bronze Star, among other awards. Gunner SP4 Arturo D. Montion was twenty-one years old and from Stockton, California. He received a Bronze Star, among other awards.

"Well, Eric, it's a shame that Captain Luke did not take advantage of learning from pilots with more experience. It might have saved the life of that entire crew."

"You're right. It pays to gain a little time on the stick before attempting to take control."

Rebstock followed up CPT Luke's fatal crash by telling Falcon about another crash that occurred on June 5, 1968. "Another similar case was the crash that killed Warrant Officer One Jeffrey Yarger and Crew Chief Specialist Five Harold Shelby Wood Jr. The AC flying that bird banked left low to the ground and the blades hit. That close to the ground, the AC should have known to temper his angle of bank. This mistake killed Yarger and Wood."

The AC, WO1 Hawkins, and the gunner, SP4 D. L. Potter, survived the crash. The copilot, WO1 Jeffrey Yarger, hailed from Edgerton, Ohio, where he had attended the Spartan School of Aeronautics before being called up to serve his county. He was just shy of his twenty-third birthday when he was killed in this crash. The crew chief, SP5 Harold Shelby Wood Jr., was twenty-five years old and hailed from Kentucky, but traveled often in his youth since his father was a chief warrant officer in the US Army. Both Yarger and Wood had received numerous medals, including Distinguished Flying Cross and the Bronze Star.

Falcon mentally filed away the wisdom in Rebstock's words and applied *lessons learned* to his leadership role in his new position as second flight-platoon leader. Quietly he thanked his lucky stars for being assigned to a unit with the command and staff talent possessed by the 191st.

And no one knew that better than the XO under Griggs, MAJ John Jones. Although filling a company position in a higher echelon than Falcon, as a C&C pilot flying combat assaults, he faced similar life-or-death circumstances. Assigned to the company with only fixed-wing experience as an O-1 Bird Dog pilot, Jones was overwhelmed when first introduced to combat assaults. "When MAJ Jones arrived," Griggs recalls, "he flew with me in the C&C ship, to begin his training as a C&C commander. Well, it turned out to be a really bad day. Several aircraft were hit by enemy fire, and the C&C ship went in and out of hot LZs several times to insert and extract infantry commanders, plus their wounded. The following day, Jones flew with the operations officer and experienced very similar battle conditions. Then, a day later he flew with me, and *again*, the results were the same. Purely as an incidental part of war, some days are more difficult than others. Jones just happened to get three really bad ones in a row, and his nerves were shot."

On his third night at Bearcat, Jones sat at the bar in the club—his head in his hands. Griggs walked into the club and approached him.

"Cal," Jones said, "I can't take a year of this. There is no way I can survive."

Realizing Jones had seen more combat in three days than during his entire previous tour, Griggs knew he needed encouragement. "He perked up a bit," Griggs recalls, "after I told him he would not be flying every day and that he had incidentally hit three hard days in a row, which was not the norm. He eventually assimilated the airmobile tactics and became a great XO and effective mission commander."

Again, Griggs's compassion won out. Other commanders might have taken issue with Jones's shaky start. Not Griggs. He nurtured the newbie's fears into a sound performance.

Unbeknown to his troops and his commanders, Griggs drew from an extensive background of combat operations. Serving as assistant operations officer with the First Airborne Brigade of the First Cavalry Division, he had an excellent foundation of infantry and airmobile tactics, and he took advantage of this experience and knowledge.

"Sometime during the July through August time frame of 1968," Griggs recalls, "the unit suffered combat losses that caught the attention of the assistant division commander of the Ninth Infantry. Both LTC Paul Anderson, the 214th Aviation battalion commander, and I were called to his office. Not knowing the nature of this summons, we were both apprehensive. As we both entered the general's office and saluted, the general jumped out of his chair and came over to give me a big manly hug. It was then that I recognized Brigadier General [BG] Elvy B. Roberts, who had been my brigade commander in the First Cavalry Division. He received LTC

Anderson and myself in a casual and friendly tone, giving both the LTC Anderson and myself a measure of relief from what we expected."

Griggs and Anderson both relaxed a bit as the general continued.

"Major Griggs, I didn't know you were the commander of the Boomerangs," General Roberts said after giving him a warm hug. Roberts looked at LTC Anderson and shook his hand. "Colonel, you are really lucky to have Major Griggs as a commander of one of your companies."

The meeting culminated into an uplifting experience for Griggs. Before it was over, Roberts asked Griggs if there was anything he could do to assist him. Griggs knew exactly what he needed to mesh the tasks and responsibilities between the 191st AHC's airmobile asset and the Ninth Infantry Division troops.

"Specifically," Griggs recalls, "I explained that if the infantry units we supported would assemble in open areas that provided some standoff distance from tree lines and jungle habitats that could potentially conceal enemy troops, it would provide a tactical advantage. I explained that our ships were sitting ducks while in LZs and PZs. By forming in the center of the larger openings in the jungle, it might offer some advantage from small-arms fire. I suggested we keep the exact point of touchdown approximately one hundred meters away from the edge of trees. He agreed and said he would look into the matter. As he adjourned the meeting, General Roberts thanked us for the outstanding support we gave the division and offered an open door if we needed him. I never told LTC Anderson that I had served with BG Roberts while assigned to the First Cavalry Division."

On another similar occasion, during an era when *Hawk Whip 6*, the call sign for the First Aviation brigade commander, would have a dramatic effect on his subordinates, Griggs got a call from operations saying that BG Paul F. Smith was inbound to visit the 191st.

"Immediately I called and informed my battalion commander, LTC Anderson," Griggs recalls. "LTC Anderson knew that the general had a reputation for using a heavy hand during these unannounced visits. LTC Anderson could not make it to my location to share in the outcome, so he promptly wished me well and said he would 'pray for me.' As the general's bird landed at Bearcat, I instructed operations to vector the general's helicopter to the maintenance ramp, where I met him with a sharp salute and a solemn composure. When he exited the aircraft, I recognized the general as someone I had served with during my earlier days with the cav. At that time, the general had been a lieutenant colonel in command of the supply-and-transportation battalion of the First Cavalry Division. His battalion had responsibility for the defense of a certain portion of the First Cav base-camp perimeter. As a captain assigned to a brigade that, on occasion, had overall base-camp perimeter–defense responsibility, I would frequently be sent to inspect his defense sector."

Recognizing Griggs instantly, General Smith returned the salute with a warm smile. "Well now, it appears that it is my turn to inspect *you* today."

The general's soft and reassuring words relaxed Griggs for a brief instant. Being in inspection mode, Griggs returned a guarded smile. "Yes, sir," he said, responding in his most respectful tone.

Griggs elaborated on the incident years later: "My thoughts were still in inspection mode, and I was very tense when he asked that I take him to the mess hall for a cup of coffee. We sat and discussed First Cav operations and 191st AHC combat-assault operations for about an hour before the general departed with complimentary words about the good job we were doing. He thanked me and left. Immediately following the general's departure, LTC Anderson appeared at my office for a full report. He couldn't believe that the general's visit had not brought down the wrath he had expected. I never gave the battalion commander the whole story."

MAJ Griggs successfully completed his command assignment on October 10, 1968, when he was replaced by MAJ John Petric. Many of Griggs's policies and customs remained in effect long after his departure, a high tribute to any departing commander, and his contributions to the unit were viewed by all of his subordinates with high esteem that remains through today. In recognition of his leadership style and performance, he was promoted to lieutenant colonel below the zone, and he went on to become a full colonel before retiring.

Completing his thirteen-month tour with the 191st, Griggs returned to the US, gathered his family, and moved to Fort Benning, Georgia, to continue his Army career. Retiring in 1987 from the Army as a colonel, Griggs accepted a position as director of Army instruction with the Indianapolis Public School System. Remaining there ten years, he retired in 1997 and moved to Fremont Hills, Missouri, where he now enjoys full retirement with his wife, Marguerite. Their oldest daughter, age eleven when Griggs returned from Vietnam, became Doctor Belinda Symmes and is now retired as the director of the Missouri Math Academy. Their son, Gary Michael, age eight upon his father's return, retired as an Army colonel. Their youngest daughter, Cathy Carney, at the tender age of four when her daddy returned safely home, presently heads volunteer functions for her church in Tulsa, Oklahoma. Indeed, a great American family.

Retired COL Griggs and his wife, Marguerite, remain joyous for such a blessed family and the blissful gifts of life. But in Griggs's heart beats the memory of the men who bravely served—who lived and died—under his command.

"As a commander," Griggs explains, "the hardest thing in the world is to write the next of kin and tell them about the death of their loved one. There are no words that can possibly relieve the pain. And after seeing it happen so many times, you become even more sensitive to the loss. It has a cumulative effect on any leader who cares for his troops."

CHAPTER 15

Crew Trust

No regret for the relationships built on trust and forged in the skies above Vietnam.

If all pilots, crewmembers, and support personnel who served with the 191st were asked to identify one element that fueled their combat effectiveness, most would cite *crew trust*. The key to the success of every combat mission in Vietnam was relationships. The ritual of a finely tuned team that trusted one another was paramount to their life-and-death struggles. Each day in combat strengthened this trust so much that when a crew change occurred it was almost traumatic. A crew death was especially debilitating. It not only destroyed a key element of the team's physical chemistry, but for a while it radically changed the synchronization of their combat employment.

All eyes focused on the replacement of the unit's lost comrade. Each life was at stake when a newbie or FNG was on board, because no one could be sure if he could be trusted with the lives of his fellow soldiers. Although combat has a way of meshing personalities into a unified effort, on occasion diametric characters would react out of sync, especially in gunships where killing is the mission. This mission can be particularly troubling to some. Not all minds have the psyche to execute a human being without having, or despite having, regret. Regret, however, was a potentially deadly feeling to court, especially when bullets were chewing up a slick's underbelly as it climbed to safety with a load of extracted ground soldiers. A moment of hesitation from any crewmember could end tragically for all souls on board. So, it's no wonder that the crews eyed the new guy with cautious skepticism until he was fully accepted. Acceptance could take days, weeks, months. But for some, acceptance never got a chance to be earned.

Planning, in every aspect, had to take into account the replacement, whether he was experienced or inexperienced. Critical elements of employing a gunship—preparing it for battle, attacking a target, breaking off from a gun run, choosing which side of a slick formation to cover—had idiosyncrasies, making each crewmember's function and experience level a crucial matter. Little compares in immensity to entrusting one's survival to the combined performance of a combat-assault aircrew. Those of the 191st AHC exercised this ritual of trust daily as if it would mean life or death. On most occasions, it did.

Among many examples of crew trust is one that occurred on June 1, 1968. On that day SP4 Richard Calton was awarded the Air Medal with V-device for valor. His award citation commended his actions as "heroism while engaged in aerial flight in connection with military operations against a hostile force: Specialist Four Calton distinguished himself by exceptionally valorous actions while serving as door gunner of an armed UH-1C helicopter engaged in combat-assault operations near Tan An. While he was delivering devastating suppressive fire on enemy emplacements, his M60 machine gun jammed. He immediately attempted to clear the weapon when a live round exploded, wounding him in the right arm and shoulder. With complete disregard for his bleeding wounds, he cleared the weapon and directed devastating suppressive fire on the enemy." Calton performed under the dicey circumstances that all aircrewmen trusted one another to perform. Only *he* could cover his side of the ship, and he did so while bleeding from wounds received in action. That is the type of behavior that earned crew trust.

Getting the bejeezus scared out of you was simply part of the job as an assault-helicopter crewmember. This reality turned crystal clear when confronted by an army of enemy soldiers in prepared battle sites and predisposed to kill you at first chance. In microseconds, this nightmare of a job took on a new meaning when, before your eyes, the enemy terminated the life of the guy beside you—the comrade with whom you shared a drink and a laugh just the night before, who showed you a picture of his sweetheart he was hoping to come home to in a few months, whom the whole crew counted on to get them out alive. The shock was earth-shattering. The jolt would take multiple passes through cognitive thought before the brain recognized it for what it was: his death was final. He would never again joke around, toast a cold brew, or return home to his family or sweetheart.

Human losses among young Americans bonded by war temporarily affected continuity of operations. Separated from home at a tender age, their call to service left a familial void readily filled by barracks roommates. Next to blood kin, the loss of fellow comrades summoned pain that struck at the whole gamut of emotions. The pain was almost indescribable and assailed the minds of survivors. The faces of those closest to the dead displayed a deep sadness seen by all, and it remained in some for weeks on end. In others, the experience literally changed their personalities. According to older service veterans, these soldiers finally adopted their soldier maturity and built up emotional blocks against death. Those warriors self-treated their mindsets, knowing such frequent losses were unavoidable. The aura spilled over onto treatment of replacement crewmembers. The newbie or FNG assimilation underwent trust issues that required time to overcome, time for survivors to cork emotional seepage caused by previous deaths of close friends. Transposed into a tactical scenario impacting new arrivals, the test for newbies was measured by their actions following "Show us why we should vest emotional matter in you." Each defensive and offensive part of the combat-assault maneuver was vested individually upon a certain crewmember. Any weakness thereof placed the entire crew at risk. All aspects of the assault posed different death propensities, and it took several battles to ferret out the intrepid composition of a new warrior. Once accepted as a battle-worthy member of the team, his place among the established crew was given earned respect.

Combat defies description, and short of having been there, the emotional blow is indescribable. With the possibility of death an everyday threat, trust in one another to react as a team made the decisive difference in survival. Who better to share thoughts about this aircrew reliance than SP4 Gerald "Jerry" Kahn?

Kahn was one of many brave young soldiers who lived it and now wears the scars of war. He served his country as a gunner on a UH-1C Huey gunship, perhaps the most action-packed occupation of the Vietnam War. Born March 6, 1949, in Long Island, New York, he grew up as the second oldest among a family of five boys. His experience at Lindenhurst High School included football and wrestling. His father, a WWII veteran retired from the Army, served as a role model of high military standards for him to emulate. Kahn Senior, recipient of numerous decorations, including the Silver Star and the Bronze Star for valorous actions, had hoped that one of his children might follow his example. His son, Jerry Kahn, stepped up to the plate and served admirably.

As a Bounty Hunter, the young Kahn witnessed the wide-eyed view of the battlefield experienced by attack-helicopter crews—a view often harrowing but sometimes spectacular. He placed his life on the line with each mission to protect the troop-carrying Boomerang flights from ground fire during combat assaults. In an equally deadly risk, Kahn and the Bounty Hunters supported the infantry when they were in close combat with the enemy. Attacking fortified enemy emplacements was, in his words, a "tough row to hoe." It required Bounty Hunter backbone, and Kahn, with a strong backbone and a heavy dose of American grit, was a premier gunner in the heat of battle. Having joined the unit at Fort Bragg before its deployment to RVN, Kahn extended his combat tour several times in order to continue serving in this high-risk position; he was one of only two 191st soldiers known to have done so. It wasn't until an enemy bullet shattered his right wrist so severely that it never regained complete function that Kahn left the combat zone.

"Looking back and describing my experiences in Vietnam after so many years is a challenge," Kahn explains. "While some of the more poignant memories have softened with time, others have slipped into the mental recycle bin. Yet, the distinctive *whop-whop-whop* of a Huey rotor blade still causes our heads to turn in unison to locate the source of that familiar sound. Similarly, an unexpected detonation of fireworks, a volley of gunfire, or even a whiff of expended gunpowder during hunting season can trigger instinctive reactions developed for survival during a Vietnam tour. All too often those memories we thought were gone return with crystal clarity when prompted by an image, a sound, a smell, or an adrenaline rush.

"Choosing to go back and examine these experiences was not one of my smarter undertakings. Trying to do so without forming an opinion about some of those episodes was impossible. For helicopter crewmen who served on UH-1C gunships with the 191st AHC, the training included being able to complete the mission in a hostile environment long before the first shot fired by the enemy. We accepted, and some even thrived on, the smell of burnt gunpowder or being splattered by the greasy spray of the LSA gun lubricant blowing back onto our faces and uniforms as we directed our M60 machine guns to fire at the enemy. Contributing to this high-adrenaline experience were the *whoosh* of rockets leaving the tube, the occasional smack on the leg from the cap flying off as the fins deployed a foot away, the ear-shattering roar and the physical assault of the sound waves hammering your body, your flight helmet rattling around on your head when the minigun fired an arm's length away.

"More passive, but equally stimulating, was the gentle *thump* of the rarely used [in UH-1C gunships] but devastating forty-millimeter grenade launcher firing from the nose of the ship. The 'falling elevator' maneuver, when the power is chopped and the helicopter drops like old Wile E. Coyote off a cliff, is reminiscent of a steroid rush. It's one hell of a ride. Equally energizing are the explosions of adrenaline coursing through your body when your helicopter screams down a road barely ten feet off the ground with the engine roaring and Steppenwolf's 'Born to Be Wild' floods your earphones from the Armed Forces Vietnam [AFVN] radio coming over the ADF.[1] And you're heading back into a firefight. Or when just before reaching the AO, the ship snaps up into the sky, straining for altitude, and with it standing on its tail, nearly stalled, it drops over sideways, completing a wingover that slips into a gun run, and you fight the g-forces to bring your machine gun to bear on the enemy. All this time, there is nothing but a thin, ten-foot monkey strap keeping you from falling to oblivion. This is an example of just another gunship day with the 191st AHC.

"With these sights, sounds, and sensations playing in the background, the enemy actions are thrown into the equation. You lean out the door or you step outside the crew compartment to put fire where it's needed, and you feel the slipstream snapping your pant legs. Sometimes it feels like a sledgehammer pounding your ship as bullets penetrate the helicopter's thin skin. This is the heart of the matter. At this point, you are decisively engaged with the enemy. Every action by each crewmember counts toward survival. It's either *you* or the bastards who are trying to kill you.

---

1 ADF, or automatic direction finder, is a type of radio navigation system. The ADF receiver will pick up music when tuned into a local AM radio station.

"The other side of that exchange comes when an unlucky crewman or pilot feels the sudden impact and the spray of blood as an enemy round finds its mark on his body. For some, it is fatal; and with death, the pain disappears. For others, it begins like a slap in the face—the bullet traverses flesh, pushing the blood and pain away from the wound. But with the returning blood flow, the pain surges again, building until it almost becomes unbearable. Like most things, it also passes, or at least you hope it will.

"These were the things we lived with, the things that became carved into our memories. If you were smart you accepted them and tried not to think about the land of the big PX,[2] as some thought of home. Neither was it healthy to think about 'Susie easy lay,' a new fast car, or going back to school and getting rich. These thoughts were all fine and well *after* you got home, but thinking of them during a lull in a combat mission didn't serve any constructive purpose and meant you weren't really paying attention to your environment. Thoughts of home, of your future, could lead to your death, or worse, your entire crew's demise. These are some of the faded memories awakened unexpectedly by a familiar sight, sound, or smell, which refresh thoughts of those days so many years ago with the 191st AHC."

Trust made the difference—and the speed at which that trust was delivered was a matter of life and death. Gunships moved much faster than ground attacks. Each crewmember had to function efficiently and react quickly. There was no time for lengthy communications. All had to function in synchronized actions. A new guy's inexperience or even his inability to quickly mesh with his aircrew affected this hard-won trust, which affected speed and performance.

"To begin with," Kahn continues, "a Huey crew is made up of four individuals, usually from different regions of the country, with their accompanying preconceived notions regarding other regions and backgrounds. They bring different skill sets, likes and dislikes, and usually different reasons for being in Vietnam. The Army must take many pegs and fit them into a corresponding number of holes. With appropriate training, it produces aircrews with average skills. But to achieve the synergy of a well-oiled machine, it takes time and experience with the same individuals, to develop mutual trust that the combined team will do exactly what is needed at precisely the right time.

"There is usually a marked difference between gunship pilots and slick pilots. Most of the pilots who flew in the gun platoon had already cut their teeth in slicks and proved they were decent pilots. The lift platoons, on the other hand, received most of the new pilots. This is not to say that lift platoons didn't have good pilots. They did. However, it took time and experience to learn how to react soundly at critical moments, and some pilots simply took much longer to learn in this environment. In my book, it was difficult to entrust my life to a green pilot, or some hotshot, who thought it was fun to overlap rotor blades while flying in formation or who

---

2 Post Exchange, an Army base retail store

would pull some other bonehead stunt that cut down on my chances of surviving my tour of duty.

"Now, like most Americans, I've had some firsthand experience dealing with assholes, so in my introduction to combat with the 191st AHC, I wasn't interested in dealing with an idiot in the front seat who not only might kill himself but also the entire crew. I've heard it said that 'there are old pilots and there are bold pilots, but there are no old, bold pilots.' I decided that if I was going to be killed, I much preferred that it be the result of enemy action rather than stupidity. So, I joined the gun platoon without a second thought. This occurred in either October or November of 1967, while CPT Stack was the platoon leader. He was as tough as they come, a great pilot, and fearless. I would later come to realize that he was the model for a good gun-platoon leader. Some had it, others didn't.

"Before my first flight with CPT Stack, I had an opportunity to crew a gunship as gunner with a well-seasoned and good-natured crew chief. That was my beginning of learning crew trust. I vividly recall my introduction to the aircraft. It was a minigun ship, tail number 715, which had a butterfly painted on the doors. It was done in a psychedelic style, and I'm fairly sure SP5 Richard Weske, from one of the lift platoons, painted the artwork. He did so for Crew Chief August 'Gus' Kramer. Each side of *The Elusive Butterfly*, as it was subsequently known, carried a minigun and seven 2.75-inch rockets in an XM158 launcher mounted to external racks. And each minigun was fed by a continuous ammo belt carefully placed on a series of metal cans that ran the length of the crew cabin. A metal chute ran from the outermost can to the feed intake on each minigun. Each time the gun was reloaded, ammo belts needed to be carefully checked for any misaligned links or rounds and then smoothly laid on top of each can so there would be no drag or hang-up when the belts were fed into the gun. The slightest misalignment could jam the weapon at a critical time. Great care was given to preparing the 'feed trough' for this beast. Depending on where we rearmed, whether it was a forward infantry firebase, a major divisional base camp, or an airfield, we sometimes needed to connect fifteen 100-round belts together for each gun. Each minigun normally fired 1,500 rounds per minute, which put a great deal of strain on each of the six bolts inside the gun. A little too much wear on the bolt could impede the extraction of expended rounds from the gun and also cause a jam.

"NASCAR fans thrilled by the performance of pit crews during races would appreciate watching a gunship crew rearming and refueling during a firefight. The crew chief held a refueling hose over his shoulder from a blivet [a rubber fuel bladder] to top off the fuel tank while either the AC or the copilot, along with the gunner, hotfooted it to gather up the rockets and ammo cans needed to rearm. After the ship was topped off with fuel, the pilot hovered it over to the rearm point, and the gunner dropped the barrels from the minigun, replaced any failing bolts, and then lubed and reassembled the gun. Then they slung fourteen rockets into the pods, checked the ammo belts for alignment, and laid in six thousand rounds of 7.62-millimeter ammo for the miniguns and the door guns. Simultaneously, they checked the ship for battle damage. The goal was to be in the air and on the way back to the AO in ten minutes or less. That's the teamwork that saved American lives on the battlefield.

"Gunships usually flew in what was called a light fire team made up of a lead and cover ship. For each mission the 191st AHC was required to supply eleven slicks: one C&C bird and five birds from each of two flight platoons. Plus, two light fire teams [two pairs of gunships]. During a mission, *one* light fire team covered the flight of *ten* slicks while they picked up troops and escorted them in transit to the AO. The second light fire team flew straight to the AO to complete a reconnaissance of the area and clear it for the flight's next troop insertion. It was a well-rehearsed and well-coordinated operation down to the last bullet, rocket, and minute."

Again, it was trust in your crew that got a Huey in and out of a hot LZ. For Gunner Kahn, building confidence in those he flew with started back at Fort Bragg before the unit deployed.

"I first met 'Heinie' [Heinmiller] at Fort Bragg, North Carolina," Kahn explains, "when the 191st AHC was being assembled from bits and pieces of other aviation units. This included pilots, crew chiefs, and gunners, many fresh out of school. Heinie and I were as different as night and day. Me, I was fairly quiet and introspective with a quick temper that had landed me in trouble on more than one occasion. Whereas Heinie was one of those bright, friendly, and easygoing kind of guys who could talk to and get along with anyone. As far as I know, there wasn't anyone in the company who didn't think highly of him. Herein again, trust comes into the picture. Heinie had it by simply exhibiting a character no one questioned. In Hollywood, he would be typecast as a Jimmy Stewart in a *Mr. Smith Goes to Vietnam* sort of movie. Hollywood would describe my character as brooding. I had to earn my trust the hard way, delivering strong weapon maintenance and field performance. Truly I loved the challenge.

"Heinie had been assigned to the company after graduating from the crew-chief school at Fort Rucker, Alabama. He hailed from California. I came from infantry advanced individual training [AIT] at Fort Polk, Louisiana, a.k.a. *Tiger Land*. The reason I was assigned to the 191st AHC? Well, my guess is it had to do with the fact that I qualified as an expert with the M60 machine gun when I was still only seventeen years old. I couldn't be shipped to Vietnam as an infantry replacement until I was eighteen. Heinie and I met each other right after I arrived at the 191st AHC, and we remained friendly. But since we were in different platoons, we didn't interact much. At that point, there were only two things we had in common, our approximate ages and both of us enlisted in the Army.

"Once we arrived in Vietnam, I was assigned to slicks in the first flight platoon [*Yellow Flight*] while Heinie flew cover in the gun platoon. Looking back, I was still very green and surprisingly immature. In Army lingo, I had my head up my ass.

One dark morning, while still half asleep, I had just finished mounting my machine gun on the slick's pintle, and without thinking, I loaded the gun. This action of course violated the SOP: *never* load the gun until you fly beyond the installation boundary. Then, while attaching the brass catcher, I knocked the safety off and the brass catcher slipped and hit the rod from the butterfly trigger—I almost killed myself. Fortunately, the muzzle end was not quite aligned with my head, so only my whiskers received the muzzle-flash burns.

"That evening after the mission, I had the pleasure of getting my ass chewed off by MAJ Patnode and then again the next day by the Ninth Infantry Division commander. These ass chewings were a real turning point for me. They drove home the realization that if I didn't pull my head out of my ass, I was going to get myself and perhaps some other people killed. I then stopped thinking about anything else that didn't have to do with being a door gunner, and I focused on being the best.

"Shortly thereafter, I found myself infused into the Pachyderms, also known as the Two Hundredth ASHC. There I joined a few others from the 191st AHC, gainfully boring holes in the sky and sling-loading supplies and artillery pieces around the Mekong Delta aboard a CH-47 Chinook helicopter. I valiantly fought off nosebleeds from flying much higher than I was used to, and I shot up rivers when the [senior] CW3 and CW4 pilots were bored and just wanted to hear the sound of the guns. I lasted about two months before I quit flying *Shithooks* and put in a request for a transfer back to the 191st AHC. At that time, I extended my tour for six months. When I returned to the 191st AHC, I was assigned to the slicks again. As I told the first sergeant at the Two Hundredth ASHC, if I was going to be in a war, I at least wanted to be able to see it.

"I still remember Heinie approaching me shortly after I returned to the company. Heinie's personality made him a natural roving ambassador, and he asked if I wanted to fly with the gun platoon. Enlisted crewmen have no say as to which pilots fly their aircraft. As far as the Army is concerned, if a pilot completes flight school, he is qualified. During my six months of flying with what I judged to be some less-than-adequate pilots, I disagreed with the Army's assessment. In retrospect, I truly believe that many young pilots were thrown into battle long before they were fully capable of handling the responsibility. Flying skills be damned! To go into battle, the *brain* needs training and preparation as well, and some new pilots simply weren't yet ready, something most any experienced crewmember could sense.

"For new pilots, their first combat encounters must have been the most unnerving experience they'd ever had. If they happened to be flying in the lead gunship, contact with the enemy was close and personal. You could literally see the other guy—the enemy—trying to take you out. At that moment, the emotions that go through your head are blood-freezing. It's as if you are living a nightmare where your body can't move fast enough and some monster is fixing to clamp humongous jaws on your ass to cut you in half—except that it is real, and death is staring you right in the face. It comes down to you or him.

"During my time flying in gunship 715," Kahn continues, "I often flew cover for the lead ship. Sometimes when my ship was down for inspections or major maintenance, I flew as gunner on other ships. Occasionally, I even got to fly on the lead ship. A few of those lead-ship missions stand out rather vividly in my memory, especially during the Tet Offensive of 1968. One such mission took place down on the Mekong Delta where I remember coming upon a village around Ben Tre. We buzzed in over the treetops. NVA flags were flying all across the area. Hundreds of people gathered in what appeared to be a big victory or indoctrination event right outside the village. This was obviously an enemy gathering, and I immediately focused on the command frequency to await orders from the C&C ship flying above us. Certain to have seen the same gathering, I assumed the delay in orders from C&C must have been indecision on the part of the command pilot or the ground commander.

"In the meantime, our lead pilot decided he wanted one of those flags. I leaned way out across the weapons systems as he flew by at around twenty knots so I could grab one for him and, of course, one for me. On each pass, I snatched the flags flying from what appeared to be a tall gateway. I was very happy that none of the flags were booby-trapped, or else it would have turned out to be a really bad day, indeed.

"When the C&C command group ultimately decided what they wanted done, I was told to fire at one individual in black pajamas who was surrounded by hundreds of other people as he ran toward the village. I fired a burst from my M60 beyond the crowd to see if I could scatter them away from the target. The pilot then began screaming at me not to hit the other people. Of course, I was perplexed. How was I supposed to hit this guy in the middle of a hundred people? Even if I could pick him out and hit him with every round, the bullets would probably go through him and hit the people running in front, in back, and beside him.

"Finally, the guy in black PJs made a break for it and hid in the corner of a rice paddy. We flew over him, and the pilot closed around him in a very tight circle. I began to fire at him but the skids were in the way. The fairly new pilot didn't realize, but he was flying virtually over the target while looking almost straight down so only *he* had an unobstructed view. Still, he continued to scream at me to hit the guy. What could I say? I let him scream. But once the pilot flipped the ship around, my crew chief got to kill the guy. In cases like that it simply doesn't pay to open your mouth; just let him scream. In this case, the pilot was not allowing enough angle for me to engage the target. He chose to give himself a front-row seat on the kill and sacrificed effectiveness from my side of the ship. This decision was clearly a case of pilot inexperience.

"Another time while flying with an AC, whose name I can't remember, again somewhere in the Mekong Delta, we were returning from a mission and I happened to glance below and toward the rear of the helicopter. I saw two guys in black PJs, with weapons, running down a paddy dike. I advised the AC on the intercom, and he broke back around and had me take them under fire. I shot one guy but the other ran into a hootch. Then both ships armed their weapon systems and rolled in with rocket and minigun fire on the dwelling. It seemed that most of the hootches in the Mekong Delta had built-in bunkers inside where the inhabitants could take cover in event of nearby military action. This custom came from many years of war against the Japanese, French, and later, the Americans. Unfortunately, it seemed the VC and NVA who took cover in the hootches pushed out the docile civilians who lived there and took the shelter for themselves. I assumed this after a woman, holding a baby in her arms, looked up at us. The AC simply said words to the effect, 'Oh well, these things happen in war,' and he went on to say that he would call in medical attention. But I truly believe he had no more intention of helping that woman than 'the man in the moon.' The AC then proceeded to roll in on the house with more rocket fire. The woman and baby disappeared. I never heard any more about the incident. Not knowing what orders my AC may have received from his higher commander, I can only assume it was a communication breakdown and not intentional. In any event, I truly hope the woman and baby survived the attack.

"Later, another pilot (I shall not name) became the AC for Bounty Hunter 715. We were still stationed at Bearcat, and the next day we were scheduled to fly an *ash-and-trash*. The mission derived its name as a gibe among the combat-assault crews who mocked the task for not having the machismo equivalence of battle. Ash-and-trash days were rare and well earned. On this occasion, our light fire team flew down to the Fifth SF camp to spend the evening. The idea was to give them ready access to our gunship support early the next morning. 'Mr. AC' spent the night hobnobbing with his old comrades. He and the other pilots went to dinner with the SF but left the enlisted crewmen to eat C rations and sleep by the ships. Such was the variability in character from one pilot to the next. A good officer would have looked after the crew accommodations before taking care of himself, but not Mr. AC. Now forty years later I can tell the truth: he was a jerk! Mr. AC exhibited a character so vile toward enlisted crewmembers that very few of us respected him. On one occasion, while we were on the flight line, he even tried to pick a fight with me—a physical scuffle. That day the little relationship we had ended. He must have sensed that I didn't like him from the get-go. But he was just one pilot. Many were really good and looked out for their crews.

"The next morning, Mr. AC and the other pilots returned somewhat worse from hangover-wear, and we flew out over some triple-canopy jungle to locate a patrol that was trying to break contact with a superior enemy force. The SF patrol on the ground popped smoke and had me put fire on top and around the smoke. I proceeded to fire close to 1,500 rounds into the target area. The SF were very appreciative. I also pretty much burned out the bolt in my M60 because I had been firing continuously without let up to keep the bad guys away. From what I was told, contact was broken. This was a prime example of how combat stresses equipment and the situation frequently dictates the action. I realized I was overstressing the machine-gun system. But the cost of its repair would not equate to the value of saving the American soldiers on the ground in their hour of need, locked in mortal combat with the enemy. At that moment, they needed all the fire support we could muster.

"On August 18, 1968, which I remember fairly well, I was still flying in 715 with my crew chief, SP5 Gus Kramer, and CW2 Bruce Campbell and WO Ronald M. Cederlund, AC and copilot respectively. That day, the 191st was having a hard time putting up and keeping up enough gunships to be able to provide cover for the slicks while also covering the infantry on the ground. It took all we could do to put up *three* Charlie-models that day, and gunship 715 was left to be the single gunship on-station to cover the flight. Being a lone gunship on-station to cover the entire flight of slicks is an uncomfortable situation. If you get shot down, there is no one to cover you. A lone gunship is especially vulnerable when it breaks off its gun run.

"That day, the pilots wanted their doors off, presumably to get more fresh air in the cockpit to stave off the heat. We were up around 1,500 feet AGL, keeping an eye out for anything out of place. Everything was nice and quiet. Of course, visibility from that altitude is nowhere as good as flying close to the earth. So, we really couldn't keep a *good* eye on things. But without a cover ship, we had no choice. It seemed to be about midday when we were bringing in another flight of infantry, and somehow an AH-1G Cobra gunship appeared on the scene to fly as our wingman. That truly boosted morale because they carry enormous firepower. But when the flight was on short final to the LZ, all hell broke loose. Slicks began calling that they were receiving fire, and the gravity of the situation was highlighted when an enemy bullet caused a minigun sight to explode in Platoon Leader Cederlund's hand.

"We broke off our gun run, and while I was putting fire under our ship to protect our vulnerable underbelly, I saw the Cobra, well up at *nosebleed* altitude. It was so high that its rocket fire was ineffective. Even worse, it broke off the gun run long before we were anywhere near clear the hot LZ. While we were coming around for another pass, I unhooked my M60 from its bungee cord and stepped around outside of the aircraft. I stood in the space were the pilot's door normally would be if we had left them on and dragged the ammunition belt behind me. We broke back around, and I swung my M60 forward to place fire directly in front of our ship hoping to suppress the enemy position that had shot out the minigun sight. Protecting the pilot was certainly self-serving, since his death could also mean mine as well. On this run, none of my pilots got hit so I guess it worked, but as we broke back around again, we took a hit in the transmission, and the master caution light illuminated. A shot-out transmission is usually a death knell for a Huey. As transmission oil drains, the gears heat up from lack of lubrication, and the transmission, which provides power to the main rotor, eventually seizes. If that happens, aircraft control is lost and that is seldom survivable.

"Campbell's ass experienced a super pucker factor when he called the Cobra and asked for covering fire while we withdrew from the area. They answered with words to the effect of, 'We have troubles of our own—we took some hits, too.' At that point, the suspense ramped up for our entire crew. We all knew that our rotor blade only had so many rotations before the transmission would likely freeze up. As the slicks departed the LZ after dropping off the troops, we headed for nearby Vinh Long on a wing and a prayer.

"As we flew over the river we were ordered to keep a few hundred rounds and throw the rest out with the ammo boxes and anything else that could become a missile if we went down hard. The problem with gunships, at least where door gunners were concerned, is that there were no seat belts. We only had monkey straps. We needed to be able to move around to put fire under or in front of the ship or reach out to hold the jettison handles for the weapons systems on takeoff. All we could do was hope that the monkey straps could keep us from the big fall. But in a crash, they didn't serve much purpose because they were generally slack. Besides, most of us at that time sat on a cushioned plate strapped across our ammo boxes, which were attached to a floor tie-down point. With no seats this day, we sat on the floor and simply hoped it was not our time to die. With incredible luck, we reached Vinh Long and quickly shut down. The sigh of relief exhaled by all of us could be heard from twenty meters away. AC Campbell and the peter pilot headed for the officer's club, most likely to wipe themselves, while Gus and I stayed with the ship.

"That day the 191st took one hell of a beating. If memory serves me right, we had fourteen ships either shot down or grounded for battle damage. Even the C&C ship, which flew at 1,500 feet AGL, went down. Later that day, as the sun was setting and I was flying back to Bearcat as a passenger on one of our slicks, I was proud of what the 191st AHC had done in that battle. Even though we did get our asses kicked, we stayed in the fight. We never turned away from the gunfire and continued the mission, calling in spare aircraft to put more troops on the ground. I could easily identify with grunts in such a high-volume firefight. It was murder in that LZ. Had we failed to deliver more reinforcements for the grunts on the ground, they would have been decimated. The odds against the ground soldiers and us were enormous, but we stayed the course and saved that day for the grunts. For his actions on August 18, 1968, Aircraft 715's AC, CW2 Bruce Campbell, received the Distinguished Flying Cross. Others on his crew received lesser awards although the fight included *every* man on board. The next day, for the first time since we arrived in Vietnam, the 191st AHC was unable to field the required eleven slicks and four gunships. The action did not let up; in just a month, we lost three gunships.

"Flying in the lead gunship meant nap-of-the-earth low, just barely clearing the trees or skimming over the ground with only a scant four or five feet of space between you and the hard earth. These are some really hairy maneuvers. Then add enemy fire raking your ship, and you got a pucker factor that sucks in some real underwear. The teamwork in this maneuvering was exceptional. Normally, the lead gunship would go low while the cover ship stayed high to provide fire support in event the lead gunship started receiving fire. Most often the minigun ships were the high bird because of the broad target area it could spray with bullets. Imagine a giant shotgun that could put a bullet in each square foot of a football field inside of a minute—and with only one burst. The lead ship, usually piloted by a platoon leader, was armed with two rocket pods that carried nineteen rockets on each side, plus the door guns used by a crew chief and gunner. Most times the low ship went in around ten to twenty feet off the ground. And when something caught the attention of one of the crew, the low ship sometimes came to a hover. Needless to say, that was a high-risk job. Despite the danger involved, this remained the most effective means of checking out LZs. On one such mission, CPT David C. Burch, who was the gun-platoon leader at the time, was killed by a gunshot to the head."

CPT Burch, the Bounty Hunter platoon leader, was an exceptionally brave, lead-by-example gun jockey. On September 3, 1968, Burch risked flying his gunship low over the hotly contested countryside to inspect a possible enemy emplacement and was shot down. His Huey crashed and burned, immediately killing CPT David C. Burch, Copilot WO Ronald M. Cederlund, and SGT Paul Reid Frazier, the assistant platoon sergeant. Only one of the crew survived, Gunner SP4 Edward Eugene Davis, who was thrown clear of the wreckage. Davis was evacuated to a medical facility with severe burns.

CPT Burch was twenty-four years old, hailed from Faison, North Carolina, and graduated from NC State University. He received the Distinguished Flying Cross, Silver Star Medal, and the Bronze Star, all posthumously. WO Ronald M. Cederlund grew up in Chicago, Illinois, and attended the University of Illinois until he was called up for military service. He was twenty-one years old and received the Distinguished Flying Cross, the Bronze Star, the Air Medal, and the Purple Heart, among others. SGT Paul Reid Frazier was nineteen years old and was from Milwaukee, Wisconsin. He is honored at the Honolulu National Memorial Cemetery of the Pacific's Courts of the Missing.

"Once again," Kahn continues, "Heinie approached me and asked if I wanted to fly with him and CPT Bruce Palmer. I didn't think twice before accepting the offer and immediately moved my gear over to my new ship. I learned somewhat later that Campbell threw a fit when I left his ship to fly with Heinie and CPT Palmer. He ranted and raved that 'the two best gunners in the company were now flying on one ship, and if it went down they would both be killed.' Of course, I kept my mouth shut while he vented and simply let the issue die over time.

"I was now flying on the lead ship with the new platoon leader, and I was able to bring all my experience to bear. It seemed that each day the crew bond grew stronger and stronger. The chemistry on this ship was a night-and-day difference from my previous bird, not just in the way the crew bonded but also in the mission itself, which was decisively different. We knew that getting down into the LZs and beating the bush was a dangerous undertaking. And we knew that the only way we were going to survive was by everyone being at the top of their game—and that meant every single day from the time we first fired up the helicopter to the time we shut it down at the end of the mission. Getting down below twenty feet and moving slowly across the LZs began to pay dividends. We were able to pick out things that didn't fit: colors which were off just a bit or piles of brush floating upstream against the current in canals and rivers. We soon discovered, more often than not, that there were people behind those oddities of color or under that pile of brush. The tactical AO was also changing. It seemed that most of our new missions took us west of Dong Tam, out where we ran into that buzz saw on August 18, and even farther northwest into the Plain of Reeds.

"One day while flying from one area in the Plain of Reeds to another, we were over a group of trees on a small stream and caught two enemy soldiers in a sampan wearing a full complement of combat webgear, powder-blue uniforms, pith-type helmets, and AK-47s. CPT Palmer snapped the helicopter up and around, and I brought them under fire, killing them before we finished our course reversal. That was some fairly hairy shooting, as I needed to nail them before they could unass the sampan and get back to the cover of the trees. I also had to keep track of my fire to keep it from hitting the rotor blades while we were in a steep turn. Many years later, I was told by one of my old platoon leaders that the individuals in the powder-blue uniforms had been Chinese advisors. Who would have known?"

There were many such things that had been left unknown to the pilots and crews during the Vietnam War. The point is, SP4 Kahn's fancy footwork would not have been possible if it wasn't for the trust he accorded each soldier aboard that flight. They had worked as a finely tuned team. Crew trust was paramount to their success—and their survival. Furthermore, crews had to trust their equipment as Kahn explains.

"Heinie and I did all sorts of experiments with our guns to make them fire faster and to make them lighter and easier to swing into action. We cut down guide-spring rods and added another spring to the ends of a full rod. We then cut off the bipods and flash suppressors on the barrels we used during the day. We tried mechanical buffers from the old M60 machine guns that were used prior to miniguns on UH-1B/C models, on OH-13s, and on OH-23s. We blew through a lot of bolts. One good thing about flying on a platoon leader's ship: we got better ash-and-trash missions to locations where we could trade up on machine-gun parts and other essentials. We traded some captured AK-47s to the Navy for a treasure trove of M60 parts."

In Vietnam, equipment parts were desperately needed, especially with missions into the land west of Dong Tam. At Dong Tam, the enemy had proved to be bolder and better equipped. Without question, trips out west took their toll on equipment. Heavy time out west had the potential of taking a toll on morale as well.

"Finally, we saw some relief," Kahn recalls. "After the 191st AHC had been pulling heavy blade time on rather difficult missions west of Dong Tam, we were given some time off for good behavior. We didn't get *actual* days off, but they were the next best thing: those coveted ash-and-trash missions. The best I remember was flying down to Nha Be, on the west bank of the Saigon River, approximately six nautical miles south-southeast of Saigon. This base housed a light fire team from the Seawolves, Navy SEAL teams, and Naval support activities.

"What was so great about this mission was the food at the Navy dining facility. Those guys knew how to live. In fact, the very first time I flew in there, we were told to go get something to eat before the missions. Now an Army breakfast isn't exactly something to write home about; it's kind of what we expected. But at Nha Be, as soon as we walked into their chow line, smiles lit up our faces. They served *real* eggs, not the powdered kind. It was a shock when the Navy cooks asked us how we wanted our eggs rather than just dishing out a scoop of greenish-yellow powdered eggs that you got in a normal Army mess hall. Then there were trays of ham, bacon, and sausage. It actually looked like it *hadn't* been cooked three hours ago. Plus, good coffee and even a milk machine. Yes, real milk! I thought I'd died and gone to heaven. These down days with their ash-and-trash missions provided a very welcome and much-needed respite. Combat assaults day in and day out wear heavily on the crews, not to mention the toll on the equipment.

"Our mission at Nha Be was to support the SEALs and to patrol the waterways south of Saigon in the Rung Sat Special Zone. The Rung Sat was an area consisting of the deltas of the Dong Nai, Nha Be, and Saigon Rivers, which were heavily infiltrated by the enemy. A vast mangrove swamp and tidal bog appeared to me like an endless uninhabited space where no civilization could exist. But through this area flowed vital shipping up the Saigon River to the waiting supply points in Saigon. General Westmoreland called it 'one of the most savage pieces of terrain in world.'

"When we finally went out to conduct our aerial patrol, we were told that the area was a free-fire zone and that anyone we found in the area was considered enemy and should be shot. As we flew around the area, we couldn't imagine how anyone could live in there. But a short time later, we came upon a stovepipe rising out of a mud island that looked like it was submerged during high tide. A very light wisp of smoke was coming out of the pipe. We became believers and fired rockets around the stovepipe and put machine-gun fire into the water around the island to try and catch anyone coming out of any tunnels. They might have been our enemy, but if they could live in that mudhole and continue fighting, they certainly had *my* respect.

"As we continued our patrol, we came across suspicious sampans sculling along the meandering channels that we took under fire. If we saw no weapons in the boats, we did our best to discourage them on the chance that they might have been innocent fisherman. Sampans were wooden boats, so we simply sank them with machine-gun fire without harming the occupant. If they were fishermen, their boats could be repaired, and we hoped that coming that close to death and losing their boat would discourage them from entering the zone again.

"On another occasion in the zone, we stumbled upon a number of armed VC or NVA that we took under fire. We got a few of them, but one soldier hid behind a tree. When we circled around, he kept on moving to the other side, always putting the tree between him and us. It was a game of 'Ring around the Rosy in the Rung Sat Special Zone.' So, we did the only thing we could: we shot the tree down and killed him. Although he became a statistic in a kill diary that I maintained, along with Heinmiller, I respected his tenacity. He had no quit in him. Just from his behavior, I suspected then, and even now, many decades later, that this guy was an NVA regular.

"After the Tet Offensive of 1968, the VC, as a fighting unit, had been destroyed, and the enemy units were then made up of NVA regulars—a totally different character, temperament, and disposition from the usual enemy resistance we were accustomed to with VC firefights. While the VC were basically a hit-to-scare-you-and-run force, the NVA would dig in their heels and fight like there was no tomorrow—and perhaps for them there wasn't.

"This guy that circled the tree just happened to get caught with his pants down, so to speak, but there was nothing cowardly about him. I have no doubt that if he had been carrying a weapon he would have done his best to kill me.

"After accumulating a few kills, I began to rehash in my mind the specifics of each individual enemy soldier. What was the individual doing when I engaged him? What was his reaction? What could have been different about the outcome? Personally, I always looked at the inverse order of things and tried to second-guess how he could have killed *me* if circumstances fell in his favor. It's scary as hell when you think about that too much. But it never hurts to role-play to be ready for the next engagement.

"One of my strangest memories of crew trust tested to the maximum occurred while working in the Rung Sat Special Zone. For that flight, it was Heinie, myself, CPT Palmer, and CPT Falcon. Falcon and Palmer were fellow Texans and carried on like two brothers. In that mission, trust between the two pilots was evident to all of us on the crew. CPT Falcon was the 191st AHC XO and had experience flying slicks. Palmer enjoyed his company. Besides, Falcon was tied to his desk with the never-ending boredom of logistics and administration, and he welcomed the opportunity to get away from the office and, better still, get the opportunity to fly a gunship.

"On this occasion, we returned to an area where, the week before, while flying with the same crew, including Falcon, we'd killed a pig in the reeds to deny it as a food source to the enemy. It was a wild animal because it was nowhere near any village, farm, or other habitable area, and it had the bristly appearance of a wild boar. As we overflew the area, we saw what appeared to be a giant crocodile eating the remains of the pig. This crocodile or whatever it was, appeared, from the air, to be well over ten feet long and about three feet high with four legs and very large claws. Its jaws were humongous with teeth to match, and it looked like it could cut a human in half with one bite. It looked to be a good source of food, but at the same time it was probably a danger to any human or animal in the area. We killed it and after expending about fifty rounds to make sure it was definitely dead, we landed beside it to get a closer look.

"Next to our helicopter, it appeared long and heavy with a height that came close to level with the deck in the crew cabin. The thought of vacating the bird to examine the croc closer was a bit troubling. But I wanted a piece of it for a souvenir, and I knew if the animal came alive I could rely on any of my crew to jump in and help. Nonetheless, leaving the gunner position and comfort of my M60 was like inviting death. Anything wrong occurring would literally be a self-inflicted wound since I didn't have to do this. But mentally I worked up the courage and leaped out next to the enormous reptile. A giant compared to me, I kept my eyes on him throughout the ordeal. CPT Palmer was looking out his window, and I was about a foot and a half away from it looking into its dead, cold eyes. I shivered a bit. My father had given me an original 1918 trench knife that had been given to him by his father. I took that knife out of one of the storage bins in the cabin, and with all the force I could put behind my 170 pounds, I stabbed down on the back of this creature. The blade didn't pierce its tough hide or even make a dent. We flew away scratching our heads and just a little bit awed by the beast. We were very glad we hadn't met it face to face on the ground. Years later, I read something suggesting that this may have been a relative of the Komodo dragon. In another reference, I also learned of an incident during WWII, when American troops had reportedly trapped a large group of Japanese soldiers down in mangrove swamps in the Gulf of Thailand a few hundred miles from where we were. During the night, the American soldiers said they could hear screams coming from the surrounded Japanese soldiers. It turned out that saltwater crocodiles, drawn by the smell of blood from the wounded, had sneaked up and were eating them.

"Perhaps the scariest incident during my initial tour and two extensions wasn't during a big firefight; it was a shootout between me and an enemy soldier about fifteen meters away. The crew was Heinie, CPT Palmer, and I think CPT Cook. It was, of course, partially due to my own stupidity and a lapse in concentration. We were in the Mekong Delta flying around checking out the area when I had to have a smoke. I rested my gun in my lap, took out my pack of cigarettes, and lit up. Just as I was putting my Zippo away, we flew over an enemy soldier with an AK-47 in his hand. With the lighter still in my right hand, I grabbed my M60 with my other hand and fired left-handed. The guy stood there, with his feet firmly planted, firing his rifle directly at me. So here I am, the only person in a position to fire at him. This wasn't the first time this type of thing had happened, but it was the first time I had to do it with my left hand. Anyone who has ever fired an M60 knows that the hot brass is extracted out the right side of gun.

"Hot brass from my gun zinged down the front of my shirt and was pressed against my chest and stomach by my chicken plate. The more I fired, the hotter the brass got until my skin started to blister and burn. But I can't stop firing, and I'm trying to keep focused on killing him. I moved the gun slightly as I watched my rounds hitting all around him while more hot brass flew down my shirt, the pain intensifying. Finally, the enemy shooter had enough and dove into a stream overgrown with vegetation. I stopped firing and was able to transfer the M60 back to my right hand. I lit up the place where he dropped into the water. I'm not sure if I finally hit him, but I stitched all the surrounding brush and water and saw no telltale activity or piles of brush floating away in the stream as was the standard practice. We finally left the area and headed back. After shutting down, I peeled off my shirt and finally saw all the burns on my chest and stomach. I never again let my machine gun rest on my lap, and I always kept the pistol grip in my right hand when I lit a smoke. When I checked the steel plate I was sitting on, I expected to find bite marks on it from my serious pucker factor."

Being the lone source of cover fire for survival of his entire crew, Kahn's actions were the true essence of crew trust. Exhibiting the grit necessary to keep firing while enduring the pain of brass burning his body, Kahn performed as his crew had expected and trusted he would.

Kahn continues: "Among the most spectacular exhibits of firepower on the battlefield were the Air Force fighter/bombers when they were working against enemy ground troops. Any occasion to watch those guys in action was entertaining. This particular incident might go under the heading of 'The Luckiest Air Force Fighter/Bomber Pilot in Vietnam.' Working in IV Corps, south and a bit west of Saigon, we were shut down at one of the Ninth Infantry Division base camps (it might have been a 3rd/39th camp around Rach Kien), when we first heard an Air Force fighter/bomber in a dive. The pilot ejected from his canopy and hit the silk. In seconds, we had untied and fired up our helicopter along with at least one other gunship and a few slicks. We were in the air in less than a minute. We left the ground so quickly that no one had the time to put on shirts, helmets, chicken plates, and flak vests. We began donning them as we headed for the pilot.

"We arrived over the guy before he even hit the ground with his chute. The gunships took up an orbit above the pilot, while one of our slicks went in to pick him up. The slick was released to take him into Saigon while the gunship went to check out the area where the jet crashed. We weren't sure if the jet had been shot down or had had an engine failure, so before we headed for the site we made sure that everyone in both crews had time to put on their chicken plates, flak jackets, and helmets. What we saw was perhaps the biggest hole we had ever seen. We were all fairly familiar with what the ground looked like after an artillery barrage, an air strike, and the even more impressive B-52 strikes, but *this* hole was at least twenty feet deep and about fifty feet across.

"Adding to that disturbing picture, just outside the hole lay the remains of an outer wall of what appeared to be a village church. I doubt the village or the church was the target, but a fully loaded fighter/bomber full of fuel and out of control has no friends. The devastation was enormous. There was no telling how much collateral damage had been done. If people were in that church, there would have been numerous casualties. You couldn't help but get a heavy feeling about the whole thing. When we returned to our base camp that evening, while on short final, we looked down and saw two burned enemy bodies on the wire, but that didn't even phase us anymore.

"There was one instance I remember in which we were extracting a unit from one PZ and assaulting into another LZ. The crew again was Heinie, CPT Palmer, and me, but I've forgotten who the copilot was. We were engaged in the extraction when the troops in the PZ came under sporadic small-arms fire. At that moment, we rolled in and were putting some fire on the area we believed was the source. Suddenly, mortar fire began impacting in and around the PZ. We pulled up from our gun runs to get some altitude and spotted the actual mortar that was firing. CPT Palmer quickly maneuvered the ship into position to attack the mortar crew.

"As we lined up on them, they lowered the tube and aimed the mortar at our aircraft. Murphy's Law seemingly always rears its ugly little head when you least expect it. The bolt on my M60 failed to extract an expended round, causing a jam. I quickly opened the feed tray, let the ammo belt fall, and dropped the gun to the floor. Snatching the M16 hanging over the back of the pilot's seat, I simultaneously grabbed the ammo box we kept in the same area, which was full of loaded magazines. I pulled back and released the charging handle, which chambered a round, and stuck it out the door. I fired the M16 on full auto, aiming at the mortar crew. A peculiarity with firing the M16 on full auto is that you go through a magazine in about five seconds, and it took more time to change mags and chamber a round than it did to expend one.

"Now I knew I had to keep up the fire to either take out the crew or those supporting the position, but I was overcome with the ridiculousness of the situation. Here I was, spraying nineteen rounds of 5.56 ammo downrange, and they were dropping mortar rounds into the tube and trying to aim at *us*. As we broke off our gun run and I expended the last magazine under our tail boom, I snatched up my M60 and cleared the jam. I felt much more useful with a real gun in my hands. We didn't have to make a second run on the position, as our light fire team's rockets, miniguns, door guns, and yes, those 5.56 rounds, had eliminated the threat.

"If you used a machine gun frequently, the one thing that you could always count on was a jam at the least opportune moment. If your gun became too hot you could get a *cookoff* in the barrel. If a round wasn't seated just right in its link, it could jam. If there was too much drag on the linked ammo as it fed from the ammo box to your door gun, it could jam. You always checked your ammo and the links, laid the ammo smoothly back and forth so it fed correctly. You kept your gun clean and checked all the moving parts for wear, but no matter how hard you tried, jams were an inevitable part of being a door gunner.

"One memorable jam occurred when I was flying down in the delta with CPT Palmer and, I believe, CPT Falcon and Heinie. We were cruising around at about twenty feet AGL when we came upon a Vietnamese national with a weapon. The person was leaning up against a tree with the weapon across his chest. The contact was called in to C&C, and we were given permission to fire on him. I had been keeping my M60 aimed in his general direction, and as soon as the order to shoot him was passed on to me by CPT Palmer, I snapped the gun around and fired off three rounds before the gun jammed and the enemy fell dead in a rice paddy. I changed the bolt on the M60 and had the gun back up in about two minutes. Hardly ever can a gunner, no matter how good he is, hit a man-sized target from a moving aircraft inside of three rounds. He was meant to die. As the day went on, it turned out to be a rather busy one, and we ended up with a number of confirmed kills. I fixed my gun and we flew back over the enemy I had shot earlier. We hovered low, and I jumped out to retrieve his weapon. It turned out to be an WWII-era M1, a good, accurate weapon when fired by someone who knew how to use it. But compared to more modern weapons, unless he was a sniper, he was truly outgunned.

"Looking back on this entire experience has been an exercise in frustration and one of emotional ups and downs. One never gets over the loss of close friends, and reliving those events only brings more grief at an age when it takes a different kind of toll. It becomes a memory download of harsh realities. It's amazing how you think more of those who died than those who lived. Those souls whom you knew like brothers are gone from this earth but not from your memory. Unless you are closely associated in normal everyday affairs with someone you served with, you actually think more often of the dead than the friends you visit at reunions. In fact, when you relive these events, you actually picture the departed as they were back then. You see their living young faces as if they had never left this earth, and you can vividly recall their mannerisms and voice tones. Reunions help a bit when reality brings you to see the contrast of old bodies and faces much changed from the person you knew in Vietnam. But those who died never age in your memory. They remain alive and well, and those recollections are with you forever. War does that to you. You bond in a way unlike any other association, fraternity, or good-old-boy group. It's a lifetime of blood brotherhood—no other trust is like it.

"The strength of your memory of the pilots and crews you flew with comes from the narrow scrapes with death that your collective actions experienced. The amazing part of this is that you don't see your own actions as the pivotal ingredient in your survival. Your actions come naturally, as an instinctive reaction to the powerful threat of combat death. When it knocks on your door, it's the actions of other crew members that surge to the forefront in your survival memory. This is where crew trust carves its way into your eternal memory bank. You forge the bonds that remain in your mind for the remainder of your life. This bond of trust is unbreakable."

Upon his retirement, Kahn returned to Long Island, New York, to settle down. He fished commercially to supplement the modest assistance the US government provides its disabled veterans. The Great South Bay, on the shores of Long Island, was his cash cow with harvests of scallops, crabs, and fish. Kahn continues to be a survivor with no regret for his service or his wound—and no regret for the relationships built on trust and forged in the skies above Vietnam. Today he will quickly tell you, "I'm a happy American who remains proud of my country and would serve again if called."

Among many other young men who served the 191st, SP4 Kahn performed admirably in a position where teamwork and team trust were an essential part of aircrew survival. Most amazing, the majority of those who served had just graduated from high school. Yet they made life-and-death decisions with enormous consequences for themselves and others. America is truly blessed to maintain a population of young lives so willing to risk death for the sake of our freedoms. Hence, they deserve our country's trust. But trust must flow both ways. It becomes us to occasionally remind our Washington politicians of this mutual trust.

CHAPTER 16

Maintenance Crew Crash

The aircraft's speed and altitude rested on the dead man's curve.

Two days before Valentine's Day in 1969, a maintenance crew left Dong Tam and headed two hundred miles northeast to Dong Ba Thin. They were heading out to inspect and, hopefully, ferry back a new Huey for the 191st AHC. Receiving a new aircraft was always a happy event. The unit was flying an aging fleet of battle-ravaged Hueys, described by some as "holy." This endearing nickname emerged from the usual holy-shit expression that came to mind when new pilots experienced the initial shaky and rickety first ride in a Boomerang vintage bird.

On this clear and pleasant morning, Janes, the senior pilot among the crew, wisely took the AC seat on the left side of the Huey. The rest of the crew positions were filled by Copilot WO1 James Patton and Crew Chief SP5 Stanley Allen. Also aboard were 1LT Michael Hannan, Specialist Six (SP6) Charles Dellinger, and SP4 Jimmie Sauls, all part of an experienced technical inspection (TI) team that would examine and approve the various components of the new Huey. The mission, as originally planned, called for Janes, Patton, and Allen to deliver the TI team to Bien Hoa for an Air Force hop to Dong Ba Thin and then fly to Vung Tau Aviation Repair Depot on a parts run. After a thorough preflight inspection, the group loaded into the bird with expectations of an uneventful flight. A few of the crew onboard hoped to steal some coveted time for leisure snoozing.

Janes had been flying combat assaults for eight months prior to his maintenance assignment and was very familiar with the flight route and the communication protocols. He hovered the bird out to the active runway and called the tower at Dong Tam for takeoff clearance.

"Dong Tam Tower, this is Boomerang One-Six-Nine-Three, ready for takeoff."

"Boomer Nine-Three, this is Dong Tam Tower, you are cleared for takeoff, sir. Have a nice day."

"This is Boomerang Nine-Three, roger. Thank you."

The flight departed and climbed to 1,200 feet AGL. After verifying flight conditions normal and all the gauges in the green, Janes called Capitol Center in Saigon on the UHF radio to report that he was departing with six souls on board.

"Capitol Center, this is Boomerang One-Six-Nine-Three, departing Dong Tam en route Bien Hoa, presently level at twelve hundred feet AGL, initializing transponder for ID."

"Boomerang Nine-Three, this is Capitol Center, transponder ID confirmed. Have a nice day, sir."

"Boomerang Nine-Three, roger, thank you. Out!"

Switching to the FM transmitter, Janes checked with Dong Tam Arty, the local artillery advisory, to ensure the flight route was clear of friendly artillery. Satisfied, Janes settled in for a routine flight. The flight path followed a commonly used corridor through Tan An and Saigon, which was advised for single-ship missions. Frequent US traffic on this route offered a measure of security in event of a forced landing or mechanical failure. Flying past Tan An, Ben Luc, and then along the river on the south side of Saigon, the bird had been in the air about an hour when it passed the water plant on the southeast side of town. Here, Janes picked up Highway 1A and followed it northeasterly. Twisting the radio transmitter selector to UHF, Janes reported his position to Capitol Center.

"Capitol Center, this is Boomerang Nine-Three, reporting water plant."

"Roger, Boomerang Nine-Three, still have you on radar. Have a nice day, sir."

"Boomerang Nine-Three, roger!"

A minute later, a loud grinding sound rumbled from behind the rear cargo-bay bulkhead. A high-pitched vibration and chatter came up through the floor and the tail-rotor controls. 1LT Michael Hannan, one of the TI team members riding in the back seat, tapped Janes on the shoulder. Janes reduced power and started a descent. Meanwhile, Hannan voiced his grave concern for the source of the noise.

A few seconds later, the racket ceased. Perhaps all was okay. *No such luck.*

The Huey violently yawed forty-five degrees to the right. With the Huey's nose out of the relative wind, the air-speed indicator dropped toward zero. Janes shoved the cyclic stick forward and right but to no avail. Again, he shoved the cyclic stick forward and farther and farther to the right, trying to follow the turn, which was now accelerating faster. With his controls not responding to his inputs, the months of combat-flying experience surged forward in Janes's mind. As common in these types of dire situations, his cognitive thinking raced while everything else appeared to be happening in slow motion.

Janes recognized the situation as a complete tail-rotor failure. The only means of survival: trust your training or trust divine intervention. A picture of the emergency section of the operator's manual popped into his mind. In the event of the total loss of tail-rotor thrust, the best solution *may* be to close the throttle and enter an autorotative glide. At the same time, Janes visualized the height/velocity chart in the manual. The aircraft's speed and altitude rested on the *dead man's curve*. At his current insufficient forward speed, the likelihood of a successful, power-off landing was significantly reduced below 250 feet AGL. Janes knew the situation was critical. His life, and that of his crew and passengers, was in serious peril.

"Mayday, Mayday, Mayday!" Janes announced over the radio. "Capitol Center, Boomerang Nine-Three is going down two miles east of the water plant with a tail-rotor failure. Can you assist?"

"Roger, stand by!" Center made an emergency broadcast on their frequency, asking for any aircraft in the area to assist the flailing Boomerang.

"Roger," a nearby aircraft replied. "Have the Boomerang in sight and will follow him down."

Instinctively, Janes closed the throttle and bottomed the collective-pitch control to attempt a power-off emergency landing. While the main-rotor rpm remained sufficient, the forward airspeed was nearly nil and the vertical-speed indicator was nearly pegged on the bottom side. The bird was falling. It descended in excess of 1,500 feet per minute, rotating clockwise out of control.

Experienced helicopter pilots view this scenario as the makings of a "real bad day." Janes was certain this one would be no exception. He spotted a plowed field of firm red soil nearby, but all efforts to maneuver in that direction failed. Power lines along the road beneath him loomed foremost in his mind. He knew they were going to hit hard, and he was resolved to their collective fate. The only thing left to do was hope that the Bell Helicopter engineers had allowed enough design margin to save the crew from certain death in a high-g vertical impact.

The earth rushed up to meet the crippled Huey, and Janes held the collective stick down. When the bird was abeam the power lines, he pulled the collective-pitch lever to its upper limit. For a split second, it looked like the vertical brakes had worked. But the bird hit hard while still turning to the right. On impact, the rear crosstube on the landing gear gave way, and the ship dropped to the left rear and rolled onto its left side. The main-rotor blade smacked the ground.

***

Janes woke up to the clattering *whop-whop-whop* of a Huey lifting off the ground. He was conscious and alive. Shaking his head and blinking to clear his vision, he eyed a pool of blood on the floor of the aircraft. Within seconds, he realized the blood was his. Pain reentered his consciousness. He made eye contact with one of the rescue crewmen. Momentarily, he gathered a measure of comfort in knowing that someone else also knew he was alive. His body relaxed, and he slipped back into unconsciousness.

Janes awoke again, but only barely, once the flight reached the Twenty-Fourth Medical Evacuation Hospital in Long Binh. Hands reached out and lifted his limp body onto a gurney and ushered him into a building. He felt his clothes and boots being cut away, hands touched, fingers probed.

"You're lucky!" a voice said. "You almost lost that eye."

An orderly came into view and holding Janes's dog tags. "Will you tell me your name and service number, sir?"

Janes responded with a half-conscious effort.

The gurney rolled again and arrived at the next station. Not unlike an assembly line in Detroit, this line was designed to fix broken human bodies. Needles pierced his flesh. More voices filtered in and asked where it hurt.

"Everywhere! I hurt everywhere!" The painkillers had not yet kicked in. The dog-tag orderly reappeared and asked Janes to recite his name and service number again. Begrudgingly, he responded.

Again, hands ushered Janes to another location. This time needle pricks stung like a swarm of bees. The doctor sutured his open wounds. Luckily, by this time, the painkillers had kicked in. Janes barely sensed the procedure. No sooner had the doctors finished when the dog-tag orderly came back and asked for his name and service number for a third time.

"Read the damned dog tags!"

The orderly laughed.

"Got a cigarette?" Janes asked him.

The orderly stuck a cigarette in his mouth and lit it. "You're going to be okay," he said and disappeared. Apparently, the orderly just wanted to make sure he was coherent enough to communicate the information. Janes never saw him again.

After recovering sufficiently, the first thing that entered the AC's mind was to inquire about the crew and passengers. He did not rest until he had visited each of the other 191st personnel and saw that they were alive and stable. All six of his fellow Boomerangs had survived the ordeal. In his mind, the Army lost a quarter-million-dollar piece of equipment, but nothing can equal the price of the lives that were spared.

During the tail rotor–failure event, Janes had only one control with which he could affect his destiny: the collective stick. The collective stick controls the pitch of the main-rotor blades. Without forward airspeed, the cyclic stick, which controls steering, was only partially effective. Even so, he managed to keep the aircraft level. The pedals, which are designed to maintain directional control, proved useless, however. By keeping his cool and fighting off the temptation to slow his descent with pitch, Janes saved enough rotor-blade inertia to significantly cushion the enormous rate of descent. His actions allowed him to survive the crash and save his fellow Boomerangs from certain death.

The aircraft accident report documented that UH-1 #64-13693 crashed at grid coordinates XS933981 with no fatalities. Death in war is not always about battle. Janes knew that he, his crew, and the maintenance passengers had just been spared. Providence? Perhaps! But he could not argue with any premise—he was alive.

Janes was grateful he and the crew survived the crash. The 191st had enough combat wounded and fatalities to contend with already. Janes finally relaxed a bit. As far as ferrying back a new Huey from Dong Ba Thin? Well, that happy event arrived on another day.

CHAPTER 17

Petric Commanding

"Boomer, can you land close to him? I'd like to body-snatch this guy if we can."

On October 10, 1968, MAJ John Petric, a tall, dark-headed, neatly dressed, Ohio native, replaced MAJ Carlvin Griggs as commander of the 191st AHC. Following the usual change-of-command ceremony, MAJ Petric immediately held a staff meeting with the unit's commissioned officers and the primary staff NCOs to explain his command philosophy and policies. The staff listened carefully; however, as usual, they adopted a wait-and-see attitude before forming an opinion of their new commander.

Petric assumed the helm of the 191st without first having spent time in the unit. Normally, officers from within the ranks of the company were chosen to replace their predecessors as COs. Thus, the assuming commander would have a working knowledge of the unit and its personnel before officially filling the new position. A measure of trust would have been already established, making the transition to a new commander a smoother ride. Only one other before Petric had taken over the unit without first having that working knowledge and trust. MAJ William Spurlock took the reins under similar circumstances behind the solid performance of MAJ Clarence Patnode, who had left a very positive and lasting impression with the troops. Some never saw Spurlock in the same favorable light with which they had regarded Patnode, who had assembled and trained with the unit at Fort Bragg for months before it deployed to Vietnam. With Petric's arrival, some crewmembers feared their future with Petric may be reminiscent of the Spurlock regime. Regrettably, some of the newer and younger 191st personnel were more inclined to be misled by some who had been with the company longer. Waiting to see the actual outcome of Petric's policies and leadership did not cross their mind. Instead they adopted the bias passed on by Petric's critics.

As a former fixed-wing pilot flying cargo planes, Petric entered the unit with no rotary-wing combat-assault experience, a common situation during that era. The Army had a process for selecting and developing officers with exceptional potential by assigning them to tactical command positions. These commands, at times, did not mirror their background and training. Petric evidently earned his command assignment by demonstrating outstanding leadership qualities at some point before coming to the 191st. Nonetheless, his limited tactical knowledge soon became apparent to the battle-calloused veterans and, therefore, placed the new CO in the awkward position of having to rely on his subordinates for direction.

What they didn't understand was that the 191st just happened to be lucky enough to get Patnode as its first CO. Patnode, who actually participated in developing the airmobile concept, was one of a kind. Other combat-assault units started with non-Patnodes. In effect, for the most part, assault-helicopter COs started with little or no airmobile experience. The concept was relatively new in the Army. Being assigned a new commander who did not have airmobile experience was actually the norm in most AHCs. Simply, those most critical of Petric were banking on their own combat-assault experience to degrade Petric's background. Little did they know they wouldn't make a freckle on his backside. Their experience and knowledge couldn't compare to all the critical command subjects that Petric had mastered.

A bright and able man, Petric could have easily mended these negative perceptions if he had not chosen his admin officer, 1LT Carl Radtke, for tactical guidance. A stroke of bad luck. An affable fellow, Radtke was a likeable soul with a gracious personality. But regrettably, although an outstanding and efficient admin officer, he possessed very little combat-assault time in a lift ship and virtually no experience in a gunship. Unbeknown to Petric, Radtke was ill prepared to offer wise counsel in tactical matters and was understandably reluctant to disclose that to his new commander. So, he chose to make the best of it. And Petric, new and inexperienced in an assault-helicopter company, responded to enough misguidance to reflect in his field performance. CPT Falcon could see the problem building but chose not to interfere between the CO and his admin officer. There were far more capable and experienced officers whom Petric could have turned to for counsel. Falcon assumed that Petric's superb mind would, soon enough, reach that conclusion. This would preclude the XO having an issue with the unit's admin officer. In fact, there were highly experienced combat-assault pilots in the 191st that Petric could have chosen as sounding boards.

The XO at the time, MAJ John Jones, was highly decorated and had combat experience. But for reasons unknown to the troops, Jones had not been offered the unit command. Another major, Rick Moore (pseudonym), assigned to the maintenance detachment, had also not been selected in favor of Petric. Jones and Moore represented the most senior commissioned experience in the unit. Many of the ol' salts wished to see Petric closely align himself with Jones and Moore, hoping that they could help the new commander to acquire the necessary combat experience faster. Their foremost concern was to help Petric learn the tactics that would enable him to safely coordinate airmobile operations with infantry commanders. Whether by choice or by circumstance, Petric remained distant from both majors, at least that's how the ol' salts in the 191st saw it. As a new commander, Petric remained under the watchful eye of the battle-hardened soldiers, a challenge in and of itself.

Another bump in the road that faced the new commander was relocating the company to Dong Tam, the Ninth Division's new base camp approximately fifty-six air miles southwest of the current base at Bearcat. In accordance with the preferences of the Republic of Vietnam, the presence of an American division in each ARVN corps region was politically significant. It represented commitment on the part of the United States. On that basis, the Ninth Division was ordered to Dong Tam and the 191st relocation followed close behind. From this point forward, the 191st AHC would be under the OPCON of the Ninth Infantry Division headquarters.

Petric selected CPT Falcon, the second platoon leader, to orchestrate this required move. With much forethought, Falcon carefully organized the convoy, arranged all communication links, including Bounty Hunter gunship cover, logistics, and administration for the big event. On "game day," Falcon safely led the procession without incident from Bearcat, across eighty miles of high-risk enemy terrain, to their new home situated on the north bank of the Mekong River adjacent to My Tho. Petric was delighted by how slick this important and complex move came off. Falcon's just reward for this accomplishment was soon to come.

MAJ John Jones, the XO, rotated back to the States, and that left only one other major in the unit, Rick Moore. Most believed that Moore would move up to fill the vacant XO slot. But Petric, far wiser in organizational dynamics than many of his underlings, appointed the unit's senior captain, John Falcon, as his XO. When called to the commander's office, the second flight-platoon leader had no earthly idea why he was being summoned.

"Come in, John. Sit down. You probably wonder why I've called you here," Petric said. Although greeting Falcon with warmth, Petric wasted no time getting to the point. He looked Falcon squarely in the eye. "John, you've been doing some good things. I need you to be my XO, I can see that you have the organizational skills I need here. I think you're equal to the challenge."

Falcon's mind raced. He imagined his workload increasing tenfold and his flight time taking a nose dive. Yet he welcomed the opportunity and recognized that it was an honor to be selected. However, he also recognized that he would go from a trusted member of a flight platoon to hatchet man for the boss. He only had to think about it briefly before he gave his response.

"Sir! It'll be a pleasure to serve as your XO. I'll give you my best effort."

Having chosen Falcon as XO, Petric had a combat-arms officer with some combat-assault experience and also one who already had a leadership following among the 191st troops.

When Petric announced his choice, it came as quite a surprise to the unit, especially to those who felt they deserved the post instead of Falcon. MAJ Moore in the maintenance detachment was thought to have been a shoe-in, and several other majors working at battalion headquarters would have jumped at the chance to fill Jones's vacancy. Nevertheless, it was a done deal.

Things will be very different tomorrow, Falcon thought.

Falcon's appointment had one redeeming benefit: he was now privileged to hear all the complaints the unit officers were reluctant to take to the commander. It gave the unit a relief valve that was always open. But the old cliché "familiarity breeds contempt" would soon manifest itself and place the new XO squarely at odds with MAJ Moore and Radtke, the admin officer, who just so happened to be roommates. Radtke, being the soft heart that he was, identified with Moore in the mix of things. Because he feared showing disloyalty to his roommate, he remained reluctant to show strong support for the new XO. To smooth things with the new XO, Radtke admitted this dilemma to Falcon. Since he had to room with Moore, he hoped Falcon would understand the bad position he was in. Falcon assured Radtke that it mattered little to him as long as he did his job, and he took the time to briefly commend Radtke for his admin performance.

"You're doing a great job, Carl, and besides, you and I don't have enough rank to sweat the politics between the two majors. Just keep doing the good work you're doing—you'll be fine."

Meanwhile, Petric relied on his XO for all the unpleasant tasks that XOs typically perform. Building a huge bunker for the officers of the 191st was the first of many—unpleasant mainly because it kept the XO out of the air and on the ground most of the time. Not only did this make for a very unhappy new XO, it also pushed him toward the combat-assault platoons for fellowship. In the evenings, Falcon sought out the flight-platoon pilots while Petric consulted Radtke about 191st administration. At least in this fashion, Falcon could stay in touch with what was happening in the field. When enough pilots reached their flight-time maximums for the month, the XO would get a chance to fly by virtue of the pilot shortage. Only then would Petric relent and allow Falcon to fly without pressuring him about his ground duties.

Being very orderly, Petric maintained an organizational schematic in his mind, with components that to him represented an ongoing production cycle. "Good planning and execution equals results," Petric would often say. He frequently shared these thoughts with the younger XO, in a nurturing manner. The young captain appreciated Petric's depth of perspective in logistics management, but he still yearned for the cockpit. Originally commissioned in the Ordnance Corps, Falcon had branch-transferred to infantry just to get back into combat arms. Having served in the infantry for several years before going to OCS, by comparison, Falcon viewed the XO slot as boring and harmless to the enemy. Like most pilots of his age, Falcon preferred to be amidst the action.

During the early feeling-out process, the new commander did not initially gain the appreciation of his officers and men. Though he meant well, Petric stumbled a few times before he won a following of his troops. One of his setbacks occurred after receiving a drink invitation from a group of Bounty Hunters, which included CPT Bruce Palmer, a small but fiery, action-packed gunship pilot from Texas; 1LT John Cook, a New Jersey Italian with iron-clad vertebrae; and 1LT Mike Arruti, a tall, quiet, sandy-haired youngster who could kill with the coolness of a stoic crocodile. The collective group of Bounty Hunters invited Petric to the Long Branch Saloon for a drink. To be sociable, Petric accepted. But the following morning, Petric called the XO to his office and ordered that all the lewd pictures of naked girls be removed from the walls of the Long Branch Saloon. Reluctantly, Falcon passed the order on to the Bounty Hunter platoon leader, CPT Palmer, who was, to put it nicely, livid.

"What the fuck does he expect—monks? They're *men* for Chrissakes!"

Radtke overheard Palmer's booming voice echoing all the way from the other end of the orderly room. When Palmer left, Radtke appeared at the XO's door to ask about the commotion, but Falcon, with a casual shrug, dismissed the incident.

"Never mind, Carl," Falcon said. "This is not something that you need to get involved with."

Palmer, Cook, and Arruti collectively represented the command element of the gun platoon for three tours, each succeeding the other with Palmer replacing CPT Burch after he was killed while flying his gunship at a low level to inspect a possible enemy emplacement. All of these Bounty Hunter pilots were known for their aggressive engagement with the enemy. They seldom regarded their own lives in the mix of combat. Protecting the Boomerang flight was their badge of honor, and they wore it proudly. And rightly so, for they were held in high regard by all pilots and crews of the 191st, who appreciated the substantial supporting fire they could wield. Their gunners were also tough as nails, but not the hardware-store variety. These gunners were tough as fléchettes, the sharp-pointed, hardened steel darts on folding-fin rocket warheads, better known as "nails." And they loved to kill VC. Among their kind, it was a them-or-us attitude—and they were out to make damn sure it was *them* and not one of their brothers.

From this devil-be-damned style of fighting emerged the idea for engraving a pair of brass testicles on a plaque as a keepsake for departing Bounty Hunters. Petric was invited to make the first presentation. A by-the-book commander, Petric viewed the plaque as crass and unprofessional. Incongruent with this humor, Petric squelched the celebration, or so he thought.

"The Bounty Hunters will have to find another way," he said. And they did. They simply held their own going-away ceremonies at the Long Branch Saloon—without Petric.

Handicapped by inexperience, the well-meaning Petric couldn't grasp the futility of attempting to force morality on a spirited bunch of fight-to-the-death warriors. Had he accepted the Bounty Hunters' offer to participate, he would have likely gained respect amongst this prideful group. More than likely it would have made them more inclined to follow him and support his policies. But it was not to be.

Petric would not subjugate his values for acceptance, and the Bounty Hunters begrudgingly went along without him "for the hell of it!"

Most any casual observer watching Bounty Hunter activities day in and day out would realize that people who go out daily and kill other human beings develop a certain mindset that separates them from other, more polite and civil people. Petric seemed unwilling, however, to make allowance for the nature of combat in an assault-helicopter company. As a logistics officer, he simply wasn't conditioned to the combat-assault frame of mind.

On the technical-service side, Petric was a superb logistician and ranked among the top in his officer class. Petric conducted meetings with exceptional management acumen and thereby elicited outstanding technical productivity from his staff. His task organization was well planned, and he followed up consistently. At meetings with the officers, Petric specifically asked Falcon for progress reports on all projects, and the XO diligently reported the status of each without ever assigning these responsibilities to his subordinates. Soon it became apparent to the platoon leaders that Falcon, although not shy by any stretch of the imagination, was reluctant to use his authority to delegate some of these details down to them. Coming from a flight platoon, Falcon understood the need for placing the mission needs first and recognized that he must be willing to accept whatever assets were left after filling the flight assignments. This allowed the platoon leaders to remain primarily focused on the mission, but it also instituted a rare phenomenon: the pilots began to volunteer their help.

A tribute to the quality of people Petric had under his command, the officer's bunker began to take shape. CPT Rugg, first flight-platoon leader, volunteered first, followed by 1LT Henry F. "Fred" Walburn, who had replaced Falcon as the second flight-platoon leader. Rugg brought with him a group of his pilots, and Walburn followed suit. Needless to say, Petric exhibited a happy demeanor as the project took shape. Walburn, an easygoing Alabamian, liked and respected by all his fellow pilots, eventually assumed the lead role in completing the bunker project. During his down days, the pleasant Southerner diligently appeared at the bunker site and hammered away with a bunch of his officers by his side. Once in a while, when the platoon leaders were both flying, the XO took a walkabout through the BOQ and snagged the poor unsuspecting souls who had the misfortune and poor judgment of having stayed in bed until well after sunup. Being snagged for bunker duty was not a pleasant affair. Petric, a stickler for an honest day's work, was pleased.

During the bunker project, word came of an impending inspector general (IG) inspection. Again, the 191st XO was tasked with responsibility for the preparation. It wasn't long before the pilots learned to hightail it out of the company area early on down days lest Falcon, whom the pilots had nicknamed "The Hawk," volunteered them for bunker duty.

Gradually, Petric bonded with the new XO, and Falcon accepted his logistics and administrative role in the tradition of a unit XO. By moving his personal belongings into the BOQ room vacated by Jones, Falcon lived next door to Petric. The two parleyed on company matters during evening lulls. At one of these sessions, Petric asked Falcon for his recommendation in filling the soon-to-be-vacant operations officer position. Immediately, Falcon recommended CPT Bruce Palmer, the gun-platoon leader, a good friend, and fellow Texan. Palmer and Falcon frequently tipped a few suds together and the two carried on like two frat brothers, constantly heckling one another. Above all, Palmer was whip smart and an experienced tactical planner—just what Petric needed to turn his command assignment around.

Indeed, this move proved to be a turning point in Petric's command. Palmer was neither bogged down with administrative duties, which had hamstrung Radtke, nor overloaded with the heavy dose of logistics carried by the XO. Almost immediately, Palmer instituted visible improvements to the unit's operations. He added an assignments board to the operations center that was easier to maintain. Then, taking advantage of his close relationship with the XO, he acquired materials to create a planning room for the pilots. Pleased, Petric began using the room for mission briefings. Soon, the new commander emerged as a solid combat-assault planner.

Palmer then added a new twist to Petric's immediate talent pool. He recommended CW2 Dave Schwartz, a fiery, redheaded slick pilot from Eureka, California, to fly C&C. Schwartz, although loud and boisterous, was an outstanding pilot, and this wise move gave Petric two seasoned vets to consult for tactical planning and coordination. Despite his constant chatter, the redheaded Schwartz was liked by all. His raucous but affable personality added a measure of informality that softened the regimented appearance of the Petric regime. Being recommended by Palmer, Schwartz automatically won the favor of the XO. And Falcon seized every opportunity to fly C&C with the savvy Schwartz. With a direct link to Palmer, Falcon slipped into these combat-assault missions more frequently than before.

"When you gonna let me fly with your redheaded stepchild again?" Falcon asked Palmer one day, goading him when the frustration of logistics was getting the better of him.

Palmer cracked a side-mouthed grin. "Yeah! I bet that redheaded fart can teach *you* a thing or two."

"No doubt! That's why I enjoy flying with that shitbird. Now get me outta here for a day, Bruce. I'm going batshit in here!"

Flying a mission with Schwartz, Falcon experienced a near-death experience. "One mission that was so out of the ordinary," Falcon recalls, "it raised the hackles on my back from sheer fright. It was perpetrated by a well-equipped and well-supplied enemy soldier who nearly destroyed our aircraft and crew when we tried to capture him."

Falcon had been flying C&C with his operations officer, CW2 Schwartz, near the Cambodian border. That day, as senior pilot, Schwartz flew as the C&C air-mission commander. Falcon, being inexperienced in body-snatching and C&C flying, occupied the copilot position. Supporting a Twenty-Fifth Infantry Division battalion south of the Parrot's Beak, Schwartz observed an enemy soldier dive into a tall rice field to escape observation. But too late. Schwartz radioed Infantry Battalion Commander LTC Don Schroeder in the back seat.

"Sir, I just saw an enemy soldier dive into the grass in this rice field to our left. Do you want me to set up a low orbit over his position so you can take a look?"

"Roger that, Boomer. Go ahead," Schroeder replied.

Schwartz maneuvered the Huey close to the enemy soldier, who could clearly be seen between the rice stalks from above.

"Boomer, can you land close to him? I'd like to body-snatch this guy if we can."

While flying previous missions with CW2 Schwartz, Schroeder had perfected this method of acquiring real-time intelligence.

"Roger that, sir," Schwartz replied. Hovering the bird right over the soldier, Schwartz eased the Huey down waiting for the snatch team to jump out and capture the enemy at gunpoint. All eyes were on the enemy. Unfortunately, Schwartz, seated on the opposite side of the bird, had restricted vision and didn't see what was happening.

Without as much of a hint or a wink, the enemy jumped to his feet and tugged at a pistol belt loaded with grenades.

Seated on the action side of the bird, Falcon witnessed the scene and quickly radioed his gunner. "Kill him!" Falcon shouted. "He has grenades—kill him!"

The enemy solider pulled a grenade off of his belt and drew his arm back to throw the grenade into the chopper.

"Damn it, Swenson [pseudonym]! He has a damn grenade in his hand. Kill him! Kill the son of a bitch!"

A burst of automatic weapon fire folded the soldier, and Schwartz initiated a fast vertical takeoff.

CPT John Cook, the gun-platoon leader in Bounty Hunter Six, observed the whole incident and called Schwartz. "Boomerang Three, this is Bounty Hunter Six. Give me a little space, and I'll finish that bastard off for you. I think he might still be moving—he may still be alive."

"Roger that! Blow his fucking head off!" Adrenaline rushed through Schwartz's and Falcon's bodies from the near-death experience.

Cook's door gunner finished the job.

"Boomerang Three, I think it's safe to approach the body now. Most of his head is missing."

"Roger that, Six. Thanks for covering my back."

After returning to home base at the end of the long day, Falcon approached Schwartz. Mindful of Schwartz's extensive combat-assault hours, Falcon picked his brain for his own enlightenment. "In hindsight, Dave, I need some rehash of what happened today," Falcon said.

"Sure, sir. What can I do for you?"

"First, I apologize for having my head up my ass today. Knowing you could not see the gook, I should have initiated the emergency takeoff immediately when I saw the danger. What's worse, I qualified with my .38 Smith & Wesson revolver several times. Hell, as close as he was, I could have shot the scoundrel myself."

"Sir, you did fine. You alerted the gunner and that's what he's there for."

"Thanks, Dave. I appreciate your experience and regret I didn't react more resolute today. I've learned a lot. One question. Since task-force commanders may choose to operate from different sides of the bird, do you suppose it might behoove the air-mission commander to sit on the same side? This will give both the same vantage point."

"That's already decided for us. It's great that you're asking these questions. It shows that you were paying attention and learning something. In your position as XO, it's damn important that you do. You will be flying these missions, and the lives of all pilots and crews will rest in your hands by your command-and-control."

"Yes, sir. That bastard today meant to take us out—and fought to the death trying to do it. Without question the closer we meet the enemy toward Cambodia, the bolder they fight. What I'd give if I could get some of those damn politicians in Washington a lesson on what we learned today. Wouldn't it be nice if we could get a few of those candyasses to come fly a few missions with us?"

Schwartz shrugged off the comment with a smirk and a laugh. Then invited Falcon to the club for a beer.

Falcon grinned. *So, that's how these experienced combat pilots deal with this stress.* Sometimes close calls were the best instructors.

Despite the near-death experience, Schwartz had found a place in the XO's favor. Falcon liked the way the young chief warrant officer related to the ground commanders and the positive visibility his competence brought to the unit. Schwartz's presence in the tactical-planning sequence of the 191st combat-assault missions became readily accepted up and down command lines. This soon caught the attention of Petric, who then began flying with Schwartz as well. Thereby, the former fixed-wing aviator transformed into an acceptable combat-assault pilot. Schwartz bridged the faith gap between Petric and the assault platoons and significantly contributed to Petric's command.

One evening, over a beer, Palmer and Falcon engaged in a quiet discussion about the redheaded Schwartz and the CO Petric. "The redheaded fart is earning his keep," Palmer said.

"Yes, he is! And Major Petric has made a hell of a change since he began flying with Schwartz. It's a good thing you brought that redheaded fart into ops."

Although Petric had made great strides in his command, in the field, as well as in garrison, he still had his ups and downs. In one of his worst episodes of bad luck,

Petric was flying with the superb and well-liked Infantry Battalion Commander LTC Don Schroeder, who had perfected that method of body-snatching to acquire real-time intelligence.

On this day Petric and Schroeder performed a body-snatch operation. Petric swooped down with expert precision into an extremely tight, confined area. Landing to a hover, Petric smoothly settled the aircraft onto the ground while Schroeder and his artillery officer jumped out to hustle to a nearby hootch. Intelligence had reported the presence of a high-ranking enemy officer, and Schroeder wanted to capture the "son of a bitch."

There was one problem: the LZ was superhot. Gun Platoon Leader CPT John Cook alerted the C&C ship that the area was crawling with enemy soldiers. Schroeder knew this, but the gutsy battalion commander had faced enemy fire many times before, and he ordered the snatch anyway. No sooner did Schroeder's and his artillery officer's boots hit the ground when the enemy opened up with withering machine-gun fire. The enemy wounded the artillery officer and killed LTC Schroeder instantly.

Bravely, Petric kept the bird on the ground while the C&C crew leaped out to recover Schroeder's limp body. To his credit, Petric held fast throughout the whole ordeal and finally got the bird out under vicious machine-gun fire.

When word of the loss of Schroeder reached the rest of the 191st pilots, Petric's popularity among the unit officers suffered a setback, a classic example of being at the wrong place at the wrong time. It is doubtful that this outcome would have been any different regardless of who had been flying Schroeder that day. Schroeder was a brilliant infantry tactician who commanded the respect of all C&C pilots, any of whom, more than likely, would have done what Petric had done that fateful day. Nonetheless, Petric took the rap, and even the inexperienced pilots began believing that a pilot with only fixed-wing experience should not command an assault-helicopter company. In fairness to Petric, his tactical liabilities were no greater than what war brings upon anyone in his position. But many guys, like SP4 Kahn stated, had a hard time trusting new or "green" pilots, and many considered Petric, despite his long history in fixed wing, green as they come.

In battle, bad luck can affect anyone. With his turn to fly C&C that day, Petric simply drew a bad hand. Feeling the effects of the incident, the XO Falcon quietly retreated to his room in the evening, hoping Petric would not call him. Falcon remained isolated from the complaints he knew would be voiced at the evening's libation session in the new officer's bunker. The bunker had been completed and turned into an officer's club for the pilots who made it a ritual to soak up a few beers each evening and discuss the state of the company. That evening, with trust in the commander low, morale teetered on the edge and then unfortunately dropped to a new low.

Nevertheless, as with all things in life and war, good things began to happen again for Petric. The Boomerangs and Bounty Hunters successfully supported the

Ninth Infantry Division in the heat of battle every day, and the commanding general poured on the appreciation in the form of awards and decorations for the pilots and crews. Petric took a personal interest and assembled the unit to present awards and decorations with considerable pomp and ceremony. Petric launched into a formal reading of the citations as each medal was pinned on the recipient. The whole event was uplifting, and the day typically ended at the officer's club with a strong bonding session that included a lot of free-flowing beer and pizza.

Life in a combat zone eventually turned in Petric's favor. Since the move to Dong Tam, Mess Sergeant SFC Robert Pagel procured his own mess hall and, therefore, was able to focus his immense cooking talents on the 191st alone. Frequently, Pagel would cook up a pile of steaks and trimmings to top off one Petric's award ceremonies. Pagel, a superb cook, knew how to please the troops. Most importantly, with the 191st having its own mess hall at their new base camp, battle-weary pilots and crews never again went hungry after a long day in the fight. Never would the mess hall close while the flight was still out in the field. Somehow, no matter how late the hour, the diligent Pagel always supplied food, hot and waiting, when the flight arrived back home after a long day in battle. Pilots and crews appreciated a well-cooked hot meal, and the unit, as a whole, benefitted from the new image of someone caring for their well-being. Morale lifted.

Falcon seized on the chance to create more morale-boosting opportunities. With the same nurturing manner that Pagel put into preparing hot meals for battle-tired crews, Falcon arranged promotion ceremonies with care and consideration. It worked. While traditionally held in the commander's office, promotions were thereafter announced in company formations, where they had the same uplifting effect for the recipients. Petric was delighted to participate in these events, and it offered the troops a more relaxed image of their commander. Petric had begun to enjoy the hard-won trust of his battle-hardened troops.

CHAPTER 18

Quiet but Deadly

Since that experience, I have not forgotten to give thanks and praise for each day that I live.

CPT Michael Arruti's personality was invariably placid compared to most 191st pilots. He possessed a quiet and peaceful nature until he occupied the AC seat in a gunship. Lethal as a cobra, his battle focus never faltered. Although remarkable in many ways, his combat successes remained a subdued entry in the 191st journal. Most regrettably, Arruti was never properly decorated for his battlefield performance. Until now, his story has remained untold.

Upon Arruti's arrival at the 191st during the last week of November 1968, he was one of few Huey pilots who were directly assigned to the gun platoon. Usually, 191st commanders preferred that gunship pilots first learn a little bit about what the lift ships did in combat assaults before these pilots were thrown into defending them. They needed to gain understanding of the urgency in gun cover. Lift-crew lives hung in the balance, and Bounty Hunter action affected their survivability. Hence, assigning a new pilot to a lift platoon before moving him to a Bounty Hunter position gave the pilot the experience and battle focus needed to save 191st lives. For that reason, it was rare for a new pilot to be assigned directly to the gun platoon.

Arruti's assignment to the Bounty Hunters stirred his penchant for action. He knew gunships stayed in the mix of combat daily, and CPT John Cook, his gun-platoon leader, made sure Arruti got his share of excitement. The timing of Arruti's arrival at the 191st coincided with the enemy's preparation for the second Tet Offensive. Peace negotiations in Paris remained stagnant and frustration among Washington politicians heightened. However, little of this world pulse made a difference to the mindset of 191st combat crews. In fact, little of that scenario was even known by frontline warriors. Simply, soldiers on the battlefront remained prepared for the worst. Peace negotiation didn't repel bullets; bunkers, chicken plates, and return fire did. That was the method by which 191st crews stayed alive.

Arruti came well versed in this them-or-us existence, having served with A Troop, 3rd/17th Cavalry, and having earned his first Air Medal for twenty-five combat hours.

With only a brief introduction to 191st combat, Arruti captured the attention and respect of his fellow pilots when he acquired his first kill. Crusty ol' combat veterans who witnessed the event marveled at the greenhorn. Although wet behind the ears, Arruti had passed initiation by these "tribal elders," as he called them.

"I believe it was my second mission as a gunship copilot when we engaged a group of VCs," Arruti recalls. "We saw one individual crawling through the rice paddy, and my AC told me to 'take him.' I cut loose with the minigun and must have put two hundred rounds through him, nearly cutting his body in half. My adrenaline rushed like never before. Killing this guy gave me great satisfaction because I had eliminated at least one threat to the American soldiers fighting these guys. The ground battle was raging by that time, and I was extremely pleased to be given the opportunity to participate."

Returning to base, Arruti had learned about a man his fellow 191st members called John. Settling into the compound after the postflight work, the pilots drank beer and celebrated the successful day. A fellow pilot approached.

"You need to participate in a knock-knock joke," the pilot said.

Everyone yelled, "Knock! Knock!"

"Who's there?" Arruti asked.

"John the Baptist!" came the chorus reply.

To Arruti's cold surprise, the group had doused him with beer until he was sopping wet.

"I hadn't a dry thread on me," Arruti recalls. "This was my initiation into the brotherhood for getting my first kill."

Arruti participated in numerous engagements where he had fought to the death with a determined enemy. "Over the first five or six months," he recalls, "I actually took pictures of the dead enemy and kept track of how many I had killed."

But soon Arruti realized he didn't want to take these pictures back to the States for his wife to see, and so he ended his souvenir practice and burned the graphic images.

"Attacking and killing enemy soldiers is redemption for their intent to kill Americans," Arruti continues. "As a gunship pilot, to allow any enemy warrior to kill our fellow brothers-in-arms is not an acceptable alternative for conscientious objections. I come from a home of strong Christian values; however, there's no way that as a gunship pilot assigned to cover a flight of birds carrying Americans or crewed by my 191st brothers, I would hesitate to kill anyone threatening the flight. Heck, I wouldn't even give that idea a second thought. I had no problem killing those that needed killing."

One particular engagement sticks out in Arruti's memory. It occurred as they were checking out an area where Americans had been inserted. Overflying the LZ, enemy soldiers popped up everywhere. Enemy fire splattered the gunships—and the fight was now on.

"Bounty Hunter Six, this is Charlie-Charlie; there are two VC running down the dike in front of you—get them!"

"Roger that!" Arruti squeezed off a rocket that penetrated the first VC soldier and exploded as it passed through the second, sending a spray of red into the air and body parts tumbling.

The intense fight had lasted for hours. When the battle was over, the Bounty Hunters were credited with thirty kills, with another five coming from the infantry. Arruti was proud of his company's performance.

Although killing enemy soldiers remained a principal objective for Arruti and his fellow Bounty Hunters, there were circumstances that taxed the mind spiritually and ethically. It was simply too easy to kill humans that were so tragically ill equipped and supplied. Most firefights and even extended battles produced enemy soldiers that were clearly indoctrinated beyond their capacity to present fair opposition. The miniguns literally chewed the human bodies to pieces in seconds. The poor souls on the receiving end knew absolutely nothing of what to expect. It was like being thrown into a meat grinder by the hierarchy of enemy brass, who witnessed the massacre from a safe distance. One couldn't help but feel compassion for the sacrificial lambs thrown into the American death machinery for the sake of Communist ideology. At times, it was almost sickening.

"As the war continued, the killing became routine," Arruti recalls, "but nonetheless, mentally taxing. One doesn't know the wife and children who are left without support."

Arruti knew what he had done, but like all the pilots and crew, he understood what had to be done and was proud to serve his country and protect the troops on the ground.

"Even enemy troops were forced into war scenarios that I'm sure they would rather have avoided," Arruti explains. "Similar to our nation's war draft that involuntarily forced Americans into war, enemy soldiers had it worse. Being that their equipment was far less effective, they faced greater odds at meeting their death. Yet history seems to redeem them. Although they lost all major battles against Americans, they persevered in the end. They won the Vietnam War by default. Our country simply stopped giving the South Vietnamese the necessary support to properly defend themselves."

The skeleton crews left behind to support South Vietnam's soldiers and civilians in their quest for freedom from Communistic rule continued fighting with all they had—including the 191st AHC.

"An action that had a profound effect on me occurred as we headed back to home base after a day of combat assaults," Arruti continues. "We spotted a VC running on a rice dike and my door gunner said he would get him. So, I dropped down to about thirty feet off the ground and flew parallel to the enemy soldier. Stopping abruptly, the enemy aimed his AK-47 at us, but instead of hearing my gunner's M60 firing at him, I heard a loud click and a thump as the door gunner fell back to avoid getting shot. The M60 jammed!

"At the same time, I saw a puff of smoke come out of the enemy's weapon—I was staring directly into the barrel of his gun. Time stood still as I reckoned with death. I made a radical control move to the left to avoid further risk, and my copilot grabbed the controls. Thinking I'd been hit, he was trying to resume the directional course when I told him to let go—politely of course. We found no bullet holes on the aircraft, and to this day I have no idea how I escaped being shot.

"Following our postflight work after landing at home base, I had a long interlude thinking about my maker. No doubt He was with me and my family on that day. Incredible but real, the enemy soldier simply failed in his attempt to kill me. The point-blank range made it appear as if divine intervention had a hand in it. I prayed silently to God for giving me another day on this earth. Since that experience, I have not forgotten to give thanks and praise for each day that I live.

"In assessing my tour with the 191st, I vividly recall a remarkable organization with people who cared and delivered their best. Both commissioned and warrant officer pilots demonstrated a high degree of pride in their work and believed in the war. They valued the objectives of our nation to support democracy in Vietnam and commit America's war machinery for the cause. It was truly disheartening to see it end as it did. I honestly cannot give our country credit for the final decision to pull out. I feel as if the politicians were more concerned with squelching dissention among the younger generation than our country's honor to fulfill its commitment to the people of South Vietnam. I hope we never do that again to any allied nation.

"The worst part of my Vietnam experience was coming home to a country that despised us as 'baby killers' and murderers. It has taken nearly forty-five years for that attitude to dim. It's galling to think of the sacrifices made by so many for the sake of freedom and then be treated so indignantly. The families of those who died certainly didn't deserve that."

Arruti rotated back to the States in October of 1969. He then pursued and completed a twenty-three-year Army career. Retiring as a lieutenant colonel, he raised three children with his lovely wife, Leslie, and now they have eleven grandchildren. With the passing of Leslie, he now resides in New Mexico.

Arruti's tour with the 191st produced unequivocal results. With his achievements and battle performance, Arruti, despite systemic failure to properly decorate him, ranks among the top gunship pilots in the Army, without question. Eventually assuming command of the Bounty Hunters from CPT Cook, Arruti amply filled his predecessor's place with authority and distinction.

During Arruti's service with the 191st, his superb influence imprinted remarkable success for the Bounty Hunters wherever they fought. Under his leadership, the gun platoon delivered flawless and precise fire support. Throughout his service with the 191st Bounty Hunters, Arruti set a remarkable example for those who followed. Truly deserving, this rendition of his success in combat does little to make up for his gift to the war effort. Arruti was a remarkable soldier and a strong champion of freedom. His exemplary performance has earned him a place of honor among the best of the 191st pilots.

CHAPTER 19

The Hardest Blow

"But sir," Heinmiller said, "this is what we love to do."

From December of 1968 through March of 1969, the enemy around Dong Tam, home of the US Ninth Infantry Division, stepped up their attacks on the US forces. Getting mortared several times during the hours of darkness became a ritual in the lives of pilots, crewmen, and personnel at their new base camp, Dong Tam. After considerable pounding, the division commander issued an order to organize a counter-mortar force and "neutralize the bastards."

The Bounty Hunters had already experienced this type of duty while stationed at Bearcat, the previous Ninth Division base camp. There, a standby-alert gunship crew had slept fully clothed in a flight line shack within a few steps of the runway where their Bounty Hunter gunship was parked. At first sign of a mortar attack, the crew's alarm would go off and the sleeping Bounty Hunters would hit the floor and bolt to their fully armed Huey. In a matter of four to five minutes, the bird was in the air, lethal and prepared to kill the enemy mortar crew. Getting airborne quickly was to deny the enemy unlimited attack time.

Every soul inhabiting Dong Tam wanted the enemy's blood. If, by some fluke of fate, the enemy mortar crews had been captured and skinned alive in public, it is doubtful that any resident of Dong Tam would have complained of war crimes. Harsh, but such are the emotions of war when explosions jolt and rock the one safe place in this shit-hole paradise. You can't sleep—you can't even take a piss without your insides rattling. The nightly battering of enemy mortars tightened the mood at the Ninth Infantry Division base camp like high-tension wire, ready to unleash its energy at the slightest touch. Any hint of a mortar attack prompted a series of coordinated actions designed to find, fix, and flatten the enemy gunners.

As frequent thrashings on Dong Tam had increased, the reaction time for the counter-mortar crew was upgraded to a short fuse—a get-airborne-quick status. Instead of sleeping on a bunk in a line shack, the standby-alert gunship crew was now ordered to remain in the bird, on the active runway, fully armed, with blades untied, poised for immediate departure from dusk to dawn. The Ninth Division commanding general wanted the enemy mortar crews dead before they had time to do serious damage or take the lives of the people under his command. He wasn't alone with his sentiments.

The priority for this duty was upgraded to parallel one of the oldest traditions in the military: the night duty officer. However, since the number of pilots in the gun platoon was a small percentage of the total 191st officers serving the company, the CO instructed the admin officer to take the Bounty Hunter pilots off the night duty–officer roster. This balanced the tasking somewhat. Their duty-assignment calendar was maintained by the admin officer as diligently as the night duty–officer schedule, and with equal priority.

This counter mortar–attack plan was well known among the personnel of the 191st, and it represented hope that it would soon deliver bloody justice and bring relief from the persistent, soul-rattling attacks. As soon as the mortar attack alarm whipped up its blaring siren, 191st personnel trained their ears in the direction of the flight line and listened for the whine of the Charlie-model engine cranking up. The clattering *whop-whop-whop* of the armed Huey lifting into the night air was the sweet sound of revenge. The entire population of Dong Tam wanted the constant nightly barrage to stop, and there was only one way for it to end—with the enemy mortar crews dead and quiet.

On Christmas Eve 1968, one of the guys at Dong Tam rushed into the bunker. "Hey, guys! You got to watch this. The cav is fuckin' over the VC big time!"

The 3rd/9th Cavalry had launched a counter-mortar fire team of Cobra gunships that treated the 191st troops to a fantastic, morale-boosting, firepower demonstration. The stage for this action covered a large area northeast of Dong Tam, within sight of the 191st hootches. Cavalry decision makers had laid out an elaborate search plan, including dispatching flare ships for illumination and Flying Eggs (Hughes OH-6 Cayuse), the light observation helicopter (LOH or "loach" as they were universally known), for locating the enemy mortar crews. With flare ships illuminating from above, the cav's Flying Eggs zipped around at treetop level while the two fire teams of Cobra gunships dished out the heavy muscle of the battle plan. The tactics of this counter-mortar force caught the enemy by surprise.

Suddenly, enemy tracers filled the night sky. The LOH gunner returned fire as his little Flying Egg quickly banked hard to escape what they knew was coming. From out of the dark above the flares, a flash of rocket ignition burst through, heralding lethal doses of rockets and minigun fire like no other aircraft in the Army's inventory could dispense. Specifically built as a high-speed weapons platform, the AH-1G Cobra had power to spare. It could hover high out of ground effect for extended periods of time. Seemingly suspended in space above the flares, the invisible "Snake" had enormous advantage for quickly gaining fire superiority over the doomed enemy. Seldom would a VC or NVA soldier challenge a Cobra.

As soon as the ground tracers stopped flying, the Little Eggs were back over the area, dancing around the palm trees as the night sky was illuminated by the flare ships. No concealed enemy would dare flinch until darkness engulfed them once again. The flare ships delivered excellent illumination over the exact spot where the enemy had set up their mortar tubes, including the several hundred meters surrounding their launch sites. With the Cobras circling above the flares and the cav's loaches buzzing just over the treetops, the enemy had nowhere to hide. To their credit, when cornered, the enemy gunners fought viciously.

The battle was intense, but in a paltry thirty minutes the sky fell silent. It seemed like the action was over before it started, and the 191st troops were pleased to retreat back into the officer's club to resume their Christmas Eve celebration until the next night when the enemy would surely return. Sleep was a hard commodity to come by.

Sleep deprivation is among the worst mental tortures and morale-draining conditions a soldier can endure. The enemy knew exactly what its ritual of mortar attacks did to the sleep-deprived bodies and minds of American soldiers. The enemy kept up its night attacks like clockwork. By December 27, 1968, two days after Christmas, the North Vietnamese had moved 120-millimeter mortars across the Mekong River from Dong Tam and launched a steady barrage of attacks every three or four hours, night after night. Stress and irritability from lack of sleep reared up in the Boomerangs' and Bounty Hunters' crews. After each day of flying, the usual high-pitched libation sessions, which were customary in the 191st officer's club, grew shorter and quieter.

Some men, who were due to rotate back to the States soon or were scheduled for R&R within a few days, chose to sleep in the bunker. An Ohioan, SP5 Bill Faucett, was not about to risk getting hit by an enemy mortar so close to his R&R. He was scheduled to meet Kathleen, his new bride, in Hawaii in ten days, so he made the bunker his quarters. Each night he dragged his mattress into the bunker and dragged it back to his hootch in the morning. The brain-rattling, morale-destroying attacks continued relentlessly for months.

From December of 1968 through March of 1969, the enemy mortar crews kept the pressure on Dong Tam, eventually blowing up the ammo dump in a spectacular midnight explosion that rocked the entire compound. The nightly attacks became a way of life, and most troopers adjusted to the threat in their own way. Some learned to judge the proximity of the mortar blasts by sound, and when the rounds *thunked* on a distant part of the base, they wouldn't even leave their bunks. They simply rolled over, waiting to evaluate the proximity of the next impact. All the while, they considered possible courses of action: make a beeline for the bunker, grab a beer on the way out the door to the bunker, skip the beer but grab cigarettes, or belay creature comforts and "gitcher young ass under substantial cover rat now."

Dong Tam residents became expert at recognizing the sound of outgoing versus incoming artillery fire. At times, artillery batteries were positioned at the end of the runway to fire on enemy targets several miles away. Their loud explosions of outgoing fire rocked the bejeezus out of the barracks area, but soon they became part of the expected friendly war noise—perhaps even comforting. Occasionally, these cannons would be moved away for several weeks. Upon their return, the 191st personnel would experience anxious moments when the cannoneers suddenly fired a volley, which sounded as if they were eight-inchers barely clearing the 191st barracks. Easily recognized as friendly fire, the sudden explosions would, nonetheless, momentarily tighten the assholes of everyone in the company area.

The mood among the 191st troops reached its boiling point when in one of the worst eruptions of disharmony a recently infused captain, Raymond Cunneen, was nearly mobbed in the officer's club. With good intentions and in friendly conversation, Cunneen shared his experience from his day of general-support flying, commonly referred to by assault pilots as an ash-and-trash mission. One could have heard a pin drop as Cunneen explained that he had spotted an enemy mortar crew setting up close to the end of the runway but was unable to quickly get clearance to fire from Second Field Force headquarters. The newbie expressed dismay that his crew chief, experienced in combat assaults, was incensed with his safety precautions and correct engagement protocol. From out of a back corner of the officer's club (a.k.a. bunker) exploded a barrage of insults.

"You doofus son of a bitch! Those are the sorry bastards who've been blowing the shit out of us every fuckin' night. What the fuck makes you think you have to ask some dumbass straphanger up in Saigon for permission to kill 'em? You fuckin' asshole!"

Another voice chimed in: "Somebody get that dumbass the fuck outta here before we kick the shit out of him. Stupid bastard!"

The mob mentality quickly escalated and several other pilots joined in the backbiting. Fortunately, MAJ Petric entered the bunker, and the relieved Cunneen escaped with only a bruised ego.

On or about February 28, 1969, the pilots and crew of a counter-mortar gunships were trying to snooze in their ship, parked but ready, on the active runway. The pilots on board were CW2 Bill Grebe, a clean-cut youngster from central Texas, and WO1 Ralph Curtis "Curt" Embrey, a tall and slim fellow with a rich, dark complexion. Filling the crew chief and gunner positions were SP5 Bill Flores, a tall and lanky Californian, and SP4 Ronald Lovellette, a stocky, fighter type. At approximately 2200 hours, the sound of base sirens split the air. The pilots and crew sprang into action.

The division counter-mortar radar had picked up several enemy mortar rounds flying through the air and headed for Dong Tam. Almost as soon as the first round landed, Grebe and Embrey lifted their bird into the night sky. They made contact with the radar crew that plotted the incoming fire. Grebe got a quick vector to the general area west of Dong Tam, just in time to see some firing residue spewing from one of the enemy mortar tubes. On the spot in seconds, Grebe dumped rocket after rocket into the exact spot from where the enemy mortar crews had pumped out their lethal dose.

After the last round of the enemy's volley exploded on Dong Tam, some of the angry 191st troops rushed out of their bunkers to watch and cheer for the much anticipated and spectacular Bounty Hunter show. A few climbed up on top of the twelve-foot bunker to get a better view. From a distance, the plumes of fire from each rocket could be clearly seen as they ignited in the gunship pods and streaked down into the darkness, exploding in a powerful blast that lit up the deep night. Unrelentingly, the enemy fired back. Enemy green tracers filled the sky, giving away their position to the crew chief and gunner, who quickly took advantage.

Crew Chief Flores and Gunner Lovellette could clearly see where their tracers were hitting the ground and quickly adjusted for effect. The enemy, on the other hand, had little visual reference. As was standard practice under such circumstances, the savvy Grebe had turned off the gunship's navigation lights to make it impossible for the enemy gunners to pinpoint the gunship's position until the gunship began firing again. As the green tracers passed behind the Huey, the enemy had no way of knowing how far behind the bird they were or how many rounds had missed. Their bullets traversed the airspace where the bird had been just seconds before and harmlessly sailed off into the night. As the gunship broke off from each gun run, almost immediately Flores and Lovellette stuffed red tracers back down into the enemy's face. Back and forth, the firefight lit up the night like Boston Harbor on New Year's Eve. After Grebe expended his load of rockets, Embrey proceeded to hose down the area with his 7.62 minigun. Exploding out of their rotating barrels, nearly solid streams of pink fire splashed onto the landscape with ricocheting rounds flying back into the air until burnout. With hot lead flying everywhere, no witness could fail to be awed—except maybe Charlie, who bet his mortality against incredible odds when fighting an American gunship.

The 191st gallery witnessed the entire "turkey shoot." To the boys tortured by months of explosions disrupting their sleep, the show was ecstasy. Each minigun burst or rocket ignition produced a loud rally of *ooohs* and *ahhhs*. And some onlookers hurled some special expletives directed toward Charlie and the ideological conflict that had brought the two forces to war. With sixty seconds of continuous fire, the minigun could land a 7.62-millimeter round on every square foot of earth across an area the size of a football field. Caught in the open, no human could survive this vicious leaden onslaught. While the minigun laid down a continuous fire, Flores and Lovellette spewed their full load of M60 machine-gun ammo into the enemy. In a matter of minutes, the enemy fire stopped, and Grebe reported the outcome.

"Boomerang Ops, this is Bounty Hunter Three-One."

"Three-One, this is Ops. Go ahead."

"This is Three-One, the mortars are suppressed. We were able to see residue from the firing tubes in time to get some heat right into their position. I feel certain we killed some of them. Suggest we ask Division to get someone there as soon as possible to confirm kills."

"Roger, Three-One. Understand probable kills. Good news. Come home and get some rest."

"Roger. Three-One, out!"

Disappointed that the show was over, the 191st troops recovered from wherever they had chosen to view the action and returned to their bunks with uplifted hearts. Each wished he had been in that gunship. The next day, an infantry unit from the Ninth Division combed the area. They found parts of enemy mortar equipment and a cache of unfired rounds. Several blood trails disappeared into the nearby jungle. That particular mortar crew would *not* be hitting Dong Tam again any time soon. But that did not stop the pounding. Dong Tam remained a high-priority target for the enemy. In less than a week a new mortar crew was again shelling out a nightly dose of mortar rounds.

To dilute the effectiveness of the airborne counter-mortar mission, the clever enemy adopted the tactic of coordinating simultaneous mortar fire on a common target but from scattered locations. What they lacked in accuracy, they more than made up in volume. Dong Tam was large enough to offer many targets to the opportunistic VC. It was not unusual to count as many as thirty mortar rounds in a single barrage. When scrambled, the gunships might be able to find *one* of the firing locations, but the others would likely escape the gunships' turkey hunt.

On the evening of March 1, 1969, the XO, CPT Falcon, dressed in jeans, T-shirt, and running shoes, met with MAJ Petric in the commander's quarters for a brief coordination session. Petric would be flying C&C in the morning, and he had made a list of tasks for the XO to complete in his absence. Petric noticed Falcon's new running shoes. "Hey, looks like you're serious about jogging in the evenings," he said.

"Yes, sir—it's risky, though. All the streets are bordered by ditches with gooey stuff that smells like shit and probably *is*. As I'm jogging, I often think about where I might have to take cover if the friggin' VC start mortaring the compound. I'd hate like hell to have to jump into one of those stinky ditches."

Petric laughed at Falcon's humor and then proceeded with the briefing. "John, here's a list of things I'd like for you to do tomorrow while I'm out flying. Also, if you would do me a favor—tell me, where did you get those running shoes?"

"At the PX, sir."

"Great! Would you please get me a pair? Is twenty bucks enough?"

"Yes, sir, no problem. I'll get your shoes if you'll just jot down your size."

"Thank you. Would you like a beer, John?"

"No, sir, but thanks! If it's okay with you, I'd rather get started on my run before it gets too close to mortar time."

Petric laughed again. "Sure thing."

Falcon thought getting the CO's running shoes was a bit much to ask; however, XOs were "go-to" people and he did it without complaint. Basically, it demonstrated that Petric had confidence that Falcon was a friend, and the XO would not have wanted it any other way.

The next day, March 2, 1969, started as a routine day in the 191st mission sequence. The aircrews exercised their morning ritual and got off the ground with the usual ten slicks and three *limping* gunships. Charlie-models, synonymous with gunship, always seemed to be down for maintenance, probably due to their regular daily battering. During airmobile operations, the D-model slicks would shut down and wait somewhere at a friendly loiter area while the grunts beat the jungle for enemy contact; whereas the Charlie-model gunships were always in the mix of the action. Anytime the grunts ran into anything suspect, the guns were called in to search and destroy. If it turned out to be enemy, the fight was on.

The Bounty Hunters loved to be in the mix. Bloodthirsty, testosterone-charged gunship pilots viewed themselves as a breed apart. And indeed, they were the real deal—bona fide combat pilots. All one had to do to learn this fact was to pop into the Long Branch Saloon and knock back a few beers with these guys. It didn't take long before even a casual observer would feel as if he had been tossed into an arena of pit bulls—each dog trained to fight to the death and living every breath for the kill. But on March 2, 1969, there was no firefight to pump their adrenaline, at least no significant enemy contact. The flight was released in the late afternoon and returned to Dong Tam unscathed.

It was a good day. No one was wounded or killed, and the flight took no hits. Petric and the rest of the flight crews taxied to their respective revetments and shut down their aircraft. Before retreating to the mess hall, they performed the initial postflight maintenance in preparation for the next day's mission, A full belly would make the rest much easier Mess Sergeant Pagel had prepared one of Petric's favorite meals: spaghetti and meatballs with garlic toast.

Leaving his aircraft, Petric strode straight to the orderly room to catch up on the day's ground activities. Upon learning that Pagel had prepared Italian, the commander invited Falcon to dine with him so they could recap the day over a hot supper. Entering the mess hall, someone sounded off with the usual protocol afforded a commander entering the dining facility.

"At ease!"

At that moment, all the forks clinked on the plates and the men sat up straight in their chairs looking forward until they heard the commander's response.

"Carry on," Petric said. Wanting his troops to relax and resume eating, his response landed quick. Taking a seat, the CO and the XO waited for the dining room orderly to serve them.

"Okay, John, tell me what went on today."

"Sir, I got your running shoes and put them in your hootch. Here's the receipt and your change."

"Thanks, I appreciate that. Now tell me about the motor pool. I've been wondering about that problem all day. How did it turn out?"

"Sir, our PLL[1] is really weak. There's no way we can sustain ninety days of operations with the parts we have on hand, much less one hundred eighty days. Sergeant Silva complains that he can't get much out of Battalion, and I believe him. I think I'm gonna have to go to Long Binh and see what I can scrounge."

Falcon was hopeful that Petric would suggest he take the maintenance bird and fly to the parts depot, but no such luck. Petric stayed focused on the problem expecting his XO to arrive at the solution. And rightly so, since Falcon had a maintenance background. The task would require that Falcon take a Jeep and traverse fifty-plus miles of enemy territory to retrieve the parts. But Falcon was used to the task. He had done it frequently after arriving at Bearcat. The fact that the main roads to the supply sources were busy with military traffic gave Falcon the confidence that he was riding on favorable odds. *Surely*, he thought, *the enemy won't pick a pissant Jeep over a five-ton full of supplies.* The road was full of them.

Before the meal was served, Petric spoke rapidly as if pressured to get supper done so he could get to the orderly room to read his mail and staff notes. Plus, he was a dedicated father and husband, and his communications to and from home weighed heavily on his mind. On days that he flew, if Petric had not received mail from home, the admin officer knew to leave him a note on his desk. Otherwise, Petric would track him down to ask.

"Supply's three-quarter-ton rig has been down with a bad clutch for over *three months*," Falcon said, "and they really need one. Maintenance uses their three-quarter-ton to pull birds on and off the flight line, so they can't really lend theirs to supply. The TJ Taxi is doing fine, but the flight platoons need it for the morning and evening runs to the flight line. The best we can hope for is for me to MRE[2] through the depot at Long Binh and see if we get lucky. Also, the wire cage around the tool room is getting an electrical charge." Falcon paused and snickered. "And it shocked the hell out of the battalion maintenance sergeant today."

Petric's face lifted into big smile. "You're kidding?" he asked and let out a subtle laugh.

"No, sir. Somehow, one of the wall sockets has a hot wire that's touching the tool-room cage and the whole damn thing is hot. It shocks the hell out of anyone who touches it. Sergeant Silva believes it might be a good thing, though—nobody's gonna steal our tools!"

Petric laughed again. "Well, we need that fixed. ASAP!"

"Yes, sir! That's already in progress."

---

1 Prescribed load list of spare parts
2 Maintenance-request expedite

When the food was brought out to their table, Petric finally unwound a bit. "Man! This is the only thing that even remotely reminds me of home," Petric said with a gleam in his eye. "My wife makes the best lasagna you could ever dream of. There's nothing like her lasagna, right out of the oven. *This* spaghetti sauce isn't in her league, but it's pretty darned good."

"Yes, sir. Pagel knows his stuff. He's the best morale boost this unit has had in a while," Falcon said, his tone sincere. "All the troops are very complimentary toward this guy. We're lucky to have him."

After finishing their meal, the two parted—Falcon slated for the motor pool to check on progress being made in preparation for the full-scale IG inspection and Petric heading to the orderly room to catch up on paperwork. Even at war, the Army generates a vast flow of paper, and Petric remained diligent about his administrative duties.

Leaving the motor pool around 1830 hours, Falcon took his daily jog. Refreshed at times when the wind blew from the river, he nonetheless paid the price when he ran next to the barracks and breathed in the foul air from the crappy ditches. Falcon was amazed by the difference between the ecology of good ol' USA versus Dong Tam. In US installations, trees and landscaping dressed the road borders and ditches drained into a subterranean sewer system, eliminating the stagnation and stench. In Dong Tam, however, almost nothing green existed. Worse, the stagnant ditches were filthy and smelled of feces. Whether actual excrement or not, the gagging smell hastened Falcon's jogging pace where it permeated the air. Reaching the fixed-wing runway, Falcon turned south toward the river and breathed in a better atmosphere. The odor around the fixed-wing strip was improved by its PSP cover, and the worst smell one would notice there was an occasional whiff of spilt fuel. Gasping for clean air and restricting the enormously foul odors was an on-and-off-again exercise in Falcon's Dong Tam jog.

Throughout his entire three-mile jog, Falcon reminisced about home and about his tasks for the next day. Sometimes on these jogs, he chose which Boomerang or Bounty Hunter barracks he would visit the next morning. Frequently switching objectives kept his target audience off guard. It tickled the XO when he caught a group idly chatting in the barracks as he approached and heard a very common phrase: "Ohhh shit!" They knew they had work coming but seldom made excuses. For the most part, all pilots knew the extra duties had to be accomplished. However, as is in any social group of mixed personalities, some of the more hardcore deadbeats shirked responsibilities and quickly bowed out right after breakfast. Mornings turned into a ritual of catch-as-catch-can.

Falcon returned to his room approximately thirty minutes later. Sometime around 1900 hours, he heard Petric arrive at *his* hootch. After ten minutes or so, Petric knocked. Falcon opened his door and noticed the commander was wearing his new jogging shoes. "Yes, sir?"

"John, where do you run? What route do you take?"

"Sir, I usually run west to the end of the road that passes here in front of the company area, then south, in the direction of the river, along the fixed-wing strip to the end and back. I don't know how far that is, but it's as long as I care to stay exposed here in 'mortar city.' Some guys run around the airfield, but I think that's asking for it. I'd rather stay away from the aircraft at night. I think it's safer."

"I suspect you're right. Thanks, John."

Around forty-five minutes later, Falcon heard Petric arrive back at his hootch, close to 2000 hours, and shut his BOQ door. The evening faded into a soft stillness.

Later that night, the first mortar round split the dark air. It hit hard and close to the company area. So close, it knocked soft-drink cans off the shelves in the hootches. It could not have been more than fifty meters away in the direction of the grunt companies to the south of the 191st barracks. The sudden explosion was a swift boot in the ass; nobody needed any encouragement to scramble for a bunker. The close proximity of the blast kicked all 191st personnel into high gear, cussing as they hustled along. Usually, the enemy gunners aimed for the airfield, with intent to damage the aircraft, a much more lucrative target than the hootches. But this time, they had coordinated their attack so that several mortar tubes struck the barracks area and others simultaneously nailed the flight line.

SP5 Bill Faucett ducked his head and make a quick beeline to his bunker as mortar rounds hissed by overhead. The rounds were aimed to strike the ground between the 214th CAB headquarters and the 162nd Aviation Company, not far to the east. The headquarters was the first to feel the effects of the 120-millimeter mortars with their delayed fuses.

Startled by the nearness of the blast, MAJ Erwin "Dutch" Schmidt, the battalion operations officer, immediately ran to the battalion bunker to join the rest of the battalion staff. The pounding lasted longer than usual, and the troops were forced to stay in their bunkers for more than the normal ten to fifteen minutes before the "all-clear" siren blew. Probably due to the intensity of the attack, after the all-clear signal, many of the 191st officers and men gathered at the company's operations center to exchange insights about the damage. Curiosity prevailed.

Located in the headquarters building of the 191st, the operations center occupied the eastern half of the building. Seated at the operations desk, SP4 Carl Douglas, a courteous and soft-spoken young man, fulfilled his charge-of-quarters (CQ) runner duties under the direction of SP4 Lovellette, the CQ. Lovellette was chatting with SP5 Heinmiller, a gunship crew chief. The operations desk was typically the nerve center of 191st activities. All mission assignments were handed out from this desk.

Among the crowd gathered were MAJ Petric, in a T-shirt and his brand-new jogging shoes; 1LT Carl Radtke, the admin officer, properly dressed in his flak vest and steel pot; 1LT Sean LaRue (pseudonym), also wearing his steel pot and flak vest; 1LT Dennis Coker, the duty officer; and other bystanders, including CW2

Bill Janes, CPT Ray Rugg, 1SG Tom Schaffer (pseudonym), and an unidentified crater-analysis crew of three who were speaking with MAJ Petric. Amid this activity, Falcon entered the room. Petric immediately motioned for him and then instructed him to accompany the crater-analysis crew out to the flight line to collect a mortar fin that he wanted for a souvenir.

"And while you're out there, John, run down the flight line and see how many birds will be flyable for tomorrow. Maintenance is out there going over the birds now. I need to know if we have enough aircraft to put up a flight tomorrow, otherwise I need to alert battalion."

"Yes, sir!" Falcon accompanied the crater-analysis crew to their Jeep. Reaching the northernmost end of the 191st flight line, the crew parked and went to work. Falcon set off to the west end of the flight line to catch up with the 191st maintenance crews.

"Sir!" one of the crater-analysis crew called out to Falcon. "Where do you want us to leave this mortar fin?"

"Just leave it right there by the crater. I'll come by and pick it up on my way in. Thanks." With that said, Falcon turned and headed toward the flashlights on the west end of the flight line, which he assumed were the 191st maintenance personnel MAJ Petric had mentioned. The attack left debris scattered throughout the entire flight line. Even in the darkness, the ferocity of the attack was clearly evident. Falcon could see that some rounds had landed right in the midst of the 191st aircraft revetments.

When he had covered half the distance to the flashlights, mortars whizzed over his head; their high-pitched whistle pierced his ears. Again, the rounds hit on the west end of the 191st revetment area. The sounds of mortar explosions and debris dropping back down to the ground worked its way toward the east. Remembering the Jeep, Falcon turned and hotfooted his 190-pound frame toward the east end of the flight line. Before getting there, the crater-analysis crew jumped in the Jeep and hauled ass to safety. The mortar rounds continued to advance east.

Turning toward the operations building, Falcon bolted in a direction perpendicular to the G-T line. He hoped to get past the anticipated impact area before the rounds got too close. Just east of him, approximately 250 meters downrange, MAJ Erwin Schmidt got caught out in the battalion aircraft revetment area when the incoming rounds started landing. Schmidt, too, was trying to outrun the enemy mortars. The mortar rounds hammered their way closer to Falcon. He knew he was not going to get clear of the blasts. He ducked into an aircraft revetment where he was quickly joined by several of his brothers trying to outrun the blasts. Not able get clear of the airfield, they hunkered down beside the revetment's blast walls. The two blast walls of the aircraft parking area gave little comfort as a protective cover.

"We're all going to get killed!" one of the guys yelled. His voice struck, searing and high-pitched like a tuning fork, an unnerving cry of desperation.

"Hell no!" Falcon yelled. "Just stay here and hug the ground as close to the corner of the revetment as you can—we're going to be okay. Just stay here for a minute!"

The shudder and bellow of incoming mortars drew closer. Each explosion shook and rumbled the ground. Falcon and the others pushed their bodies into the floor of the revetment covered by PSP material that formed its base. Each trying to make themselves as small and flat as possible. Blast fragments showered down, pelting the group with debris and hot mortar fragments. Each froze and gritted his teeth as the next round hissed over the revetment and exploded thirty meters to the east. Almost in unison, the group leapt to their feet and scrambled in the direction of the company bunkers.

The enemy had cleverly disguised their attack strategy. Their firing sequence was coordinated with delayed fuses. The 81-millimeter mortar crews walked their shells from west to east, blasting the long axis of the flight line, while the 120-millimeter mortar crews walked their ordnance in the opposite direction, from east to west, blasting diagonally across the aircraft parking area and into the barracks.

Falcon continued to bolt toward the operations center. He knew the 120-millimeter explosions shifted toward his path. He heard their muffled blasts drawing closer as they buried themselves into the ground and exploded. Unfamiliar with the enemy's new bombardment strategy, Falcon did not believe the muffled explosions to be nearly as menacing as the loud surface blasts of the 81-millimeter shells. Therefore, he did not change his pace or direction.

MAJ Schmidt, also caught out on the airfield, dashed toward the battalion bunker when a 120-millimeter shell burst and debris opened a small shrapnel wound in his forearm. Falcon, still beelining it to the operations center, was tossed into the air—flung airborne by the tremendous pressure wave from a mortar blast. His body slammed back onto the ground, and he lay unconscious. Coming to, dazed with the wind still knocked out of him, the XO stood back up, his legs wobbling. He wiped the sand from his face and stumbled into the operations center to witness a horrifying scene.

"Still swinging from a direct hit of a 120-millimeter shell," Falcon recalls, "the fluorescent light fixture that serviced the operations center had been blasted loose from the ceiling and was dangling on a three-foot span of wire, with one bulb still lit. As it swung from side to side, it briefly illuminated the scene. The bodies of several men were piled up almost in one spot, their limbs still twitching as the last vestige of life ebbed away."

Still dazed from his near-death moment, Falcon stood motionless, surveying the macabre sight, his mind in denial of what his eyes were showing him. As the one fluorescent light swung, it flashed over 1LT Radtke's body.

"He was still moving," Falcon recalls. "He was below two other bodies with disfigured faces that I could not identify. As I tugged Radtke loose from the pile of bodies, he stopped breathing. He lay motionless. I was still half-frozen with shock, and I half-consciously shook Radtke, as one would shake a sleeping person, hoping that might bring him back to life."

The scene gradually filtered through Falcon's consciousness, and he recognized the running shoes he had bought for MAJ Petric earlier that day. He momentarily focused on the shoes in the rubble. Then his gaze shifted from one body to the next: the curly blonde hair of SP5 Robert "Heinie" Heinmiller, the dark complexion of SP4 Carl Douglas, the mustachioed face of 1LT Dennis Coker, and the husky form of SP4 Ronald Lovellette. The familiar smell of cordite, together with the odor of human matter, left a battle-death stench that only war can produce. It hung thick in the gritty air.

Falcon's cognitive functions, blasted numb by the mortar round, regained clarity, and he slowly processed what had just happened. After a round exploded and knocked him unconscious, the next shell struck a direct hit on the operations center. With a delayed fuse, the round penetrated the metal roof and exploded at arm's length from his fellow soldiers gathered there.

A scuffling noise came from the orderly room. Falcon shuffled through the debris and dim light. 1LT Sean LaRue (pseudonym) struggled to get out through the orderly room door that had been locked. One of LaRue's eyeballs dangled out of the eye socket. The eye's sticky vitreous pasted it to his flak vest. LaRue's arms and legs appeared to be hamburger, but he was standing on his own and trying to walk. Immediately, Falcon swung one of LaRue's arms over his shoulder to help him to the medical dispensary. CPT Kalamber, the battalion surgeon, burst through the door. Seeing that the XO was assisting LaRue, he screened the other bodies lying in the pile. Shining a light into the eyes of each individual one by one, he pronounced each dead, a bitterly depressing announcement for Falcon. Holding LaRue up, Falcon stood in disbelief until the doctor finished. Kalamber grabbed LaRue's other arm, and they carried him to the battalion aid station.

After assisting the surgeon in placing LaRue on a gurney, Falcon hightailed it to the 191st officer bunker for help. Arriving there out of breath and still rattled from the shock, he could hardly find the words to explain to those wondering men, sitting in the dark, what had just happened. Seeing their XO covered with blood, CW2 David Schwartz grabbed Falcon by the arm.

"Captain Falcon, are you okay?"

"Yes," Falcon said—his voice unsteady, his thoughts still shaken. "But a bunch of our guys are dead in operations. I'm going to need some help."

At that moment, with neither hesitation nor regard for their own lives, each man in the bunker was willing to assist. CW2 Dave Schwartz, never at a loss for words, quickly chimed in and picked out several people to assist Falcon. The rest remained in the bunker, in case the enemy attacked again. Falcon, Schwartz, and the helpers made their way to the operations center where their commander lay. They began assessing the full extent of the damage.

Regrettably, after he finally had a firm grasp on his company, Petric's command philosophy was never fully implemented, much to the dismay of his XO John Falcon, who had grown to appreciate the major's superb mind and talent. Equally tragic, the commander died before he could fully demonstrate his love and appreciation for the extraordinary company of American fighting men he was commanding. In hindsight, many of his early critics came to regard MAJ John Petric as a solid, well-respected CO.

That same night, the 191st was assigned a new commander, MAJ Erwin Schmidt, the battalion staff officer (S3). Schmidt directed the unit to fly its routine mission the very next day.

Early morning found Falcon sleepless and still anesthetized by shock. Determined to get the unit operations center back in full swing, he made his way over to the blasted-out building to find the first sergeant already busy with a cleanup crew and carpenters beginning the reconstruction. Falcon walked through the site, examining the hole in the roof, and he relived the surreal events of the previous evening. Stopping at the east door, through which he and CPT Kalamber had evacuated LaRue, he paused for a few moments and stared at a spot, just to the left of the door. There, plastered on the wall, was a piece of skull, its curly blond hair still attached. Robert "Heinie" Heinmiller. Falcon winced. A surge of emotion gripped his soul.

To Falcon, it seemed like only yesterday that the meticulous Petric had reviewed paperwork and noticed that Heinmiller and Khan had both been in-country since the 191st first deployed from Fort Bragg. Concerned for their long exposure, MAJ Petric directed Falcon to advise Heinmiller and Kahn that he would not approve any further extensions for them. He wanted them to go home and take a break from the war. When Falcon carried out Petric's order, he commended both men for their dedication to duty and informed them of Petric's decision, explaining that they needed to go back to the States for a breather before volunteering to come back to Vietnam.

"Your families deserve to see you," Falcon had told Heinmiller and Kahn, "and the 'Old Man' believes it's important that you not get target fixation on this place. You guys need to go back to 'the world' and live like normal human beings for a while. Spend Christmas at home for a change." Falcon smiled, demonstrating his appreciation for the enemy-kill ratio that both of these soldiers had accrued. Heinmiller and Kahn were among the world's finest marksmen and performed their duties as crew chief and gunner with distinction, each well respected in the unit. Heinmiller, still a curly-haired youngster, cracked a wide smile back.

"But sir," Heinmiller said, "this is what we love to do. Where else can we kill VC, get three hots and a cot, *and* get combat pay for doing what we love to do?"

The stoic Kahn, who seldom showed any emotion, even in the heat of battle, also smiled, nodding his head in approval.

"I understand," Falcon said. "You guys represent the best our country has to offer, and this unit is damn lucky to have you, but the old man is right; it would be sad to see something happen to you because you stayed here too damn long."

Falcon's last words kept ringing in his memory, and his gaze remained fixed on the curly blond hair stuck to the wall. *Because you stayed here too damn long . . .* Fighting back a surge of emotion, he shuffled out of the building and beelined back to his room. Only after a few minutes of quiet reflection did the "business-as-usual" wisdom of the new CO, MAJ Schmidt, sink in.

"Still, at that moment," Falcon recalls decades later, "I wished I was out flying with the company, doing what we did best—fly guns."[3]

---

3 On January 15, 1969, two months before Heinmiller was killed, SP4 Jerry Kahn was wounded in battle and evacuated back to the States, where he was medically discharged with a permanent disability. He now lives in Ghent, New York, with his wonderful wife, Karen, and son, Zachariah. On March 2 of each year, Jerry Kahn takes a few moments to remember his good friend, Heinie. In the end, Petric's hunch was right; Heinmiller and Kahn had both extended their combat assignments, beyond the odds of survivability for combat assault-helicopter crewmembers.

CHAPTER 20

Schmidt Commanding

"Bounty Hunter Six, this is Boomerang Six. I've got two enemy running in rice paddies left of you."

It was near midnight on March 2, 1969, when MAJ Erwin Augustus "Dutch" Schmidt was handed the reins of the 191st AHC. The transition had been swift and deliberate without the customary fanfare of a change of command. Schmidt, along with the battalion commander, LTC Wallace Dietrich, XO John Falcon, and several others, surveyed the mortar-attack damage and confirmed that MAJ John Petric was dead.

Falcon eyed Schmidt's shrapnel wound from the night's mortar attack. Blood trickled from Schmidt's forearm. *Must be destiny*, Falcon thought.

Schmidt, a burly fellow born and raised in the Texas hill country, was comprised of a tough and tenacious fabric—the same fabric that inspired self-driven commissioned officers to reach their highest potential in the Army's intensely competitive career system. When he first arrived at the 214th CAB, Schmidt shared with the battalion commander, LTC Wallace Dietrich, his desire to command a company. With his good performance in command assignments, Schmidt's career progression was fast-tracked. However, Schmidt had no clue that he was destined to assume command under the most trying conditions an assault-helicopter CO could fathom.

The night's devastating enemy-mortar bombardment killed the CO; left for dead the admin officer, the duty officer, the operations specialist, and two of its most experienced gunship crew chiefs; critically wounded the intelligence officer; severely damaged some of the 191st aircraft; and obliterated the 191st operations center.

Standing side by side, Schmidt and Falcon gazed at their jumbled surroundings. Bodies torn beyond recognition. Flesh and blood splattered over the entire room. Their raw emotions were heightened by the visual impact of a human face torn in half—exposing the tongue split across the middle, teeth torn away with a piece of jawbone protruding. A young body with the rear portion of his skull missing and brain matter flowing onto the floor. Curly blond hair soaked with blood and the solemn young face almost untouched with a peaceful expression that pierced one's living soul to see. Another body with flak vest on, the face looking up to the ceiling, an enormous shrapnel hole exposed at the base of his neck, eyes open as if the young lad was ready to talk.

The pungent odor of blood dominated Schmidt's and Falcon's nostrils. Like a bad sea wind, the stench forced unofficial curiosity seekers to turn and leave. Worst of all, blood dripping from the rafters splashed onlookers with repulsive effect.

It was then that LTC Dietrich immediately assigned Schmidt to take command of the 191st AHC. Schmidt, with a straight face, contemplated his next move as the new CO.

LTC Dietrich turned to leave. "Dutch, call me if you need anything."

"Yes, sir. Thank you," Schmidt responded. "I'll give you a damage report as soon as possible."

"That's fine. Just do what you can."

Schmidt remained calm and well composed. Seeing the group of onlookers growing, he motioned Falcon to accompany him toward the door. Stopping short, Schmidt placed his arm on Falcon's shoulder. "Captain Falcon, where are the rest of the men in the company?"

Amid all this devastation, the XO and the new commander had to coordinate to get things in order. Although Falcon's mind needed a moment to recompose, he felt urgency in Schmidt's words. With his new boss exhibiting a strong persona, Falcon recognized that Schmidt was a no-bullshit kind of guy and one who needed answers right away. Complicating matters, Falcon was in physical and emotional pain; however, MAJ Schmidt, having not been close to the dead, did not immediately sense Falcon's discomfort.

With blood spread throughout the operations floor sticking to their boots, and the smell of cordite and human excrement still thick in the air, the room was a death chamber. Worse, with eyes still open, some of the deceased were facing toward the direction where Falcon and Schmidt were standing. Most nauseating, brain matter from one of the dead crew chiefs was spread on the floor next to his body, rendering a scene like no horror movie could possibly recreate.

Being a highly intuitive individual, Schmidt soon sensed the XO's anguish for his dead comrades and walked slowly to the door as Falcon followed. Once outside he repeated the question. "Captain Falcon, where are the rest of the men in the company?"

"They're in the bunker, sir. I didn't want them exposed to any more of *this* in the event we get hit again."

The new commander took note of Falcon's bloodstained clothes. "You okay?" he asked, his voice soft and low.

"Yes, sir, the blood is First Lieutenant LaRue's, the intelligence officer; he was wounded pretty bad, and I helped carry him to the battalion aid station."

"Well, what about your arm?" Schmidt asked, speaking with a little more firmness. "It's still bleeding, isn't it?"

"Yes, sir, I was running to the operations center when I was hit by mortar shrapnel, but it's nothing serious."

Maintaining a calm demeanor, Schmidt looked at his new XO and directed, "Captain Falcon, please take me to where the rest of the 191st officers are taking cover."

"Yes, sir."

Calmly walking to the 191st officers' bunker, accompanied by a few 191st pilots who had volunteered to help the XO with the dead and wounded, Schmidt entered the bunker and introduced himself as their new commander. Briefly describing the circumstances and the events that had just occurred in the 191st operations center, Schmidt chose his words tactfully.

"Gentlemen, I am Major Schmidt. I have just been assigned command of the 191st," Schmidt said, speaking in a soft and gentle tone. "A one-hundred-twenty-millimeter shell has just made a direct hit on our operations building and killed or wounded a number of people. Major Petric was among them, and it is not known if he is dead or alive, but he and the others have been evacuated to the battalion aid station."

Schmidt paused briefly and then continued. "I have directed Captain Falcon to give me an aircraft-status report, as soon as maintenance personnel can determine how many birds we can put up tomorrow. I need to meet with the XO and the operations officer immediately after that, and I would recommend that the rest of you try to get some sleep. We will, more than likely, fly our scheduled mission in the morning."

The bunker fell silent. No one could understand the rationale behind Schmidt's order to fly the next morning. With all the devastation and death that had just occurred, plus the yet unknown extent of aircraft damage, to try to get the unit airborne in just over six hours seemed ludicrous. At that moment, among captains and lieutenants who were combat veterans and intermediate leaders of the 191st, the wisdom of the older artillery pilot, freshly thrown into command of an assault-helicopter company, was in serious doubt.

But in a mere twenty-four hours, Falcon realized the extraordinary value in Schmidt's thinking. While sifting through the human remains and blasted-out pieces of the 191st operations center the following day, Falcon relived the impact of the prior evening's events. Twice, he had to stop what he was doing and take a few moments to clear his mind and soul as he attempted to reconcile the losses. As he walked over the bloodstains on the floor, the image of the dead came to life in the last communication he had with each one.

His closest bond with any of the dead had been MAJ Petric. Falcon could still see his face as if he was talking to him at that very moment. He could also hear

Heinmiller's voice and see his face from the last mission that they flew together. Invited by his close friend, gunship pilot CPT Palmer, Falcon had flown missions with Heinmiller, a likeable crew chief with a big heart and a personable nature. The outstanding admin officer, 1LT Radtke, and the gentle-natured operations specialist, SP4 Carl Douglas, were also among the people with whom the XO bonded daily. Equally embossed in Falcon's mind was the loss of SP4 Lovellette, a gunship crew chief with exceptional performance. Soft-spoken 1LT Dennis Coker, an officer of extraordinary quality and a true gentleman, would be missed by all who knew him.

Coker's crew chief, SP5 William L. Sawls Jr., was among those who felt Coker's loss the greatest. Both Southerners, Coker from Georgia and Sawls from Alabama, they frequently shared Southern values of customs and culture. On the door of their Huey, Sawls had drawn a map of Georgia and Alabama with a cotton ball and a Southern belle and named the aircraft *Southern Pride*. With one decisive blow, the enemy had snuffed out the lives of several precious human resources of the 191st, but had forever strengthened the brotherhood bonds felt by all who lived in their midst. Following the death of Coker, Sawls crewed a Bounty Hunter gunship and performed gallantly under fire in numerous engagements. He served under the pilot skills of CW2 David Hamilton and CW2 SanFillipo. Residing with his family in Atlanta, Sawls remains in touch with his fellow 191st brothers. He recalls vividly the day Coker advised him that his foremost goal should be to get home alive.

After the attack, Falcon had known exactly where each of the bodies lay when he stumbled into the ops office, still dazed from his own narrow escape with death. Six brothers were dead, and XO Falcon was tasked with obliterating the last vestiges of life they left on the floor. It had to happen; the ordeal had to be cleaned. Falcon's mindset went from pain for the loss to rage for the enemy. Most disturbing, the only mode by which he could release this rage had gone flying without him: the gunships. Occasionally, Falcon was invited to fly with his Bounty Hunter buddy, CPT Bruce Palmer, who was now the new ops officer. But the gunships were in the air doing what he wished he could. With Palmer on R&R in Australia, the XO felt helpless.

However, amidst the morbid scene—the smell of dead bodies, the blood and brain matter drying on the floor—Falcon now understood why it was better for the company to be out flying combat assaults. Schmidt ordered his unit back in the air to avoid the risk of his men reliving the horrific events of the previous night. The new CO, like a wise father, discerned that when his youngster is thrown from a horse, it's best to get back on the steed and regain confidence. The new commander made an immediate impression on the XO, and from his initial wisdom, Schmidt garnered Falcon's devoted loyalty. Thereafter, a close working relationship thrived between Falcon and the older artilleryman.

Experienced in managing men and equipment, it did not take long for Schmidt to reach full throttle. He knew how to think like his men. And his initial, gentle direction turned into a vigorous assimilation that had quickly earned him the following of the company's officers and men.

"Right from the start," Schmidt recalls, "I knew I could rely on the officers and men of the 191st to know their jobs and get the mission accomplished with minimal interference from me." His warm smile fills his cheeks. "The unit did, in fact, fly combat assaults the next morning."

Under these *unusual* circumstances, the company went into battle with less than their full complement of aircraft. But the pilots and crews were, for the most part, productively employed away from the site of all the death and destruction that occurred the night before. Prior to departing on the morning of March 3, 1969, Schmidt briefly met with the XO and issued several orders, among which the new commander wanted the memorial ceremony for the dead to be held in the company area the following morning.

"We need quick resolution, John," Schmidt said. "It won't help to have this hanging over our heads any longer than necessary. It's hard enough to deal with it as it is. The men need to move on with the mission and try to put this behind them. Flying combat assaults is far too hazardous to have anyone's mind preoccupied or numbed by this tragedy. I really need your support on this, and I'm relying on you to take care of these things. Also, I have already spoken to the first sergeant about cleaning up the operations center, and getting things in order, as much as possible. I would appreciate it if you could oversee that to make sure he has the resources he needs. I would rather the men not see any more of that devastation than they have to."

"Yes, sir!" Falcon affirmed once again Schmidt's intent to minimize emotional anguish for the survivors.

Memorial ceremonies always jolted the emotions of the survivors. The deceased were their brothers. The intimate bonds forged in combat are deeply seated in the very nature of what it means to be human. Humans as a communal species gravitate toward a collective tribe, and there is no more powerful evidence of our nature then at times of war, when we come together to fight and defend against a collective enemy. When death preyed on members of the 191st, the loss stunned as if it had been the loss of one of your own limbs. No one can explain this better than WO1 Jack L. Lammers, 1LT Radtke's roommate.

"The worst task I ever had with the 191st was packing a soldier's belongings after his death," Lammers recalls. "That had no equivalency in my book."

At the memorial ceremony, helmets of the deceased comrades were placed on an altar, and the battalion chaplain, trying not to seem fatalistic, did what he could to preside in what was a solemn monotone, with words that honored the fallen soldiers. For the 191st brotherhood, it was a final farewell. Some said their goodbyes in the American tradition and saluted those who gave their lives for their country. Some, however, took a different view. To say that anyone *gave* his life was a misnomer. In the real-world perception of the survivors, none of the deceased gave their lives—their lives were *taken* in the heat of battle, killed by a vengeful enemy.

The VC, driven by a fanatical belief in their Communist cause, were viewed as a threat to humanity, in the same way that one might consider a pit viper in your backyard as something to be eliminated in order to protect your family. The killing of these Americans incensed those who were bonded closest to the dead. A rancor penetrated the innermost souls of the 191st brotherhood, remaining latent until the opportunity emerged to kill the enemy. In Bounty Hunter fashion, there was only one way to relieve the pain: *kill more of the enemy*—such were the thoughts of the men honoring their dead brothers that day.

The swell of emotion surged through the attendees of the 191st memorial ceremony as they passed through the phase of grief for the loss of their brothers and then anger at an enemy that now seemed cowardly elusive—an enemy that struck at night like vermin. At the end of the ceremony, "Taps" was played on a recording, and those notes pierced each attendee's heart. Most choked down the emotions they were feeling and maintained composure by clearing their throats or otherwise blinking their eyes under sunglasses. The sound of the bugle truly signaled the end of a life. Within each member of the unit was a deep feeling of emptiness and sorrow. Mental visions of the living faces of the dead, smiling or talking or doing the mundane things they regularly did, were still fresh on the minds of the survivors who daily bonded with those now deceased. It was mental anguish. Schmidt was right. This whole scene needed to be over quickly.

Memorial ceremonies are supposed to be an instrument of reverence, to honor the dead. But in a war zone, where retaliation was so close at hand, they simmered just below the boiling point of vengeance. The brutal bereavement for this human loss did not end in Vietnam but instead made its lengthy journey from the hearts and minds of the 191st brotherhood to the Stateside communities, where the families of the dead awaited the return of their loved ones' remains. Eventually, the bodies of the fallen comrades were laid to rest in a cemetery plot, their last earthly domain. Their mothers, fathers, wives, or sweethearts were handed the United States flag, its red and white stripes wrapped into the blue and folded into a tight triangle with only the white stars visible—their final salute.

As had been the case after previous battles, the unit recovered from the loss and readjusted to the new faces replacing those killed or wounded in action. CPT Palmer, who had previously been reassigned from gun-platoon leader to the operations officer position, had been on R&R in Australia on the eve of March 2, 1969. Upon his return, he was stunned by the devastation. He had personally taken an interest in upgrading the operations planning area, and now, he had to start all over again. Fortunately, the first sergeant moved rapidly with a crew of carpenters, and in two weeks, the 191st operations center was back in full swing, good as new.

Palmer, relieved that he had been in Australia during the enemy attack, shared a beer with Falcon.

"Damn! John. Had I been here, I would have been blasted to pieces with the rest of 'em. There's no doubt in my mind, I would have been in there."

"You were lucky, Bruce," Falcon said. "Not only were you spared your life, but you were spared the mental anguish of seeing the bodies of our buddies lying there, torn to shreds. The damn mortar went off at arm's length from the whole bunch gathered there. You were lucky in many ways. The scene was as horrific as you can imagine. As I stumbled into the room, bodies were still twitching. Radtke was still alive. But in the short time it took for me to get to him and try to dig him out from the pile of corpses, he died. It wasn't your time, bud. You were spared much agony."

The two men sat silent for a moment, both knocking back another swig of beer, before talking again. "What do you think of our new commander?" Palmer asked.

"I personally think he's excellent. He has a good grasp of combat operations, and he doesn't shirk any risk. He's flying combat assaults as we speak."

"I know, and I appreciate that." Palmer chuckled. "At least we won't have to *train* him from scratch like we did his predecessor."

Falcon grinned, welcoming Palmer's lighthearted humor. "Yeah, but Petric turned out to be a good commander, nonetheless. The unit has certainly had worse. He had a heart for the troops, and in my position, I saw him do some great things for some who needed his attention." Falcon paused for a moment, remembering Petric's concern for Heinmiller and Kahn. "Anyway, in answer to your question, I think you'll like Schmidt."

Schmidt held a series of meetings with the staff and familiarized himself with the various operations and tasks of the company. Among his highest priorities: the proper accounting and disposition of personal belongings for the mortar-attack casualties, replacements for those killed or wounded, and repairing the aircraft and facilities that were damaged. Furthermore, he instructed Falcon to continue with unit preparation for the imminent IG inspection.

Within three weeks, Schmidt had flown at least two combat-assault days with each of the two Boomerang lift platoons and with the Bounty Hunter gun platoon. In between, he sandwiched days flying the C&C bird, where he brought together all his previous experience as an artillery officer, and gave the infantry commanders a premier aviation performance. Just four days after assuming command of the company, Schmidt was awarded the Distinguished Flying Cross for extraordinary leadership and bravery under fire.

On March 6, 1969, the engagement that earned Schmidt the Distinguished Flying Cross started with a routine insertion of American troops in a suspected enemy stronghold. Enemy tracers immediately alerted that the enemy was ready. Flying in the C&C bird, Schmidt witnessed the entire sequence of events as it unfolded. The Bounty Hunters focused their rocket fire to suppress the enemy machine-gun fire. Meanwhile, Schmidt saw two black-pajama figures running from the vicinity of the LZ. Knowing the gunships had missed seeing the fleeing enemy, he called the Bounty Hunters: "Bounty Hunter Six, this is Boomerang Six. I've got two enemy running in rice paddies left of you. I'm going down to check. Please cover me."

"Boomerang Six, this is Bounty Hunter Six. Go ahead, we'll be there in a jiffy!"

Landing the C&C bird in a blocking position in front of the fleeing enemy, Schmidt ordered the crew to fire their M60s in front of the running figures. Failing to stop, the two VC changed direction and kept running. Schmidt ordered the crew chief to take them. As close as they were, one quick burst from the M60 and both enemy soldiers were rolling to the place of their final breaths. They died where they landed, without moving a muscle.

A search of the enemy bodies produced some documents concerning the mission of their operation in the region. Schmidt quickly turned those over to the task force commander riding in the back of the C&C bird and went about marking the LZ where enemy emplacements were hidden. Having been at ground level, he got a good look at the defensive positions of the enemy stronghold.

Withdrawing back to altitude, he directed rocket strikes on his smoke markings. Straightaway, rockets exploded on the enemy emplacements with a large splash of fire raining on enemy bunkers. The entire complex in flames and smoke rising to the clouds indicated the concentrated American aggression. With the whole compound burning, the enemy were seen surrendering to the American troops on the ground.

The task force commander, seeing that Schmidt was instrumental in defeating an enemy unit without yet being fully acquainted with his new command, recommended Schmidt for award of the Distinguished Flying Cross. Schmidt earned it.

Schmidt was the type of commander who wanted to *personally* see how each of the unit's flight components collectively executed the mission. Taking a hands-on approach, he quickly assimilated the established tactical protocols of the company and gradually inserted his influence where it would improve unit performance. As a CO, Schmidt was innovative. One of his first innovations: invite combat-assault pilots to the weekly battalion briefings.

Having served as the battalion S3, Schmidt knew that the exposure to the weekly briefings would professionally benefit the young officers and help them gain a better perspective of the overall airmobile concept. CPT Palmer took advantage of the opportunity. Recognizing that combat-assault missions were, at times, assigned several days in advance of the actual OPORD, the clever Palmer, on a daily basis, stole a peek at the battalion assignments board. This proved invaluable for the flight-platoon scheduling officers, who could then better manage blade time for ACs who were approaching their monthly maxima. On days when the AO would be far from "home plate," Palmer notified the XO. This assured that all logistical and support elements under XO Falcon's direction remained on duty if the flight returned late. And best of all, it didn't matter how late the flight arrived back from their combat-assault missions, the mess hall stayed open so food would be warm and plentiful. Morale soon picked up. Schmidt was making headway with the troops. Eventually, those intermediate leaders, who were initially concerned with the new commander's ability to lead, relaxed in his presence and enthusiastically sought his guidance. That's all Schmidt needed.

A natural-born leader who preferred to lead from the front, Schmidt would make rounds through all parts of the company and stop to communicate with the troops. Most appreciated his presence. But some, who were prone to indulge in what some coined as "devil weed," experienced discomfort with his unannounced visits to the barracks.

Falcon recalls one such event. "One evening, in the latter part March 1969, after a hot day, just about dusk, the gun-platoon leader, John Cook, and I were standing behind the maintenance hangar, swigging a beer, when we saw MAJ Schmidt enter the front door of the enlisted barracks. After a loud 'Tench-Hut,' the back door of the barracks suddenly flew open and out sailed three lit marijuana joints, landing in the dirt, just a few meters from where John Cook and I were standing. Shortly afterward, three enlisted men casually stepped out the back door of the barracks. In the near darkness, they headed for the lit joints when they caught sight of Cook and me. With amazing theatrics that could have earned an Oscar, they changed direction without breaking stride and nonchalantly headed in the opposite direction."

Amused by their behavior, Falcon couldn't pass up the opportunity to jerk their chain a little.

"Hey! Where you folks going?" Falcon yelled.

"Uh . . . we're just headed over to the club for a beer, sir!"

"Aaah! Okaay!" Falcon said, a chiding tone in his voice.

Surprised by Falcon's humor, Cook nearly choked on a mouthful of beer and was overcome with convulsive laughter.

The three enlisted men never once turned back. They quickly disappeared behind the next building. No doubt, looking for better cover to get high. Swigging down the last sip of his beer, Cook looked sideways at Falcon.

"Over in my hootch, I have a goodie package that my mom sent," Cook said. "I'm willing to bet there's some plant and cheese in the box, if you're interested."

Falcon understood what "plant" meant: canned eggplant in tomato sauce, a delicacy that both Falcon and Cook relished.

"Yeah, man!" Falcon sucked down the last of his beer. "Let me swing by my office and see if the Old Man left me any messages. I'll be up there in a short minute."

Falcon made his way to the orderly room. But right before he entered the building, a mortar round exploded. It hit about a mile away, on the far side of the compound.

"Initially, I assumed the enemy was aiming for the Riverine Force," Falcon recalls. "With rounds landing that distant, I would have normally checked my inbox and then headed for the bunker. But with the March 2 attack still fresh on my mind, and with the enemy now mixing their attack strategy to include bombarding the barracks, I thought the better of it and immediately headed for the bunker. MAJ Schmidt arrived shortly afterward and stood just outside the bunker door, momentarily talking with 1LT Alvin Hogsett, the recently appointed admin officer. With the mortar rounds landing so far away, there was no urgency for the two officers to take cover. Suddenly, the whole night sky lit up, bright as day, in a tremendous explosion that rocked the entire compound. Both Schmidt and Hogsett darted into the bunker and joined the rest of us."

Although the detonation occurred over a mile away, the blast created a pressure differential that momentarily pushed the air out of the bunker. As the sky lit up, CW2 Janes, thin and small framed, was caught a few feet from the hangar-side entrance to the bunker. Frozen by the brightness, he stood in awe. Regaining his composure, he scrambled for the entrance. A tremendous shock wave passed through, lifting up Janes's body and throwing him into the bunker—along with several pounds of sand. Bewildered, Janes picked himself up from the floor and dusted the sand off himself, laughing.

Watching with concern, several pilots reached to help him, but he waved them off. "I'm okay," he said, "but what the fuck was that? For a minute, I thought we were getting *nuked.*"

The enemy had scored another major hit. Their mortar shell landed squarely in the center of the ammo dump, precisely in the middle of a stack of eight-inch howitzer warheads. The resultant chain reaction of secondary explosions was the most spectacular demonstration of fireworks ever seen by inhabitants within a forty-click radius. Approximately forty kilometers to the west, WO1 Steve Kinnaman, a pilot serving with the 114th AHC at Vinh Long, witnessed the explosion. Later, he shared his observation with Janes, his flight school buddy. According to Kinnaman, he knew something *big* had exploded at Dong Tam because the fireball soared several hundred feet into the air and lit up the entire eastern sky.

For almost an hour, small-arms munitions and artillery shells, of various yields and calibers, cooked off into the night sky. They rained down on Dong Tam in a shower of fire and glowing metal. The Ninth Division headquarters, which was just beyond the ammo-dump berm, received the full brunt of the blast, as did the nearby PX and the water plant. It wasn't known until later that Dong Tam took eighty-eight Purple Heart (wounded in action) casualties that night.[1] Although no names were given, this statistic was reported by an Army news chronicle that covered that region of South Vietnam. All eighty-eight came from other units stationed at Dong Tam. In effect, it had no debilitating impact on any of the units to continue their operations, nor were base operations stymied.

---

1 COL (Ret.) LeRoy "Lee" W. Dyment Jr.

However, the considerable damage sustained by the PX took a toll on morale. The mortars destroyed every bottle of booze and every can of beer, much to the dismay of the pilots, crews, and support personnel of the 191st. It was no laughing matter. Being without hot food for a day or so was no big thing; one could eat C rations. Cutting off the running-water supply was also not an issue; after all, the only flushable toilets were in the division headquarters. It didn't concern most men if the CG would have to crap in a sawed-off fifty-five-gallon drum like the rest of the underprivileged. And showers? Oh well! But being without beer and booze was a *serious* matter. Something had to be done, and quickly. Sure enough, the next day, a courier flight left Dong Tam, en route to the Vung Tau Aviation Repair Depot with an emergency parts requisition. Of the 1,300 pounds of cargo that the bird carried on the return trip, 380 pounds were parts. And the rest? Bootleg alcohol.

Mess Sergeant Robert Pagel fired up the outdoor grills. With power generators limited to providing electricity for only the essential terminals (such as refrigeration units, the company headquarters, and sensitive communication gear), Pagel seized the opportunity for a cookout.

"And man, what a cookout!" Falcon recalls. "Grilled steaks and trimmings were the menu of the evening, hot off the fire, with Pagel himself standing behind the chow line serving steaks sizzling hot and asking each man who went through the chow line how do you want it—well, medium, or rare?"

Chowing down on good food—and knocking back a few drinks—was how the 191st reacted to the ammo-dump explosion. After what the men had been through several weeks earlier, little could faze them. Hardened by months of combat, and mentally toughened by periodic losses of fellow Boomerangs and Bounty Hunters to the enemy, the 191st was hickory tough and showed it when they flew combat assaults. With Schmidt at the helm, the 191st AHC was now headed for new horizons.

Under Schmidt, aircraft maintenance underwent significant changes. MAJ Rick Moore had rotated back to the States, and CPT Michael Hannan became the new maintenance officer. This allowed Schmidt an opportunity to again influence change for the better. He formed a close working relationship with Hannan, and together the two instituted adjustments to the night shift. They increased the number of night test flights so that these tasks could be done when the airfield pattern was less crowded. This granted the test pilots more freedom with airspace and better support with ancillary services, such as air-traffic control and fire-truck coverage. The smart move increased aircraft readiness and made a significant impact on availability of gunships. Charlie-models were mechanically notorious for not being ready to cover the flight at departure time each morning. Frequently, the slicks would leave Dong Tam with less than optimum gun cover, and sometimes they even flew combat-assault missions for the entire day with less than adequate gunship security.

The workload was immense. SP5 James D. Fouse, an avionics specialist, maintained a seven-hour-a-day work schedule seven days per week. Yet one never heard anyone complain. Schmidt himself put in some exceptionally long hours to keep the unit in top shape. With dedication for the unit's well-being, people like Fouse volunteered to fly combat assaults to give the aircrews some reprieve from the sting of battle.

"On my very first flight as an aircrewman on a slick," Fouse recalls, "we landed in a friendly PZ where we were surrounded by children selling cold drinks. Throughout the day, they made rounds by the aircraft parking area to sell their goods and kept asking for the time of day. They insisted they had to be home by four o'clock. Shortly after 1600 hours the parked flight came under enemy mortar attack. Trust in those kids went out the door thereafter."

Under Schmidt's direction, teamwork among all segments of the 191st came together to rapidly enhance Boomerang operations. Most significant, protection for the flight was substantially elevated. Gunship support improved and all pilots and aircrews celebrated on the eve of the first aircraft-readiness report that verified the functional upgrade. A hangar party ensued. Beer by the gallons.

By mid-April of 1969, Schmidt had honed his skills as AMC and was delivering exceptional support to the infantry commanders. However, Falcon grew concerned that the older artilleryman might be overenthusiastic about moving into the full swing of combat assaults too quickly and might get shot down. Then, during a May morning of 1969, Falcon was alerted that Schmidt's bird was down at Firebase Schroeder with significant battle damage and a replacement aircraft was needed. Falcon assumed the worst.

"Was anybody hurt?" Falcon asked.

"We don't know, sir. The message came through infantry channels."

Quickly, Falcon issued the order for maintenance to prepare a replacement bird, plus a chase bird to recover the replacement crew. While the operations specialist rounded up a copilot, Falcon hotfooted it to his hootch and grabbed his flight gear.

In ten minutes, Falcon lifted the Huey into the air and headed northwest from Dong Tam at full throttle. Arriving over the fire support base, Falcon spotted Schmidt standing by the downed bird, seemingly okay. Gently, the XO landed his aircraft next to the battle-damaged Huey. He instructed the copilot to remain on the controls and he quickly exited the aircraft to meet with the CO.

Falcon and Schmidt exchanged salutes. Schmidt and his crew were unharmed, and a wide Cheshire-cat grin formed on the CO's face. Schmidt was humbled by the experience, and he fully expected Falcon would have something witty to say about the incident.

Falcon spied the long stitching of bullet holes. "Damn, sir!" The holes, about eight inches apart, spanned from just behind the crew chief's station, extending along the tail boom, to the vertical fin. The experienced XO knew that the only way this could have happened was for the bird to be at a dangerously low altitude. Falcon respected his commander and used a friendly tone so not to appear condescending.

"As tight as those stitches are, you must have been down there pretty close. Trying to kiss and make up with the enemy, huh?"

"No, it wasn't me," Schmidt said. His tone, jovial. "It was the task force commander who asked for a closer look—and I gave it to him! Of course, Charlie didn't like that. But we nailed the bastards anyway. We got three of them, before they could di di mau out of there with the rest."

Relieved that all was well, Falcon assisted the crew chiefs with the transfer of C&C gear while Schmidt went into the operations center and reconnected with the task force commander. In minutes, Schmidt was back in the air and on his way to seek and destroy more enemy.

On May 17, 1969, Schmidt was again decorated with a Distinguished Flying Cross for heroism. That day, while flying as AMC, he descended abnormally low and observed enemy soldiers running away from an area where the Boomerangs had inserted infantry troops. With quick reactions, Schmidt directed door-gun fire into the fleeing VC, killing several and pressuring the others to throw down their weapons and give up. He landed the C&C bird close by and took them prisoner. Afterward, he promptly delivered them to the US forces. On the same day when the grunts became pinned down by enemy fire, Schmidt attacked the enemy and relieved the beleaguered troops. Without question, Schmidt served his country as a hands-on commander, setting an inspirational example for his troops.

Amidst rumors that the Ninth Infantry Division ("Old Reliables") would be going back to the States, the 191st AHC underwent a gradual shift in its support role of the Ninth and began working more with the ARVN. In August of 1969, the Ninth departed Vietnam, leaving behind a contingency of infantry to maintain the security of Dong Tam while the ARVN moved in. Virtually deserted, Dong Tam had only the Boomerangs and the Bounty Hunters as aviation assets.

In September of 1969, the 191st AHC received orders to relocate to Can Tho, where it would support the ARVN IV Corps exclusively. Loaded onto LSTs (landing ship, tanks), docked on the riverine ramps at Dong Tam harbor, the 191st heavy equipment and vehicles were transported by river passage. Schmidt led the company formation of aircraft as they departed the Dong Tam home base for the last time and headed out for their new home at Can Tho.

Two weeks after arriving at their new location, Schmidt's command tour was complete, and his departure would mark the beginning of the end of the 191st mission as it had evolved over the preceding three years.

"It was the most memorable assignment of my entire career," Schmidt recalls. "Looking back, I see the entire event as if it took place only yesterday. The tragic beginning of my taking command of the company made me extremely aware of the high loss ratio of personnel in the airmobile combat-assault arena. Consequently, as CO I made it my number-one priority to bear down on the things that I thought would minimize death and casualties in the unit. And whether by luck or by design,

I was extremely pleased to complete my command tour with only one casualty [from the 191st]. To this day, I thank God for that and for the contribution of the officers and men. They performed admirably. The 191st was an exceptional unit blessed with exceptional talent, which made my job easy. In retrospect, the 191st stands out among all the outfits that I have served with as the quality of American fiber that Army units should all possess. I would hope that if my grandchildren must ever go to war, that they have the bond among their fellow warriors that existed in the 191st AHC."

Retired LTC Erwin Augustus "Dutch" Schmidt died peacefully of natural causes on September 11, 2013, in El Paso, Texas. Retired MAJ John D. Falcon was asked to speak at his funeral.

"No greater honor has ever been asked of me," Falcon said. "Dutch was truly one of a kind. I learned so much from the man and felt a bond typical of the heartfelt relationships shared by warriors of that era. His character, his human kindness, his phenomenal instincts, his endless valor—seemed at times too risky and worrisome to others. Dutch Schmidt will forever hold a place in my soul. He earned it the hard way—as a warrior."

CHAPTER 21

Battle at Ap My Thuan

"There is no monument that can properly measure the debt of gratitude owed these warriors."

At 0500 hours, March 25, 1969, the 191st AHC operations center buzzed with activity. Dong Tam meteorologists forecasted a hot day, with air so thin that pilots pulled the guts out of their battle-weary birds just to lift normal combat loads. Although it was certainly a workhorse, little could reduce a Huey's lift capacity more than tropical heat, and Vietnam was cursed with a triple dose. Hot and stiflingly humid days jacked up the pucker factor of even the most experienced Boomerangs. The mere thought of crashing with a full load of fuel and passengers made all pilots shudder.

CPT Falcon stood in the middle of the operations center. He could still smell the new lumber from recent mortar-damage repairs. It was a grim reminder that barely three weeks before, a 120-millimeter enemy mortar shrieked into Dong Tam and punched through the center's roof.

Falcon scanned the flight assignments. He was scheduled to fly as copilot on the C&C bird with CPT Palmer. Assigned as operations officer, Palmer actually worked for Falcon on the ground, but a shortage of pilots required dispensing with formalities, and the XO volunteered to fill in as copilot. Falcon appreciated the chance to get off the ground, while Palmer, of course, relished the opportunity to strut his stuff in the presence of his boss. Decades later, wearing his characteristic goofy corner-of-the-mouth grin, Palmer would admit to Falcon, "When I saw Falcon on my crew list, I finally realized you were a pilot."

The two pilots made a formidable pair, with Falcon experienced in airmobile troop insertions and Palmer experienced in flying gun cover. Having more flight hours than Falcon, Palmer would be boss for the day, and that was something the lucky bastard relished even more. Palmer, a man of short stature, reveled in the distraction of ribbing Falcon, who towered over him and was twice as broad. The Texan drawls of both could be heard from one end of the flight line to the other as they carried on with their antics and prepared for the day's mission. At every opportunity, as common with pilots, they taunted each other in friendly rivalry.

Palmer chuckled. "Hey John! You'd better perform the ground check and let me do the head. I'd hate to see your big lumbering ass come crashing through the greenhouse and fuck up our bird."

"Yeah, yeah!" Falcon's voice was loud enough even for the crew chief to hear. After all, when two pilots get to ribbing each other, as customary, it's more entertaining to have a captive audience. "You just don't want to leap your midget ass up on that tail stinger to check the tail rotor."

"You little fart! I'll have maintenance get you a fuckin' ladder so you won't be too scared of falling off and bustin' your puny ass."

Falcon's and Palmer's mission that day assigned them to work with the 4th/39th at Fire Support Base Danger (FSBD). Deploying a reinforced, platoon-sized reconnaissance element, the infantry would be sweeping a small region of the Mekong Delta for remnants of a VC battalion that the 4th/39th had severely battered two days prior. FSBD was right smack in the middle of some of the largest enemy strongholds in South Vietnam. After the devastating mortar strike on the 191st ops center on March 2, even the most intractable souls were motivated to occasionally contemplate their maker. And the mission to FSBD that morning certainly had Falcon thinking about his destiny.

Preparations for the 0630 lift-off were uneventful. The last-minute scurrying about of crews who occasionally found their aircraft unfit for flight did not happen, fortunately. After start-up and receiving the up-status report from each aircraft, Palmer eased the C&C bird off the pad and the ten Boomerang lift ships hovered into position on the active runway. Three Bounty Hunter gunships joined them. When the trail ship signaled the entire flight "ready," the whole armada took to the air.

Palmer and Falcon exchanged little conversation during departure. It was customary to focus on the mission until the flight was on its way and stable, since departure was typically when dicey maintenance problems appeared. After they had flown west a few miles, Palmer broke the silence with his usual friendly ribbing. Falcon was quick to shoot back.

"All right, you half-grown smartass. That's enough of that bullshit, unless you want to join the bunker-building crew when we get back on the ground."

For Falcon, a flying day meant temporary relief from the foul air of Dong Tam. His XO duties kept him on the ground more days than not. Palmer knew that flying was a break for Falcon, and being the asshole he loved to be, Palmer couldn't pass up a chance to rub it in.

"Must be good to get a breath of fresh air, once in a while, eh, John?"

"Man, you'd better believe it! But you better hope like hell I don't rotate before you do or I'll recommend they move your midget ass into the XO slot so *you* can smell that burning shit all day long."

Burning shit was an additional duty 191st pilots loathed. Fifty-five-gallon drums, cut in half, were used as crapper receptacles. Those lucky enough to be assigned this detail took the loaded drums to a common location, doused them with diesel, and set them on fire. Flaming shit! The resulting nauseating stench greeted each arriving GI with a "Welcome to Vietnam!" Therefore, words cannot describe the joyous celebration when 191st officers learned that a second lieutenant from the 214th Aviation Battalion had been assigned that nasty task. The 191st personnel wondered who the lucky lieutenant pissed off—and what stories he would tell his grandchildren. Still the stench permeated Dong Tam.

Falcon moved in for his final jab at Palmer. "As low to the ground as you are, those fumes would probably pickle your little ass." In true Falcon fashion, the rib was laid down in a matter-of-fact way with only a light snicker.

In the back, the crew chief damned near busted a gut with laughter. Palmer was tough on crewmembers, so it pleased the crew chief to hear Falcon ribbing the little fart.

After about fifteen minutes of flying westerly, FSBD was just becoming discernible on the distant horizon.

Arriving at the fire support base, Falcon and Palmer found Hackworth's grunts unprepared. Normally, by the time the 191st arrived, the 4th/39th had already grouped for a trail formation, ready for pickup. LTC David Hackworth commanded a good bunch of grunts in the 4th/39th. Always well organized, they wasted no time exiting helicopters in hot LZs. Knowing that combat-assault pilots are literally sitting ducks on the ground, this efficiency appealed to Falcon. But this morning was different. There was confusion about which unit would load first. Palmer quickly exited the bird, leaving instructions for Falcon to shut it down but keep the flight on standby with blades untied for a quick departure. Half an hour went by before the grunts finally filed out of the compound. Ten minutes later Palmer appeared, along with the battalion operations officer and the rest of the C&C party.

"Ah! No Hackworth this morning," Falcon said and turned to his crew to mumble the rest of his words. "That might explain the clusterfuck."

Hackworth was up at Ninth Infantry Division headquarters, and his operations officer was temporarily in charge. Still, the first lift of the day went well. After receiving reconnaissance advice from CPT John Cook, the Bounty Hunter platoon leader, the mission shifted the LZ a click to the east to avoid suspected enemy positions. At this point, Falcon settled into his role as copilot flying the aircraft while Palmer wrestled with maps and the rigors of directing combat assaults. Falcon's part was fun. All he had to do was point the aircraft on a given azimuth and maintain airspeed and altitude. Occasionally, he glanced outside to scan the beautiful Vietnamese countryside. Though riddled with shell craters, the lush green environment portrayed a fertile ambiance of a laid-back agrarian landscape. Later that day, this serene image would radically warp.

As the lift ships approached the designated LZ, the grunts, who seemed disorganized earlier, suddenly came alive. When they landed, they scrambled into the tall grass in seconds. Conditioned to getting their asses shot off during insertions, these troops wasted no time in making like ghosts and disappearing into the lush greenery. The 4th/39th functioned as a well-trained combat unit and moved with the dispatch of having had many bloody encounters. They were good—severely good—and Falcon liked what he was seeing in the 4th/39th.

This LZ was a huge expanse of harvested rice paddies with only sparse cover and crisscrossed by dikes that appeared a foot or so tall. To the west of the LZ, approximately one thousand meters away, a rectangular-shaped fortification sat situated with heavily reinforced bunkers. Judging from the neatly cut parapets, the emplacements had been improved with two or three feet of packed earth and positioned with a commanding view of the rice field. Even at a distance, the firing parapets appeared well maintained and menacing to an approach from the LZ. With canal resupply access and a strip of heavy jungle protecting the west boundary, the compound layout appeared well planned and well established. When Gun Platoon Leader John Cook reported taking heavy automatic-weapons fire from the canal, Falcon doubted the wisdom in the young major's decision to insert his troops into such an exposed area. Falcon's concerns slightly dissipated after the grunts began to move about with no enemy resistance. Mentally, at this point, he cast aside worries of the bunkers, assuming the major knew what he was doing, or so Falcon hoped.

Following close behind, the second insertion hit with boots on the ground in minutes. Within half an hour, the entire column of 4th/39th troops snaked its way toward the bunkers. In the meantime, the Bounty Hunters scoured the surrounding lush countryside, destroying enemy positions and racking up kills. As soon as the flight that brought the second insertion cleared the LZ, Palmer took over the controls of the C&C bird and made a slow pass about eighty feet above the bunkers. Showing signs of recent usage, the question of *who* used them lingered in Falcon's mind, but he soon shrugged it off, again assuming all was well since no shots were being fired at the troops. Satisfied that all was clear, Palmer handed the controls back to Falcon and refocused on his C&C duties.

Waiting for the situation to develop, Falcon took the bird to one thousand feet and made holes in the sky. *This could turn into a boring day.* Thirty minutes to an hour elapsed with only sporadic reports of enemy contact from the gunships. All was clear.

Suddenly, the 191st radio frequency crackled alive and a frantic voice reported a 191st bird down. Almost simultaneously, the ground forces reported a gunship on fire and going down. Amid all the battle confusion, it was not clear whose ship had been hit and was burning. Later, Falcon and Palmer realized that Cook's chopper took some rounds through the floor, igniting a box of smoke grenades used for marking LZs. With the crew chief reporting the ship on fire, Cook immediately headed for the deck and ordered the crew to kick out the burning box. They had only a second to spare. When the box hit the ground, the white phosphorus grenades exploded in a shower of white-hot fragments. Thousands of white phosphorous bits of fire scattered in every direction.

"Holy shit!" Cook rejoiced with typical pilot-issued expletives. "We made it by a gnat's ass! Man! We didn't have a second to spare." Cook turned to the crew chief. "If that *ever* happens again, kick the fuckin' thing out the instant it starts burning. You don't have to wait for me to put the bird on the deck." His tone carried an air of a scolding.

The crew chief was feeling a bit sheepish. "Yes, sir," he said. "I thought the whole aircraft was on fire, sir. That stuff was burning really bright and I couldn't tell for sure."

Falcon had no inkling the 4th/39th was searching for the remnants of one of the largest enemy units in the South. By standard procedure, Falcon had stayed with the bird and crew when Palmer had gone into the 4th/39th Battalion TOC for the mission briefing. Furthermore, Falcon was not always able to tune in to Palmer's conversations with the ground force commander. Although unaware of the enemy situation, Falcon was getting concerned over the amount of enemy fire that was hammering the gunships. Due to maintenance problems, they were working with fewer than the prescribed six gunships (two heavy fire teams), which offered optimum protection for the flight. The 191st airmobile force was down to only three gunships, barely enough to cover insertions into light enemy resistance. If confronted with a tac-e of moderate to large enemy contact, the entire flight would be at risk. The reality weighed on Falcon's mind. Nonetheless, getting a Bounty Hunter ship shot up was a relatively common occurrence, and once Falcon learned that the fire had been extinguished and Cook was back on station covering the flight, he breathed a sigh of relief. After several passes over the bunker complex and close scrutiny of the ground surrounding the bunkers, all seemed clear.

But in Vietnam a routine, boring day could turn deadly within milliseconds. Just as soon as the leading ground elements cleared the last rice dike between them and the bunkers, the parapets suddenly exploded with a hail of machine-gun fire. The surprise fire cut down the forward-most squad, which trapped the lead elements behind skimpy cover with nowhere to go. No one in the C&C party, including Palmer and Falcon, gathered even the slightest clue of the lurking enemy presence. Lying deathly still and camouflaged like a brood of hungry vipers, the enemy force didn't make a move until the 4th/39th troopers walked into their lethal trap.

Three grunts hit the dirt on the bunker side of the dike. With no cover between them and the enemy guns, in seconds their bodies were reduced to bloody pulp and twisted into lifeless forms. Presumed dead, the enemy gunners spared them further damage and switched to other Americans, who were maneuvering into attack positions. The enemy fire was relentless and quickly froze all movement by the 4th/39th. One American soldier tried to reach over a dike to retrieve a radio and his arm was torn to pieces by enemy fire. As soon as a 4th/39th trooper would attempt to maneuver again, the enemy cut him down. This very grave situation continued to worsen over the course of several hours.

The close proximity of the wounded soldiers to the enemy machine guns rendered American artillery unusable for fear of killing the nearby friendlies. The bunkers' close proximity to the wounded grunts stymied any air strikes that could pulverize the enemy emplacements. Each time Cook and his gunships flew over the bunkers, heavy enemy fire erupted. Ignoring the threat, Cook's Bounty Hunters descended extremely low in order to continue placing effective fire on the enemy positions without hitting the trapped Americans. Green golf ball–sized tracers appeared to rise slowly from the earth and did not burn out until well above the range of small arms—a telltale sign that the enemy was using heavy antiaircraft weapons. The enemy's .51-caliber machine guns were usually organic to battalion- or regimental-sized units. At this point, it became unnervingly clear that the small, platoon-sized American unit was no match for such a large enemy force.

The voluminous radio traffic generated by the battle quickly attracted top brass to the area, and by approximately 1100 hours the sky above the fight filled with higher-echelon commanders anxious to influence the action. The ensuing outcome created mass confusion for the C&C party trying to regain control. The major filling in for Hackworth seemed relieved when Palmer announced the need to break off from the fight to go refuel. The C&C ship returned to the battle thirty minutes later to find the situation had worsened. Other inserted units had also become pinned down and were unable to move. The enemy had executed a perfect ambush and was methodically disemboweling the American effort.

Radio traffic from the grunts was filled with desperation. A high-ranking officer could be heard threatening to relieve one of the trapped platoon leaders if he did not take immediate action and break off the engagement.

Looking down from 1,500 feet above the battle, Falcon could see bullet strikes raising dust all along the leading rice dike protecting the 4th/39th forward echelon of troops.

"Man, they're catching all kinds of hell down there, Bruce," Falcon said to Palmer over the intercom. "I feel sorry for that poor lieutenant."

Palmer had seen a lot of combat and knew a bad scenario when he saw one. In this case, all advantages were on the side of the enemy. The tactical layout of the bunker complex was well planned and built to withstand a superior ground attack. In this case, the enemy was facing a much smaller unit and had it pinned down to boot. The NVA had the advantage of field of fire, excellent cover, concealment, and fire support immediately behind their front positions. The enemy was well prepared.

The line of enemy bunkers bordered a canal, thick in nipa palm and foliage. The dark, heavy growth easily covered the second line of bunkers arranged to support the outermost machine-gun emplacements. As many times as the 191st had overflown the position, the pilots and crews had all failed to spot the hidden bunkers.

Falcon recalls: "A small figure with a radio mike close to his ear and mouth was lying behind the second dike facing the enemy. Above the battle noise, when he keyed the mike, one could hear a weak voice trembling over the air. Overcome by fear of death, the young lieutenant's voice broke every time a barrage of bullets hit close to him. Adding to the confusion, a senior officer of unknown origin, to Palmer and me, repeatedly directed the lieutenant to pull his men back a safe distance from their present position to allow artillery strikes on the enemy. Frozen with fear, the young officer pleaded for help instead. I remember the young officer replying, 'I can't move, sir!' He tried to explain that bullets were hitting all around him whenever they made the smallest move. His voice growing meek, he begged for reinforcements to break them loose from this trap."

The trapped lieutenant's urgent radio call came through with sounds of the ferocious firefight that left him no escape. With no safe route to break off the engagement, the youngster's desperate plea for help socked Falcon and Palmer in their guts, giving them a horrible sinking feeling. Safely in the sky, three thousand feet above the cornered platoon leader, the unsympathetic senior officer kept growling at the youngster.

Decades later, Falcon still remembers the officer's threats. "He was hollering at the boy and not understanding. Something like 'Danger Two-One, this is Reliable Five-One. I am ordering you to immediately pull your troops back so we can place effective artillery fire on the enemy. Failure to do so will require that we relieve you of your platoon command and insert someone who will respond to orders. Do you understand me, Lieutenant? Over!' The youngster came back again saying, 'Sir, I can't move!' I may not remember the exact exchange of words, but I'll never forget the young lieutenant's trembling voice."

Although Falcon and Palmer remained silent, they rooted for the kid to simply stay alive—to hell with his career. This scenario continued to unfold for what seemed like an hour. They couldn't help but wonder how the day would have been different if Hackworth had been present.

When the battle erupted, LTC David Hackworth, commander of the 4th/39th, was at Ninth Infantry Division headquarters with his brigade commander, COL John G. Hayes. Hayes, a battle veteran steeped in human values, placed a high priority on troop survival and had extraordinary tactics for dealing with determined enemy attacks. Countering enemy threats with aggressive application of men and equipment was a constant predisposition in his mind. Endowed with acute deductive reasoning, Hayes ranked among the finest military risk managers when weighing combat odds in battle scenarios. Like the photo memory of a card counter at a high-stakes casino, Hayes played an expert hand when enemy forces shuffled and dealt out new cards.

Years of Far East experience (two combat tours in Korea and three combat tours in Vietnam) had given Hayes firsthand knowledge of Asian battle tactics and

Asians' fight-to-the-death mentality. On their flight back, following the meeting at Division, radio traffic revealed the circumstances besieging Hackworth's troops, and Hayes didn't hesitate to snap into action when Hackworth begged for immediate transportation straight to the battle site.

Arriving over the scene of the action, Hackworth was anxious to take control of the situation. Not wanting to wait for his own C&C ship, he requested to be inserted into a rice paddy on the fringe of the battle. Hayes reluctantly approved the landing but instructed his pilots to fly a low orbit over Hackworth until he was safely picked up by his C&C ship.

His voice edged with deep concern, Hackworth radioed Falcon and Palmer over the tactical frequency: "Boomerang Three, this is Danger Six. I'm standing by for pickup approximately two clicks northeast of your present position."

"Danger Six, this is Boomerang Three. Understand two clicks northeast of my present. Willco!"

Hayes's bird eased onto the ground, and Hackworth jumped out. Wind from the blades whipped at his shirt, and the Huey lifted off again. Hackworth waited alone in the rice paddy. Continuously, gunship rockets exploded and small-arms fire crackled through the air just across the enormous open rice field where his ambushed guys were locked in an intense firefight. The old infantry officer knew what the sounds meant, and he was anxious to enter the fray.

Hayes continued a low orbit over Hackworth. In ten minutes, Falcon and Palmer picked up Hackworth, and both C&C birds took positions over the battle area. Hackworth's C&C bird orbited freely above the battleground at 1,500 feet, and Hayes's C&C bird orbited higher to allow sufficient flexible airspace for Hackworth. From these vantage points, both field commanders swiftly brought the full force of their assets to bear against the enemy.

While monitoring the 4th/39th tactical frequency and observing from his C&C bird, Hayes instinctively grasped that his 4th/39th troops, hunkered down and trapped, were in severe trouble. Being pinned down at the center of an enemy battalion's main battlefront at point-blank range by machine guns was characteristic of a well-designed and executed defensive plan by a determined enemy force. The ambushed friendly troopers were totally subdued. Green .51-caliber tracers from positions several hundred yards behind the enemy battle front confirmed that the small American platoon faced a whole battalion—not good odds. Hayes knew in his bones that the stakes in this battle were piled high.

Meanwhile, a company of American soldiers was inserted to the north of the enemy and directed to approach the bunker complex along a stretch of jungle that bordered the canal. The section was saturated with booby traps, and American casualties continued to rise. Pinned down by the enemy guns and frustrated, the 4th/39th could neither disengage nor bring decisive firepower to bear on the enemy emplacements. Having arrived amid the tactical scenario after conditions had seemingly deteriorated beyond repair, Hackworth pondered his options. With phenomenal advantage on the side of the enemy, compounded by the excruciating suffering of his wounded troopers, Hackworth faced the most devastating conditions a field commander can possibly encounter. His troops were being cut to pieces and there was little he could do.

At midafternoon, in a desperate attempt to ease pressure on the trapped squad, Hackworth had directed artillery and air strikes into the western edge of the enemy position.

"Bounty Hunter Six, this is Boomerang Three, please use *Willy Pete* to mark the LZ. The task force commander wants to bring in super-zoomers to put serious heat on the enemy."

"Boomerang Three, roger. Understand Willy Pete."

"Roger that, Six!"

During the marking run, Cook's ship was again tattooed with machine-gun fire, this time wounding his copilot, WO1 Chris Patterson. Although he assessed Patterson's wounds as minor, Cook's aircraft damage was anything but. It suffered too many hits to remain airworthy, and Cook requested a replacement bird to meet him at nearby Vinh Long Airfield.

After requesting and being granted permission to break away from the fight to connect with his replacement bird, Cook landed at Vinh Long to await his new aircraft and copilot. Patterson was taken to the nearest medical facility, and Cook inspected his shot-up bird. He counted fifteen holes. One bullet perforated the fuel cell, and JP-4 leaked profusely.

Much to the amazement of Cook and his crew, the airfield commander at Vinh Long complained that the fuel leak was damaging his brand-new *Peneprime* taxiway. Peneprime is a high-penetration, cutback asphalt that stabilizes the soil and cuts down on dust being whipped up by rotor wash.

Cook ignored the white-headed lieutenant colonel and called Falcon (Boomerang Five) on the 191st tactical frequency. "Boomerang Five, this is Bounty Hunter Six. I just landed at Vinh Long to wait for my replacement bird and copilot when some white-headed lieutenant colonel told me to fly my bird out of here because my fuel leak is damaging his Peneprime, over."

"Bounty Hunter Six, did I hear you right, that a white-headed lieutenant colo-nel asked you to fly your battle-damaged bird out because it's leaking fuel on his Peneprime?"

"Roger that, Five, what should I do?"

"Tell that asshole to take his Peneprime and stick it where the sun don't shine!" Livid, Falcon screamed into the radio. "We have a replacement bird coming into Vinh Long for you along with another copilot. Tell that dumbass REMF[1] that we have a tactical emergency in progress and Boomerang maintenance will arrange

---

1 Rear-echelon motherfucker

evacuation of the damaged bird as soon as possible." Falcon's face blazed red with anger. "And tell that stupid white-headed asshole to go fuck himself!"

"Roger that!" Cook responded.

Outranked by the crusty old, white-headed lieutenant colonel, Cook casually ignored his order and continued with the aircraft and copilot exchange. He knew better than to tell the AC exactly what the XO had said, and he understood perfectly well the combat pressure under which the XO had snapped out his directive. No more was said about the leaky bird, and in a half hour Cook was back over the battle zone with a fresh copilot and a new gunship.

During the air strike, Palmer flew the C&C bird three clicks to the east in order to give the tactical fighters enough room to maneuver and release their ordnance. Meanwhile, Falcon was giving the remaining Bounty Hunters instructions to *get the hell out of Dodge*.

"Bounty Hunter Six, this is Boomerang Five. Super-zoomers are incoming with seven-hundred-fifty-pounders. Please exit to the east at least three clicks."

"Roger that, Five. Will do ASAP!"

Seconds later, huge explosions uprooted trees and obliterated the landscape on the western edge of the enemy positions. From a vantage point one thousand feet above and three thousand meters away, the spectacle eclipsed even the most awesome fireworks display. As if in slow motion, bombs weighing nearly half a ton separated from the wings of American F-4 Phantoms and sailed through the air like weightless objects in space before rocking the earth with fireballs reaching 150 feet in the air. Shock waves hurled huge clods of earth several hundred feet in all directions. Emanating from the center of the blast, huge dust clouds emanated in circular patterns. Time slowed down, and the whole scene held a furious sense of beauty that inspired admiration.

It seemed like nothing could crawl out of such stunning destructive power, nothing could survive to do more damage or take more lives of young Americans cornered in the sandy dirt of dried-up rice paddies below. Yet, after each pass by a fighter, the enemy guns defiantly filled the air with green tracers. Well fortified, this enemy unit was an efficient fighting machine. Finally, after a series of napalm attacks roasted some of the enemy bunkers, the hostile fire subsided enough to encourage Hackworth to take another look at the trapped squad.

CPT Cook, back on station with a new gunship and a new copilot, was again asked to go in first and check the damage. Descending to about fifty feet above the wounded, his assessment brought more bad news. Cook reported friendly troops still alive and dangerously close to the enemy bunkers.

Falcon called Cook on the 191st tactical frequency: "Bounty Hunter Six, this Boomerang Five. Exactly which danger-close troops are still alive?"

"This is Six. The troops nearest the bunkers. They're completely exposed. One moved his foot as I passed low level. Probably to let me know he was still alive."

"This is Boomer Five. Roger that!"

The air strikes and artillery simply couldn't finish the job without risking American lives. Again, Cook warned of taking heavy fire during his pass. With RPGs exploding directly beneath his aircraft, he advised extreme caution to the C&C ship carrying the battalion commander and staff.

Allowing time for the smoke to clear, Palmer took control of the C&C bird and flew as close as possible over the target while Cook's gunships unleashed a barrage of covering fire. Bullets sporadically smacked the C&C aircraft with loud crashing and banging sounds that made the crew feel as if the bird was coming apart. The bullets left no discernible effect, and the crew managed to overfly low enough to get a good look at the trapped grunts. Barely eighty feet below the Huey, one grunt was facing the sky and the other two lay on their sides. The one facing up was nearest the enemy and continuously moved his foot. Enemy bullets had torn a hole through the entire length of his left cranium, which explained his unconscious foot movement. Safely behind him were survivors lying behind the rice dike and keeping a low profile. Among them was the lieutenant whose senior officer had threatened to relieve him of his platoon command. Remarkably, the head-wounded soldier's life was spared by the enemy because they knew leaving him alive would encourage high-risk rescue efforts and therefore give them opportunity to kill more Americans. The poor soul remained alive for hours before his extraction. It was a miracle he lived as long as he did, eventually dying in a med facility after rescue.

Inspired by the wounded soldiers' astounding courage, Hackworth leapt into action. He immediately communicated his intentions to the brigade commander, COL John Hayes: "Reliable Three-Six, this is Danger Six. I'm going to insert into the battle site to personally take charge of the situation on the ground."

"Negative, Danger Six. Instead pull what you can of the Fourth/Thirty-Ninth troops back away from the battle and consolidate your losses."

"Roger, Three-Six. Understand pull back and consolidate losses, out."

Falcon glanced back and caught a painful expression on Hackworth's face. Knowing the man from numerous previous missions, Falcon understood the idea of leaving his men on the ground to die did not sit well with his style. Hackworth was fit to be tied. By this time, it was evident the whole situation was out of control. The enemy dominated with a decisive tactical advantage called *hugging the belt*, where they trapped Americans so close to their position that American firepower was rendered ineffective. With all apparent options expended, the tactical conclusion was that the lives of the trapped squad would be lost without some sort of recourse. Exhibiting a collage of emotions, Hackworth vented anger, grief, and frustration. He refused to yield or concede that all was lost.

Infectious to epic proportions, Hackworth's agony deeply touched the entire C&C crew. His influence captured the heart and commitment of all, and they formed one body of purpose. In short order, Hackworth energized that purpose.

As C&C orbited the battle area, Falcon looked down to see the ground ablaze with tracers, most of them green and headed east in the direction of the 4th/39th. It was at this point that Hackworth proposed the most daring rescue conceivable. Recognizing the enormous risk and the insurmountable odds he was proposing, Hackworth chose his words with care and tact, seeking consensus.

Hackworth keyed his intercom mike. "Boomer," Hackworth said, addressing Palmer. "I doubt there is any way we can get those boys out of there unless we land this bird close enough to load the wounded. Ask your crew what they think about that, babe."

Falcon, in the meantime, tuned Hackworth out so he could stay in touch with the Bounty Hunters. Palmer turned his head and locked eyes with Hackworth. Hackworth was dog-ass serious. Suddenly, Palmer whipped his head toward Falcon. "John what do you think? Should we try to extract the wounded with our bird?" Without thinking twice, Falcon nodded his head in approval and resumed his communication with the Bounty Hunters.

Palmer could have legitimately refused the request as being outrageously suicidal. But instead, he radioed his intentions to Cook: "Bounty Hunter Six, this is Three. We're going to try to extract the wounded with the C&C bird. Please give us all the fire support you can muster."

A pause on the other end. "Are you sure you want to do that?" Cook asked.

"Roger that!"

The wounded lay approximately fifty meters from the enemy machine guns. For the C&C ship to extract the trapped Americans, they had to land in the crossfire. The odds of successfully touching down directly between two forces locked in mortal combat within a stone's throw of each other were, to say the least, slim. However, the risk was miniscule by comparison to the risk of losing the entire crew, along with the battalion commander and staff. Nonetheless, at approximately 1600 hours, Hackworth issued the order to go.

Palmer flew the C&C bird northeast several kilometers to take advantage of wind direction and cover before lining up for the approach. CPT Cook and his gunships followed close behind in a support position.

Correctly interpreting the movements of Hackworth's aircraft, the savvy Hayes was now deeply concerned with the option Hackworth had chosen to pursue. Hayes felt certain that the decision, cleverly made before he could disapprove it, would end in a tactical disaster. Under heavy enemy fire and within point-blank range of well-entrenched enemy positions, Hackworth's proposed maneuver was reminiscent of a very similar action experienced by Hayes a few years earlier.

"At that moment," Hayes recalls, "my mind flashed to an incident which had occurred while I was serving with the Fifth SF. It popped into my memory as if I were seeing it again in a similar situation that I had experienced before. This disaster occurred during an extremely bad weather day when a very thick layer of fog hovered over mountain peaks on the Laotian border. Due to such poor visibility, the helicopter bearing one of my SF teams overflew the intended LZ inside Vietnam and erroneously inserted my team into Laos, literally on top of a North Vietnamese battalion. My entire team was annihilated and there was nothing I could do to stop it. Although I had a battalion of South Vietnamese rangers at my disposal for a rescue attempt, US Department of State's political border restrictions discouraged any such maneuver. It was like a nightmare when you are peering into imminent death and powerless to act. Years of healing have done little to ease my pain about that incident."

Once more, Hayes watched what he hoped was not a repeat of the Laos incident. Hayes considered Hackworth one of America's prime infantry officers. Entrusted to him, he feared that Hackworth was engaging in a harebrained rescue mission that he considered "tantamount to suicide." If it failed, Hayes had no doubt that it, like the Laos massacre, would plague him for the remainder of his days. Hackworth, too, was well aware of the odds.

An approach to the LZ from the northeast placed Falcon on the side facing the enemy machine guns. Both Palmer and Falcon remained on the controls in event one were killed. As the bird began the approach, the whole scenario unfolded as something surreal. What the pilots were about to attempt was not in the manuals of war or any part of the tactics taught at flight school. Unconventional or not, it was too late for discussion. They were collectively committed. To abort the rescue attempt now was to sign a death warrant for the troops on the ground.

At approximately 150 meters from touchdown, rounds crackled as they ripped through the Huey. Bullets hitting hardpoints banged with a force strong enough to shake the ship as it descended. Falcon looked over at Palmer and could hardly believe what he saw. The little man cracked that goofy side-mouthed grin. Of course, the macho part of Falcon was not about to reveal to that little shithead that he was feeling knots in his belly and an astronomical pucker factor. He just shook his head and smiled back.

When the Huey was fifty feet from the ground, Cook's gunships began pounding the enemy bunkers. Using extraordinary tactics and bravery beyond measure, Cook employed his fire teams in a right echelon formation, which allowed all gunships to fire simultaneously on the enemy once C&C was on the ground.

Rockets burst right in front of the parapets. Remnants of the trapped squad, along with the rest of the 4th/39th on the ground, poured small-arms fire into the bunkers. The explosions and deluge of gunfire noise penetrated Falcon's flight helmet. Although flight helmets muffled *some* of the noise, the din was deafening. Ignoring the gravity of the moment, Falcon stayed busy instructing the C&C crew to make sure they had a full belt of ammo in their machine guns with safeties off.

Muzzle blasts boomed from the parapets in the direction of the ship. Falcon watched helplessly as one enemy gunner walked his bullets directly into his C&C

bird, raking across the engine compartment several times. Frustrated that he could not shoot out the engine, the enemy gunner reoriented his fire directly into the cockpit at Falcon and Palmer. Falcon ducked his head and gritted his teeth. The impact didn't happen. Miraculously, the gun stopped firing as the last bullet hit the skid of the Huey directly below the copilot's seat.

Right before touchdown, Falcon stole a last look at Hackworth and his C&C party. They leaped out of the bird while it was still four or five feet in the air and scrambled in the direction of the wounded. Cook and the gunships fired simultaneously on the enemy and then reverted to a tight daisy-chain pattern that took him and his crews directly over the enemy bunkers. His gunships acted as decoys to draw some of the enemy fire away from the C&C ship.

Sprinting through a wall of tracers, Hackworth reached an unconscious soldier and dragged him back to the bird. Then he turned and brazenly rushed to a second. Bullets punched through the aircraft sounding off like popcorn in a Jiffy Pop bag but without the magic treat. Falcon directed door gunfire into the enemy bunkers, barking orders to the door gunner for adjustment each time fire erupted from a different parapet. In less than a minute, Hackworth returned to the bird with the last wounded.

With the chopper now full of soldiers and bodies, Hackworth jumped on the skid, waving his hand and screaming at Palmer. "Go! Go! Go!"

Just as Palmer lifted the C&C bird into the air, Falcon spotted an RPG round headed straight for the bird. The round detonated in the dirt, literally where Hackworth's boots had just been before the Huey had left the ground. The explosion shook the entire aircraft as it began to climb through a gauntlet of enemy fire, with Hackworth still on the skid and hanging on the side.

The wind direction forced an initial lift-off parallel to the enemy bunkers. Heading into the wind, along the entrenched enemy bunkers, it wasn't clear to the crew if they were going to make it out of this crazy rescue mission alive. With enough speed and altitude, Palmer turned the nose away from the enemy, and everyone in the C&C ship held a glimmer of hope, believing that they could make it.

After traveling about a click away from the guns, Palmer slowed the bird down to cruise power long enough to check its pulse. Multiple warning lights flashed, but the engine was still running like a champ. By that time, Hackworth had been pulled farther into the bird by his C&C party and somehow piled in with the rest of his men. With the worst over, all that remained now was to nurse the battle-wounded Huey to a friendly PZ.

The old bird had taken one hell of a beating but continued to fly. Falcon's eyes stayed glued to the engine instruments, amazed that the powerplant still turned. Right then, Falcon wanted to kiss the hallowed ground at the Bell Helicopter plant. Clearly, the engineers who designed this magnificent bird knew what they were doing. It was unimaginable that any aircraft could take so many hits and still hang in the air.

Falcon finally looked back at the wounded. A black trooper lay with a bullet hole on one side of his forehead and pieces of bone from his skull protruding from the exit wound. A huge welt had formed along the entire side of his skull, clearly marking the path the bullet traveled through his head. But he was still alive and moving. Others were lying lifelessly on the floor, bleeding out. The lucky ones grinned as humans do when they've cheated certain death.

Hackworth, with amazing resilience, immediately rekindled his intense focus on the enemy and asked to be inserted to the rear of the infantry. Finally, for the first and only time that day, the aircrew advised against his wishes lest the aircraft be unable to get airborne again to deliver the wounded to medical attention. The crew flew back to FSBD, where they arranged medical evacuation for the wounded and a change of aircraft. The bird they were flying looked like a piece of swiss cheese. Boomerang maintenance flew a replacement bird to meet the C&C crew, and in less than an hour, they had Hackworth back in the fight.

With the stalemate now broken and the trapped squad out of harm's way, C&C arrived to see American air power at work again. Combat aircraft swarmed over the battle like angry bees. This time, the jets were pulverizing the entire bunker complex, piece by piece. Cook's Bounty Hunters orbited the periphery. They kept a sharp eye out for enemy soldiers, waiting for them to break and run from the bombing when the Bounty Hunters would then dive for the kill like goshawks preying on rats running from a grass fire.

One hardcore NVA soldier jumped out of a hole not fifteen meters from where a five-hundred-pound bomb had detonated moments before and proceeded to run for his life. Falcon watched as 2.75-inch rocket trails and explosions followed him all the way to the canal where he disappeared into the foliage. It was not his day to die. Five VC that took refuge in a bomb crater were not so lucky. Cook scored a direct hit with a ten-pound warhead right in the middle of the five, blasting their coolie hats, weapon pieces, and bloody gore into a shower of debris that lifted Falcon's morale from the depressing events of the day. Falcon watched the debris fall back to earth, and his Texan heart sang. He was rest assured that those five would never kill one of his guys—not one more American.

After the pain and suffering Falcon saw inflicted on the beleaguered troops, he couldn't hold back his emotion. He keyed the mike on Cook's radio frequency and vented. "Right on, John! Pound the shit out of them!" At that moment, Falcon would have given anything to have been piloting a gunship. While killing numerous enemy soldiers, the gunships paid a high price that would later require a three-day maintenance stand-down to repair the battle damage.

After the harrowing events of the day and how quickly Hackworth turned the outcome around, Falcon reached a conclusion that stuck with him the rest of his life: "Call it intuition, deductive reasoning, brilliant strategy, timing, or just plain ol' luck, but some people are gifted with the right kind of stuff that works where others fail. In Hackworth's case, it was as if he'd been thrown into a pile of dung and come out smelling like a rose."

That day, Hackworth glowed with this rare kind of good fortune, and Falcon and Palmer were happy as hell to ride on his good luck. Unconventional? Perhaps, but nonetheless, Hackworth delivered results when his men needed them most.

Feeling in control and safe after surviving the miraculous extraction, Hackworth went back to work delivering his best to the enemy. Flowing with intensity again, Hackworth directed low-level passes over the enemy to devise a plan for their final destruction.

With the infantry resupplied, the wounded evacuated, and the sun barely hanging over the horizon, a hard day was over. Or so Falcon thought. Suddenly, the freshly commissioned C&C aircraft shuddered. Bullets ripped through the cockpit and cargo areas, slamming into the bulkheads above. The crew in the back seat screamed. Falcon looked back to see LTC Hackworth holding his calf while another member of his staff was bleeding from the armpit. Immediately, Palmer turned the aircraft away from the enemy fire and took evasive action. He took the pitch out of the rotor blade and slipped the helicopter out of trim. The bird shook, as if it were disintegrating, dropping like a rock. Palmer's clever tactic and quick thinking increased the difficulty for enemy gunners to reacquire, but what a wild ride for the injured and dying in the back.

A lone tracer round passing through temporarily filled the cabin with smoke, but fortunately did not incinerate the ship. At approximately three hundred feet AGL and still dropping, Falcon sized up Palmer to be sure he was all right. He was relieved to see Palmer recover the Huey from the dive and resume straight and level flight.

Dong Tam Hospital was approximately thirty minutes away, and the wounded were showing signs of expiring. Palmer wasted no time making a beeline for Dong Tam while coordinating the flight's release for the day.

After delivering Hackworth and the other wounded to the medevac pad at Dong Tam, C&C repositioned back to the 191st flight line to watch the rest of the Boomerangs and Bounty Hunters bring in their battle-torn birds. Despite the hails of bullets aimed at the birds that day, the 191st didn't lose a single soul.

"Today was a damn good one!" Falcon concluded. Looking back on the events of the day, the XO admitted that Dong Tam looked pretty inviting to him—even though it still smelled like burning shit.

Later that evening, over supper, the visuals and din of the day played on a reel in his mind. He visualized the 4th/39th grunts forty clicks to the west, in darkness, wondering if they would see the light of day again. At that moment, Falcon knew that the battle at Ap My Thuan on March 25, 1969, would remain forever etched in his memory as a picture of those hardcore soldiers, facing imminent death with a resolve that only America's best can endure. The experience of being on the ground with the 4th/39th in a death trap with virtually no escape, as well as seeing their faces light up once they were airborne and headed to safety, is one he will cherish the rest of his days.

"There is no monument that can properly measure the debt of gratitude owed these warriors," Falcon explains, "and warriors they were—literally, to their last breath."

Falcon admits that once free of the enemy fire, he realized God doesn't make all men equal. And keeping with pilot tradition, Falcon couldn't help but give a quick ribbing to his old comrade, CPT Palmer. "I truly believe God left something out when he assembled Palmer."

In June 1969, Falcon got orders to rotate back to the States, so Schmidt was faced with the task of finding a replacement XO. CPT Hubert Brinson was one of the most senior O3s in the battalion, and he was chosen to fill the vacancy. With only a few days of overlap, the two captains conferred over the logistical and administrative tasks assigned to the XO before Brinson took over. Not long thereafter, Brinson gave up the XO slot to fly gunships with the Boomerangs' sister company, the 172nd AHC. Within a month, Brinson was dead—killed in action while attacking an enemy stronghold.

CHAPTER 22

The Natural

"Wake up, meathead. You're no longer flying a bird with blades as wide as your coffin."

Some believe genetic endowment in a living body can beget *natural* skills or behavior. Athletes gifted in this regard are believed to bear innate qualities that produce extraordinary human feats. Perhaps such is the case with 191st AHC pilot, CPT Kenneth R. Carlton. His flying skills were extraordinary and seemed innate.

Carlton arrived on the doorstep of the 191st the day after the fatal mortar attack that shook the company to its core in March 1969. Crossing the threshold of the AHC operations center, Carlton halted—his senses assaulted by the repulsive odor of decay inside. The sight of human remains and blood splattered on every visible wall and floor space stunned the young pilot. Looking at the grim face of the first sergeant, who was tending the cleanup and building repairs, Carlton spoke softly. "First Sergeant, I'm First Lieutenant Kenneth Carlton, here to sign in to the company. What happen here?"

"Mortar attack, Lieutenant—killed six people last night. Right where you're standing! The operations officer, Chief Warrant Officer Two David Schwartz, is handling administration for the time being. Go see him." The first sergeant pointed to the orderly room. "He's in the next office, through that door."

Carlton made his way to the operations officer. *What a hell of a way to start this assignment.* He figured that it must be true that a helicopter pilot's life expectancy in Vietnam was awfully short.

Carlton's concern was not unusual. Many Vietnam helicopter pilots experienced apprehension when arriving in combat zones. For soldiers, war brings a full awareness of mortality. If the signs of death and destruction Carlton had just seen in the unit's headquarters were typical of war, he deduced there would be a far more lethal environment on the battlefield. Concern for his chances to survive this combat tour turned on like a floodlight. The death scene in the operations center was far too gruesome. With that introduction, Carlton began his helicopter combat assignment as a 191st AHC pilot.

Carlton was a good, all-American youngster. Coming from a small farming community in Shafter, California, he was the type of human Army commanders valued. Brought up pumping gas and washing windshields at his dad's gas station, he had learned to appreciate honest work, especially after earning a minimum wage the hard way: by picking potatoes with his mom on commercial farms. By comparison, gas station work was a snap. Carlton experienced the right upbringing to fully appreciate opportunity. It was evident to his fellow Boomerangs and Bounty Hunters that Carlton was delighted to be a part of the 191st AHC. His flying career became chief among all of his other ambitions. The desire, deeply embedded in his heart and mind, was binding. He knew this is what he wanted to do for a lifetime, if possible. Of course, surviving the Vietnam War was foremost in this mind. Nothing in his Army training up to this point had prepared him for the shock of war. Words from Army instructors could not prepare a soldier for the noise, stench, and concussion of battle—nor the chemistry that blends shock into reality.

After attending basic training at Fort Polk, Louisiana, followed by flight school at Fort Wolters and Fort Rucker, Carlton landed in Vietnam prepared for Army responsibilities. He felt certain he was ready for his introduction to combat. And, indeed, he was. But his life back home had traversed a soft and placid upbringing that inculcated pleasantries in his mind. Death was another matter altogether. Back home, Carlton had been a former college football player and was married to his high school sweetheart, Shirley. He had adjusted well to family responsibilities, and he excelled in flight school. Witnessing the stench and carnage in the unit's operations center, however, was a rude awakening. At the time, Carlton didn't know that the CO had been among the victims of the mortar attack. Learning this fact later instilled further death apprehensions. He recognized that rank had no privilege in the 191st mission.

Carlton's introduction to CW2 Schwartz was brief and resolute. "Lieutenant, I'm going to assign you to the gun platoon," Schwartz said with no discussion. "That may change when the new company commander gets settled. But right now, he's just barely assimilating the job." Schwartz paused and noticed the wholesome appearance of Carlton. "The previous company commander and the admin officer were killed in that mortar attack. You know, you saw the mess in the operations center."

Schwartz tried not to show undue concern. He felt it was better to be shocked now rather than on the battlefield where your ass is grass if you make the wrong move. "So, for now, Lieutenant, the Bounty Hunters are your new assignment." The old combat veteran knew the consequences of being *too* naïve. With full understanding of what awaited the lieutenant, Schwartz was satisfied the newbie would either learn or become a statistic.

Fortunately, this assignment was an excellent learning opportunity that pleased Carlton. His gunship-pilot responsibilities secured, he continued in-processing, which included getting fitted with an armored chest protector (more affectionately called the chicken plate), assigned a .38-caliber revolver, and issued a flight helmet. 1LT Carlton soon found himself receiving preparatory indoctrination, including flying with a number of senior gunship pilots in the Bounty Hunter ranks.

During this indoctrination flying on a Bounty Hunter gunship, he watched slicks fly troops into battle—an impressive show for the young lieutenant. But none of the indoctrination missions had drawn enemy bullets. Excited, he looked forward to his first baptism by fire, as the salty, experienced pilots called the occasion when all newbie pilots lost their virginity. In effect, with the first penetration of bullets through their aircraft, they got their cherries busted. That event would come soon enough for Carlton.

Carlton received his in-country check ride from his gun-platoon leader, the well-seasoned CPT Mike Arruti, and from the superb instructor pilot (IP) CW2 David Hamilton. Hamilton spared no ass chewing for pilots, warrant or commissioned. Highly knowledgeable in deadly pilot errors, Hamilton bore down with authority in checking aviator proficiency. Renowned among Boomerangs and Bounty Hunters, Hamilton was respected for his role in saving crew lives. After passing the check ride, Carlton was cleared to fly cover for the slicks.

Carlton's christening into combat occurred in early March 1969. That day, Carlton flew as copilot on Hamilton's gunship. Their mission took them west of Dong Tam, in the vicinity of *wagon wheel*, a large landmark very familiar to the combat-assault pilots. They would cover the Boomerangs, who were supporting the Ninth Infantry Division troops in combat with a large NVA force.

Hamilton clicked on the intercom. "Watch the slicks in the LZ when they start receiving fire. You'll gain firsthand knowledge of what slick jockeys experience when the enemy stitches the shit out of them. This will give you an idea of why our role providing cover is so critical and urgent."

Hamilton explained that mere seconds could mean the difference between life and death for crewmembers or infantry troops aboard the slicks. Carlton listened carefully, and soon his first battle came alive with action as the slicks landed.

"Off-loading troops with amazing patience, the slick crews remained on the ground as bullets slammed into their birds," Carlton recalls. "Firing from cover, the cold-blooded enemy gunners rejoiced in the chance to kill Americans at their most vulnerable point: the combat-assault landing. Sitting motionless in an LZ waiting for the ten-ship formation to offload troops had to be nerve racking for lead-ship crews. Landing first, or forward in the formation, required a one- to two-minute wait. I remember thinking, *With bullets flying through the bird, sixty seconds must seem like an eternity.*"

Carlton had received his baptism. After that day's firefight, Carlton asked Crew Chief SP5 Jon Brones about the battle.

"When bullets are rattling through the aircraft," Brones explained to Carlton, "you feel this powerful urge to escape. Overcoming the urge to flee is mindboggling.

The normal brain says, 'Get your ass out now!' But at the same time, the flight discipline required of aircrews in formation demands staying predictably within your airspace so you don't create a midair collision that might kill many others. Even for that short period, stability under fire is dreadful. Horrifying! You expect a bullet to come slamming into your body any second. There's no other way to explain it. It scares the hell out of you."

Carlton filed this extremely dangerous part of the mission into his brain for a lifetime keepsake. He mentally took notes for future reference: identifying the exact source of enemy fire is a remedy; relaying their specific location near the LZ to the covering gunships brings us into action; kill the enemy—mission accomplished! Needs to happen in seconds. As a gunship pilot his job was to attack and suppress enemy guns immediately upon target acquisition. In such cases, if the enemy gunners were firing from bunkered positions, only direct hits from gunship rocket explosions would suppress the enemy fire. But even then, only for a brief moment while the bunkered occupants recovered from the concussion. Carlton didn't need reinforcement to know this experience would remain embedded in his mind to his death.

Inside of a month, Carlton experienced the glumness that overshowed the 191st when a member of the unit was killed. On April 10, 1969, while supporting infantry troops not far from Dong Tam, the aircraft in which SP4 George Albert Dasho Jr. was flying crashed and killed the young gunner. Dasho was just shy of his nineteenth birthday. A clean-cut, friendly, and likeable youngster, he was always smiling and congenial with all who came in contact with him. Those who knew him personally felt the greatest pain. Attending the customary memorial service held in the company area, Carlton felt the grief of Dasho's roommates. A solemn experience. Carlton and the 191st crews were quick to adjust to the loss, knowing that a brooding mind was dangerous—a loss of combat focus could cost precious infantry and crewmember lives.

Carlton's devotion to the organization and to his crewmembers evolved enthusiastically. His attention to detail made a difference in the lives of others. On September 6, 1969, this attribute delivered commendation to a fellow pilot by a most inconspicuous form. While flying as AC of a wing gunship near Vi Thanh, South Vietnam, Carlton noticed a slick pilot, WO1 Paul P. Zawicki, exhibiting extraordinary discipline under fire. Each time the flight inserted troops in the LZ, the position of Zawicki's aircraft, chock four, was inadvertently aligned perfectly with a VC emplacement that slammed bullet after bullet into his Huey. Despite extraordinary valor by his door gunner, SP5 Daniel Morin, who kept the bird's M60 machine gun pumping a steady stream of bullets, the enemy green tracers were overwhelming. Still Zawicki repeated the process over and over again. Each time they landed, Zawicki called "receiving fire" and identified the source location adjacent to the LZ.

Immediately, the gunships pounded the enemy emplacement with vigor. But that bunker was extra thick, discernible by its extra-deep parapets. Even when the gunships descended to a dangerously low altitude to best strike the bunker, the rockets only dented the surface. The enemy was cozy and safe in its emplacement. No doubt they felt the concussion of the ten-pound warheads; nonetheless, the gunships kept firing. Experienced in infantry combat with the Eighty-Second Airborne Division and other Vietnam units, Morin, the chock-four bird's gunner, was unshakeable in the face of death. As if daring the enemy to come out of the bunker for a good ol' western-style gunfight, Morin kept up the fire. *A courageous soul*, Carlton thought.

Carlton changed his angle of attack with hope of relieving the chock-four bird by slipping a rocket into the bunker through a parapet, but to no avail. The hole was simply too small and the surface too thick. Miraculously, Zawicki's ship and crew survived the barrage of lead. When the insertion point was moved to another LZ, Carlton breathed a sigh of relief. He appreciated the battle focus exhibited by the AC and crew in the chock-four bird that day. Carlton inquired about the AC's name and filed it in his memory bank to recommend the crew for decorations.

As good fate would have it, the AC of the C&C bird noticed the same sequence of events that Carlton witnessed. In good order, by direction of the president, Zawicki was awarded the Distinguished Flying Cross for his heroism on September 6, 1969. His gunner, SP5 Daniel Morin, was also decorated with an Air Medal with V-device for valor. His heroic actions, covering the aircraft with his M60 machine gun while in the face of overwhelming enemy fire, were credited to the survival of his aircraft and crew. Both Zawicki and Morin were well deserving of their recognition.

Zawicki's ship was not the only Boomerang aircraft devastated by enemy fire that day. Up and down the line of assault ships, the enemy fire was relentless. The chock-five bird, crewed by SP5 Jon Brones, took several hits from heavy weapons. One fifty-seven-millimeter recoilless cannon round hit the aircraft just below Brones's machine-gun pintle, sending shrapnel through both his legs and into his groin area. Badly wounded but steady as a rock, Brones alerted his AC of his wounds and aircraft damage. Bleeding and in pain, he returned fire with his M60, fiercely defending the ship and crew. As the bird departed the LZ, Brones advised the AC of hot spots to skirt enemy gunners. Upon arriving at the medevac pad for his own evacuation to emergency treatment, still bleeding and in pain, he calmly guided the AC for landing over the wire obstacles surrounding the facility. A stern example of the great American fabric in young men who served with the 191st, SP5 Brones was properly decorated for his bravery—blood earned and well deserved. On December 14, 1969, by direction of the president, Jon B. Brones was awarded the Purple Heart for wounds received in action and the Air Medal for heroism in connection with his exceptional valor under fire.

Carlton was pleased with the unit's performance and elated with being a part of it. In cumulative form, Carlton's excellent performance as AC placed him in position for promotion. Upon CPT Arruti's departure, and by the good graces of the 191st unit commander, MAJ Vic Conner, the newly promoted CPT Carlton was given command of the 191st gun platoon.

Assuming the position from CPT Arruti was a huge plus. Arruti left the unit with a strong performance in logistics, tactics, leadership, personnel management, and valorous action. His was the perfect example for the newly promoted CPT Carlton to emulate.

Delighted with his prize assignment, Carlton relished in his new opportunity to excel. His promotion enhanced his appreciation for the Army and America's military establishment. It opened lots of room for upward mobility. Carlton was now basking in his element.

Adjusting well to the many nuances of commanding the gun platoon, CPT Carlton stayed busy with a laundry list of responsibilities. Flying was the fun part. But gunship maintenance, on the other hand, could become a daunting experience, especially in an organization with such a high demand for flight hours and combat exposure that took its toll on men and machines.

"In action nearly every single day," Carlton recalls, "the Charlie-models took a beating. Bullet holes were easily patched with sheet metal. But damage to an aircraft's major arteries were most debilitating. Internal damage required close follow-up and significant time spent tracking part numbers to assist and expedite maintenance. For me, this was among the biggest pains in the ass I had to live with. For optimum protection of the flight each day, I needed to furnish at least two fully armed heavy fire teams consisting of six gunships. Hell, I was happy with being able to put up two light fire teams requiring only four Charlie-models. This was very minimal protection for the combat-assault choppers that usually numbered ten in a formation.

"Personnel were also a premium among gunship crews. Extensions for ACs who exceeded their monthly limit of 140 flight hours were not easy to come by. Such a decision could end the flight surgeon's medical career; hence, the responsible physician was very tough in this regard. Ordering an overworked pilot to fly combat assaults could easily lead to combat fatigue and fatal pilot error. Investigators have typically examined this aspect foremost in their checklist of possible accident causes. Therefore, flight surgeons were obliged to support the maximum flight-hour limitation. It normally took some woeful pleading from platoon leaders to gain such favors. Flight surgeons carried a heavy burden, and little could be done to relieve their responsibilities. Combat simply demands more than what a full complement of aviators can reasonably deliver. I had to learn this exceptionally well; thus, I managed my bench of ACs' employment carefully. It also helped a lot to have good people under me to keep me straight. I relied heavily on my platoon sergeant and section leaders to keep me alerted."

Departure of the Ninth Infantry Division from South Vietnam squeezed the remaining allied forces, increasing their workload covering a larger portion of the war zone. The 191st AHC also formed an additional platoon and mission, the Green Delta operation. On demand, the Green Deltas would fly high-ranking US and ARVN officers. Requiring experienced ACs, the Green Delta requirements strained the already thin 191st pilot roster.

Traversing the southernmost portions of South Vietnam, missions over the U Minh Forest would often encounter well-prepared North Vietnamese troops, who possessed advanced weapon systems that could easily shoot down UH-1s. This fact complicated tactics; hence, Green Delta pilots were extra careful to properly measure terrain risks in the dense growth. Carlton knew this and paid heed when directed to cover Green Delta flights over the southernmost war zone.

Recalling one unforgettable experience, Carlton explains: "Hell, I remember one occasion when we were flying, oblivious of any danger. Then enemy camouflage nets suddenly flung open beneath us exposing heavy antiaircraft guns that slung huge pumpkin balls at us. Scared the shit out of me! I saw where the birds in our formation dove for cover—a good move that gave me flexibility to take evasive action. As I saw the situation, rolling in on those bastards with rocket fire would do nothing to stop the lethal barrage of heavy metal coming our way. I ordered all gunships to remain low level until we cleared the field of fire covered by those lethal bastards. Those aircraft killers fired large-caliber rounds, the kind that tightly puckered Boomerang and Bounty Hunter rear orifices."

Enemy thirty-millimeter rounds easily covered several thousand feet of sky in seconds whereas a lumbering UH-1 took minutes to reach a safe altitude. Diving for cover below the tree line as opposed to ascending to greater altitude seemed a defiance of logic. But in the absence of jet propulsion, hitting the deck was the most practical option to evade this threat. No comparison, the enemy guns had the advantage, and they loomed in the area as a death-delivering menace. Bounty Hunters operating in the region remained alert.

"The U Minh Forest reeked of enemy presence," CW2 Ray Ayala recalls. "Flying over that Godforsaken place made your hair stand on end. While the environment was beautiful, the death that lurked beneath the tree canopy was horrifying. Stories of the cav crews getting their asses handed to them by heavy antiaircraft fire made us sweat BBs when traversing that hell hole. Many cav choppers ended their combat employment crashing in that area. The amazing part was flying low level at treetop altitude, which gave you a fresh smell of the forest. Kind of reminded me of home. But in reality, that's the only redeeming feature it offered. It was a horrible place to engage enemy. The odds were in their favor. They had years to fortify that region, and they used it well to their advantage. To make matters worse, the on-call wait period for tac air increased considerably with departure of the Ninth Infantry Division. Tac air was the strongest response available against the NVA advanced weapon systems emplaced throughout the U Minh. When jets dropped their heavy payloads on the enemy, you wouldn't hear a peep out of the bastards. But let the jets depart the area, and death would leap out at you with a vengeance."

With US combat units leaving Vietnam, response to enemy activity fell on fewer allied forces. Increasing need for fighter-bomber support prompted new tactical priorities. During some battles, bombing and strafing demands reduced air cover to a crawl.

"When tac air finally arrived on station," Crew Chief Jon Brones recalls, "they made a decisive difference. Enemy units typically froze activities to avoid the mass napalm frying that suppressed their attacks. The smell of burning flesh and screams of humans being scorched alive at times struck a soft spot in your heart, knowing that the human suffering such a harsh death was more than likely not the decision maker who placed him there."

But napalm made believers of enemy brass. Having experienced firsthand the potential of US tactical bombers, the enemy avoided exposure to air attacks. Carlton took all this into account when employing the Bounty Hunters. As the new gun-platoon leader, he learned well and fast. One day, October 2, 1969, remains a benchmark in Carlton's memory.

"We were working in the Moc Hoa area, supporting an American unit," Carlton recalls, "when the enemy attacked with heavy weapons. Pounding the US soldiers with artillery and .51-caliber machine guns, the massive enemy fire effectively pinned down the friendlies. Unable to maneuver, and with casualties mounting, decisive action was urgent or we would lose the entire force. Medevacs were working over-time extracting wounded and couldn't proceed faster. The enemy fire intensified. Of greatest danger, the .51-caliber machine guns were nothing to play with or ignore. They were literally chewing up the friendly positions. As I expected, the C&C ship called for us to engage the enemy. The target areas were slightly crosswind for optimum direction of attack. Nonetheless, I instructed all gun crews to follow me in establishing a 150-degree attack azimuth with a 330-degree downwind."

After talking with C&C, Carlton called his wing ship pilot, CW2 Ray Ayala, with his plan of attack.

"Bounty Hunter Two-Nine, this is Bounty Hunter Six."

"Six, this is Two-Nine, go ahead."

"Bounty Hunter Six, follow me through the first pass, be prepared to support. I don't want to set up the daisy chain at high altitude. Those .51-calibers won't forgive us. I'd rather attack right off the bat and not give them a chance to prepare."

"Roger that, Six," Ayala replied. "I'll follow close and be prepared to cover your attack."

"This is Six, roger!"

In his first pass, Carlton fired rockets from an altitude of eight hundred feet and continued steady until breaking off at fifty feet, damn near at ground level. The wingman, Ayala, saw Carlton's last rocket hit a stack of unfired mortar rounds. The secondary explosion rocked the earth for several hundred feet. Mud and bits of hardened bunker mud hit Carlton's gunship, breaking the chin bubble with enough force to shatter the Plexiglas and send pieces into the cockpit.

Ayala followed suit and expended approximately 50 percent of his munitions. Again, the second pass hit the enemy hard, and the enemy fire began showing signs of slowing. Except for door-gun ammunition, both Bounty Hunter fire teams were low on ammo and fuel. Carlton chose to stay on station a bit longer and engage with door guns. With ammunition nearly expended, Carlton called C&C.

"Boomerang Six, this is Bounty Hunter Six. Request permission to break off to refuel and rearm."

"Bounty Hunter Six, this is Boomerang Six. Roger, go refuel and rearm with all dispatch please. We need you back soonest."

"This is Bounty Hunter Six, roger. Understand soonest, wilco, out."

Carlton headed out at one hundred knots for the nearest refueling and rearming point at Soc Trang. As usual, once the gunships were out of the firefight, the enemy grew bolder. In a short thirty minutes, Carlton returned with his Bounty Hunters to find the battle had significantly intensified.

An Air Force FAC spotted a wounded allied soldier at the FEBA, but rescue attempts by ground troops were thwarted by enemy fire. The soldier lay bleeding with little hope of rescue while his survival chances rapidly diminished. C&C called Carlton.

"Bounty Hunter Six, this is Boomerang Six. What's your location?"

"Boomerang Six, this is Bounty Hunter Six. Approximately six clicks west of you. I have you in sight."

"Roger, Bounty Hunter Six. Your timing is perfect. Please proceed southwest approximately on a two-hundred-degree azimuth. I want to vector you into a location where a wounded soldier has been reported. He may need cover."

"Roger, Six. This is Bounty Hunter Six, wilco."

Approaching the AO, Carlton was hailed again by C&C.

"Bounty Hunter Six, this is Boomerang Six. Directly to your front, approximately half a click, you'll see a small rice dike that runs north-northwest to south-southeast. Right behind it you should also see the soldier lying on his back, approximately two hundred yards from the canal to your front. Bunkers along that canal have the soldier trapped. He can't move in any direction without drawing fire from those canal bunkers. See what you can do to neutralize those damn bunkers?"

"Roger that, Boomerang Six. Understand, neutralize the canal bunkers. Out!"

Carlton then called Ayala. "Bounty Hunter Two-Nine, did you monitor the Charlie-Charlie message?"

"Roger that, Six. I got you covered. Pound the shit out of them!"

Carlton aligned all four gunships in a right echelon formation so that the heavy-weapon systems of all four birds engaged the target simultaneously. In seconds, one hundred yards of canal bunker occupants were feeling the concussion of seventeen-pound warheads rocking the ground they stood on. Blasting huge earthen chunks from their bunkers, the HE shock temporarily disabled enemy gunners. Though a wonderful sight to the friendlies, the bunkered enemy were absorbing the HE shock with debilitating pain. Ear drums fluttering and brain matter stunned, the enemy continued to receive brutal punishment. The pounding brought the desired effect. Carlton instructed his pilots to load the heavy seventeen-pounders instead of the usual ten-pound warheads. He intended to attack the enemy fortifications.

Bright orange explosions accented the backdrop of green foliage along the canal as one might see in an artist's rendering. The blasts uprooted palm trees, and in two passes, the enemy gunfire was almost suppressed. After the second pass, Carlton ordered his second fire team to continue pounding the bunkers while he directed wingman Ayala to cover his extraction of the wounded ARVN soldier.

In the blink of an eye, Carlton was on the ground. Within seconds, his crew loaded the wounded trooper. The surprise move worked. Lifting off with a full load of fuel was challenging; however, Ayala, along with the second fire team, skillfully provided a steady stream of hot lead on the enemy, giving Carlton time to clear the LZ.

The wounded ARVN was ecstatic. He couldn't contain himself. Even with pain from his leg wound shooting through his body, he shook hands with the crew that saved his life. In broken English, he thanked them repeatedly.

As Carlton's ship cleared the ground, he spotted an enemy barely fifteen yards away. Apparently, the VC was intending to crawl up to the wounded soldier and finish killing him. Carlton directed his door gunner to the target, and the would-be assassin suffered that fate himself.

"I couldn't kill the enemy fast enough," Carlton recalls. His number-one responsibility, in his words, was to "keep our boys alive."

Carlton went on to explain: "When I took over the gun platoon, I always directed my gunship pilots to take immediate action. As soon as our boys called 'receiving fire,' regardless of who was nearest the enemy, 'kill the bastards soonest' was my SOP."

On December 21, 1969, by direction of President Nixon, CPT Kenneth R. Carlton was decorated with the Silver Star for his gallantry in action, performed on October 2, 1969. It was one of many decorations Carlton would receive during his tour with the 191st.

On another occasion, Carlton inexplicably reversed his engagement policy. This occurred in the shadow of the Parrot's Beak. The 191st was operating in the IV Corps region, otherwise called the Forty-Fourth Special Zone in the Plain of Reeds. Flat and wet, the area rendered no sign of suitable ground for a military camp. But it was a good place to land a combat-assault unit and assemble a search-and-destroy operation. In such close proximity to Cambodia, American brass felt certain the area would yield a large volume of enemy supplies en route to their troops in the South.

"The Boomerangs inserted a company of Old Reliables on the only dry land within miles," Carlton recalls. "Unknown to Americans, the NVA had established a regimental base camp exactly where the slicks landed. Well camouflaged, the bunkers remained undetected until the explosion of gunfire. The enemy started swarming like a giant anthill. Assaulting with full suppression from ten slicks and four gunships was an incredible stroke of luck. Any other place within three hundred yards would have been deadly for the Ninth Division troops. Firing at point-blank range kept the enemy down long enough for the infantry to organize their attack.

"What I saw of the Ninth Division troops was memorable. Seldom given positive media coverage, on that day, they deserved top billing. They were fantastic. Brave and decisive. In minutes, they dug in and were defeating the enemy on their own ground. The battle lasted all day. Incredibly, the Americans pushed the enemy out in the open where we could have a field day with them. All the slicks made it out. For certain, the lift pilots' pucker meters were redlined. Pushing the NVA to the open plain was an aggressive and powerful move. The enemy yielded. These were NVA, fully armed and equipped. Yet the stack of enemy bodies grew. The Bounty Hunters, just like all other gun crews in Vietnam, lived for a fight like this one. We were racking up kills by the dozens.

"In the midst of this mayhem, my wingman called me: 'Bounty Hunter Six, you have a gook at twelve o'clock on the dike.' Up until then, Bounty Hunter gunners were having all the fun, so I told Bounty Hunter Three-Three to take him. Falling back to give him room to maneuver and allow me to provide cover for him, I saw a rocket land close to the fleeing enemy. The explosion blew him in a forward somersault. Landing on his feet, the NVA kept running and even faster than before. Next, Bounty Hunter Three-Three's minigun raked through him, and still he continued running.

"I radioed in, 'Okay Three-Three, it's my turn now.' I flared to allow my gunner his chance at the enemy, but before I recovered the bird, I heard a long blast of M60 bullets followed by a long string of cussing. My gunner announced, 'I can't believe I missed.' The NVA soldier finally reached a bunker. But in his haste to enter, he crashed his head on the side of the entrance and dropped to the ground dazed. Enough time for me to come to a hover in front of the enemy with my gunner's M60 pointing directly at him. The enemy looked at me with pitiful eyes as if saying, 'You got me.' Not a glint of fear, no begging for mercy. Simply lying prostrate, awaiting his death. Something in his eyes stirred a human element within me that I can't explain.

"I quickly laid the cyclic on its side and turned the gunship away from the enemy soldier. This prevented the door gunner from killing him. Contrary to my philosophy of killing all enemy soonest, this individual survived under my hand. I still think about that enemy soldier and wonder if he remembers what I did for him that day. God must have smiled upon him that moment. War does have its moments."

The battle ended with US assets in full pursuit of a retreating enemy. It was a sight to behold for friendly troops. Carlton continued delivering his part in the war effort. Containing enemy aggression within his means, Carlton was a gleaming success. He eventually earned senior pilot status with the unit, which called for C&C positioning. The routine for experienced Boomerangs and Bounty Hunters was to elevate their presence into control schemes and other management policies of the company. Carlton was there and loved it.

Humor was a staple of these individuals at that level. One common gibe among senior Boomerangs and Bounty Hunters was aimed at the gunship pilots. Incited by spite and provoked by endless Bounty Hunter prodding, slicks were taunted as harmless, while they, the *mighty* Bounty Hunters, were always there to save the day for the *wimpy* lift crews. Of course, at C&C level, all that equalized.

Former slicks pilots watched with humor as former Bounty Hunters transitioned to the C&C role and flew slicks. When these former gunship pilots saw an enemy running, they couldn't help themselves and invariably gave chase, in dog-and-cat style. They even had a name for it: gunship-pilot syndrome. Slick pilots knew that Hueys with less blade width would immediately shudder a harsh warning that the maneuver was only moments from turning lethal for the entire crew. Pointing the UH1-H nose toward the ground, a common maneuver for a Charlie-model, would immediately initiate retreating blade stall with the less-maneuverable H-model. Deadly if not quickly recovered, former slick jocks would taunt the embarrassed gunship senior, even taking over the controls before the helicopter inverted and killed all aboard.

Many slick pilots believed that one can take the Bounty Hunter out of a gunship, but you can't take the gunship out of the Bounty Hunter. In effect, gunship pilots were so conditioned to pursuing a fleeing enemy by employing the maximum Charlie-model maneuverability that occasionally they would attempt the same with the C&C bird, thus risking a retreating blade stall. A Huey cannot fly inverted. A common gibe toward former Bounty Hunter pilots: "Wake up, meathead. You're no longer flying a bird with blades as wide as your coffin." A former gunship pilot turned operations officer, CPT Palmer, injected that humorous comment into 191st premission briefings. It had a softening effect on the occasional harsh mission assignment and was often repeated to soothe the moment. Slick pilots enjoyed the kidding, and everybody in the briefing room shared a moment of laughter.

CPT Carlton adjusted into his new C&C role, transitioning from gunship to the C&C bird. Though utterly different in tactics, he acclimated well. All joking aside, Carlton, unfortunately, suffered the gunship-pilot syndrome. It flared up amidst a difficult allied operation, but luckily it ended well.

On December 19, 1969, the 191st was supporting an ARVN unit northwest of Vinh Long, a traditional hot spot. Not far from the always-hostile Parrot's Beak, the action intensified. Sooner than most engagements, heavy weaponry came into action. The ARVN were battered. This was evidence the enemy had far better planning and intelligence than the allies. They took advantage of the great civil disparity among the indigent population to probe local farmers for tactical information of friendly-force emplacements and operations plans. The VC were masters of people manipulation. This outcome had all the makings of enemy being prebriefed as to details of this operation. Green tracers saturating allied positions implied a massacre in the making. Carlton saw it and swung into action. Calling on his old gunship cohorts, he ordered a full Bounty Hunter attack on the enemy line. Predictably, the devastating gunship attacks stymied the enemy advance. Once stopped, the allied force regrouped and dug in for a fight.

Descending through intense enemy fire, Carlton in his lone C&C ship followed the enemy front. The enemy was pulling back. *To reform!* Carlton thought. Among military planners "to reform" is a common term, which means to reassemble the attacking unit in preparation for another attack. This usually occurs when an intervening variable either disassembles or breaks up the attacking force but leaves it sufficiently strong to set up for another attack. And with that, Carlton called Bounty Hunter lead.

"Bounty Hunter Six, this is Boomerang Three."

"Three, this is Six. Go ahead."

"This is Three. I believe the enemy's movement to the rear of the battle area may be to regroup for a counterattack. Pound the crap out them, and don't let them form."

"Roger that, Three. Will do."

Relentless gunship pressure did the job. The enemy attack broke down in small groups and melted into the jungle—a job well done. The day ended in victory for the allies. Being snatched from the jaws of the enemy made it even more gratifying. The low-level control tactics demonstrated by Carlton added some validity to the gunship-pilot syndrome. In effect gunship pilots are trained to fly low level while seeking enemy contact. Slick pilots are tactically trained to the contrary. By this time, Carlton was fully assimilated into the characteristics of a UH-1H versus a Charlie-model gunship. So, he performed gunship tactics with the C&C ship but guardedly. Had C&C been shot down in that pressure-cooker firefight, then no extraction would have been imminent. It was a plus-or-minus outcome that incidentally produced the desired effect. Carlton's judgment prevailed and he was recognized for his valor.

His actions and bravery directing the battle from a dangerously low altitude and his continuous voluntary exposure to intense enemy fire impressed his allied task force commander. With gunship blood running through his veins, Carlton could not contain himself. Accepting defeat was not an option. He jumped into attack mode as always. Though he now had a different role, he was a gunship pilot at heart.

Flying C&C or Green Delta missions, Carlton continued to mix it up with the enemy in any capacity. He maintained this focus until his date of rotation back to the States. That day came soon enough. Carlton had long since expended his survival-probability time frame for helicopter pilots in Vietnam. God was with him. With his DEROS orders in hand and boarding a Freedom Bird for his ride to America, he woefully thought of how painful it would be if Vietnam were lost to the Communists. He remained hopeful that the United States would continue to support the South Vietnamese government in their effort to defeat North Vietnamese aggression.

On March 1, 1970, Carlton took his seat in a huge jet to end his tour in Vietnam and return home. As he headed to good ol' US soil, for the first time in what seemed like a long time, he pushed no buttons, pulled no levers, and didn't squeeze his head into a combat helmet. After takeoff, he simply reclined his seat and snoozed in a most restful and peaceful sleep. CPT Carlton had survived among many faces of death—some he'll carry to his grave. In April 1970, by the direction of President Nixon, CPT Kenneth R. Carlton was awarded the Distinguished Flying Cross for heroism in his C&C role on December 19, 1969.

CHAPTER 23

Mental Impacts of War

But for each Vietnam War veteran, the sound of rotor blades turning in flight strikes a nerve that forces at least a snap look.

Surrounded by death, the warrior mind yearns for a spare moment of solace. The persistent fear of dying imposes extreme mental pressure on battlefront souls. At times, the psychology of this mindset is inescapable. It's driven some to the brink of insanity. Medical experts diagnose the condition as battle fatigue or, if it persists for years afterward, post-traumatic stress disorder (PTSD). Every day, in the midst of bloodshed, both friendly and foe, the human brain suffers an extreme sensation, to which only those who have been there can relate. Like any other soldier, the 191st combat-assault crewmen sought relief from this emotional malady.

On occasion the ecological uniqueness of Vietnam offered a brief distraction from the emotion of combat. Nature lovers especially warmed to the magnificent vistas of the jungle environment. At sundown on a clear day, the 191st airmen returning to Dong Tam gained a brief moment of mental respite as they crossed the Mekong River. In a spectacular splendor of colors, the Vietnam sunset stretches across the horizon, and Mekong's banks take on an orange hue with a soft tone pleasing to the eye. Such a vibrant exhibit could trigger a fleeting memory in a warrior's mind, perhaps a romantic interlude with his loving spouse back home or his best girl from high school. But without warning, such tender moments were quickly vanquished by the VC. Daily pounding by mortars vaporized any quixotic notions within the Dong Tam area.

On a July evening in 1969, the 191st AHC returned to Dong Tam from a hard day on the battlefield. The river's dazzling sunlit display had long sunk below the horizon. As the flight crossed Mekong's banks to turn onto short final—a safe landing at Dong Tam only seconds away—the feelings among the crewmen were fraught with tension. On occasion, enemy gunners timed mortar strikes to detonate on the airstrip's approach threshold just as helicopter flights reached a hover for landing. The potential of death was a sobering wake-up from any romantic fantasy.

This lurking death had become a ritual for many assault-helicopter aircrews who supported the Ninth Infantry Division. Luckily this night's landing was mortar free, and the crewmen breathed a sigh of relief. It was the ending of an uneventful day; however, July 1969 would be remembered by Boomerangs and Bounty Hunters as the harbinger of ominous news.

The Ninth Division had orders to stand down in preparation for Stateside return. This order raised questions for support elements remaining behind. Not only would the 191st lose its primary tactical host, the Ninth Infantry, but also it would relocate to Can Tho. There, the new mission would be to support the Twenty-First ARVN Division and other allies in the southernmost regions of the Republic of Vietnam.

Amid all this unsettling news, Bounty Hunter Platoon Leader CPT Michael Arruti relaxed in the unit's bunkered officer's club, having a casual beer with one of his pilots, 1LT Carlton. The savvy Arruti was less than ninety days from DEROS and was taking all this upheaval in stride. Members of the 214th CAB from headquarters, company level to the battalion staff, were in a twist over the sudden change. Departure of the Ninth Division was also raising questions in the progressive mind of Carlton, who wondered about the future of the 191st.

The young lieutenant assumed his platoon leader had been briefed on the subject. "Captain," Carlton said, "do you have any idea when the 191st will be standing down for Stateside departure? I was hoping I could complete a whole tour with the 191st and have an opportunity to lead the gun platoon. If the 191st leaves soon, that may not work out for me."

"Ken, I wish I knew," Arruti said. "But I haven't the foggiest idea when the 191st will return Stateside. I haven't heard anything to that effect. All I know is that we need to prepare the platoon for relocation to Can Tho. That means packing all men and equipment for the trip as soon as possible. It also means inventorying of all equipment. It's a good opportunity for you to get familiar with all the TO&E gear that comes with each aircraft. Might get ahead of the game by gathering up all the manuals and checking the inventory lists."

A concerned look formed on Carlton's face, but he said nothing more. At the time, he had no idea he would eventually become the Bounty Hunter platoon leader. After delivering an exemplary gun-platoon performance, he would be selected for the role a week before Arruti rotated back to the States.

Amid the dysfunction, promised by ongoing changes, the 191st CO, MAJ Erwin "Dutch" Schmidt, knew what to do. Compared to getting the unit back on its feet before the light of day following the horrific bombardment that killed his predecessor, the 191st CO Petric, and five others, moving to Can Tho and changing mission requirements was a *simple* challenge. Schmidt gathered his company officers and assigned tasks needed to effect the changes. CPT Arruti was correct in his remarks to 1LT Carlton. In preparation for the move, gathering and inventorying the equipment was the primary task at hand. The new support requirements and mission would take effect after the 191st relocated. In the meantime, an out-of-the-ordinary personnel matter called for Schmidt's attention.

The issue, a name-calling incident, included the platoon leader of the first lift platoon, 1LT Bill Leipold, and his newly assigned pilot, Second Lieutenant (2LT) Joe K. Roberts. Leipold casually wrote the acronym FNG, slang for Fucking New Guy, before Roberts's name on the platoon's assignment board. Although a commonly used term among 191st senior pilots, the label was unacceptable to Roberts, who changed it back to 2LT, giving Leipold reason to approach Roberts. The confrontation ended with Leipold terminating Roberts's assignment to the first flight platoon, in effect, placing disposition for Roberts's new assignment back in the hands of MAJ Schmidt.

Exercising his suave style, Schmidt induced wisdom that would defuse the issue. Having been informed earlier of Roberts's desire to fly gunships, Schmidt called the new lieutenant into his office, where the Bounty Hunter platoon leader and section leader were present.

"Lieutenant Roberts," Schmidt said. "How would you like to fly gunships?"

A surprised look came over Roberts, which quickly turned into a smile. "Sir, I would *love* to fly guns!"

"Okay, consider it done. Effective immediately you take orders from your platoon leader, Captain Arruti, and your section leader, First Lieutenant Carlton. Any questions?"

"No, sir!"

Schmidt nodded with a smile. "Problem solved."

In Roberts's mind, Leipold fired him as a ploy to dispel any notions of favoritism. "Leipold knew I wanted to fly guns," Roberts recalls, "and I believe he did it as a favor. Though it might have appeared like a disagreement, I never took it that way. In any event, I was grateful for the opportunity to fly guns. Those memories will remain with me for the remainder of my life."

Roberts quickly assimilated into the Bounty Hunters and joined the preparation for the September move to Can Tho. At this point in their combat tour most aircrews of the 191st dedicated little attention to the political conflicts back home that were impacting their war effort. But with departure of the Ninth Infantry Division causing the change in mission and relocation, they were now feeling that impact—physically, mentally, and emotionally.

Within the following two weeks, the 191st loaded what assets could not be flown onto riverine force barges and completed the ordered relocation to Can Tho. With new installation procedures to learn and no American infantry to rely on for combat support, some of the seasoned Boomerangs and Bounty Hunters remained concerned. Nonetheless, under the leadership of MAJ Schmidt, the move was completed without incident. The resettlement process was rapid, and in very short order, the 191st was back in action flying combat assaults with ARVN forces.

2LT Roberts assumed his place among the Bounty Hunters as the gun platoon settled in Can Tho. Blissfully missing the cause, which bothered other gunship pilots who had developed mutual friendships within Ninth Division units, Roberts added a new dimension to the gun platoon's operation. He went about his mission unconcerned with how Washington politicians were conducting the war. He had already tasted combat with infantry units in Vietnam.

Roberts came to the 191st AHC decorated with the Combat Infantryman's Badge. Before being commissioned by the Army and rated to fly helicopters, Roberts served as an NCO in the infantry, where he was decorated for his combat performance. Hence, he joined the 191st with experience under fire, which manifested value to the Bounty Hunters, who operated under fire more frequently than other helicopter crews. Roberts was well received among the 191st gunship pilots and eventually became a solid asset for the gun platoon. To his benefit, he did not feel the loss of the Ninth Division combat strength perceived by others.

Experienced Bounty Hunters and Boomerangs, although generally not vocal about the subject, remained disappointed with the US withdrawal. Leaving reduced fighting capability in the face of growing enemy pressure didn't seem like the correct move. For those in the mix of combat every day, it worked on the psyche of some of the most experienced. Nonetheless, fighting hard, many wondered how it would end. Enemy aggression continued and spilled over onto friendly installations. New American technology fielded for testing was designed to help contain this reinvigorated enemy aggression. Two such heliborne setups were separately introduced as the Nighthawk and, somewhat later, the Iroquois Night Fighting and Night Tracking (INFANT) system, which equipped birds with powerful night-fighting capabilities. These upgrades would soon make a significant impact on enemy night movements, but not before these changes presented some hairy experiences. Night refueling at remote locations by Nighthawk crews was no longer safe. Enemy attacks became more frequent. Locations and specific details of these incidents were frequently mentioned and reiterated in staff meetings and premission briefings for safety emphasis. For many, the changes required additional mental alertness—on an already mentally taxing workload.

One death attributed to this new threat and frequently reiterated in crew gatherings was that of SP4 Timothy Clay McCarthy. On June 24, 1970, McCarthy was killed at Ben Tre while trying to prevent the enemy from overrunning the area where he was refueling a Nighthawk bird. He fought valiantly, killing several of the attacking VC with his M60 machine gun until he ran out of ammo and was shot and killed. McCarthy was nineteen years old and hailed from Biloxi, Mississippi. He received the Distinguished Flying Cross, the Air Medal, and the Purple Heart, among other awards.

Roberts was made aware of this incident as part of his 191st indoctrination for new pilots. Prior to receiving Roberts in the gun platoon, CPT Arruti flew with the newbie on a familiarization ride. Roberts passed with flying colors and soon became a respected AC, participating in numerous battles. Known for his toughness under enemy fire, he established a laudable example for others.

"While flying with my platoon leader, CPT Bob Lifsey," Roberts recalls, "I was wounded in the left leg. After spending four or five days in the Can Tho hospital, the tending physician appeared in my room with good news. My bullet wound was diagnosed severe enough to merit evacuation to the government's advanced medical facilities in Japan. Both CPT Lifsey and my assistant platoon leader, 1LT Jim Kennedy, were present when I told the doctor I didn't want to go to Japan. They both looked at me as if I was crazy. The doctor asked why, and I explained this was the best unit I ever served with and I wanted to stay in it. To my benefit, he approved and placed me on light duty for a month. Thereafter, I received minor wounds twice more, and the same physician treated me on each occasion."

On Roberts's fourth trip to the hospital, the same doctor was walking in the hallway when Roberts entered. The doctor abruptly stopped and called out to Roberts. "Roberts! What happened this time?" He sounded frantic.

"I have fifty-two pieces of plastic in my legs from getting my chin bubble and windshield shot out, Doc."

The doctor sat Roberts down and swabbed iodine on one of his legs. "How much longer do you have in Vietnam?" the doctor asked.

"I have eleven days left, Doc."

"Eleven days!" the doctor practically shouted. "Then you're grounded for eleven days. You will *not* fly again in Vietnam."

With that exchange, the doctor dispensed iodine for Roberts's other leg and sent him back to his BOQ. He was given strict medical instructions to remain in his room until he left Vietnam.

Roberts reluctantly agreed. He left Vietnam never fully understanding the Ninth Division combat void that concerned others. Though he had heard plenty from veterans whose DEROS preceded his, Roberts's performance remained consistent with his everyday warrior mindset. His focus remained on the job at hand and ignored the strategic shifting in Washington. Too vague to make a difference in his opinion, Roberts knew there was little *he* could do to impact those changes. The fact that the full measure of strategic thinking by Washington was not explained to the troops meant little to Roberts. He simply took the war one day at a time and fought to win. This living in the moment was his way of handling the mental fatigue of war. Troops that thought too much of home or wondered what was going on in Washington beyond their control were ripe for battle fatigue.

For security reasons, not only are battlefront troops seldom privy to strategic planning that determines when the US commits to war, but they also are seldom aware when the US will terminate that commitment. Among the lower tiers of 191st personnel, little was known of the planning sequence approved by the commander in chief of the United States to begin pulling combat troops out of the Republic of Vietnam. It caught most veterans by surprise and affected unit morale.

The 191st supported the Ninth Division for three years, and many unit crewmembers had established comradery with the grunts. Some of each had exchanged small mission sequences with one another. Infantry troops enjoyed flying as gunners on Boomerang ships, and some air crewmembers occasionally spent a night on ambush squads, seeking opportunity to kill the enemy on the ground.

Before CPT Falcon, the unit's XO, rotated back to the States in the summer of 1969, he informally visited firebases with his close associate, CPT Palmer, the unit's operations officer, to call upon task force commanders, such as LTC David Hackworth. Although impromptu, the visits were well received by the battalion staffs, and the exchange of tactical information was invaluable on the battlefield for both grunts and 191st crews. As such, the relationship was a sincere extension of the brotherhood shared by American soldiers at war. Hence, the sudden separation impacted more than just the support relationship and diminished tactical interface— it impacted the morale and mental grit needed to keep up the fight.

Seldom in war stories depicting the lives and times of Americans dying in battle are the political reasons explained in detail to the troops. Driven by America's trendy democratic process, Washington's elected officials preferred to steer clear of such unpleasant accountabilities. The truth of why US forces were ordered to Vietnam rests somewhere between Communist aggressions in the Gulf of Tonkin (where North Vietnamese gunboats were said to have attacked American military ships) and discretion on the part of President Johnson's administration. Many argue that the matter could have been settled with diplomacy instead of bullets. President Johnson chose war.

The resultant 191st battle deaths affected the lives of numerous families related to the forty-four who were killed in action. Eleven of those forty-four died by enemy action after April 12, 1970. The year prior, with the Ninth still in Vietnam, only one 191st crewman died in combat. Considering that the major portion of Ninth Division assets left Vietnam in September of 1969, one can say it took the enemy approximately twelve months to raise the kill ratio of 191st personnel from one in twelve months to ten in twelve months. A considerable difference. Some experts attribute this loss to the missing American infantry support. The increased losses certainly accelerated battle fatigue.

Flying out of Can Tho, CPT George Clogston, a 191st slick pilot, offered firsthand witness of a battle where three Bounty Hunter crewmembers were killed by enemy fire. The morning of May 9, 1970, found the Boomerang flight sitting on the Go Cong airstrip loading ARVN for combat assaults south into the Tra Vinh area. CPT Clogston was flying the chock-two bird. The usual pre-assault prep, which typically called for loading the infantry and waiting for C&C to call with launch instructions, was underway. The morning was placid with crews telling jokes, reading books, and discussing other mundane events when a sudden mortar blast sent the 191st flight scrambling for takeoff. Abbreviating start-up procedures amid mortar-round detonations, the birds left in a hurry. Once in the air, they joined up and formed an impromptu eagle flight. After a few minutes airborne, flight lead broke the silence.

"Boomerang Flight, this is Flight Lead. Check your crews and report wounded status. Trail, let me know how many birds you count in formation."

"Boomerang Lead, this is Trail, roger. I see five birds in trail formation."

"This is Lead, thanks. Boomerangs, render your wounded reports."

Respectively, all five slicks reported. "No wounded."

"Boomerang Flight, this is Lead. We're going to head south to vicinity of Tra Vinh where we will orbit until Charlie-Charlie calls with further instructions."

Again, all five Boomerang slicks acknowledged.

C&C called for insertion. Enemy fire was encountered, and the slicks executed the combat assault as normal.

"All slicks made it in and out of the LZ," Clogston recalls. "As the flight gained altitude, a near hysterical Mayday call came through the 191st tactical frequency: 'Boomerang Six! This is Bounty Hunter Two-Six—I just lost power. We're going down!' I craned my neck, being careful to maintain formation. And I saw smoke coming from the trees on my left. The gunship flown by CW2 Deacon 'Deak' Jones, with Copilot WO1 Terry Lynn Henry, Crew Chief SP4 Kris Mitchell Perdomo, and Gunner SP4 Stephen Harold Haight, crashed, killing all but Jones. Deak was never the same."

Copilot WO1 Terry Lynn Henry was twenty-one years old and grew up in Clarion, Pennsylvania, where his family owned and operated the Finotti Beverage Company. He received the Distinguished Flying Cross and the Bronze Star, among other awards. Crew Chief SP4 Kris Mitchell Perdomo was twenty-one years old and from Newport Beach, California. He received the Air Medal and the Purple Heart, among other awards. Gunner SP4 Stephen Harold Haight was twenty years old and from Cazenovia, New York. He received the Distinguished Flying Cross, the Air Medal, and the Purple Heart, among other awards.

Witnessing the deaths of fellow crewmembers struck an emotional chord in Clogston. WO1 Henry, his previous roommate, had grown on CPT Clogston. As only war environments can do, the warriors bonded—and empathy for your brothers-in-arms lasts a lifetime. Still reeling in the pain of Henry's death, he learned that WO1 Steve Cashin, another one of his previous roommates, had also been killed by the enemy. Clogston's easygoing mindset transitioned into rage.

Qualified to fly the Nighthawk bird and rotating the duty with other pilots, he seized the opportunity to seek out the enemy with a purpose. Intensified by the losses of his brethren and buddies, Henry and Cashin, Clogston's anger remained insatiable for weeks. While flying Nighthawk missions, he used the bird's potent weaponry to destroy as many enemy troops as the combat situation permitted. He killed with a vengeance and added sizeable body counts to enemy kill ratios attributed to the 191st AHC. This persisted with elevated personal commitment for several weeks following the death of his former roommates. The mental impact of losing fellow crewmen who were bonded as brothers took a toll. However, warriors don't have the luxury of a gentle transition through the stages of grief—grieving can be dangerous in battle; anger is often the safer response.

Expended energy against the enemy seemed limitless to Clogston. However, WO1 Henry was no longer on earth, and those most affected, sooner or later, must recognize his interred state—his final resting place, a fate reserved for all humans, some before others.

Long after Vietnam, Clogston continues to exhibit anger over Henry's death. A loyal subject to his warrior bonds, CPT Clogston shares this attribute with many 191st veterans. Some behavior scientists believe that such ardent manifestation of anger exhibited by Clogston also grows from social confinement in war camps. Being unable to mix and socialize with the foreign population at war may strengthen the relationships among those entrapped by hostilities. Barracks life, such as the daily routine forced upon Clogston, was unnatural by the normal order of average American family environments. Interacting with immediate family captivates a large portion of a parent's day clock. This allows far less time for friends, and quite contrary to the scenario that Clogston experienced in Vietnam. WO1 Henry was his family away from home, so to speak. Under the circumstances, Clogston reacted as he would for a close blood brother.

The war fought by Clogston and his 191st teammates was rooted in international instability. Known worldwide as Indochina, the region once contained fiscal interests from world powers, covering a broad spectrum of capital investment. Some, from socialist-dominated countries, clashed with Western enterprise in irreparable fashion—having no remedy except war. Such conflicts normally have a final call to battle that settles disputes once and for all. In the case of the French government, which preceded American intervention in Vietnam, the effort to establish and maintain democracy ended in May 1954, at the Battle of Dien Bien Phu. Thoroughly defeated, the French surrendered. Logistically outperformed by the enemy, both the French and the Viet Minh organizations, which led the struggle for Vietnamese independence, learned the value of war material sufficiency. For the French, it was a tactical catastrophe that ended scores of free-world interests and thousands of French lives. But for the Viet Minh, it was a logistics lesson the Communists would not forget. And for CPT Clogston and his fellow 191st crewmembers? They learned that a well-equipped enemy requires an ever-constant adjustment in tactics and advanced weaponry. In that regard, America excelled. But the NVA continued to advance their cause as well. They remained determined to unite the two countries and invested enormous human resources and hardware into the fight.

The tenacity of North Vietnamese military thinking is truly remarkable. Their willingness to commit lives in the face of enormous opposition becomes of far less concern than that of US decision makers. War as they know it is a way of life that has endured for eons. A continuation of the same makes little difference in their political and military objectives. As an adversary, the US was no different than all other forces who threatened their way of life.

In effect, Communist aggression existed in Southeast Asia long before the US intervened. While war was routine for the enemy, for the 191st the ever-growing enemy strength was clearly a result of the Ninth Infantry's departure. The enemy previously tried to invade the region defended by the Ninth but failed. Now, the enemy engagements were far more ferocious and effective. Despite the increased Communist aggression, CPT Clogston and his crew stubbornly engaged the enemy.

Though facing the same enemy that had defeated powerful French forces years before, the 191st never yielded to enemy pressure. Even when severely battered by enemy fire, the Boomerangs and Bounty Hunters continuously reentered the fray. Their diminished assets were committed until reinforcements arrived. American will and commitment assured sufficient strength for all contingencies. Continuing the fight in the face of adversity was encouraged by the understanding that reinforcements were on their way. Boomerangs and Bounty Hunters were well aware of this. It was a world of difference between US strategies and those of other world powers. Nonetheless, once committed, public opinion in a democracy such as America can derail such promises. That weakness, and how it impacted 191st personnel, should serve as a hard lesson learned for future war planners and American political decision makers.

A good example of that hard lesson was the price of 191st blood, which increased nearly tenfold over previous combat years. Clearly, this American bloodshed was a result of US government executive-level refusal to act on intelligence made readily available to the United States political machinery. It was evident that the enemy buildup was ongoing when the US government decided to remove combat troops from Vietnam. Those support units left behind, including the 191st AHC, were suddenly exposed to far greater enemy threat without the support they previously experienced.

When war strategy and battlefield tactics fail to synchronize, it's usually a temporary shift for strategic reasons. Pulling the Ninth Division out of Vietnam was a political decision made by President Richard Nixon. Resultant harm to combat troops that evolves from such political decisions normally becomes breaking news soon after. This is how political decisions of war become the accountability of the commander in chief. Regrettably, in this case, the entire nation was tired of war and applying enormous pressure on Washington to bring the troops home. This strategic change is what threw the system out of synchronization. It can be argued that America was winning the war, but the American public simply ran out of patience.

A typical mend for faulty tactical protocols is in adjusting to good battlefield order: the order of battle. This very important component of battle preparation was upset by the hasty departure of the Ninth. In America, depending on battle contingencies, established Army fighting units are organized in a tooth-to-tail fashion required to function in coordination with one another. The 191st AHC was a part of this assembly. The cutting edge of Army units, the teeth, is intertwined with elements of infantry, both mechanized and nonmechanized, along with artillery and armor. Among these three combat-arms branches, American offensive and defensive measures are assembled and employed. Force development comprising combinations of each branch is merged for whatever military threat or contingency the US faces. This represents the Army's combined-arms team. After that, there exists a tooth-to-tail ratio of support elements providing the logistical needs of frontline troops—the supply and service units.

Herein lay the combat role of 191st AHC crews who flew infantry soldiers into battle. Then they followed these insertions with resupply or medevac support as needed. Bounty Hunters reigned supreme in close air support for frontline elements. They delivered ordnance with pinpoint accuracy into tight battle lines where artillery variables were too risky for friendly troop safety. Short of any one of these war-making components, the risk of battle loss increases exponentially. Ecological variables among the populated regions of the world also present different force demands. Vietnam jungles posed their own challenges.

Commitment of military force anywhere in the world requires well-planned contingencies, including the tactical reasons for the combination of tooth-to-tail elements. The Ninth Infantry Division provided these protocols, and enemy forces are equally aware of these factors. Boomerangs and Bounty Hunters operated in this environment and in this order of battle until the Ninth Division went home. Thereafter the force-development procedures explained above were no longer observed by allied forces, leaving the 191st highly exposed. Simply stated, the ARVN did not have the capacity to employ the same force-management protocols. Neither did the US provide them with all supplies and equipment necessary to maintain the security needed by US support elements left behind.

The 191st entered the war well after other US forces established secure areas in the Republic of Vietnam, yet it remained well after a large contingency of US combat arms units departed, pulled out for political reasons back home. However, allowing American combat troops to depart a war zone before the enemy was contained meant severe consequences for the 191st crews and support personnel left to shoulder the burden. The weakened defenses, in areas where the Ninth Division had protected friendly installations, increased the consequences suffered by 191st soldiers. Mortar attacks were more frequent and attacks on friendly installations increased. Deaths continued to rise—and the battle fatigue escalated. The emotional pain from tragic losses inflicting the unit and their American families was a severe imposition of a failed US policy.

Seldom were 191st insertions made into LZs where enemy plotting of prearranged fire missions occurred. Enemy occupants were kept on the move by Ninth Infantry Division pressure, rendering little time for this type of preplanning by the enemy. A late 1969 battle near the southern Cambodian border demonstrated the negative impact of American combat troop withdrawal from the Republic of Vietnam—including the mental impact on the surviving crewmembers still in the fight.

WO1 Darrell Stigler recalls: "The order came for inserting fifty ARVN troops in an area thick with nipa palm. The LZ was situated just east of friendlies already on the ground, giving a false pretense of enemy absence, an assumption far from accurate. The ARVN were to establish a blocking force for enemy fire directed at a line of hootches bordering a tributary of the Mekong River. I was flying as peter pilot with CW2 Aufi Maxx, a senior pilot and a very cool and seasoned combat aviator. The usual pre-insertion gunship prep and slick suppression was nixed, giving us little cover on approach. Flight lead called for staggered right formation, and all was quiet until just before touchdown. As we flared to decelerate, I noticed some brown columns of dust ahead on the LZ. With uneven ground sloping right at touchdown, we slid toward chock four slightly, and I refocused on our safety distance between birds. Suddenly, the top of chock four opened upward as if a giant can opener peeled it back—all the way to the engine cowling. When the chopper hit, the aircraft blades flew off and the skids vaulted fifteen feet in the air. Landing upright, I could see the mass of what appeared to be dead bodies in its cargo compartment and both pilots slumped in their seats. 'Mortars!' I finally realized. And we were right in the middle of the impact area.

"I immediately reacted on the intercom and ordered the crew chief and gunner to exit our bird and go retrieve chock four's wounded crew. Hesitant to abandon his M60 machine gun, the gunner needed a second scream from me to exit our aircraft and go help the crew chief. Both performed as I have never seen brave men do before. Running through a hail of bullets and mortar explosions, they carried the wounded to our bird, and we made a miraculous lift-off with CW2 Maxx remaining cool as a cucumber. An amazing pilot. We flew at max speed, 120 knots, to the nearest medical facility. Both chock-four pilots were bleeding profusely from shrapnel wounds on their feet, ankles, necks, and the back of their heads. In route, I called the Navy hospital at Binh Thuy to prepare emergency treatment and then, on and off, watched the passengers as Maxx flew the bird.

"Blood impacted the windshield and soaked our flight suits, building a nauseous odor in the aircraft. But we kept our stomachs down and pressed on. On one of my glances to the rear seat, I noticed the wounded copilot teetering on the verge of passing out. There was a real possibility that if he passed out he would fall out the side. Screaming to the gunner to help stabilize the peter pilot, I reached back and caught the copilot's shoulder harness, barely keeping him from falling out the bird. Saved by a stroke of luck, we got him to the hospital, where he recovered sufficiently for medical evacuation to a facility with the specialized care he needed. All crewmembers survived the enemy attack, and at the end of the day, we drank ourselves to sleep in preparation for another day of combat."

This whole episode of enemy action had been strengthened with the supply of weapons and equipment made possible by the safety margin provided for the enemy. Shortsighted US planning did not account for this threat when planning the extraction of American forces. Not allowing American ground forces to enter Cambodia and Laos early in the war gave the enemy a logistical advantage. American military had the wherewithal to clean out the enemy supply depots prepositioned by the NVA, but failed to act. This gave enemy forces the logistical strength to occasionally close the gap with American airmobile capacity, especially when high-caliber anti-aircraft fire was directed at heliborne forces. It also gave the enemy overwhelming combat power over South Vietnam. Ultimately it provided total domination over the Republic's military. Many experienced combat veterans attribute this outcome to the political decisions made in Washington DC.

By 1970, the NVA had extended its logistics throughout Laos and Cambodia. Facilitating its invasion plans for uniting North and South Vietnam under Communist rule, the NVA continued stockpiling war material. NVA supply routes comprised ten entry points into the Republic of Vietnam. Six of these entered through the Ho Chi Minh Trail from the DMZ to the central part of South Vietnam. The remaining four entered through the Sihanoukville Route of Cambodia and dispersed from central Republic of Vietnam down to the Parrot's Beak.[1] A learned fact from many decades of war, the NVA remained aware that logistics made the difference in their final defeat of the French at Dien Bien Phu, and they made sure their logistics proved infallible in that episodic battle. Thus, in 1970, the lower half of the Republic of Vietnam remained a frustration for enemy logistics teams. It represented the last bastion of resistance to enemy logisticians seeking to complete their invasion prep. Heretofore, the enemy knew what they needed to do, but the Ninth Division was simply too powerful to allow the enemy to act decisively. Conventional engagements with the Ninth had proved catastrophic for them. When the Ninth was still operating in-country, aircrews of the 191st AHC clearly saw enemy body counts soar by comparison to American casualties. This was affirmed by Howard K. Smith of American Broadcasting Company when he reported that "Viet Cong casualties during Tet 1968 were one hundred times ours."[2] Enemy numbers killed during the 1969 time frame were just as numerous. American units on the northern front were equally lethal. But the shorter distance to northern battle zones made it easier for the NVA to replenish and recompose men and equipment. The area where the 191st operated required a different priority for

---

1 LTG Phillip B. Davidson, USA (Ret.), *Vietnam at War: The History: 1946–1975* (Novato, CA: Presidio Press, 1988), 31.

2 Davidson, *Vietnam at War: The History: 1946–1975*, 31.

the enemy. The distance from North Vietnam made it more difficult to reach. That changed when the Ninth Division left the Republic of Vietnam.

Convoy after convoy of heavily laden Russian and Chinese trucks carried tons of NVA war material into southern Cambodia. Easy distribution to enemy units in the South, coupled with the absence of the Ninth, substantially leveled the playing field for enemy action. Now, from the DMZ to its southern coasts, the Republic of Vietnam was targeted for takeover by the Communists. This massive invasion plan and execution was occurring all around the 191st operational zone. Yet little or no intelligence to that effect reached the lower echelons of 191st crews. The stage was set for en-masse attack by the enemy. But for the 191st AHC, it remained business as usual. Slow, but persistent, enemy preparations for the final invasion were closing for action. From captured caches of enemy supplies, the 191st crews clearly saw the upgrade in enemy weapons and munitions. Most pleasing to Boomerangs and Bounty Hunters were the American rocket fléchettes buried in the captured gunstocks, as proof that 191st INFANT ships did their job.

The enemy invasion path into the southern reaches of Republic of Vietnam traversed the 191st operational zone precisely at center of mass. As US ground forces vacated South Vietnam, the 191st was left behind—smack in the middle of harm's way. Not only was the 191st AO expanded, but the enemy forces leaving the Parrot's Beak area were much better equipped and their fighting capacity far stronger. Casualties among the 191st AHC crews increased significantly when these enemy forces traversed the central part of South Vietnam directly into the Boomerang and Bounty Hunter combat zones. The War, as the 191st had come to know it for several years, was changed dramatically.

Near the far-north end of South Vietnam, dust trails raised by massive columns of NVA rolling stock on the Ho Chi Minh Trail could be seen for miles. Almost daily, US Air Force and Navy bombers scored big attritions on some of these convoys. SF often inserted into Cambodia by 191st AHC crews shared observations of the lethal impacts of these air attacks. Though for security reasons they didn't offer their names, shared discussions of their clandestine observations were numbing. One individual who gave a pseudonym, SSG Bill Jill, described the following while sharing a beer with Bounty Hunters the evening before his insertion:

"Napalm blasts seared equipment and enemy soldiers by the hundreds, often setting off secondary explosions that were lethal and enormously destructive. You could see burning human bodies leaping from enemy vehicles and collapsing nearby. Twisting and contorting while dying as their flesh seared on desolate jungle roads. Like us in countries we were not supposed to be, who knows if their identities and death notice ever reached next of kin hundreds of miles to the north."

While information offered by SSG Jill gave 191st crews an uplift, it did little to raise morale knowing the scale of enemy effort building. The onslaught of war material was too immense for US fighter strikes to make a decisive strategic difference. Megatons of war supplies were being prepositioned in enemy logistic centers along the entire length of South Vietnam. Staged just inside the Laotian and Cambodian borders, logistical preparations for the enemy's final assault into the Republic of Vietnam were nearing completion. Availability of the necessary supplies and munitions, for the extended battle to come, were only months away. The NVA were determined. Many adversaries, before America, had been dispatched in the same way. The last among their victims were the French, no less.

Mentally, the enemy were conditioned to stay the course; they always had. The 191st was one small, peppery element that stood in their way. But with American ground combat forces being removed from the Republic of Vietnam, Boomerangs and Bounty Hunters, who followed US policy, felt confused about war objectives. Unlike the enemy, who saw the war as a way of life, Americans were conditioned to do what was necessary to win. At this point in the war, US policy simply didn't appear to support this premise.

In some units where pilots were receiving *pink slips*, ordering their outright release from active duty upon completion of their tour, some aviators refused to fly. Logically, it made sense. While in Stateside labor forces, such a career-ending notice might be received with intent to remain on the payroll as long as possible, but in combat, it was a bumbling failure. A comment frequently heard during that process was, "Who in their right mind would want to risk their lives in such a lethal environment for a few months of Army pay?" Dismissed by all frontline aviators as simply more political idiocy from Washington politicians, it became evident the Vietnam War had reached its downward turn for American interests.

In the minds of 191st warriors, both in the Republic of Vietnam or Stateside assignments, these turns of events were demoralizing and regretful. Among the most hurtful impacts were memories of Boomerangs and Bounty Hunters who died fighting with the unit. CW2 Terry J. Wilund, a Huey pilot who arrived at the 191st with sufficient flight time to begin his tour as an AC, recalls an incident that even in decades later impacts his mind with deep-seated remorse. On June 5, 1968, while flying combat assaults in the vicinity of Dong Tam, following numerous formation-flight insertions and extractions, Wilund's bird and one other were assigned single-ship missions.

"Well familiar with the area," Wilund recalls, "my ship was one of two directed to break from the flight and proceed to certain locations to pick up supplies or personnel and deliver them to certain points of need. The second ship, crewed by AC WO1 Ricardo 'TJ' Robert Tejano, Copilot WO1 Norman Michael Turone, Crew Chief SP5 Richard Larry Vines, and Gunner SP4 Dennis Owen Akers, was assigned a mission into unfamiliar ground. TJ called and asked if I would trade missions with him since he was familiar with my pickup and delivery locations and I was familiar with his. I said yes, called C&C for approval, and then proceeded along TJ's course of action. At approximately 1630 hours I completed my delivery and landed adjacent to a fire support base to grab C rations for our supper, leaving my bird running on idle and the crew strapped to their seats. Monitoring our tactical frequency, I overheard several calls from C&C made to TJ with no response.

"C&C called me and asked if I'd been in contact with TJ. 'Negative,' I responded. I suggested that I depart my present location, climb to altitude, and attempt contact in event he landed at his point of delivery and yet remained on the ground. C&C approved. I departed, climbed to 1,500 AGL, and spotted a column of black smoke in the direction of TJ's point of delivery. After notifying C&C, I proceeded to the location and found TJ's aircraft crashed and burning. Landing nearby, we could only see TJ's body in the bird. The rest were burned beyond recognition. Extricating TJ from the wreck, we were ordered to stand by for help to arrive. To this day, I've had occasion to visit the names of TJ and his crew at the Vietnam Veterans Memorial Wall and feel in my heart that had TJ not asked to trade missions, it would have been me and my crew's names on that wall. I bow my head and wonder why."

AC Tejano hailed from Spokane, Washington, was twenty-four years old, and was married to Wanda. They had two children, Ricardo Jr. and Deborah. From Chicago, Copilot Turone had been the captain of his high school's football team and joined the Army right after graduation. He was a couple weeks shy of his twentieth birthday. Crew Chief Vines hailed from Bakersfield, California, and was nineteen years old. Gunner Akers came from Louisville, Kentucky, and was twenty-one years old.

In worst cases, the survivors who are left to wonder and carry on without their buddies suffer varying degrees of mental disability. And while mental experts seemed in doubt when first presented with the premise of combat fatigue in Vietnam, they failed to understand the effects of longevity at war. Prior to Vietnam, most other wars engaging US forces did not endure for twelve years. Since then, as a nation, we have come to realize the mental damage wrought by the seemingly never-ending rotations of the same soldiers to the battlefront, a sad but real political cause.

No one walks away from war unchanged or unscathed. Many 191st pilots, crew, and personnel understood then and do now that they shall carry horrific scenes in their mind for life. Some manage to resume an outward normal appearance but hide the dark side well enough to seem unmoved. Others manage to keep the living faces of the deceased in their minds as bright beacons of what it means to be human, to be an American, to be a brother.

To this day, a great American asset unshaken by his Vietnam experience, CPT George Clogston continues to grow his estate for his family and maintains close bonds with his friends and loved ones. After CW2 Terry Wilund left Vietnam, he married his fiancée, Rita, returned to college, and flew helicopters for the Missouri National Guard and the St. Louis Police Department, accruing twenty-two years of flying service. He then resumed rotary-wing duties with ARCH Air Medical Service, where he remained a helicopter pilot for an additional nineteen years. Retired after logging 18,600 accident-free hours, Wilund lives gleefully with Rita, and they both enjoy quality time with their adult children, Erik and Dana, and their families. WO1 Darrell Stigler completed a thirty-three-year career as a commercial airline pilot, retiring from American Airlines. Thereafter, he served as a flight-safety instructor training both rotary-wing and fixed-wing pilots. He plans to retire in 2018, volunteer to assist the US Olympic Ski Team in Utah, and enjoy his family of four children and eleven grandchildren with his lovely wife, Sandy.

Every American who served in the 191st AHC during the Vietnam War carries the experience with him in his own way. But for each Vietnam War veteran, the sound of rotor blades turning in flight strikes a nerve that forces at least a snap look in the direction of the noise, accompanied by a blood surge that warms the body.

CHAPTER 24

Conner Commanding with Bearden as Top

In Vietnam life changed in a micro-heartbeat Soon, bullets stitched within inches of Bearden.

On a clear morning in mid-March 1970, the 214th CAB commander, LTC William Saur, visually followed a 191st Bounty Hunter gunship below him as it slowly made its way at treetop level over enemy-infested ground. Intelligence sources indicated the area was occupied by a large and well-equipped enemy force. With nerves pinging, Saur kept a sharp eye on the gunship, not knowing it was the 191st CO, MAJ Victor S. Conner. The anticipation that he may lose another gunship and crew kept Saur's stomach tied in knots. Having made a surprise visit on the scene to observe the 191st AHC operation, Saur's presence in the air above the flight remained unnoticed by 191st pilots.

In the gunship below, MAJ Conner cautiously searched the landscape for the slightest hint of enemy presence. As AC of the heavily armed UH-1C gunship, he carried on with seemingly careless exposure, intent on drawing enemy fire. Conner ambled the gunship at a dangerously slow pace and at point-blank range to any ground-level weapon emplacements. Saur, inexperienced in combat-assault tactics, knew little about the feint move he was witnessing below. Conner's tactic was common among gunships' search-and-destroy operations. Baiting the enemy into action, the gunship team positioned themselves to launch a salvo of death and destruction, and the wing ship remained poised to attack.

Using all his faculties, Conner keyed the mike for WO1 John Thomas Orrico, his copilot. "Orrico, keep your eyes on that nipa palm line to your right that follows the canal, while I search the brush and hootches on the left. Any sign of Charlie—and we score. But we need to move fast or we might get stitched by the bad guys below. Let me know the minute you see anything that might be enemy troops."

"Roger that, sir!" Orrico's voice rose with excitement.

Meanwhile, unable to contain himself any longer, Battalion Commander Saur, assuming Conner was flying the C&C bird he saw circling at 1,500 feet, called the CO on the tactical frequency. "Boomerang Six, this is Cougar Six."

"Cougar Six, this is Boomerang Six, go ahead."

"Boomerang Six, this is Cougar Six. You have a gunship *loaching* around in the treetops. I suggest you call him immediately and order the Bounty Hunter to a safe altitude where he belongs."

With no consternation in his voice, Conner replied, "Cougar Six, this is Boomerang Six. I'm the one flying the low-level gunship. Please let me visit with you later, and I'll explain the premise of this tactic." Not known to the battalion commander, MAJ Conner often flew missions not just from the safety of the C&C bird, but in the fray as a gunship pilot, and was well versed in assault tactics.

"This is Cougar Six, roger." With that final communication, LTC Saur departed the scene trusting the combat-assault business to those who did it every day.

The search-and-destroy operation continued over the ground where intelligence sources had pinpointed an elite NVA unit. Approaching a canal junction, the gunship drew the anticipated enemy fire. The attack plan immediately swung into motion. Flying the wing ship, Bounty Hunter Two-Nine, the well-seasoned CW2 Ray Ayala, was ready.

"Bounty Hunter Two-Nine, this is Six. Did you see the fire?"

"Roger, Six—rolling in now. Stay clear!"

Within thirty seconds the earth around the canal junction was erupting from ten-pound warheads blasting holes in the thick growth below. From out of nowhere, a second gunship team appeared and joined the attack. The beautiful jungle growth below soon became green matter mangled together as if it was run through a shredder. The four gunships in the daisy-chain pattern continued to bombard the canal junction with a continuous barrage of rocket fire until blast after blast devastated the suspected enemy position. Hidden bunkers, exposed as their cover was blown off, became prime targets. Loaded Hogs (UH-1Cs), each carrying two nineteen-shot rocket pods and seventeen-pound warheads, attacked the earthen mounds and parapets. They pounded the fortifications into dust.

Minutes after the pounding, Ayala's crew chief, SP5 Kenneth Lavern Brown, commented to the crew over the intercom. "Man, did you smell that residue from explosive chemicals? It was so thick, it burned my nose and eyes."

As the smoke cleared, four dead bodies were counted—bloody pulps lying dismembered on the ground surrounding the canal junction.

The action was fast and furious but lacked the expected response. A gunship attack against a large enemy unit normally brought a ground swell of enemy fire. If that had occurred, an eagle flight of troops orbiting nearby would have landed in blocking positions to surround and destroy the enemy unit. But no such luck in this case. The NVA anticipated correctly and moved their main body of troops just before the search-and-destroy force arrived, leaving behind only their cleanup crew.

"Damn!" Conner keyed his mike and loudly exclaimed his disappointment to Orrico. "I was hoping we'd found the big enemy outfit. This is why it's so important to move on intelligence information quickly. The enemy knows not to stay in one place for long, for fear that we find and destroy them. Take the controls for a moment while I look at the map again."

"Roger that, sir."

Just as Orrico took control of the gunship, Boomerang operations called on the unit's secure frequency: "Boomerang Six, this is Ops."

"This is Six, go ahead, Ops," Conner responded.

"Sir, a First Sergeant Donald Lee Bearden came by to see you. He said he's been assigned to the unit and wants to visit with you. The sergeant major recruited him to replace First Sergeant Screven [pseudonym]. We told him you were out flying. He'd like to know what time he can visit with you tomorrow."

Conner scheduled a meeting with his new first sergeant over the airways and then, without missing a beat, continued with his search-and-destroy mission. The ground unit found a small cache of enemy weapons and munitions, which were evacuated by the lift ships, but otherwise the remainder of the search-and-destroy mission waned into the late hours of dusk before the ARVN gave up the chase. No enemy contact to speak of. The four enemy kills at the canal junction gave the crew gratification that at least those four individuals would no longer kill Americans. Exhausted, the crews headed back to Can Tho.

An extraordinary commander, MAJ Conner graduated from OCS in 1960. After earning his wings in 1965, Conner completed a tour in Vietnam with the Sixty-Eighth AHC (1965–66). Therefore, combat assaults and enemy fire were no surprise to him. He had felt the sting of battle long before he became an IP at Fort Wolters, Texas (1966–69). Assigned as the S3 of the 214th CAB, he assumed command of the 191st AHC in February 1970. Without question, Conner came to the 191st well versed in aviation and Army protocol. His experience made a progressive impact on the company. It complemented the strong points of the unit's already elite performance and exemplified his poise and control when needed.

The next day, Conner dug into the reports and mail that he was too tired to bother with the night before. *Hell, there are never enough hours in the day for all this paperwork.* Having terminated the previous day's mission late in the evening, he decided to retire to his bunk so his worn-out body could recover. The stress of low-level flying over enemy territory mentally fatigued and drained the average soul. He hoped that his new first sergeant could pick up the administrative slack. First sergeant is the official Army title bestowed upon the human linchpins at the very head of enlisted soldiers at company level and are respectfully called "Top" by all. Overseen by the CO, the first sergeant works in close proximity with the CO, and their responsibilities are divided. The unit's commissioned personnel respond to the CO while enlisted individuals work under the first sergeant.

The meeting with the new 1SG Bearden came quicker than Conner anticipated. It would have been proper for a CO to remain seated when a first sergeant walked into his office; however, out of respect, Conner chose to stand. Conner returned Bearden's salute with a friendly smile.

"Have a seat, First Sergeant, you're a sight for sore eyes. Look at this pile of reports and paperwork that I've had to contend with since First Sergeant Screven left."

Conner's comment brought a snicker from both before the interview started. It softened the stiff, military atmosphere in the room, which is typical with occasions of this type. Conner knew exactly what to do to learn all he could about Bearden.

Conner got right down to things. "Top, what type of aviation training have you had?"

"Sir, I've been in aviation for about fourteen years. Started as a rotary-wing mechanic, became a tech inspector [TI], was selected to serve on the Seventh Army Accident Investigation Board as a tech inspector. Then I was selected to serve on the United States Army Board for Aviation Accident Research [USABAAR]. That followed with assignment to the Accident Investigation Board at Fort Rucker, Alabama, from where I investigated accidents in Alaska and Germany. I was sent TDY [temporary duty] to Africa where I inspected aircraft for the corps of engineers stationed there. Subsequently, I was assigned to the 240th Mohawk Company in Vietnam on my first Vietnam tour. Then to the 121st Assault Helicopter Company in Soc Trang on my second tour. Two days ago, I was sent here to finish my second Vietnam tour, sir."

Conner liked what he was hearing from Bearden—by the way Bearden spilled out his achievements and accomplishments, he suspected Bearden was a no-nonsense type of guy and certainly highly qualified. "Let me give you the fifty-thousand-foot-level view of what we do here."

Conner sat back, smiled, and then continued. "An assault-helicopter company in Vietnam has some of the most sophisticated weapon systems in the Army inventory. And without question, one of the most hazardous missions of the war. Our troops face death almost every day they fly combat assaults. On occasion, there are days when no enemy contact is made, but those are rare."

Bearden's body language, leaning forward in his chair with his back upright, satisfied Conner that his new first sergeant was concentrating on the briefing.

Conner ran through what he expected of Beard as his top soldier. "You will need a little time to get used to our routines. So, I'll let that happen before we sit down to plan how to merge our efforts to run this outfit. In the meantime, I want to make sure we do what's necessary to get you settled in here. Is there anything we can do to help?"

"No, sir, the sergeant major has me accommodated at the battalion senior NCO quarters, and I'm ready to go to work. There are a few questions you could answer for me, if you have time?"

"By all means, Top. Fire away."

"Sir, I pulled the 191st manning report from battalion and saw the unit's personnel status, and it looks pretty good. But among the personnel actions, I noticed quite a few substance abuse charges that, with your permission, I'd like to focus on for a bit."

"Glad you mention that, Top. As time permits, I'd planned to bring that to your attention. In a week or so we'll sit and revisit this subject. But in the meantime, put your experience to work as you deem appropriate. You certainly have my support in that realm." Conner paused and waited for Bearden's next question.

"Also," Bearden continued as he saw Conner yield the floor, "I see where the maintenance detachment is using crew chiefs to assist with the PE inspections. Is there a reason why we can't use those personnel during that time frame?"

"Good question, Top." Conner was impressed with the details that Bearden had scrutinized in the reports. By this time in the interview, Conner was well satisfied the sergeant major had delivered a superb individual to the 191st.

Conner explained to Bearden that the unit SOP was initially written by MAJ Patnode, who was assigned as the first CO of the 191st in Vietnam. Conner was proud that the 191st was high on the list of aviation companies with the strongest aircraft-availability rate in the entire First Aviation Brigade, and therefore he wasn't going to tamper with crew chiefs assisting maintenance with inspections. Nevertheless, Conner appreciated Bearden's scrutiny. He would make a fine first sergeant.

Walking out of the commander's office, Bearden rolled up his sleeves and went to work. He felt that somehow the company needed to reinforce discipline as needed to minimize drug abuse. *That should not be too difficult.* Furthermore, Bearden recognized that as the unit's first sergeant, it was his job to shape or maintain this body of troopers into a combat force capable of maintaining amazing organizational integrity amid horrendous battle death and destruction. Bearden knew about the early 1969 mortar attack that killed six in the 191st operations office, and he knew the role that the first sergeant played in the cleanup and reorganization. Bearden saw himself to be center of mass in that realm.

"That was our job," Bearden recalls, "and I was happy with the outcome. I was pleased to have a staff of great NCOs who did their jobs efficiently. Within a few weeks, I realized my oversight role was minimal; they knew what to do and excelled in that regard. They were good! But nothing good comes easy, and I would soon learn that the hard way."

Bearden's first hard-learned lesson came when one morning a soldier, experiencing a fried-to-the-max drug high, unexpectedly charged into the orderly room while attempting to insert a loaded magazine into an M16. As Bearden recalls: "Immediately reacting, I grabbed the weapon stock with one hand and the barrel with the other and proceeded to wrestle with the soldier until an NCO, who happened to be passing by, came to my aid. Together we finally subdued the drug-crazed individual until the military police escorted him away in handcuffs."

Conner wasn't surprised about the incident and maintained a calm demeanor when Bearden briefed him.

"Misplaced aggression," Conner said. "Where is he assigned? In a ground job or does he fly?"

"No, sir, he doesn't fly. He works in supply."

"Well that makes sense. If he was out flying combat assaults he would have less time to mess with dope. While that's not necessarily a solution, it identifies the problem to a point, anyway. We simply need to do what we can to minimize it. And for sure, we need to keep our ear to the ground on the flight crews. We definitely cannot have it among our flight crewmembers."

"Well, sir. I think I can help in that regard also. I plan to start making unannounced inspections in the barracks frequently enough that I might discourage some of that behavior."

Unbeknown to Conner at the time, Bearden also entertained the idea of setting an example for the troops by flying as gunner during combat assaults. He figured this would certainly give him a firsthand experience of what the troops were facing on the battlefield. Bearden's thinking amply filled a strong leadership regimen. Now, he had to make it happen.

A battle-hardened soldier who led by example, Bearden surprised many when he volunteered to fly as gunner on the 191st combat-assault ships—setting a rare example. Hearing of Bearden's plan from the operations officer, CPT Carl Jeffrey, Conner held his breath but initially refrained from interfering. Then after reconsidering the risk of losing a very key figure on his staff, Conner decided to have a word with Bearden. Impromptu, Conner visited Bearden's office to diminish the rigidity of calling his first sergeant to his office.

Immediately as Conner entered, Bearden stood up. "Yes, sir, what can I do for you?"

"Top, I'm concerned about you flying combat assaults. I really am. You are way too critical to this unit to place yourself on an assault bird. The risk is extraordinary!"

"Well, sir, I appreciate the concern, and I've given it considerable thought myself. I would never go against your wishes, and I certainly don't want to be a casualty. But for sure my risk is no greater than yours. And I see the respect you've earned from the troops by flying guns on occasion. What I hope to achieve is to set an example for the troops as you have. In all other units, the first sergeant humps right along with the troops. Aviation has the distinction of separating the senior NCO staff from pilots and their crews. How can I possibly know what my troops experience without sharing the risk, at least sufficiently to know what they feel? Don't get me wrong, sir, I don't plan to make a routine of it, but I would like to learn more of what the flight crews know. I can't think of any other way."

Conner couldn't argue with his Top. After all, like Bearden pointed out, Conner flew missions sometimes on a C&C bird, but often on a gunship in 191st combat operations—another rare example. Most unit commanders flew only the C&C

ship and remained well out of small-arms range. But far from typical, Conner dwelled in the action and spared no opportunity to engage the enemy face to face. Nevertheless, he did express concern for his first sergeant following suit. "Well, Top, you've been around aviation long enough to know what you're doing. But I would feel better if you would minimize your exposure. I'd keep it down to the absolute minimum."

Soon thereafter, the operations officer, CPT Jeffrey, assigned Bearden his first mission as a door gunner. Bearden accepted. But he needed a call sign. A call sign for Bearden's position, however, was not in the unit SOP or tactical manual since in the past, the first sergeant didn't fly missions. A new call sign was created: Echo-One, which stood for Enlisted One, in effect the top enlisted man in the unit. So, Bearden became *Echo-One*, the only one of its kind.

Bearden was briefed by the crew chief and then by the AC. Bearden took it in stride and buckled himself in for his first combat assault. The mission was a routine search-and-destroy operation with ARVN troops doing the grunt work. A highlight of the day was refueling at Soc Trang.

Some news travels fast among aviation companies and several folks from the 121st came to the refueling station at Soc Trang to see their old first sergeant flying as gunner on an assault ship. The meetings were cheerful and heartwarming for the 191st crew. To see Bearden's former troops rally to him and wish him well was an indicator of good leadership and caused the faces of the 191st to light up.

Surprisingly, the day's mission ended with no enemy contact, but it racked up the usual long hours aloft. By the time the flight returned to Can Tho, Bearden was a little more aware of what his troops endured in labor on a daily basis. And as he thought would happen, word among the 191st personnel quickly circulated about the first sergeant's combat-assault flight as gunner. Thereafter, several crew chiefs approached Bearden to invite him to fly on *their* ships. Bearden had made the impact he wished.

As expected, his follow-up briefing with Conner went well. The CO had already received a point-by-point briefing from CPT Jeffrey. All indicators pointed up. Still, Conner warned Bearden that the enemy was growing more aggressive since the Ninth went home, and he agreed to keep that reality fresh in his mind. Bearden had accomplished his objective for the moment, but he knew more combat assaults were ahead before his example would have a lasting effect.

By late 1969 and early 1970, the 191st AHC, with its Boomerangs and Bounty Hunters, was among the diminished combat assets left in place for ARVN support. An additional platoon, the Green Delta provision, was thankfully added to the ranks of the 191st. Committed to flying high-ranking US officials and South Vietnamese officers conducting the allied war effort, the Green Deltas employed some of the most experienced 191st pilots. Flying dignitaries demanded the best in service. Conner and Bearden oversaw this component with high priority. But little did they know their combat mission would escalate beyond the load previously bestowed upon in-country airmobile assets.

With the US Ninth Infantry Division redeployed back to the States, the enemy seized the opportunity to expand its regional holdings. Large enemy troop movements became prominent. Engagements grew in ferocity with enemy support services well manifested among VC and NVA units. From the Parrot's Beak down to the U Minh Forest, the Cambodian border region extorted enormous threat to the southern reaches of Vietnam. The predictions made years earlier by General Westmoreland and Admiral Nimitz to the Washington establishment under President Johnson became reality. Cambodia escalated as a lethal menace. The Ho Chi Minh Trail affirmed its strategic worth to the enemy, and thousands of young Americans died as a result. Logistically fit, the enemy was far more effective. Conner and Bearden had their work cut out for them, but both faced the challenge with sheer determination.

These two old salts represented the upper echelon of leadership in the 191st AHC—with Conner often flying gunships and Bearden often flying along as gunner. Their presence during missions tightened up 191st performance because their simple act of being in the fray with the troops was a status symbol and gave emphasis to mission importance. In effect, from top to bottom, the Boomerang flight had a key person amid the unit's presence in the field. These observations offered opportunity for the first sergeant to suggest operational improvements to MAJ Conner and CPT Jeffrey, who had assigned Bearden to his first gunner mission. Often thereafter, Battalion Commander Saur received compliments on the professionalism exhibited by the 191st in the field. When such commendations were announced, during morning formations, incentive for becoming a flight crewmember grew among the 191st personnel. As this elite status became contagious, top performance escalated.

Nevertheless, Conner grew concerned about his flying top soldier. "Among my greatest command challenges," Conner recalls, "was dealing with the truly outstanding 1SG Bearden, who pushed the envelope a bit. Frequently enough to cause me some consternation, he would leave the orderly room to fly as door gunner in one of our gunships. However out of the ordinary it appeared, I understood his zeal for the adrenaline rush and for his desire to demonstrate his willingness to mix with the troops and share in the exposure they endured each day. His example was a highlight among the flight crews, and they enjoyed having him along for the combat assaults. Occasionally, I would be asked by some of the battalion staff officers if it was true that my first sergeant was flying combat assaults, and I always loved the opportunity to rub it in a bit. My response was that he was unlike the *paper hangers* at some of the higher headquarters; Bearden was a real combat-assault trooper. This was further reinforced when on August 24, 1970, Bearden was awarded the Distinguished Flying Cross for heroism.

"This occurred while on a night mission near My Phuoc Tay. His aircraft was supporting a ground unit being attacked by a sizeable enemy force that was threatening to overrun the friendly compound. Bearden unleashed all the firepower at his disposal in the aircraft, including his own individual weapon, which he used as tracer fire to guide the .50 caliber onto the enemy positions. With all door guns firing and with the big fifty taking its toll, the enemy retreated. Without question, Bearden's actions were in keeping with the finest traditions of the United States Army, and he earned the award with my strongest recommendation. As if that was not enough to quell his thirst for action, seven days later he was awarded the Bronze Star with 'V' device for engaging the enemy in another heated battle where he covered an attacking jet fighter that experienced difficulty with intense enemy fire. Although I never discouraged Bearden from flying combat assaults, I was relieved when the battalion sergeant major began using Bearden for some battalion-level NCO tasks that kept him on the ground periodically."

During the Vietnam War, Army troops were conditioned to seeing the unit's top soldier in the orderly room overseeing logistics and administration that keep the unit battle ready. In effect, the first sergeant implements the unit commander's agenda through the enlisted chain of command, which is a tradition that carries considerable weight among the Army's NCOs. The 191st AHC operated in this order. But battle-hardened 1SG Bearden sought higher ground. When MAJ Conner recruited a new XO, CPT Fred Evors, who contributed immeasurably to the unit's administration, Bearden could fly more often, perhaps to Conner's dismay. Evors, true to form, indeed carried his weight, not only with his admin responsibilities in the orderly room but also in the field, where he earned a Silver Star and three Distinguished Flying Crosses for gallantry in action. He became Bearden's ticket to flying combat assaults and a strong example for the officers and soldiers of the 191st AHC.

Flying combat missions in a gunship and manning an M60 machine gun was something Bearden loved doing. By his own volition, he earned a place of honor within the ranks of the 191st AHC by volunteering to fly combat-assault missions as a door gunner or crew chief. There were few warriors endowing the ranks of the US Army who could compare to 1SG Bearden and the CO, MAJ Conner. Together, they made an inspirational team.

As enemy aggression grew, the 191st fought against mounting odds. But the Conner-Bearden team responded with purpose. Bearden and Conner set a precedent never before experienced by the 191st AHC. Highly regarded for extraordinary performance under fire, the 191st story would not be complete without an excerpt of 1SG Bearden in battle.

West of Dong Tam near the Plain of Reeds, enemy infiltration from Cambodia was wreaking havoc on friendly installations in and around the Mekong region. A large ARVN force was assembled for this assault, and battle planning was ongoing for several months based on intelligence reports from Mohawk surveillance aircraft. The flight during the morning prior had located and photographed a large NVA force making its way southeast. Coming from the vicinity of the Parrot's Beak, the enemy unit was well equipped and prepared to attack installations along the Mekong.

Recognizing the mission risks and seeing the first sergeant to crew a gunship, the operations officer, Carl Jeffrey, approached Bearden the evening prior to the mission. "Top, you are aware the mission is taking you where the old man prefers you not go?"

"Yes, sir. But it's time I experience that risk."

Jeffrey rubbed the back of his neck. "Very well. I appreciate that, and good luck tomorrow."

"Roger that, sir, and thanks for your concern."

Flying the mission near the Plain of Reeds, West of Dong Tam, was the operations officer, CPT Jeffrey (Boomerang Three) in the C&C bird; flying as the gunner for CW2 Ayala as his AC (Bounty Hunter Two-Nine) was 1SG Bearden (Echo-One); flying as Ayala's wingman was CW2 John Thomas Orrico (Bounty Hunter Two-Seven); and flying as gun-platoon leader was CPT Carlton (Bounty Hunter Six). The CO, MAJ Conner, call sign Boomerang Six, remained on the ground in operations for this mission but would check in on 1SG Bearden later in the flight.

Flying at low level behind the slicks, Ayala's gunship carrying Bearden housed two fifteen-shot pods of rockets and two miniguns, each capable of firing up to six thousand 7.62 rounds per minute, complemented by the free guns manned by the crew chief and gunner, both carrying several cans totaling six thousand rounds of 7.62 ball/tracer belts. By this time in his tour, Bearden was well seasoned in combat assaults. But he had never been this far northwest of Can Tho, and little did he know of the tactical explosion that awaited their arrival.

But for the moment, low-level flight gave Bearden a brief respite from the challenges of LZ hazards, and he took in the beautiful scenery offered across the Plain of Reeds. These reeds grew tall and reminded Bearden of Corpus Christi, his hometown, where the salt grasses grew along the Gulf Coast. His mind wandered over the life he knew in Texas.

As the offspring of devoted Christians, Walter and Naomi Bearden, Don Bearden entered this world in 1937 in Overbrook, Oklahoma. The first of seven children, five boys and two girls, he grew up leading his siblings in the traditional kindred role of an older brother. He accepted the responsibility and stayed the course throughout his growing years and later exercised those same principles in the Army.

With strong parental guidance, Bearden also developed a dedication for ethics and good order, which were further reinforced by his Christian learning. This also played a role in his Army performance and his mannerisms with troops. He learned to respect other people, regardless of rank, ethnicity, or color.

Relocated to Corpus Christi, Texas, by his father's employment, Bearden enjoyed growing up along the Gulf Coast, where he fished and *gigged* flounder. In coastal areas of Texas, a spear with a three-prong head is called a gig. Using a night lantern, wading in shallows, flounder are easily spotted in the sand. Seeing Vietnam's coastal environment of the Plain of Reeds pulled Bearden into a fleeting daydream of those good times on the Texan coast.

Bearden's spell was broken as a call from Jeffrey in the C&C bird to Carlton, the gun-platoon leader, crackled over the airways.

"Bounty Hunter Six, this is Boomerang Three. What's your present location?"

"Boomerang Three, this is Bounty Hunter Six," Carlton responded. "We're following the flight about ten clicks west of Dong Tam, presently coming up on Vinh Long."

"Roger, understand approaching Vinh Long. Break off one of your fire teams and tell him to fly heading 347 from present location and advise when he has C&C in sight. We have something that looks suspicious and needs a low-level pass to confirm."

"Roger, Bounty Hunter Three, wilco."

The gun-platoon leader hailed Bearden's Huey: "Bounty Hunter Two-Nine, this is Six. Did you pick up Charlie-Charlie's communication?"

"Six, Two-Nine," Ayala responded. "Yes, I did."

"Break off and do a low-level pass. Keep me posted on the secure frequency."

"Roger Six, breaking right to gain altitude. I'll keep you posted, out."

Bearden knew this could mean trouble. He checked his M60 to make sure the safety was off and his ammo box was full. The gunship flying at max speed was rapidly approaching the C&C bird when the radios crackled again and Jeffrey hailed Ayala.

"Bounty Hunter Two-Nine, this is Boomerang Three. Do you have me in sight?"

"Roger, Boomerang Three. I have a Huey at my twelve o'clock position. Is that you?"

"Roger, Two-Nine," Jeffrey responded. "Have you got the canal junction to your three o'clock in sight? We just saw two sampans pull under the nipa palm adjacent to that cluster of hootches. Check those out and give us your observation, over."

"Roger, Boomerang Three. Will do! Two-Nine out."

Ayala called his wingman, CW2 Orrico (Bounty Hunter Two-Seven), for coordination. Then he proceeded low level to the canal junction. As Bounty Hunter Two-Nine approached with caution, all eyes and ears stayed alert. The only sound was the comforting *whop-whop-whop* of the chopper blades. But in Vietnam, life changed in a micro-heartbeat. Soon, bullets stitched within inches of Bearden, just missing his left foot before he could even react. The expanding metal exploded with shrapnel flying throughout the cargo compartment. The roar of AK-47s firing happened so fast, neither Bearden nor the crew chief had time to engage with their M60s.

Overflying the enemy position, Bearden had never fired cover for a gunship breaking from a gun run. This required leaning out of the aircraft as far as his safety line allowed and firing under the belly of the Huey. He had practiced it enough times but was caught off guard before he could react.

Immediately Ayala called his wingman, Two-Seven, who was already lowering the nose of his attack bird. Then Ayala called C&C to report the enemy fire. "Boomerang

Three! Bounty Hunter Two-Nine, received fire from the canal junction and took some hits. Two-Seven is rolling in on the target now."

"Roger, Two-Nine," Jeffrey responded. "What was the size of the enemy force?"

"This is Two-Nine. It happened too fast to get a good look, but they were ready for us as soon as we overflew their position."

"This is Boomerang Three, understand. Continue the attack, and let me know what we have down there."

"Roger that. Two-Nine out."

No sooner had Ayala responded to C&C when Orrico called. "Two-Nine, Bounty Hunter Two-Seven. We took several hits in the cockpit and cargo compartment. Our gunner has some shrapnel in his hand and we have several warning lights on our caution panel. Request permission to break off and head for Vinh Long, over."

"Two-Seven, roger. Understand wounded on board and warning lights. Stand by, please."

Ayala called the C&C bird. "Boomerang Three, this is Two-Nine. Did you read Two-Seven?"

"Roger, Two-Nine," Jeffrey responded. "Understand Two-Seven has wounded and warning lights on board and is breaking off for Vinh Long. Suggest you climb to altitude and wait till we get you some help. If you get shot down in that area, we have no way of getting you out of there."

"Roger, Boomerang Three, will wait for help. Two-Nine out!"

Bearden's emotions were attempting to distract him, but he remained focused and on task. When Orrico's attacking wing ship passed the canal, Bearden saw muzzle flashes and tracers coming from numerous locations among the hootches. He looked out at the Plain of Reeds again and mentally prepared for whatever lay ahead—a delightful daydream of home blasted away by the reality of war.

The ARVN task force commander also saw the enemy fire blasting from the hootches. From his altitude, he grasped a better view of the volume of tracers and recognized that they definitely had a developing tac-e that needed a larger force to produce the volume of fire needed. The task force commander immediately called for tac air.

At this point in the firefight, no one had yet seen the sampans. Deep in his belly, Bearden felt the rumble of one hell of a fight brewing. Nimble fingers on his M60, he was ready.

Jeffrey called the gun-platoon leader, Carlton, for status on their escort mission: "Bounty Hunter Six! This is Boomerang Three. What's your status?"

"Boomerang Three, this is Bounty Hunter Six," Carlton responded. "We're in sight of the friendly PZ, no enemy contact to this point."

"Roger, Six. Continue the escort until the flight is on short final to the PZ. Then break off and head in my direction. We have a tac-e developing."

"Roger, Boomerang Three. Understand tac-e! Will be there shortly!"

Bearden, flying with Bounty Hunter Two-Nine, was unaware the ARVN task force commander had called for tac air and, therefore, remained poised to attack the hootch complex again. He spotted a cluster of trees bordering the canal and felt certain there were sampans hidden beneath them. Intending to saturate it with his M60 fire, Bearden called Ayala, his AC, on intercom. "Sir, this is Echo-One. If you give me enough lateral room from those two large trees directly in front of the hootches, I believe I can find the sampans."

"Roger that, Echo-One. You got it."

Meanwhile, Bounty Hunter Six reached his destination and remained aloft while the slicks unloaded the troops they were delivering and then turned in the direction of Jeffrey in the C&C bird. Jeffrey called Bounty Hunter Six as he approached the firefight. "Bounty Hunter Six, this is Boomerang Three. Is that you approaching from the southeast?"

"This is Bounty Hunter Six, roger. I'm about three clicks out."

"Roger, Six. Got you in sight. Two-Nine is orbiting about four clicks due south of my location. Join up with him and hold there for air strike on the canal junction."

"Roger, understand. Join up with Two-Nine and orbit there awaiting air strike."

Hearing of the air strike for the first time, Bearden looked far to the southeast searching for the approaching Air Force FAC, still five to ten clicks away. Aware now that tac air support was imminent, Bearden's belly began to relax some after the close call for both gunships.

In approximately two minutes, the Air Force FAC hailed C&C. FAC pilots had no knowledge of the internal assignments or protocols of the 191st AHC; therefore, to them C&C was always Boomerang Six or the guy at the top calling the shots for the combat-assault flight. For this mission, CPT Jeffrey (Boomerang Three) was *that guy*.

"Boomerang Six, this is Jaguar Two-Six."

"Jaguar Two-Six, this is Boomerang Three, have you in sight. What type of ordnance do you have available?"

"Have two F-4s in tow with napalm and five-hundred-pounders."

"Roger understand, napalm and five-hundred-pounders. Please observe out of your left window for a marking round at the canal junction with the adjacent hootch complex. There is a sizeable enemy force occupying that locale."

"Roger, Boomerang. Have marking round in sight, suggest you give us about five clicks clearance. Super-zoomers will be making their runs from the northeast and breaking south."

"Roger, Jaguar Two-Six. Understand super-zoomers approaching from the northeast and breaking south while dropping loads. I'll clear the sky for you. Thanks, out!"

Jeffrey immediately contacted CPT Carlton, the gun-platoon leader. "Bounty Hunter Six, this is Boomerang Three."

"This is Six, go ahead."

"Bounty Hunter Six, Boomerang Three. Move your orbit to the east about five clicks for super-zoomers inbound."

"Roger, Boomerang Three. Understand orbit five clicks east of the canal junction for air strike."

Bearden, now fully versed on the tac air situation, kept his line of vision glued to the northeast for the approaching F-4 Phantoms with heavy payloads. With his gunship orbiting at one thousand feet, his visual scan of the canal junction was far broader in its geographical limits. The area behind the hootch complex was well covered in jungle growth all the way to the Mekong River, about fifteen clicks to the north. This made it easy for enemy sampans to navigate the distance under the cover of darkness without revealing their presence. Directly, the radios crackled with the voice of the Air Force's Phantom lead bird (Lightning Bolt Five) calling his FAC (Jaguar Two-Six).

"Jaguar Two-Six, this is Lightning Bolt Five approaching from your north."

"Bolt Five, this is Jaguar Two-Six. Please stand by for my marking round."

Very shortly, the Phantom lead's call crackled across the airways again. "Jaguar Two-Six. Lightning Bolt Five. Got your mark, stand by for effect, out."

Bearden did not see the Phantom jets approaching at a much higher altitude until the first one dove to the target. The F-4 released its napalm canisters that tumbled sideways end over end through the air until they exploded just short of the hootch complex. Fire engulfed the entire east side of the complex, and before the second bird could drop its payload, a tremendous explosion blew the foliage cover off the sampans, which were carrying fuel. With one fuel load up in smoke, the second fuel load detonated with a resounding blast that splintered the two sampans into pieces. Almost simultaneously two five-hundred-pound bombs released by the second F-4 exploded on the western outer edge of the hootch complex. Shock waves spread from the center of each blast, sending huge logs tumbling through the air like matchsticks.

With amazing resilience, the enemy responded sending a hail of tracers after each jet as the F-4s broke off from each bomb run. The second bomb run was just as devastating, but the enemy fire was equally aggressive. The second jet took some hits, and Lightning Bolt Five called off the attack to get the wounded bird back to Bien Hoa Air Base for repairs.

Bearden was now convinced that the enemy force would require more than air strikes and the slick's small contingency of troops. It was no surprise when C&C told Boomerang lead to prepare the slicks to load their assault troops and proceed to his location. C&C further instructed Boomerang lead to have the slicks join up with the Bounty Hunter ships and orbit to the southeast of the canal location awaiting an artillery prep of the target.

More flights from other AHCs carrying more ARVN troops arrived and orbited to the south. Bounty Hunter Two-Seven's replacement arrived and joined the 191st gunship escort just as the 105-millimeter shells were landing on target. The bombardment lasted for only five minutes, but the entire complex looked devastated. What the napalm did not burn to the ground, the five-hundred-pounders blasted clean. Unfortunately, Bearden's Texas-conjuring Plain of Reeds reverie was obliterated in the wake.

After the tac air, it was discovered that the few remnants of hootches that remained had been attached to bunkers built inside the thatched-roof huts. They were then burned to the ground. Yet somehow, the enemy managed to return fire each time a super-zoomer dropped more ordnance. Jeffrey took note of this and passed the information on to MAJ Conner at Boomerang operations.

Conner, having received word of the enemy contact, called Ayala for a status report. "Bounty Hunter Two-Nine, this is Ops."

Knowing the 191st commander's focus was to check on 1SG Bearden, Ayala reported all was well and the hotspot had been softened by tac air.

"Bounty Hunter Two-Nine, roger," Conner responded. "A replacement was called in for Bounty Hunter Two-Seven, who is down at Vin Long for maintenance and crew change. Do you need any crew change?"

"Ops, Bounty Hunter Two-Nine, stand by please." Ayala looked over his seat back at Bearden and asked, "Top, the major is asking if you need to be replaced and evacuated back to headquarters. What do you want me to tell him?"

"Just tell him I'm fine. And no! We don't need another replacement at this time."

Ayala nodded with a grin and got back to Conner. "Ops, this is Bounty Hunter Two-Nine. Sir, we don't need a replacement at this time."

"Two-Nine, this is Ops, roger, out!"

With the arrival of ten more slicks carrying ARVN infantry, combat activity picked up. The ARVN task force commander selected an insertion point center of mass and directly across the canal from whatever enemy force was on the other side. This was questionable to C&C, and so Jeffrey suggested an insertion farther down the canal to avoid a frontal assault against prepared enemy positions. But the ARVN commander insisted a frontal assault would overwhelm the enemy. Jeffrey knew that the land directly across the canal was open coastal grass and reeds with little cover. The troops would have little room to maneuver and the assault birds would be completely exposed at near point-blank range. But at the insistence of the task force commander, that area became the LZ.

Despite using full suppression and gunships pounding the bunkered emplacements across the canal, when the assault birds landed and offloaded the ARVN infantry, the Hueys were blistered with enemy fire. The second insertion was not as lucky as the first insertion, and one bird was shot down in the hot LZ. Fortunately, one of the birds picked up the downed crew and made it off the LZ.

The third insertion was the 191st lift, and Bounty Hunter Platoon Leader Carlton called for an echelon-right attack formation to simultaneously concentrate all firepower on the bunkered enemy. With the canal running southwest to northeast, the slicks were landing slightly crosswind to remain on the open side of the LZ and across the canal from the enemy positions. Bearden kept his door gun sending suppressing fire into the bunkers, which was possible only when he placed bullets directly on the parapets. But the enemy emplacements were so numerous the effort was ineffective. Although the gunship-attack results were better, they were still costly in terms of aircraft. Three of the five slicks took hits. Two were in vital areas, causing the birds to go down for maintenance when they reached the PZ.

Responding to the declared tac-e, another ten slicks arrived, results of the comprehensive battle plan prepared from the intelligence reports. When inserted, the ARVN troops quickly formed an attack formation and moved toward the canal. Though taking casualties, the task force commander kept his ground forces moving toward the enemy. Reaching the canal, the line halted while another barrage of 105-millimeter artillery blasted the opposite end of the area that was a hootch complex. Once the artillery concentration was well adjusted, the ARVN crossed the canal and aggressively moved into the blasted village. Unexpectedly, the enemy fire started diminishing and in minutes died completely. It was a mystery to Bearden and others until the infantry began reporting a large tunnel complex extending toward the Mekong River fifteen clicks to the north. Though well within the geographic influence of the Plain of Reeds, the ground was slightly higher and covered with thick jungle as far as the Mekong.

Hmm, thought Bearden. *Their intelligence is working.*

Following the artillery barrage and after crossing the canal, the ARVN checked out the tunnels while the Bounty Hunters moved well ahead to catch any retreating enemy. Bearden, already well seasoned in providing suppressive fire with his M60, caught several enemy soldiers in full stride as they bolted from the approaching ARVN. Watching Bearden's action, Ayala keyed the intercom to hail Top's marksmanship. "Echo-One, keep up the fire! You're doing a hell of a job. I've seen at least three enemy roll up under your fire. Kill the bastards!"

The day ended with seventeen enemy bodies found scorched by the napalm and a few other blood trails leading to tunnels. From the signs left behind, this location had been occupied by the enemy for a long time. *Probably an enemy headquarters*, Bearden figured.

Flying back to Can Tho, Bearden reminisced about his past, specifically about his training and the fact that it didn't properly prepare him for this type of war. Completing basic training at Fort Ord, California, Bearden had approached his Army duties with intent to excel. He set a course by which he would eventually ascend the ranks in the Army to the maximum of his ability, and he achieved his goals with high marks. By the time he arrived at the 191st AHC, he was a model NCO worthy of the highest responsibility his rank deserved, and he served admirably.

"When I first arrived at the 191st," Bearden recalls, "I was following the instructions of a sergeant major I had known for a good number of years. In fact, he promoted me to E-6 some years before in another unit. We frequently played cards, and he was a jovial character, enjoyable to be with. When he became the command sergeant major of the 214th CAB, he called me up to serve as the first sergeant of the 191st AHC. Of course, to this day I remain grateful for the opportunity. As an added bonus, I got to work with a remarkable CO, MAJ Victor Conner. He believed in teamwork and always communicated with me and others in a professional and respectful manner. His command presence promoted goodwill and loyalty. The troops respected and appreciated him—and so did I.

"Before I arrived at Can Tho, the 191st had earned an outstanding reputation as an aviation combat-assault force and was highly regarded by the infantry units they supported. The grunts loved the Boomerangs and Bounty Hunters. Discussions at the NCO club seemingly always centered on the operations of the day, and troopers who rode on Boomerang ships said good things about their performance. I was happy being a part of such an esteemed outfit. It gave me great incentive to assimilate the operation and do my part to improve what I could.

"As a whole, the unit's foundation appealed to me, but there were some small nuances that were troubling. Some enlisted men were wearing bracelets and neck ornaments that were not in keeping with standard military uniform codes. So, I took note of this and began a gradual correction regimen. Illegal drug use also appeared as another problem in the barracks, a serious threat to flight safety and mission discipline. In aviation, this is absolutely taboo. Drugs and flight crews can easily spell disaster. There was little choice in the matter; it *had* to be fixed *immediately*. After conferring with MAJ Conner, who rendered his own guidance, I moved expeditiously to conduct barracks inspections and discipline those caught with illegal drugs. In a matter of weeks, the loop began closing on those who refused to conform, and the command group began administering military justice with increasing consequences for repeat offenders.

"The discovery trend of drug abusers rose sharply in the beginning. MAJ Conner and I were both upset at the number of people who were abusing drugs. But the effort was worth it, and soon the case numbers began to fall. Keeping a good barometer on the unit pulse to ensure morale held, I was further energized by some of the more wholesome troops who advised that my efforts were having a good impact on their barracks life. They voiced appreciation for being able to get some sleep. Before, they felt they couldn't say anything about the noise from drunks and dopeheads. But now, the party animals were beginning to keep a low profile. The old bold days, when anything was fair game in the barracks, were now over."

The resultant turnaround was astonishing to Bearden. He began seeing extraordinary consistencies in the 191st mission efficiency and combat support. Conner's directives were taking effect. Bearden considered Conner's philosophy of military discipline as extraordinary.

Conner's introduction to the 191st operations section conditioned him for the unexpected, and he handled those events with a cool hand. His first experience of the type happened shortly after his arrival in the orderly room. The operations officer called him to assign tail numbers for the next day's mission. Smelling something foul, the new CO found himself in a quandary. After examining the aircraft maintenance reports, it was evident the birds had been flown well into their scheduled maintenance periods, and the operations officer was simply alerting his new commander of impending crisis. Conner speculated that "this was probably an effort to make availability look good for the outgoing commander's benefit as he vacated his command position."

At that point, Conner ordered the maintenance officer and the operations officer to schedule tail numbers based on expected flight hours per mission, and he gave the maintenance officer three weeks to fix the schedule. "He took four," Conner recalls, "but I was happy nonetheless. Both officers were outstanding assets, and the organization began to move well under their guidance."

Calling on knowledge gained from previous assignments, Conner quickly gained a firm grip on the 191st reins. Inside of a month, the unit was averaging three thousand hours per month with at least one aircraft per day entering scheduled phase maintenance. "I was happy with the results, and during a down day, I expressed my gratitude with a Jeep trailer full of beer and drinks for all to enjoy. The troops were happy, and they certainly earned my respect and appreciation."

The troop discipline under Conner was not restricted to enlisted personnel only. Commissioned officers were treated equally. According to Bearden, Conner "was always fair and just." In one incident, a captain leaving the unit had mailed home some illegal contraband, and MAJ Conner promptly referred him to the battalion commander for discipline. The captain received an Article 15, a disciplinary measure that typically ruins a commissioned officer's career. That was the way it was with commissioned officers. One had to keep a clean nose and set a strong example for the enlisted troops in order to advance. Enlisted soldiers were given some latitude, but not commissioned officers. Either you kept it straight or you ended your career. As standard SOP, the rare few commissioned-officer disciplinary actions were all referred to battalion level. The captain's Article 15 incident served notice to the commissioned ranks in the battalion that Battalion Commander Saur led by example and expected the same from all commissioned officers. Conner's reputation as fair and balanced remained steady.

"Among one of the most bizarre occurrences I recall from our operations," Conner remembers, "occurred one day when the Bounty Hunters were in hot contact with some bunkered enemy soldiers. I was flying C&C that day. Having received fire from the area of the bunkers, the Bounty Hunters were heatedly engaging the enemy emplacements when suddenly a small child appeared in the midst of the battle scene. After ordering all guns to 'go cold,' one of the crews bravely landed and picked up the tot and delivered him to an Army hospital. I couldn't have been prouder of that crew. I'll never forget the anxiety experienced by all concerned over that infant. God was with him that day."

A CO of a unit that is staffed with the wit of aviation-class personnel is occasionally challenged with issues that tax his soul. Conner had just such an occasion one day when some of his guys *commandeered* a colonel's Jeep. "An MP vehicle pulled into my motor pool," Conner recalls. "They were looking for a Jeep that had been stolen from an SF colonel. It took them awhile to find it, but finally, toward the late afternoon, they located it parked among *my* unit vehicles. Since we had a shortage of vehicles and repair parts were hard to come by, my suspicions were aroused and I immediately assumed something out of the ordinary. Sure enough, I learned that three of my NCOs snatched the vehicle and repainted over the bumper numbers to keep for their own use. It took the MPs going through each Jeep and inspecting the serial number plates before discovering the stolen vehicle. With the group commander breathing down my back about what disciplinary measures I was going to take, I told him I would take care of it, and he seemed satisfied. I then ordered the trio to repaint the vehicle with the correct markings and promptly deliver it to the angry SF colonel. I heard no more from the group commander, and the guilty trio performed thereafter like model soldiers. To this day, I wonder if I did proper justice in that case. But perfection is a virtue few humans approach. At this point in life, I believe I can live with my mistakes."

MAJ Conner and 1SG Bearden left Vietnam in late June of 1970, at a time when the unit began the long drawdown to its final withdrawal approximately a year and a half later. Although combat had not receded, the 191st AHC began losing fewer and fewer casualties, and the missions were now confined, for the most part, to operations south of the Mekong River.

"As luck prevailed," Conner recalls, "on the day I rotated back to the States, the battalion commander released Bearden so we could fly home on the same Freedom Bird. We had a great time reliving our command tour on the way home. Since then, I have visited 1SG Bearden at his home in California, and I always enjoy his company. Together, with his wife, Patricia, and my wife, Sharon, we always squeeze the most of the time we spend together. Such a bond is the most rewarding outcome of serving together at war. It creates an everlasting human yearning for closure from the perils of war that only those who have survived together can fully appreciate and provide for one another. There's nothing like it."

Many unit veterans believe that during the latter third of the unit's presence in Vietnam, both MAJ Conner and 1SG Bearden set the bar for outstanding leadership beyond any 191st chain of command of that era. Bounty Hunter platoon leader and C&C pilot CPT Carlton affirms their leadership finesse when he explains the advantage of having Boomerang Six (Conner) and Boomerang Echo-One (Bearden) aboard assault ships: "Both offered a high-level courtesy for infantry task force commanders who frequently praised the unit for its performance."

With both leaders flying combat assaults, especially at low levels, engaging the enemy, no one in the 191st AHC could recall this type of performance from any other unit commander or its first sergeant. As rare examples, Conner and Bearden were the exceptions. With Conner flying gunships and Bearden crewing them, even though not on a daily basis, the entire set of combat-assault performance was perceptually changed for the better. Respect for this pair of leaders was duly given and the outcome unprecedented.

CHAPTER 25

Nighthawk Down

The 191st aircrews could feel the synergy gathering, and it filtered and fibered their warrior blood.

In the 191st AO, the Nighthawk mission ratcheted down the VC and the NVA night movements. Night movements were the major supply source that fueled enemy war-making capability. Nighthawk missions were an expedient way to knock a big hole in this fuel source. It increased night-movement risk for the enemy by a colossal amount. One thing was for certain, the night would no longer belong to the enemy soldiers. Hence, it was easily assumed by some 191st Nighthawk crewmen that their new mission was a product of the highest command seeking a rapid end to the war.

World events frequently shape the missions of troops on the battlefield, but the faithful souls fighting the war are rarely privileged to know the how and why. Traditionally, American warriors simply respond with dedication to whatever their country orders. Such was the case when the 191st AHC was ordered to fly the Nighthawk mission.

Those of the 191st who kept up with the news back home knew of the Paris peace talks and the ongoing civil disruption that impacted Washington decision makers. The US decision to participate in the Paris peace talks was influenced by civil unrest. Most of the younger generation of Americans knew that. It was also common knowledge among American forces that Pentagon officials remained closely linked to Henry Kissinger, America's national security advisor, as a negotiating responder. Turning war machinery on and off, such as bombing North Vietnam, was a tool of Kissinger's negotiations. The Pentagon was his on-and-off valve. Soldiers at the tip of the spear understood that this relationship between Kissinger and the Pentagon most certainly impacted their status on the battlefield. For sure, Pentagon officials, pressured by the Nixon administration, frantically sought ways to expedite the end of the war. Hence, military leadership at all levels burned midnight oil devising tactics and technology to impede the enemy.

By the early 1970s, Henry Kissinger was tested to the limit by North Vietnamese delegates at the Paris peace talks. Aware of the media circus in America and demonstrations against the war, the enemy negotiators were relying on negative public opinion in America to help them prevail. The cumulative benefit for the enemy by this American unrest seemed to have the most treasonous influence. American media seemingly enunciated civil protest, which impacted Washington decision makers. Also emanating from this unrest was a strong public opinion that encouraged elected officials to expedite an end to the war. North Vietnam saw their opportunity to delay concessions.

Among the most glaring examples of public unrest were the soul-crushing receptions given our warriors as they returned home to their beloved families and country. Disembarking from Freedom Birds, returning Americans were often met by demonstrators who spat in their direction and hurled repulsive words at the war-battered souls. "Baby killers!" This unrest wrongly projected onto the brave souls who served their country pleased the enemy, who felt it worked in their favor. To them this behavior was advertising atrocities committed by Americans against the innocent people of North Vietnam. Coupled with Jane Fonda's own anti-American war campaign, the enemy felt they held influence and political support in America. Thus, for a society built on freedom, provided by the likes of these warrior-heroes being heckled, something had to give.

When diplomacy fails in such negotiations, military might is a preferred solution for breaking the stalemate. Used properly, it is fast and furious. Therein is where the transition of power shifts from the diplomat's lips to the warrior's gut on the battlefield. With political impasse, war casualties usually increase as the lives of soldiers become trading stock—*yours for ours*! Kissinger knew that with resumption of strategic bombing and elimination of border restrictions along Cambodia and Laos, the North Vietnamese would proportionately lose far more lives. In his opinion, the enemy needed some attitude adjustment. Unleashing the earthshaking B-52s to again bomb North Vietnam, along with the combat troops in the field to invade Laos and Cambodia, was the right lanyard to pull. He was prepared to expend some political capital in order to gain leverage in Paris, peace talks be damned. A resolution was needed, and action on the battlefield was the remedy. It was time to turn the dogs of war loose. Kissinger's passion was shared by President Nixon, who desperately sought closure with the enemy. According to media analysts, Nixon's political legacy was literally hanging in the balance.

With the Paris peace talks starting and stalling continuously without resolution, President Nixon forcefully decided to raise the ante on the enemy. The bombing restriction of North Vietnam and the border restrictions that protected their war-supply depots in Laos and Cambodia were finally lifted to encourage the North Vietnam negotiators to return to the table and resume talks with sincerity. In other words, either you negotiate honestly or I'll bomb the hell out of you. Whether coincidental or not, the birth of the Nighthawk mission in the 191st tactical scenario occurred about the same time.

In Vietnam, the enemy traditionally ruled the dark hours while US troops and their allies dominated during daylight. The night mission was designed to further restrict the enemy's freedom to roam the South Vietnamese countryside after sunset, and therefore restrict the NVA and VC from transporting troops, supplies, and ammunition for the next day's ambush on American soldiers. An American tactical change was brewing. The 191st aircrews could feel the synergy gathering, and it filtered and fibered their warrior blood.

Although other units had already performed this mission, its exact origin and tactics were not disseminated to the 191st pilots and crews. In circumstances of this type, it is unlikely that warriors at the tip of the spear would hear the exact words of political leaders transmitting orders to the war zones. Soldiers on the FEBAs live and die as expendable stock of political ideologists. Thus, when the 191st AHC was ordered to fly Nighthawk missions, no one in the unit really knew its origin or its tactical significance other than to interdict the flow of Communist war material and troops in the South. The 191st operations section received the order from battalion operations, and the necessary logistics and administration were left for the 191st AHC commander to fulfill.

On occasion, when a new mission was handed down through command channels, the receiving CO would be called up to the next-higher headquarters to be briefed. But this was never an inquiry to gain the lower commander's approval. Simply, details of the new mission were issued in the way of an operations plan with coordinating instructions, and the rest was up to the receiving commander to assemble and execute. The mission would be performed with no questions asked and no justifiable explanation given. This was the *modus operandi* in a combat aviation battalion. World politics didn't even come into the picture at this level.

As preparations for the first Nighthawk mission sprang forward, anticipation among the crews selected to execute this new tactic generated some anxiety. In war, the life risk of any maneuver is always a looming thought that tugs at those who deliver and take the deadly blows. No soldier worth his or her salt wishes to prolong the killing and dying. Living every day with death at your doorstep is a dominion wished for by no one. Only the demagogues, who never see and feel the agony of human loss in great numbers, remain indifferent to the prolonged pains of war.

Nonetheless, the 191st AHC crews, for certain, sizzled with excitement. All eyes focused on battle preparations. As common in the before-battle ritual, guys shared cigarettes, ribbing and one-upping each other, as they mentally prepared for the rigors that awaited them. With adrenaline and hearts primed and ever ready, they were eager to tighten the noose on the enemy and, to everyone's hope, help end the war and get out of this shithole for good. Charlie would most certainly be caught with his pants down, and what a shock the first few encounters would spring on the unsuspecting enemy.

When the Nighthawk mission first appeared on the desk of the 191st AHC operations officer, it required extensive logistical preparation. A highly modified and super-strong Huey, the UH-1H, with strengthened firepower and dedicated lift capacity, became the machine for the job. This configuration was already battle-tested. Thus, no questions were asked when the 191st AHC ordered .50-caliber machine guns with extra-heavy pintles for door gun mountings, manually controlled miniguns, and powerful xenon searchlights. The outcome was the ability to exert an awesome display of firepower, never before seen by the 191st AHC crews. Anxiety, knocked back like a beer gone warm, poured in. The crews, anxious to test the new war machinery, revved up their resolve.

WO1 Bernard Harvey was among the first 191st AHC pilots who tested the system.

"They were a very brave bunch," Harvey recalls, "since we were literally going out into the dark in a role that was only recently tasked to our unit. During normal night combat-assault operations, when our aircraft came under enemy fire, we customarily turned off our running lights, but in *this* case, we were going to shine the brightest light one can imagine, right on the enemy. In my way of thinking at the time, this would give the bad guys one hell of a bullseye to shoot at. It was a hairy thought.

"The attack group assembled for the mission consisted of a three-ship team, led by a C&C aircraft, a UH-1H, equipped with two flare pods. The crew aboard the C&C bird included an ARVN officer, who directed the geographical coverage, mostly in the U Minh Forest.

"The second bird was a loaded H-model with the extra power to carry heavy armament—weapons with awesome battle potency. In the right transmission well was a .50-caliber machine gun with the capacity to penetrate and destroy virtually any enemy sampan distributing enemy supplies and equipment. The well on the left side contained a xenon searchlight mounted on a handheld minigun that could deliver up to six thousand rounds per minute to the enemy—one hell of a lot of firepower in itself. Then, in the right-side cargo compartment, stood a gunner with a pintle-mounted forty-millimeter grenade launcher that blasted out three-hundred-plus HE rounds per minute. With a fifteen-meter blast radius, this pinpoint grenade bombardment had a demoralizing effect that broke the back of many an attacking force. The concussion itself was devastating and mind-boggling. A fourth member of the crew, armed with a free gun—an M60 7.62-millimeter machine gun, could shift support from either side of the aircraft.

"The third bird was a Bounty Hunter Charlie-model gunship that flew wing on the xenon-searchlight bird. Armed with the usual array of rocket pods and miniguns, this ship was the heavy reinforcement that snuffed out the enemy fire in difficult engagements. The force was formidable, to say the least. I felt privileged to be flying this mission.

"After the routine flight planning and the usual preflight check of the aircraft and weapon systems, we lifted off at dusk. As we departed Can Tho, I expected to head for the U Minh Forest, but we weren't airborne ten minutes when we were diverted to a firefight at a compound southeast about fifteen clicks. Arriving over the battle, we surveyed the situation and oriented on what the American advisor, an SF officer, was reporting. The compound was being attacked on the two sides that faced the most wooded cover. The trees were extraordinarily high and the forest very dense, making excellent fodder for aerial explosions that would rain shrapnel on the enemy. So, we turned the forty-millimeter *blooper* loose on the bad guys from the same side that housed the .50-caliber. The result was a series of treetop explosions as the grenades hit upper branches and the big fifty cut down tree limbs. The damned thing could literally dismember whole trees!

"At the same time, the Bounty Hunter gunship pounded the area with rockets right behind us as we broke off our gun run. To my surprise, the enemy continued to send tracers our way. Our second attack on the other tree line detonated a secondary explosion. Evidently the NVA were carrying HEs, more than likely to breach the compound perimeter. As the explosion lit up the area, it gave us a great vector to orient our fire, and in short order, the minigun lit up the sky with its own stream of fire that rained death on the bad guys. As we returned to the first tree line with the same firepower, the results were encouraging—no more enemy fire. The NVA briskly retreated. It gave us a great feeling of strength and gratitude for the technology our nation provided. There was no equal. At times, you almost felt compassion for the enemy. That is, until you saw one of your crewmembers shot or killed. Then all bets were off, and the enemy was given no mercy. These were the moments that brought reality into the war, and they were an everyday occurrence."

As remembered by many 191st veterans, the technical upgrades made for the Nighthawk missions generated some of the unit's greatest combat achievements. Years later many lamented that these improvements would have produced phenomenal results if available earlier in our Vietnam mission.

"When I first arrived at the 191st," CPT Clogston recalls, "the Nighthawk bird had a cluster light and two M60 machine guns. That was the extent of its armament. It flew under the protection of a Bounty Hunter gunship. But by the time I left Vietnam, the Nighthawk mission had gained superb tactics and firepower. A minigun with butterfly triggers was added along with an additional gunner. Other weapons included an aviation .50-caliber machine gun, plus a Mark 19 Honeywell forty-millimeter grenade launcher with gunner and powerful xenon searchlights that could light up the world below us. Tactically, we then implemented flight-altitude separation of several hundred feet to execute teamwork that produced extraordinary kill ratios. It delivered not only flight safety but excellent weapon-systems coordination plus searchlight efficiency. This upgrade reached its zenith just prior to our first incursion into Cambodia.

"Our surprise ingress into Cambodia caught the enemy moving troops by boat to the U Minh Forrest. When discovered by MACV, TEAM 56, a group of advisors, was formed and ordered to upgrade intelligence support for the Nighthawk mission. That further produced a decisive success. We discovered and tracked large enemy movements. One large group of NVA in particular turned out to be fresh troops just out of advanced training. Their slaughter was wanton—and that shocking outcome for the enemy soon stopped their night movements. Equally effective, we interdicted night extractions of NVA being picked up on the Gulf of Siam for repositioning to other battle sites. This was another surprise move that stunned the enemy.

"A turning point in our operation occurred on or about June 30, 1970, when the NVA overwhelmed allied troops at the An Bien outpost. Assuming command of the installation, the NVA seized military-age civilians and employed aggressive patrols for population control. Preparing an air assault, the allied forces inserted three sorties to conduct house-to-house searches—the NVA vanished. The problem disappeared almost as rapidly as it started. Mobility and firepower prevailed. This was another clear example of airmobile battle superiority upgraded by advanced technology.

"That Nighthawk outcome caught the attention of the command staff of the Thirteenth CAB. Allied personnel from the Kien An District senior advisor discovered from captured NVA interrogations that NVA night movements stopped for fear of Nighthawk interdiction. The losses from Nighthawk team patrols drew the attention of the NVA hierarchy, who stopped the movements until safer modes could be found. A letter of commendation was issued to the 191st AHC with specific recognition for the outstanding impact of the Nighthawk mission. The letter specifically stated, 'The Nighthawk mission substantially slowed night movement by the NVA and VC because the enemy was afraid of the threat it posed.'"

In effect, for a short period while the new technology was overwhelming enemy infiltration efforts, the 191st helicopter assets could move men and equipment throughout the southern war zone with impunity. Day or night, the 191st battle capability was highly reactive to enemy movements.

Like all new tactics, the effectiveness of Nighthawk missions began to lose its impact as the enemy assimilated the threat and began avoiding engagements. The cost of assembling and launching the trio of aircraft began to outweigh the reduction of enemy losses, so the mission was modified. It became a single-ship mission. Among the first to fly a single-ship Nighthawk mission was CW2 John "Larry" Potts, a former slick pilot, and his copilot, Robert Anderson.

When Nighthawk was reduced to a single-ship mission, much of the mutual support that originally protected the three-ship task force disappeared. This also reduced the available firepower by a large margin. Nonetheless, as the sun set in the late afternoon on the day before Easter Sunday in 1971, Potts peacefully nourished his body and heart in the 191st dining facility, preparing for his single-ship Nighthawk mission. As routine would have it, the mechanical aspects of the bird were being tended to by Crew Chief SP5 Alan Roth, and the weapon maintenance, rearming and testing the xenon light, with the assistance of Gunner SP4 Joseph Ladd. Having dined earlier, the crew chief and gunner were given priority with logistics necessary to expedite mission preparation. They were the VIPs of the moment, and all command members yielded to their needs. Typically, pilots and commanders did not rush their crews any more than necessary while they prepared the aircraft for launching. It simply wasn't a healthy thing to do. As with any other combat mission, the flight readiness of the aircraft and weapon systems played a major role in safe return of Nighthawk crews.

When Potts and his crew broke ground to begin their mission, they had no idea that on *this* Easter Sunday, a typical celebration of "Sunrise Services" anticipated by the Christians on board, would be carved into their collective memory for life. It would be one Easter sunrise they would never forget.

With considerable Nighthawk flight time logged at 191st AHC headquarters, the operations officer adjusted the Nighthawk mission to a one-ship perimeter-security patrol that included counter mortar, support for outposts that protected approaches to Can Tho, and a free-for-all witch hunt of canals with whatever available flight time permitted. Canal patrol exhilarated the crews. The action frequently generated a fantastic adrenaline rush among those who closed on and destroyed the enemy. The 191st crews believed that the greater the elimination of enemy assets, the shorter the war, and canal engagements produced significant enemy losses. *Wreak havoc on the enemy and destroy their will to fight* was a constant Boomerang and Bounty Hunter mindset. It was deeply ingrained in their subconscious and reinforced daily.

Potts reported his airborne status to Boomerang ops and began his initial routine flight path, which became a rather doldrum type of affair. Usually nothing happened during this portion of the mission, and this flight lifted off as dull as usual.

Standing by on the ramp back at Can Tho, a Bounty Hunter gunship manned by CW2s Ralph Colbert and Tony Ellison was armed and fueled, ready for any action that Nighthawk firepower could not handle. With radios tuned to the operations frequency, the hard-hitting Charlie-model was poised to strike in the wee hours of the morning still covered by darkness.

The single-ship Nighthawk mission turned outbound for canal patrol, and it came upon a sampan exhibiting every sign of enemy activity. Potts called the TOC for clearance to fire. Approval was immediate. The mission erupted into a vicious firefight. As it turned out, the enemy craft was supporting an NVA camp in the immediate vicinity.

"I called TOC and reported the engagement while the crew poured all the firepower we had on the enemy," Potts recalls. "With the xenon light burning brightly, we could see the ground crawling with enemy soldiers, reloading and firing their weapons. We made several passes. On each occasion, we received intense fire, far more than the usual we normally saw. The fight started at approximately 0100 hours on Easter morning and continued gathering intensity. Each pass seemingly brought more tracers up to meet us. Determined to gain the upper hand on the enemy, I continued to engage and descended to approximately two hundred feet AGL to intensify our killing effect. Still the enemy fire did not ease up, and I called the TOC for Bounty Hunter support.

"On the next pass, we took an intense burst of devastating ground fire from our twelve o'clock position and almost directly under the nose as we crossed to the west side of the canal. You could feel every hit the Nighthawk took. The caution panel lit up. Engine and transmission-oil pressure gauges dropped to zero. At the same time, under Ladd's seat in the left well, a one-hundred-round can of .50-caliber ammo started cooking off with loud explosions that made matters even worse. 'Crap! We're on fire, too!' I knew we were in deep shit. I called out 'Mayday' and gave my location as best I could. Ladd managed to toss the burning can of ammo overboard. Knowing that I needed to get as far away as possible from the bad guys, I headed for the nearby ARVN compound, but I had to land far short. No transmission-oil pressure could be a sure death sentence for all. With NVA certain to come looking for us, the situation hovered over a grave. A puckered-up asshole is saying it lightly—we were scared shitless. The price of survival radios could have gone to one million dollars at that moment, and I would have gladly pawned my life to keep those we had working. Lucky for us they *did*.

"Only three days earlier, the NVA attacked a nearby triangular compound manned by ARVN and advised by an SF captain. I should have known this was a hotspot. That engagement started when the SF captain called for support. Being nearby, I returned his call and quickly moved to help his beleaguered forces. With the xenon light shining super bright, we could clearly see the wood line where the enemy was taking cover. The .50-caliber devastated the sparse vegetation sheltering the NVA. Small trees shot up in the air like twigs as the heavy rounds chewed up their small trunks. In just a few minutes, the fight was taken out of the NVA and the battle was over. Saved by our support, the SF captain called and expressed his eternal gratitude as we departed the scene. Then, as fate would have it, on this Easter morning he returned the favor. His troops came to our downed ship and stood guard until we were picked up by a medevac that happened to be in the area. Once the crew was safe in the medevac bird, I breathed a big sigh of relief. That is one Easter morning I'll never forget, and I'm willing to bet my crew won't either."

Not long thereafter, the 191st began to stand down in preparation to return to the United States, its mission well done. Mixed emotions touched the soul of many. Boomerangs, Bounty Hunters, and Green Deltas alike could not fathom why the US was leaving Vietnam, literally while the country was still being ravished by the enemy. Those who believed in the purpose of the war could easily see that the US was pulling out while the job was not yet complete. These warrior-heroes fought and died for the cause, and their surviving 191st brothers felt it was a waste of human lives and effort to pull out now. To these brave warriors, it was surreal and defied understanding of how a nation as powerful as the United States could create and live with policy that would forever subject our loyal allies who fought right along our side to a future under Communism.

The 191st AHC's combat deployment to Vietnam occurred during the Johnson administration. By the time President Johnson left office, approximately twenty-six Boomerangs and Bounty Hunters lay silent in their graves, leaving behind families with lives forever shattered. Eighteen more would join them before President Nixon finally aborted his attempt to prevent the North Vietnamese from seizing South Vietnam.

CHAPTER 26

The Final Call

Death was but a heartbeat away and no one was immune.

Each warrior engaged in battle desires victory in the end. In Vietnam, American soldiers knew their country was obliged to stop the spread of Communism in Southeast Asia. What was *not* clear to US troops was when they would receive the final call to battle for that devoted cause. All commitments to the Vietnam War, whether Army wide or those of an individual soldier, were bound to an anticipated end. Not knowing when that end would come, the mindset of pilots and crews of the 191st was "fight to the end—and fight to win."

With that perspective, the 191st AHC committed its full force and effort to each engagement. And with astonishing alacrity, the crews and personnel adjusted to the departure of its host unit, the Ninth Infantry Division, performing remarkable achievements in their final phase of combat. Most incredible was the 191st AHC's ability to increase its battle effectiveness against a stronger enemy, which came into South Vietnam better equipped and fully manned. Upgrading their own war technology, the Boomerangs, Bounty Hunters, and Green Deltas amassed enemy kill ratios of staggering proportions. Although the last phase of the war for the 191st was highly successful in attrition of enemy forces, it was also bloody for Boomerangs and Bounty Hunters. With the stakes for this war rooted deeply in North Vietnamese plans for taking the Republic of Vietnam, the enemy was prepared to bet it all. In effect, North Vietnam was all in and willing to do what was necessary to neutralize any threat, including the 191st AHC.

Boomerang and Bounty Hunter casualties were destined to increase. And they did, almost tenfold, in the unit's final year of combat. Yet the Boomerangs and Bounty Hunters continued decimating enemy forces with their new weapons and technical support. Their losses served to increase the passion of surviving 191st crews who then fought with renewed intensity. Vengefully, they moved with premeditation to close with and destroy the enemy.

"I truly couldn't see any military reasoning in media reports that we were losing the war," Gun Platoon Leader CPT Carlton recalls. "Hell, almost every engagement with the enemy resulted in staggering losses for the NVA and VC. Even after the Ninth left, the ARVN units we supported amassed some remarkable enemy kills. Occasionally, they would get their asses kicked, but as a rule they killed a hell of a lot more of the enemy than what the enemy took from them. I was never more impressed with their guts and will to fight than when we took them to the Cambodian border. The enemy forces there were heavy in manpower and well equipped. Yet the ARVN waded into them like there was no tomorrow. Of course, I don't know what the outcome might have been without our support. I wasn't there for that phase of the war. But personally, I can't see how our presence there would have made a big difference. They had the will to fight and win on their own. If only the US would have given the ARVN the support that China and Russia gave the NVA."

On a lighter note, each day in 191st AHC's final year in Vietnam was not about war. One lucky bird, crewed by SP5 Robert Charles Gavette, was ordered to carry the 1970 Miss America, Pam Eldred, and her entourage to various installations in the delta. The beauty queen and her staff were a real thrill for American warriors who had not seen such a gorgeous attraction since leaving the United States. Gavette beamed at the attention his aircraft was getting at each stop. A tried and true warrior in his own right, he nonetheless offered the Miss America experience first in his list of war excerpts.

"Calling my gunner on secure intercom," Gavette recalls, "I asked, 'Hey Gunny, how would you like to spend an evening with this passenger? Quite a difference from what you're used to seeing in this bird, huh?' Gunny just smiled and sheepishly replied, 'Maaann! They're all hot! Hell, I wouldn't mind an evening with any of her company.'"

Nonetheless, with the Miss America thrill a past memory, Gavette's ship was among the first combat crews ordered into Cambodia. Engaged in battles that drew massive blood loss from both enemy and allies, Gavette's aircraft took its share of bullets. The fight was rich in advanced weapons; both sides were well equipped in firepower. The South Vietnamese forces leading the incursion lost many good troops but took huge body counts of NVA with them, an encouraging turn of events, though inconclusive. Neither side gave in. For Gavette, it was the first time in his entire combat experience he saw enemy tanks in battle.

"The mission launched from Moc Hoa," Gavette recalls, "where we landed an American one-star general for coordination with ARVN brass. Boarding the ARVN general's aircraft at Moc Hoa, the American general flew into Cambodia with our bird in pursuit—as a chase aircraft. Several hours later the birds were refueled and the American general returned to our aircraft. Returning to Cambodia, the battle raged on. Enemy tanks dominated the battlefield and Cobra gunships were called in to destroy the enemy armor. Soon, the sky above the battle area bristled with American airpower. With deadly precision, we watched a Cobra gunship attack one tank that was spearheading the enemy force. Leaving the tank in flames, the gunship pulled out of the dive but plowed directly into the underside of the ARVN general's ship. Bladeless, the sleek Cobra streamlined ninety degrees into the ground and buried itself, exploding into a huge fireball. All that could be seen of the Cobra was its vertical fin protruding from a large, smoking hole in the ground. Both pilots were killed. The ARVN bird crashed upright but killed all aboard as well.

"Seeing the whole episode, the American general commented, 'I was afraid of that.' Having luck on his side, at the end of that day, the American general returned to MACV headquarters in Can Tho, no doubt relieved that he was back on our aircraft during the collision. That mission weighed heavily on my mind for weeks. Up to that point in my tour, I hadn't seen that much death in a single day. It gave me a real view of war at its worse, and seasoned my understanding of human loss in battle. In seconds, many can die."

When announced that the Ninth Infantry Division was leaving Vietnam, speculation among higher in-country echelons of Army aviation grew concerned about security for its field assets. The 191st AHC was under OPCON of the Ninth Infantry Division for almost its entire presence in Vietnam and protected by the division's perimeter guard elements. Careful not to imply that ARVN capacity might not fill the security void, higher aviation staff unofficially suggested security reindoctrination for its field units. Yet today, not one 191st AHC living soul will say that any reindoctrination connected to the departing Ninth Infantry Division was part of the mission change they executed in Can Tho. Business as usual continued for all concerned. Orders for the unit to move to Can Tho simply meant prepare to load and relocate. Same as it did from Bearcat to Dong Tam. The only unknown component? The Boomerangs and Bounty Hunters moved unaware that this new base of operations would include their final call to battle—the end of their great aviation company's contribution to the Vietnam War. But by a large contrast, this was not so for the enemy. The Ninth Infantry Division's departure cleared a major obstacle for enemy infiltration into South Vietnam. Given such an open door, the enemy moved decisively to infiltrate and occupy.

Meanwhile, the 191st AHC was gaining heavy weapons and refined battle experience. Cumulative night-fighting capability came in the way of the UH-1S, armed with powerful searchlights and high-caliber weapons. The .50-caliber machine guns, theretofore taboo on UH-1 airframes, were modified for helicopter use, and some 191st birds gained a heavy hand. Placed in the laps of seasoned 191st pilots, the night freedoms enjoyed by enemy troop movements faded. Night engagements became frequent but rapidly dissipated. Boomerangs and Bounty Hunters literally fought day and night, imposing greater strain on their personnel, but they were far more effective in terms of enemy body counts. More and more enemy were killed at the hands of 191st crews. Over and over again, 191st SOPs were being upgraded to conform to new missions and equipment. Newly arriving personnel were subject to close oversight by experienced NCOs and officers. Training became highly technical, and newbies accepted this new battle prep with a serious self-preservation mindset.

Support for the ARVN, on the other hand, was waning. President Nixon's Vietnamization of the war was not delivering the necessary logistics to our South Vietnamese allies. Artillery basic loads for the ARVN were being reduced. Equally, not all war-making hardware employed by US forces were furnished to the ARVN. Therefore, it would only be a matter of time before the South Vietnamese Army would not be able to hold its territory. Worse, the enemy antiaircraft systems were gaining formidable strength.

In the previous twelve-month period of April 10, 1969, through April 10, 1970, only one 191st aircrewman was lost in battle. Yet during the following eight-month period, April 13, 1970, through November 4, 1970, ten 191st crewmembers were killed in action. A 900 percent increase.

It is these brave souls whose lives were lost in battle that bolstered their brothers-in-arms to stay in the fight and free South Vietnam from Communist rule. This is what they fought, bled, and risked their lives for—day in and day out. SP4 Kenneth Larry Fleming recalls one such day.

"April 13, 1970, was not a good day for me. I had the privilege of flying with CW2 Curt Embrey when he was shot and killed. I can recall that incident as if it just occurred. We were sent out on a hunt-and-kill team, and CW2 Embrey was flying as AC. We attacked an enemy bunker complex and received one shot from the enemy. I kept firing my M60 till I heard Embrey say he was hit and we were going down. Meanwhile, the copilot, CPT Van Hoy, who was hit by the same bullet in the shoulder before it mortally wounded Embrey, took control of the aircraft and flew it to Binh Thuy hospital, where he executed a controlled crash landing. Immediately, I jumped out of the bird and pulled Embrey from his seat to find a bullet hole on his chin. It exited through the back of his neck just below his helmet. He died very quickly. Embrey always treated his crew with great respect and courtesy. To this day, I think of him as one of the finest pilots our unit had. We lost a great asset."

CW2 Ralph Curtis "Curt" Embrey was twenty-three years old and had a lovely woman he called "Stick Lady." He grew up traveling the world with his family because his father was a pilot and a colonel in the US Air Force. He received the Distinguished Flying Cross, the Bronze Star, and the Air Medal, among other awards.

WO1 Bernard Randy Harvey remembers three lost crewmembers: "It was on June 24, 1970," Harvey recalls, "and I was serving as assistant operations officer under CPT Van Hoy, when SP4 Timothy McCarthy, affectionately called Porky by his friends, came into the operations center to request the Red Box. It contained the OPORD for that evening's Nighthawk mission. Knowing that Porky had only a few days before he would rotate back to the States, I questioned his logic. He said he was going home a hero because he had already received a Purple Heart plus a few other awards. But now he wanted to go home with a higher commendation for valor such as the Distinguished Flying Cross or the Silver Star. He thought Nighthawk would give him the opportunity. Careful not to show my deep concern, I handed him the Red Box and wished him well. I couldn't help but feel dread that now, so close to his return home, something might happen to him. Approximately five hours later he was dead.

"Porky's flight landed at Rach Gia to refuel and rearm, and just as the throttles were rolled back and engines winding down, the enemy attacked. Well planned, the attackers caught the flight crews unprepared and completely by surprise. Having little choice, the crews headed to the nearby bunkers when the attack began. Porky, on the other hand, ran around the aircraft to get his machine gun. Seeing the opportunity to exhibit his extraordinary bravery, Porky cut down the attackers one by one. With the tables now turned, the ground attack slowed significantly but was quickly replaced with a heavy rocket attack. Holding his ground, Porky continued pouring machine-gun fire on the enemy positions until a rocket exploded at his feet. Severely wounded, he was recovered as quickly as possible and evacuated to the nearest field hospital, but to no avail; he died en route. In a situation like that, you get a heavy feeling in your soul for not having been more forceful in advising the individual to stand down. Being so close to his DEROS, you can't help but wonder if you could have made a difference. I felt really bad for his family."

These losses made it clearly evident that enemy resolve and capability had increased by a large margin. Unfortunately, more losses were still to come for the 191st AHC. Meanwhile, American resolve in Washington was weakening. With the Ninth withdrawn, the increased 191st exposure extracted a heartbreaking price in Boomerang and Bounty Hunter blood.

Among the first to train under the new SOP was 1LT John T. Fickett. Arriving in late October 1970, 1LT Fickett, born in Athens, Georgia, and the only child of a military family, came to the 191st AHC anxious to fly helicopters in combat. He would soon get his wish. But first came the breaking-in process. His required in-country check ride would have to wait for the IP's return from R&R. In the meantime, two senior members of the 191st, CPT Alan Hotaling and SFC Jaime Restrepo, would provide his in-country maintenance ground school. The unit's strong emphasis on mechanically sound aircraft stemmed from the recent November 2, 1970, crash that killed four 191st crew members. The day of the crash, CW2 John Thomas Orrico, WO1 Douglas John Campbell, SP5 Kenneth Lavern Brown, and SP5 Oscar Maloney departed Rach Gia headed for Rach Soi to refuel—a routine flight. When the bird reached five hundred feet AGL, the main rotor suddenly separated from the aircraft. Free of the blade, the helicopter nosed down and crashed with a violent explosion, eliminating any chance for crew survival. Following only seconds behind, the trail gunship immediately circled the site searching for survivors, but the crew's death was instant.

Gunner SP4 Myron K. Guerrero in the C&C ship observed the crash. "The blade separation occurred so abruptly," Guerrero remembers. "It was agonizing to watch our fellow 191st brothers fall to their deaths. It was a fiery crash with no hope of any survivors. In the minds of anyone watching, those poor souls died a thousand times before that aircraft even hit the ground."

Flying as AC, John Thomas Orrico was twenty-two years old and maintained his home of record in Ridgefield, Connecticut. Just a few months prior, he received the Distinguished Flying Cross and earlier was rewarded the Bronze Star, among others. The copilot, Douglas John Campbell, just shy of his twenty-first birthday, was from Orlando, Florida, and was married to Teresa. He earned a Bronze Star, among other awards. Gunner Kenneth Lavern Brown was twenty years old and from Fort Scott, Kansas. He received the Air Medal, among other awards. Crew Chief Oscar Maloney was twenty-five years old, hailed from Tuba City, Arizona, and was married to Emma. He received a Bronze Star, among other awards. In high school, Maloney played football at the Intermountain Navajo Indian Boarding School, where he and his buddy Sammy would jump the fence and buy a gallon of Coca-Cola and one dollar's worth of french fries. The loss of these lives cut deep.

The mechanical failure circulated among 191st flight personnel in record time. It was a grim reminder that before each takeoff and landing, no chance for preflight inspection must be wasted. Among the company's newly adopted preventive measures, new personnel were given an in-depth maintenance indoctrination. Fickett learned from this chilling crash story. But even more so, he learned the most from his observation of the impact death had on crew functions and the remorseful mood that survivors exhibited. In some, the experience of losing a buddy literally changed their personalities. Troops eventually adopted emotional blocks against death—and against their dead comrades' replacements, or FNGs. It took time for crews to defer the FNG status of a replacement crewmember. This FNG status was made clear to Fickett.

CPT Alan Hotaling, recognizing Fickett's FNG station, volunteered to assist the fresh lieutenant to assimilate his ground responsibilities. The unit commander directed Fickett to familiarize himself with the unit's new maintenance protocols and seek advice from an experienced NCO, SFC Restrepo. Both Hotaling and Restrepo possessed information essential to Fickett's ground responsibilities. However, Restrepo was recovering from a stomach ailment, common in Far East environments. This required an additional waiting period for Fickett to get his maintenance introduction. That day finally came on the afternoon of November 4, 1970, when SFC Restrepo returned.

The initial introduction was friendly and exciting for Fickett, who sought to close the ground gap and get on with flying. Restrepo ushered the young lieutenant to a line shack, where the two sat for the initial briefing. The discussion centered on UH-1 repair-time lapses. Repair parts acquisition was problematic, and Restrepo was careful to explain the details to Fickett. The young lieutenant listened intently, nodding his head as Restrepo emphasized hard points. Completing a general overview of 191st aircraft maintenance operation, Restrepo stood up and motioned for Fickett to follow him to the flight line.

"Lieutenant, let's run down through the aircraft revetments so I can show you some of the birds with advanced hardware," Restrepo said.

"Sure, Sergeant. Be glad to. You have no idea how long I've been waiting for this moment. Ever since I left flight school, I've often wondered where I'd end up and what kind of outfit I would fly with. I got really excited when I was told at the replacement depot that I was assigned to the 191st Assault Helicopter Company. It's like a dream come true."

"Well, Lieutenant, I wish you luck in this assignment. It's a high-risk mission. You'll soon see." Restrepo didn't know what a profound statement he just made.

They continued making their way down the line of aircraft, with Restrepo explaining the recent maintenance demands of each bird. Fickett and Restrepo had only just arrived at the Nighthawk ship, and Restrepo was eloquently beginning to explain its lethality with its .50-caliber machine guns and powerful night lights. At that moment, CPT Hotaling, driving a three-quarter-ton truck, appeared on the flight line and called out to Fickett as he was about to enter the night ship with Restrepo.

"Hi, Lieutenant," Hotaling yelled. "I see you're hanging with your platoon sergeant. You couldn't have a better aircraft tour guide on this flight line."

Hotaling then called out to the NCO. "Sergeant Restrepo, if you'll allow me just a few minutes with the lieutenant, I'll release him right back to you."

"Sure, Captain," Restrepo said and opened the door to the night ship. He sat on its cargo deck while Hotaling and Fickett talked.

Fickett recalls that day years later: "I was just starting to converse with CPT Hotaling when an earth-shattering blast rocked the ground beneath us. Hotaling hollered, 'Mortars!' and bailed out of the three-quarter-ton truck to head for cover. Fire filled the revetment, and I was caught between the scorching blaze and the truck. Then a second explosion cooked off with enormous heat engulfing the airspace around me. Scrambling my way across the tarmac, a .50-caliber machine gun and ammo box blew free from the night bird, landing near me. Rounds including grenades started cooking off.

"When I finally reached the opposite end of the revetment, I took account of my injuries. My hair was singed around my hat line, and I noticed a small piece of shrapnel protruding from my hand, which caused little concern. It seemed like forever before the ammo explosions stopped. I caught up with Hotaling, and we waited for the fire truck to arrive. The fire crew appeared as the flames died. Hotaling and I ran to Restrepo and found his charred upper torso at the front of what remained of the aircraft. With all his appendages blown off, he never knew what hit him. The poor soul probably felt no pain. His death was instantaneous, but it was a mind-numbing experience to witness. Each year on my birthday, it vividly pops up in my memory when I call Hotaling to thank him for saving my life."

The investigation that followed revealed an enemy infiltrator breached security and booby-trapped the aircraft. The enemy wrapped a grenade with electrical tape, pulled the pin, and slipped it into the bird's fuel tank. As the fuel ate through the adhesive, the grenade was poised to detonate, simply waiting for the next motion to loosen the tape. The death trap was designed to blow the aircraft from the sky with crew and troops falling to their death. The irony in Restrepo's death was being the soul who died to save others. It's not certain whose lives were saved by Restrepo that day, but one clear possibility was the bird's crew chief, SP5 Dennis D. Vasko. Vasko felt and heard the explosion from the barracks. Learning it was his bird sent a chill through Vasko that remains in his mind to this day.

"The short time since we met remains a powerful stimulant to understanding life's fate at war," Fickett explains years later. "How unpredictable it can be. One moment Restrepo was advising me of the death risks connected to my pilot duties, and then minutes later his life was taken by enemy action. My introduction to combat thus came in a most unexpected way. In Vietnam, death was but a heartbeat away and no one was immune. Made one wonder, who would be next?"

SFC Jaime Restrepo, killed in action on November 4, 1970, by an enemy grenade, would be the second-to-last casualty of the 191st. Restrepo was thirty-six years old, hailed from Columbus, Georgia, and was awarded the Bronze Star, among many other awards. He was survived by his wife, Nancy, his son, John Jaime, and his three-year-old daughter, Maria.

Following the death of Restrepo, Fickett remained focused on survival. Anxious to get on with his assignment, his check ride freed him to join the rest of the Boomerangs and Bounty Hunters.

"Elated, I listened carefully and observed the ACs during each mission," Fickett recalls. "There was a lot to learn on the tactics of flying combat assaults. But regrettably, I could not shed my boring and time-consuming additional duties, which included pay officer and tech-supply officer. Those kept me grounded more than the average Boomerang. Those tasks were not a happy time for me."

Nonetheless, Fickett worked diligently and performed some remarkable upgrades in the unit's logistics. Key to the 191st passing the IG's readiness inspection, his performance impressed the unit commander, a remarkable achievement that would, one day, qualify him for a most formidable mission among his peers. He would be ordered to deactivate the unit and redistribute its TOE equipment. Unaware of what lay ahead, Fickett enjoyed his combat experiences as they evolved.

A day well commemorated in Fickett's mind occurred in early February 1971. He was flying as AC on the C&C ship.

"We were assigned to work with the Seawolves, the Navy's gun platoon along the Gulf of Thailand," Fickett recalls. "Using our most advanced hardware, the flight included the C&C aircraft and two UH-1MFs equipped with the INFANT AN/ASQ-132 systems with low-light-luminated TV cameras [LLLTV], systems that can see in the dark yet are not visible from the ground by the enemy. Also, attached to this night Phantom package was a YO-3A Quiet Star fixed-wing aircraft built by Lockheed and flown by the Army Security Agency. The bird, equipped with infrared lighting also not visible to the enemy during night tactical operations, had a tuned propeller and a muffler running the entire length of the plane for quietness. An extremely formidable package, and the enemy had no idea it existed. Worse for the souls who died by it, they had no way of defending against it.

"Tactically, the UH-1MFs were armed with two rocket pods filled with seventeen-pound fléchette rounds and miniguns with low-intensity tracers conforming to light sensitivities of the LLLTVs. Arranged in altitude echelons, the Quiet Star flew at twenty-five hundred feet so it could direct infrared light center of mass on targets ahead. With C&C at one thousand feet, they could control the two UH-1MFs flying respectively at seven hundred feet and five hundred feet. This configuration assured mass saturation of fléchettes on target for max kill ratio. Deadly! I would soon learn just how deadly."

Departing Rach Gia, the flight flew down the coast. Around twenty clicks out, the INFANT birds detected a large number of sampans, in parallel lines, moving in and out of the shoreline. At that time, Fickett received a call from the Bounty Hunter flying the low bird.

"Boomerang Double Deuce, this is Bounty Hunter Six. We have a large mass of enemy offloading supplies from sampans just ahead at twelve o'clock."

"Roger, Bounty Hunter Six. This is Boomerang Double Deuce. I'm right behind you, take them!"

"Roger that. Bounty Hunter Six, out!"

As the flight got closer, Fickett saw a boardwalk stretching across a mudflat out to the sampans. "An enemy porter workforce was carrying supplies from the vessels to the canopy of the U Minh Forest," Fickett recalls. "Given clearance to engage, the INFANT ships fired fléchettes, immediately scattering the porter force trapped between the forest and the water's edge. About fifty yards of mudflat became a killing ground. With blast after blast, numerous porter bodies were dead or dying on the low-tide mud. Human flesh and blood littered the shoreline for several hundred feet around the boardwalk, the outcome of new technology unknown to the enemy."

Meanwhile, the INFANTs were destroying the boardwalk human operation, and C&C tracked the sampans to the supply source. A large trawler anchored offshore was offloading war material onto the sampans. The trawler offered a high-yield target inside the three-mile unrestricted engagement limit. Fickett immediately called the Seawolves.

"Seawolf Ops, this is Boomerang Double Deuce. I have a large, high-value Naval target in the vicinity of our current engagement. Need fire support as soon as possible, please."

"Roger, Double Deuce, this is Seawolf Ops. We'll have some birds in your area shortly. Out!"

Arriving promptly, the Seawolf gunships made contact with C&C.

"Boomerang Double Deuce, this is Seawolf Six. How can we help you, sir?"

"Seawolf Six, this is Double Deuce," Fickett responded. "From your present location, please head one hundred ten degrees out from shore, and you'll see a large trawler offloading supplies to VC sampans. See what you can do to destroy or disrupt the enemy supply operation!"

"Roger, Double Deuce. We're on our way. Out!"

Explosions on the trawler deck could be seen for miles in the darkness. "The Seawolf gunships blasted the trawler with 2.75-inch rockets," Fickett recalls, "but we soon realized heavier ordnance was needed. Black Pony [the Navy FAC team with two OV-10As loaded with twenty-millimeter cannons and five-inch Zuni Rockets] was called to engage the trawler. But Black Pony could not inflict terminal damage before the enemy supply ship reached the safety of open water beyond the three-mile limit. A Navy destroyer was called to intercept the enemy ship, but to no avail. It arrived too late to engage. As the battle continued, subsequent detonations turned night into day long enough to see human bodies and debris floating for approximately five kilometers around the scene on the boardwalk. Some gunships were blasting the tree line along the coast to kill enemy taking cover inside the forest. The battle took us well into the early hours of the morning. Departing to refuel and rearm, we returned as day broke over the sea—a beautiful tropical sight reflected off the calm ocean."

The serene, picturesque landscape had quickly faded when Fickett and his crew returned to the battle site.

"Dismembered bodies could clearly be seen from the air," Fickett continues. "Most atrocious, sharks were having a field day with the dead humans. Body parts ripped in pieces were floating everywhere. One human head floated face up and was missing the lower portion of the jaw. Eyes and forehead were intact, but the lower jaw was one big empty hole. Severed where the neck connects with the skull, the enemy head floated face up, with eyes open in a cold, dead stare.

"On the shore around the boardwalk, sharks took running starts and slid up on the mud to grab a body, and then flapped their way back into the water. Once floating in ample depth, the corpse was attacked by several sharks, causing entrails and other human matter to float to the surface around the cadaver. A horrific scene such as only movie scriptwriters dream up. Certainly, not something one would photograph for the folks back home. After gaining some battle experience, I understood how most war veterans agree that battle scenes with dismembered humans are ghastly enough when one sees them in combat. Not only are such hideous photos repulsive for recall later in life, worse is the impact they impart on family members who, in the minds of many war veterans, should be spared such vile images. I felt relieved when I did away with those photos."

Fickett took a long, solemn pause before continuing. "The mission ended with high marks for all friendly forces who engaged the enemy. Though we never got a firm body count, minimal kills were estimated at approximately forty enemy dead. The combat experience I gained from that mission was invaluable. Especially the night-fighting skills, which applied amply in future assignments. Other missions into the U Minh Forest and vicinity offered challenging enemy action.

"The NVA moved a considerable force into the region and fought with intent to hold. The battle outcomes between their forces and ARVN units were a give and take. Occasionally, the NVA overcame allied forces with superior firepower and equipment. Disadvantaged, the ARVN often fought with less-than-adequate fire-power and munitions. The Vietnamization of the war was not all it was made out to be. Our allies did not have the same quality of equipment and supplies issued to American forces. Self-evident, this contributed to the ultimate defeat of South Vietnam by the NVA. By the time I left Vietnam, I revised my opinion of the US government's planning sequence. It seems to me that too much American combat force was pulled out of South Vietnam before the enemy was sufficiently subdued. It didn't allow the Republic of Vietnam time to do all that was necessary to hold their ground. I think we made a mistake by pulling out too soon."

During the final month of combat missions flown by the 191st AHC, the enemy increased its strength in the lower portion of South Vietnam. Well supplied from Cambodian stores and employing upgraded weapons, the enemy was emboldened by the evacuation of American combat troops from South Vietnam. Firefights came with greater frequency and intensity. The North Vietnamese government gleaned a bit of impatience from US negotiators at the Paris peace talks and assumed a position of strength in their war effort. The 191st, not knowing the full strategic picture, kept its nose to the grindstone and fought with conviction. Offensively, the Boomerangs, Bounty Hunters, and Green Deltas remained confident they possessed the upper hand in any contest with the enemy. Their upgraded weapons systems were far superior to any the enemy had. Though artillery support waned a bit, air strikes could rapidly close the gap. Still, the NVA fiercely engaged and committed to hold ground, whereas in the past they would fire a few rounds and run. It makes one wonder if their intelligence sources had some way of knowing that the 191st was the next unit scheduled to go home.

Orders for deactivation arrived at 191st headquarters in August 1971, and the process of transferring personnel to other in-country units was expedited. Meantime, 1LT John Fickett, having exhibited exceptional skills in managing material and equipment in preparation for the unit's IG visit, was ordered to handle the equipment transfers and supply distribution. A monumental task.

"When done," Fickett recalls, "I went to Saigon and met with the YO-3A Quiet Star pilots and ended up flying seven-hundred-plus night combat hours before returning home to US soil."

But before the 191st AHC returned Stateside, Vietnam would take one more young life. For those close to any of the forty-four members of the 191st killed in action, the faces of the dead remain vivid in their memories. Though the emotion has long since dampened with age, the painful loss will accompany the beholder to his or her death. Those who saw them die will never forget the horrific sense of loss. Many veterans agree that it is truly regrettable that humanity cannot find an alternative to war. Perhaps most regrettable is being the final man in your unit to die for the cause. Such was the case with SGT Thomas Preston Harvey. He bravely died a soldier's death. His brother, WO1 Bernard Randy Harvey, recalls:

"Like a typical little brother, Thomas was aware that Army policy did not allow for brothers to serve in war zones concurrently, unless one or the other signed a waiver from that policy. Thomas had signed such a waiver to go to Vietnam. When notified, I immediately contacted him and almost with a belligerent voice advised my younger brother that hopefully he would get assigned to my battalion. Fortunately, he got assigned to the Thirteenth CAB without any request from me. I then went to the CO and requested assistance to see if he could get Thomas assigned to the 191st AHC. It happened. After which the CO directed that under no circumstances should we ever fly on the same aircraft together. Thomas was assigned to the Bounty Hunters.

"On June 16, 1971, Thomas was testing a weapon system on the Nighthawk bird when he saw an enemy soldier hiding in the grass and he advised the AC. As the Huey made a pass over the area, Thomas was hit in the left eye. He was taken to a nearby field hospital, where he went into surgery, and about forty-five minutes later the surgeon came out and said Thomas would be blind in one eye. Then forty-five minutes later he again came out and said he would be blind in both eyes. Finally, the same surgeon came and announced that Tommy died.

"I can't begin to explain the empty feeling that comes over you when you lose a family member in those circumstances. Not three months before, Porky was about to ship home to see his firstborn son. Now, in short order, I'd seen two people die, Porky and my brother, and both did not have to be where they were when they were killed. It seems like such a waste. I knew, the moment I received word about Tommy, that my family would never be the same again. Ironically, this was the same area where CW2 Curt Embrey was killed, also without the bird taking a hit. It seems that somehow those bullets were meant for them."

SGT Thomas Preston Harvey was twenty-five years old and hailed from West Virginia. He had two young boys, Thomas Jr. and Michael, and was married to Priscilla. SGT Harvey earned the ultimate respect as the last brave 191st warrior who gave it all for his country.

The 191st AHC presence in South Vietnam officially ended. For those who fought under the 191st AHC banner, the life and times of that period in their lives remains etched in their memory for the remainder of their living days.

The 191st AHC was awarded the Meritorious Unit Commendation for its distinguished service. The award was affirmed by thousands of valorous medals pinned on the chests of hundreds of 191st personnel. Among the numerous letters of commendation issued to the unit, the essence of one rings loud and clear. From Headquarters, Department of the Army, Thirteenth Aviation Battalion (Combat), APO San Francisco 96296, the letter explains how, at its peak strength, the NVA in the Kien An District, on the northern edge of the U Minh Forest, were too paralyzed to move during hours of darkness because of the threat posed by 191st Nighthawk attack helicopters. An amazing transformation from its original ground-transport mission as the 2029th Quartermaster Truck Company. Reorganized as the 191st AHC that carried combat troops into battle, the 191st experience in Vietnam was truly one of a kind.

America's war history transcended centuries of social evolution before Vietnam appeared as a menace to our way of life. Before this war, Americans were highly patriotic about fighting off threats to our mainland, our freedoms, and our well-being. To this day many of our citizenry still argue that based on our established defense policy, our reasoning for committing US Armed Forces to the Republic of Vietnam was unfounded. Most tenuous is the sixty thousand young lives sacrificed for the sake of what was believed to be a truly political ideology. Many believe that America entered the war in Vietnam for the sake of a few who sought financial gains from the war effort itself, in effect, politics at work, as Americans have grown to think of our Washington bureaucracy.

***

When we were young, we were there. When we left the nipa palms and rice paddies of Vietnam, our memories traveled back home with us. The faces of those who breathed their last amid the agony of those who watched, the laughter shared over some comradery-building joke that made us all feel young and human in the middle of that shithole, and the everlasting brotherhood that war creates among those who endured the suffering together create the memories that bond us, carving them deep in our minds. Decades later, we cleave to those fresh faces and the bonds we formed. We let the laughter of the living faces of the deceased fill up those out-of-reach dark spaces in our hearts. And while stories of war render a semblance of battle, words cannot convey the actual feel of combat with its sights, smells, sounds, and horrific mental impact etched in the innermost crevices of the warrior mind. Reunions among the living provide some healing. With each gathering and each passing decade comes a gradual acceptance of the fate that took other lives but spared our own. In the end, the making and preservation of this great nation merits the sacrifice. In the mind of each 191st AHC veteran remains the pride felt in serving America's cause in Vietnam and the experience of airmobile combat as it earned its tactical worth in the nation's arsenal.

Killed in Action

In war, life has a way of turning on a dime.

In honor of those who died in battle with the 191st AHC.

There is no greater honor given a nation than a warrior's life in defense of its citizens' freedoms. Below are the forty-four names of those brave individuals who served and died with the 191st AHC in Vietnam. Since they're unable to speak for themselves, it is with deepest respect and sympathy that their surviving brethren dedicate this place of honor to the remembrance of these fallen souls. Having given the ultimate sacrifice, they truly deserve their own recognition in the 191st story.

We pray that they are resting in peace and that their families find solace in the great honor bestowed upon them by their fallen hero. He paid the ultimate price, having died for America's values. May God always bless our nation with the likes of these brave warriors.

From the surviving brethren of the 191st AHC, 1967–1971:
At long last, a grateful nation has recognized your ultimate sacrifice and praises you for your gallant service. *Rest in peace, brothers!*

May 26, 1967
CPT Norman Richard Kidd Jr.
1LT Jack Leroy Dodson

August 29, 1967
1LT Sharel Edward Bales
1LT David Colin Hall
SSG Richard Lee Scaduto
SGT Louis Charles Muser II
SP4 Peter Steven Martinez
SP4 Joseph Leon Whitaker Jr.

February 1, 1968
CW2 Tommy Gerald Sandefur

March 19, 1968
WO1 Jeffrey J. Yarger
SP5 Harold Shelby Wood Jr.

April 29, 1968
PFC Gerald David Aiton

May 21, 1968
SP4 Richard Alwin Weske

June 5, 1968
WO1 Ricardo Robert Tejano
WO1 Norman Michael Turone
SP5 Richard Larry Vines
SP4 Dennis Owen Akers

August 12, 1968
CPT Arnold Wayne Luke
WO1 Terry Roy Jens Jr.
SP5 Gerald Anthony Wilson
SP4 Arturo Daniel Montion

September 3, 1968
CPT David Carroll Burch
WO1 Ronald Michael Cederlund
SGT Paul Reid Frazier

September 30, 1968
SP4 Glenn Robert Lawfield

October 9, 1968
WO1 Morris Jerome Ross

March 2, 1969
MAJ John Anthony Petric
1LT Dennis Sanders Coker
1LT Carl Leonard Radtke

SP5 Robert Lynn Heinmiller
SP4 Carl Scott Douglas
SP4 George Ronald Lovellette

April 10, 1969
SP4 George Albert F. Dasho Jr.

April 13, 1970
CW2 Ralph Curtis Embrey II

May 9, 1970
WO1 Terry Lynn Henry
SP4 Stephen Harold Haight
SP4 Kris Mitchell Perdomo

June 24, 1970
SP4 Timothy Clay McCarthy

November 2, 1970
CW2 John Thomas Orrico
WO1 Douglas John Campbell
SP5 Kenneth Lavern Brown
SP5 Oscar Maloney

November 4, 1970
SFC Jaime Restrepo

June 16, 1971
SGT Thomas Preston Harvey

Glossary

.45 ACP: The 1911 model automatic Colt pistol sidearm adopted by the US military; renowned for its robust, man-stopping power.

1LT: Army abbreviation for first lieutenant (O2 grade).

1SG: Army abbreviation for first sergeant (E8 grade).

2LT: Army abbreviation for second lieutenant (O1 grade).

AC: Duty symbol for aircraft commander; the senior pilot (generally without regard for rank) of a two-pilot Army aircraft. This status was accorded based on tested combat behavior and maturity as a *peter pilot* with other ACs.

ADF: Automatic direction finder; one of the radio navigation receivers found on aircraft, which receive navigation signals from nondirectional beacons and AM radio stations with a maximum range of seventy-five nautical miles, depending on the power of the transmitter.

Advisors: Assignment of US officers or noncommissioned officers (NCOs) to South Vietnamese units to provide combat-arms training and staff-level guidance. This was intended to facilitate the US exit strategy from Vietnam.

AGL: Above ground level.

AHC: Assault helicopter company.

Aircraft commander (AC): Designated pilot in command of a two-pilot aircraft.

Air control point (ACP): One or more easily discernible ground checkpoints along the en route phase of a multiship flight or airlift between the initial point (IP) and the release point (RP). Each successive ACP gives flight lead an opportunity to adjust airspeed so the flight will reach the objective at a precise, planned time.

Air strike: Air-to-ground bombardment, usually by Air Force close-air-support fighters using one or more of many ordnance options.

AIT: Advanced individual training, which typically follows Army basic combat training (BCT) to qualify the BCT graduate for his next assignment in a specific military occupational specialty (MOS). AIT is typically conducted at a variety of training centers depending upon the MOS.

AK-47: Russian-manufactured, automatic Kalashnikov assault rifle designed in 1947. It was the primary weapon utilized in Vietnam by the Viet Cong (VC) and North Vietnamese Army (NVA) soldiers.

AMC: Air mission commander. Typically, this would be the commander's representative flying in the C&C bird, who would coordinate with the ground commanders and direct the air assets to best accomplish the mission.

Angle of attack: The pitch angle of an airfoil presented to the relative wind.

AO: Area of operations.

APC: Armed personnel carrier.

Arc light: The code name for high-altitude B-52 bombing strikes conducted in support of ground operations in Vietnam.

Article 15: A form of nonjudicial discipline administered in accordance with the *Uniform Code of Military Justice* (Article 15) for offenses that do not warrant court-martial.

Artillery advisory: With the volume of air traffic in Vietnam, pilots could contact advisory services at key locations for detailed information about friendly artillery firing. Information provided would include timing, origin, and impact-area coordinates along with the maximum ordinate (altitude) of the rounds. This would enable aircrews to plot the gun-target (G-T) lines for the purpose of avoidance.

ARVN: Army of the Republic of Vietnam (the South Vietnamese Army).

ASAP: As soon as possible.

ATC: Air traffic control. The military or civilian airfield tower and air-route traffic-control center (ARTCC) controllers responsible for air traffic separation, in the skies and during takeoffs and landings in supported areas. To provide their services, they rely on both visual means and radar.

Autorotation: The means by which airflow upward through a helicopter main-rotor system causes it to freewheel in the absence of engine power, thus enabling it to glide in a descent.

AWC: Aerial weapons company.

B-model: UH-1B

Battalion commander (BC): Commander, usually a lieutenant colonel, of a battalion-sized element (a unit comprising multiple companies, but smaller than a brigade).

BC: See Battalion commander.

Beep switch: Rpm increase/decrease switch on the Huey's collective stick.

BG: Army abbreviation for brigadier general (O7 grade).

Bird Dog: See O-1.

Black pajamas: Loosely fitting pants and shirt that were the generally adopted uniform of VC soldiers. While not the sole discriminator, carrying a weapon in this "uniform" would usually invite the undivided attention of American and allied soldiers.

Blivet: A durable, rubber fuel bladder, which can be airlifted to remote locations not easily serviceable by other means.

Boomerangs: The call sign used by the lift platoons (slick platoons) of the 191st AHC.

BOQ: Bachelor officer quarters (officer billeting, cf. hootch).

Bounty Hunters: The call sign used by the gunship platoon of the 191st AHC.

C&C: Command and control.

CA: Combat assault.

CAB: Combat aviation battalion.

Capital center: One of several ATC centers in Vietnam. This one was located in Saigon.

CE: Duty symbol for crew chief.

Center of gravity (CG): The point at which an object would balance perfectly on the head of a pin. The acceptable CG range for a helicopter, beyond which the flight controls are no longer effective, is very narrow and requires careful attention when loading cargo or passengers.

CG: See Center of gravity.

CH-47: See Chinook.

Chalk: Alternate spelling for "chock."

Charlie: A term used to refer to the enemy.

Charlie-model: See UH-1C.

Checkerboard squares: A shaded grid system superimposed on a topographic map by Lieutenant Colonel (LTC) David Hackworth, commander of the 4th/39th Infantry Battalion, First Brigade, Ninth Infantry Division. Used for identifying certain grids while communicating C&C information during the planning and execution of combat operations.

Chicken plate: A slang term for the ballistic vest issued to helicopter crewmembers, capable of preventing or minimizing the lethality of incoming small-arms fire. It replaced (or augmented) the older "flak jacket." It contained a slip-in chest plate and back plate, both made of a dense ceramic. The pilots didn't need the back plate because they sat in armored seats. So, they would lay their back plate in the chin bubble of the helicopter or loan it to one of the aft crewmembers to sit on for additional protection.

Chin bubble: Formed Plexiglas windows through the forward fuselage of several types of helicopters, below and forward of the pedals, to provide enhanced downward visibility to the pilots.

Chinook: Large, tandem-rotor helicopter (CH-47) produced by Boeing and used extensively in Vietnam for a wide variety of missions.

Chock: A wheel block for parked aircraft or vehicles to prevent rolling. When used with a number, it designates the position of each helicopter in a formation (e.g. chock one would be lead, chock two, the next aircraft, etc.). Commonly spelled "chalk" because it sounds the same.

Chunker: See M5.

Claymore: A command-detonated, directional antipersonnel mine frequently used to protect a defensive perimeter or to enhance an ambush.

Click: A term commonly used to mean kilometer, abbreviated km.

CO: Commanding officer.

Collective (or collective pitch): Helicopter flight-control stick to which the throttle control is integral. It increases or decreases the pitch of the main-rotor system, thus providing lift. The pilot operates it with the left hand.

Combat assault (CA): A multiship operation designed to quickly deploy infantry troop strength to overwhelm an expected enemy force. In Vietnam, such operations were typically directed by a C&C ship as one or more gunship fire teams would provide suppressive fire support along the flanks of the formation to augment the door guns of the slicks.

Command and control (C&C): The C&C mission was often conducted from a helicopter flying at a safe altitude above the battlefield with the ground-forces commander on board. This bird's-eye view of the ground operation, along with effective radio communication, enabled the ground units and air assets to react instantaneously to or reinforce against a developing threat. Also referred to as Charlie-Charlie.

Commander: The leader with overall responsibility for a unit.

Company commander (CO): The commanding officer of a company.

CONEX: Container express. A rugged, metal shipping container (size varies) in which military gear is packed or stored.

Cookoff: Premature firing of a weapon, in which excessive heat buildup causes the ammunition to detonate.

Copilot (CP): The junior pilot (generally without regard for rank) flying with an AC (often called the *peter pilot* by other ACs).

Corps: A military term with both general and specific meanings. General: A body of personnel who share a common function (e.g., Signal Corps, Marine Corps). Specific: An organizational unit comprising two divisions, typically commanded by a lieutenant general (Summers, *The Vietnam War Almanac*). However, South Vietnam was divided from north to south into four corps regions that corresponded to four tactical zones. The northernmost, I Corps (I pronounced /eye/), abutted the demilitarized zone (DMZ) and was headquartered in Da Nang; the II Corps was located in Nha Trang; the III Corps was headquartered in Bien Hoa; and IV Corps was headquartered in Can Tho. The IV Corps included the Greater Mekong Delta area and extended to the southernmost tip of Vietnam.

CP: Duty symbol for copilot.

CPT: Army abbreviation for captain (O3 grade).

CQ: Charge of quarters. This mundane duty falls to junior enlisted soldiers. The tasks include logging everything that happens on shift: making coffee for the staff duty NCO; waking the officer of the day (OD), but only if absolutely warranted; answering phones; taking messages; finding anyone with whom a caller needs to speak (unless it happens to be a well-staffed unit with a "CQ Runner"); staying awake for the entire shift; and maintaining a pleasant demeanor.

Crew chief (CE): The enlisted crewmember responsible for daily helicopter maintenance. They generally flew with the helicopter except where helicopter design did not provide for a crew chief (e.g. the AH-1 Cobra). The crew chief and gunner operated the door guns at the direction of the AC.

CWO: Chief warrant officer is a generic term for all warrant officer grades above W1.

CW1: Chief warrant officer one.

CW2: Chief warrant officer two.

CW3: Chief warrant officer three.

CW4: Chief warrant officer four.

CW5: Chief warrant officer five.

Cyclic: The helicopter flight control operated with the pilot's right hand, which tilts the main-rotor system in the desired direction of flight (the primary steering mechanism).

DA: Density altitude; Department of the Army.

D-model: See UH-1D.

Dead man's curve: The region of a chart (called the height-velocity diagram) well known to trained helicopter pilots, which depicts combinations of height (altitude) and velocity that would not permit a safe landing in the event of an engine failure.

Dead reckoning: The navigational technique by which present position is estimated using time, distance, and heading when visual references are obscured by clouds, weather, or darkness. Without on-board inertial navigation equipment or when operating outside the range of radio-navigational aids, the effects of wind can be difficult to estimate. Present position is likely to be less certain the longer the flight proceeds under such conditions.

Density altitude (DA): The altitude in the standard atmosphere corresponding to a specific air density. It is a function of air temperature, pressure, and humidity; thus it is a measure of available lift.

DEROS: Date eligible for return from overseas (expected end of a combat tour).

Di di mau: Go quickly (in Vietnamese).

Dien Bien Phu: A small village in northwesternmost Vietnam a short distance from the Laotian border. It was here that the French military was soundly defeated in 1954 by the Viet Minh led by Ho Chi Minh. This effectively terminated contested French involvement in Indochina.

Division: An Army unit usually commanded by a major general and, depending on its mission, normally staffed with upward of fourteen thousand troops configured in three or more maneuver brigades, each commanded by a full colonel O6.

DMZ: Demilitarized zone; the dividing line between North and South Vietnam, approximately coincident with the seventeenth parallel and, by treaty, agreed to exclude military installations.

Donut Dollies: Ladies of the Red Cross who served in Vietnam, visiting forward bases and hospitals to assist the servicemembers. They gave special attention to those who were wounded, for morale, welfare, and general support, often helping with the handling of paperwork required in times of emergency. Providing a welcome sense of home, they also dispensed donuts and coffee when available. They were wonderful and always a sight for sore eyes.

Door gun: Typically, an M60 machine gun operated by the helicopter crew chief and/or gunner. They were initially suspended on bungee cords that were later replaced by fixed pintle mounts to keep outgoing rounds from hitting the airframe or the rotor system. An exception was made for gunships, on which they remained suspended on bungee cords, and were also referred to as a "free guns." This provided flexibility for the gunship crew chief/gunner to place protective fire on the target by leaning out of the aircraft and firing back at the target underneath the tail boom of the aircraft, while breaking off from a gun run.

DRO: Dining room orderly. The ad hoc title for the lucky detailee who on a particular day was "privileged" to look after the well-being and every need of the commander and any distinguished guests he invited to join him at the "head table."

Dustoff: Generic call sign for medevac helicopters belonging to dedicated medical units. They are recognizable because they are completely unarmed and display a red cross on each side. Due to their vulnerability, they frequently depend on gunship cover when they must land in a hot landing zone (LZ).

Eagle flight: Small (squad- or platoon-sized) heliborne assault force used to reconnoiter suspected enemy positions. Normally, a larger assault force would be standing by to reinforce if enemy contact were established.

EM: Enlisted men.

Extraction: Removal of troop(s) from a field location via helicopter.

FAC: Forward air controller. FACs were responsible for coordinating air-ground operations either from the air or from the ground as part of the supported unit. Directing tactical air strikes on hostile targets was a major role.

FEBA: Forward edge of the battle area. The demarcation between friendlies and the enemy in conventional war, which both sides would refer to as "the front."

Final: The latter phase of a landing approach where airspeed is being gradually reduced as altitude decreases, the touchdown point is identified, and the decision whether to land is made.

Fire direction center (FDC): The controller element for an artillery battery responsible for computing firing data specifying type of ammo, fuze settings, azimuth, elevation, etc. and passing the information to the gun crew(s) to execute on command.

Fire team: Helicopter gunships are normally deployed in pairs: one as lead and the other as the wingman. A pair of gunships is referred to as a light fire team. Occasionally, a third gunship would be assigned, forming a heavy fire team.

First Aviation Brigade: One of the largest US commands in Vietnam, organized at Tan Son Nhut Air Base near Saigon, on May 25, 1966, and one of the last to leave Vietnam on Mar 28, 1973 (COL Harry G. Summers Jr., *The Vietnam War Almanac* [New York: Facts on File/Infobase Publishing, 1985]).

Flak jacket: A ballistic vest, which was the predecessor of the chicken plate. It was made of tightly woven, ballistic nylon fibers, designed to afford some measure of protection from shrapnel.

Flight lead: The forwardmost aircraft in a combat-assault flight. Also, the senior leader of a gunship team.

FM: Frequency modulation; this radio frequency band was used for internal air-to-air communication and also for selected air-to-ground uses, such as communication with ground units.

FNG: Fuckin' new guy. A term of endearment applied to individuals newly assigned to a unit. It clearly elucidated the collective sentiment that they would be regarded as "lower than whale shit" until they proved themselves otherwise.

Fox mike: See FM.

Freedom Bird: One of the (often chartered) airliners or military aircraft that took servicemembers back to the US at the completion of their tour of duty in Vietnam.

Frog configuration: Helicopter gunship configured with an M5 grenade launcher in combination with two nineteen-shot rocket pods (cf. M5).

FSC: Fire-support coordinator; this individual would often be part of the airborne C&C package assisting the ground commander during infantry operations.

G: Duty symbol for gunner.

G1: The principal, division-level or higher, general staff office(r) responsible for all human resources matters to include personnel services, readiness, and head-quarters management (cf. S1).

G2: The principal, division-level or higher, general staff office(r) responsible for all matters concerning military intelligence, e.g. counterintelligence, security, and intelligence training.

G3: The principal, division-level or higher, general staff office(r) responsible for all matters concerning training, plans, operations, and force management.

G4: The principal, division-level or higher, general staff office(r) responsible for all matters concerning logistics, which includes supply, maintenance, transportation, and services.

G-force: The force of gravity that increases when the nose of an aircraft is pulled up, relative to the rotation plane of the main rotor.

GEN: Army abbreviation for a general officer of four-star (O-10) grade.

GI: Government issue; a slang term for a member of the military, popularized during WWII.

Gook: A derogatory term for the Vietnamese, not necessarily reserved only for the enemy.

Green Delta: The call sign of a few Army helicopters assigned to fly general officers and selected VIPs at the Military Assistance Command (MAC) corps headquarters. Delta MAC was the IV headquarters located adjacent to the soccer field at Can Tho. Several Boomerang pilots were chosen for this privileged mission, and they served at the general's call.

Greenhouse: Either of the two Plexiglas windows molded into the roof of the Huey, right above both front seats, which precluded blocking the pilot's visibility in a steep turn. They are tinted a greenish color like sunglasses to reduce sun glare, hence the nickname.

Ground effect: As air is sucked into the spinning rotor system of a helicopter, it is accelerated downward ("downwash"). When the helicopter is hovering within approximately half its rotor diameter from the ground, the downwash is compressed against the ground faster than it can disperse, creating a cushion of more dense air. Because lift is directly proportional to air density, the same power setting produces more lift in ground effect.

Grunt: Slang term for infantryman.

Guard (frequency): International emergency radio frequencies: 121.5 (VHF) for civilian use and 243.0 (UHF) for military use. The UHF radios in Army helicopters used in Vietnam were configured to allow continuous monitoring of 243.0 along with any other frequency.

Gun-target (G-T) line: The arc line between the muzzle of artillery piece and the intended target, plotted as a straight line on a map between the two endpoints. See Artillery advisory.

Gunner (G): An enlisted helicopter crewman assigned to assist the crew chief and who is responsible for manning one of the door guns.

H-model: See UH-1H.

Hangfire: The condition where an aerial rocket has ignited but fails to leave the launch tube.

Heavy fire team: Three gunships working together.

Hog configuration: Helicopter gunship with four nineteen-shot rocket pods (two on each side).

Homeplate: Radio vernacular for the home installation, whatever its size or location might have been.

Hook: Nickname for CH-47.

Hootch: A generic term for "home away from home." In Vietnam, a hut created from various materials; accommodations for GIs, somewhat better than tents; a well-appointed foxhole. Also spelled hooch (not to be confused with potable alcohol).

Howze Board: A group of airmobile experts convened under the XVIII Airborne Corps Commander Lieutenant General (LTG) Hamilton Howze to bring the helicopter airmobile concept to fruition.

Huey: The early designation for what became Bell's workhorse helicopter of the US military, during the Vietnam era, was originally the HU-1A. Hence, the nickname "Huey" stuck despite a fairly early redesignation as the UH-1 series.

Ia Drang: A river in South Vietnam. At LZ X-ray, a small clearing in the Ia Drang Valley, approximately 450 US soldiers were inserted by helicopter in 1965. They soon found themselves surrounded by 2,000 North Vietnamese soldiers and committed to an intense and bloody battle. That story is told in the book *We Were Soldiers Once and Young: Ia Drang—the Battle That Changed the War in Vietnam*, by Harold G. Moore.

IFR: Instrument flight rules are the rules and procedures by which an aircraft can be legally flown with reference to on-board instrumentation if there is no outside visual reference (cf. VFR).

IG: Inspector general (overseer and insurer of Army rectitude, fair treatment, and counselor for Army personnel and operations with a charter to seek out and address fraud, waste, and abuse in Army activities.). This office has high-level investigative powers within an organization.

IG inspection: The periodic oversight inspection to which all Army units are subject. The IG charge is to ensure that everything prescribed by regulation is happening within the inspected unit. Exceptions are not to the commander's advantage.

IMC: Instrument meteorological conditions are those during which an aircraft must be flown with primary reference to the on-board instruments.

INFANT: The acronym for Iroquois night fighter and night tracker. A very effective combination night detection and armament system, utilizing a specially configured UH-1M with a pair of 500W xenon searchlights mounted atop miniguns. Image intensifiers and low-light-level TV were integral parts of the system to facilitate target acquisition with various combinations of heliborne hunter-killer teams in darkness.

Initial point (IP): An easily discernible, post-takeoff ground checkpoint at which a flight of multiple aircraft enters the en route phase at a prescribed time and in proper formation.

Insertion: Initial deployment phase of a combat assault.

Iroquois: The common name for the UH-1 Huey. All Army helicopters are named after American Indian tribes.

Jitterbug tactics: A method employed by LTC David Hackworth, while commanding the 4th/39th Infantry Battalion, First Brigade, Ninth Infantry Division, to deceive the enemy with a series of false insertions followed immediately by a combat assault in a suspected enemy location. Much like the jitterbug term used in trout fishing.

JP-4: The grade of jet-propellant fuel used by turbine-engine aircraft during the Vietnam era. The formulation was a 50:50 blend of kerosene and gasoline exhibiting a fairly low flashpoint (0 °F).

KIA: Killed in action.

Knot: The standard unit of airspeed: one nautical mile per hour, abbreviated kt (or kts in the plural).

L-11: The shortened designation for the Lycoming T53-L-11 engine of the Bell UH-1D helicopter. It produced 1,100 shaft horsepower, which often made it a marginal performer with heavy loads on hot, humid days.

L-13: The shortened designation for the Lycoming T53-L-13 engine of the Bell UH-1H helicopter, which produced 1,400 shaft horsepower—a hugely appreciated improvement over the L-11 engine.

L-19: See O-1.

LCPW: The widely adopted large, complicated pilot watch.

Lead: A shortened radio call sign for flight lead.

Lifer: A career servicemember. Depending upon usage, the term can be flattering or not.

Light fire team: Two gunships working together.

Loach: See LOH.

LOH: Light observation helicopter (Hughes 500), affectionately referred to as a "loach." It looks like an egg with a narrowed, aft-end, turbine exhaust with a tail boom situated close to but beneath and parallel to the main-rotor tip path plane. During hard landings, the main rotor would often flex downward and chop through the tail-rotor drive shaft. But due to its nearly round shape, the fuselage would thence tend to roll, such as to absorb energy and protect the occupants (the very definition of crashworthiness).

LRRP: A small team (four to six men) that undertook high-risk, specialty long-range reconnaissance patrol missions often well behind enemy lines.

LSA: Small-arms lubricant.

LST: Landing ship; tank was the designation for a variety of Naval vessels manufactured during WWII and designed to land vehicles, cargo, and troops on unimproved shorelines.

LTC: Army abbreviation for lieutenant colonel (O5 grade).

LTG: Army abbreviation for lieutenant general (three-star grade).

LZ: Landing zone. A generic term for any landing area, but commonly used to designate where the troops are inserted during a combat assault (cf. PZ).

M5: Belt-fed forty-millimeter grenade launcher mounted on Huey or Cobra gunships and capable of a cyclic rate of fire of three hundred rounds per minute. It was the wartlike appearance of the M5 nose turret on the Huey that inspired the "frog" nickname (also called a "chunker").

M14: The 7.62-millimeter infantry rifle replacing the M1 in 1957; its weight (11.5 pounds) and length (47 inches) made it awkward in the heavy jungle vegetation of Vietnam, leading to its being replaced by the M16 in 1968.

M16: The 5.56-millimeter infantry rifle replacing the M14 for the Army in 1968 with significantly reduced weight (8.5 pounds) and shorter overall length (40 inches), making it much easier to handle than its predecessor.

M60: A belt-fed machine gun used as the helicopter door gun of choice in Vietnam. Initially, it was suspended on a bungee cord from the ceiling by the door of the helicopter to give the operator an unrestricted field of fire. However, a hard mount with fixed stops came later to eliminate the possibility of outgoing rounds hitting the aircraft in the event of carelessness or target fixation by the gunner. It shoots 7.62-millimeter NATO ammunition at a maximum rate of fire of 550 rounds/minute.

MACV: Military Assistance Command Vietnam was the organization that directed the extensive military advisory effort in South Vietnam. Its headquarters was located at Tan Son Nhut Air Base adjacent to Saigon.

MAJ: Army abbreviation for major (O4 grade).

Maximum ordinate: The highest altitude reached along the trajectory of artillery or mortar rounds.

Medevac: Medical evacuation of any sort.

MG: Army abbreviation for major general (O8 grade).

MIA: Missing in action.

Minigun: A six-barrel, electrically rotated, Gatling-type machine gun mounted on helicopter gunships in Vietnam. It fires 7.62-millimeter ammunition. The maximum rate of fire is six thousand rounds per minute (although they were generally adjusted to fire at only two thousand rounds per minute to make their ammo last longer and keep the barrels from overheating), and they were generally mounted on the helicopter in pairs.

mm: Abbreviation for millimeter.

Mortar: Any of several types of indirect-fire weapons consisting of an aimed tube that shoots an explosive projectile at a high angle that creates a plunging trajectory that can be very effective against dug-in targets. They can fire multiple rounds as quickly as they can be dropped into the tube. They can be set up and dismantled quickly for effective hit-and-run tactics.

MOS: Military occupational specialty. Any of the many job assignments for which soldiers receive advanced (post-basic) schooling.

MP: Military police.

MRE: Maintenance request–expedite document to expedite resupply of high-priority item.

MSG: Army abbreviation for master sergeant (E8 grade).

Nails: Nickname for the small, very sharp-pointed, hardened steel, finned darts (fléchettes) incorporated into 2.75-inch, folding-fin rocket warheads designed for antipersonnel use. Upon expulsion, the rocket warhead opens and deploys 1,179 individual darts that assume individual trajectories in a predictable, disk-shaped pattern, similar to that of a shotgun.

Napalm: An aluminum soap of various fatty acids which, when mixed with gasoline, makes a firm jelly used in bombs and in flamethrowers.

Nautical mile: A unit of distance equal to one minute of longitude at the earth's equator or one minute of latitude. Abbreviated nm. It is the predominant distance unit used in marine navigation and aviation. Also, see knot (the related unit of speed).

Newbie: See FNG.

Nighthawk: The initially generic name for the nighttime mission, undertaken by various units, designed to deny safety to enemy operations conducted under cover of darkness. One key ingredient was a powerful xenon searchlight, which could illuminate ground activity from a safe altitude. It was used in conjunction with a minigun, set up to direct bullets at the illuminated target. A grenade launcher, a .50-caliber machine gun, and a heavily armed gunship were often used to complement the mission with an effective and intimidating display of firepower.

Nipa palm: A palm genus characterized by rising stalks with long, feathery leaves emanating from a horizontal trunk that grows beneath the surface in poorly drained, tropical areas. Often mistakenly used by GIs in Vietnam as the generic term for palm trees of any type.

Nuoc mam: A fish sauce ubiquitous in Vietnam as a staple of the diet and renowned for its pungent odor.

NVA: North Vietnamese Army. These were their best-trained and best-supplied enemy soldiers as contrasted with the VC.

O-1 (Bird Dog): A single-engine Cessna used in Vietnam as an "observation" aircraft and as an FAC platform. The FAC birds generally carried small rocket pods for marking targets with white phosphorous rockets. It was originally fielded as an L19, but was redesignated O-1 in 1962.

OPCON: Acronym for "under the operational control of."

OPORD: Operations order; the document that provides command tasking details and required supplemental information for a military operation.

OPSO: Operations officer.

Pachyderms: Call sign of the Two Hundredth Assault Support Helicopter Company.

PE: Common abbreviation for the periodic equipment inspection of the UH-1 Huey. This was scheduled maintenance required after every one hundred hours of flight time involving substantial teardown to inspect and replace vital parts as necessary.

Peneprime: An asphaltic coating applied to airfields and roads to control dust.

Periodic inspection: See PE.

Peter pilot: A junior copilot.

PFC: Army abbreviation for private first class (E3 grade).

Pintle: The helicopter mounting hard point for a door gun.

Pitch: Rotation about the pitch axis; the angle of attack of a rotor blade (i.e. its presentation to the relative wind) is also referred to as pitch. For the main-rotor system, it is controlled by the collective-pitch stick. Tail-rotor pitch, however, is controlled with the pedals.

Pitch axis: In a helicopter, it is the axis that is perpendicular to the longitudinal axis but parallel to the tip-path plane. Pitch up or down is rotation about this axis, and it is manifested by the nose of the aircraft being raised or lowered with the cyclic control.

PLL: Prescribed load list; the standard list of parts and equipment a deploying unit takes with it.

POL: In military parlance, it means "petroleum, oils, and lubricants." However, for pilots, POL is most often taken to mean fuel.

Preflight inspection: A careful aircraft inspection, generally conducted by the pilot, to determine its airworthiness prior to flight.

PSP: Perforated (or pierced) steel planking. Interlocking rectangular sheets of steel used to improve soft runway surfaces and support heavier aircraft than would otherwise be possible.

PVT: Army abbreviation for private (E1 grade).

PV2: Army abbreviation for private (E2 grade).

PZ: Pick-up zone (i.e. the loading area for a combat assault) (cf. LZ).

Release point (RP): The easily recognizable terrain feature at which point the task force commander releases control of the entire attack force to his subordinate commanders.

REMF: Rear-echelon motherfucker (a term for useless paper-pushers who managed to avoid combat exposure).

Revetment: Any of variously constructed explosive barricades designed to protect parked aircraft at improved bases throughout high-threat areas.

R&R: Rest and recuperation from duty; a vacation.

RF/PF: Collective term for the South Vietnamese Regional Force/Popular Force. The Regional Force was the locally recruited equivalent of the US Army National Guard and operated under direction from province/sector/district chiefs. The Popular Force was recruited at the village level and served under NCO guidance at the behest of the village chief, generally with little training and only scrounged equipment. They were nicknamed the RuffPuffs.

Roll: A rotation about a longitudinal axis.

RPG: Rocket-propelled grenade.

rpm: Revolutions per minute.

RTB: Abbreviated radio vernacular for "return to base."

RTO: Radio-telephone operator; the designated commo man who accompanied troops in the field and carried the bulky radio that was the lifeline for the unit. He was the first to receive tactical instructions or to summon help in a bad situation.

RuffPuff (RF/PF): A generally derogatory term for the South Vietnamese Regional Force/Popular Force soldiers.

RVN: Republic of Vietnam or South Vietnam.

S&P semitrailers: A tractor/trailer rig, with an open flatbed trailer, typically forty feet in length, and pulled by a five-ton prime mover. Used for cargo, or rigged with seats to transport troops.

S1: The principal company- or battalion/brigade-level staff office(r) responsible for all human resources matters to include personnel services, readiness, and headquarters management.

S2: The principal company- or battalion/brigade-level staff office(r) responsible for all matters concerning military intelligence, e.g. counterintelligence, security, and intelligence training.

S3: The principal company- or battalion/brigade-level staff office(r) responsible for all matters concerning training, plans, operations, and force management.

S4: The principal company- or battalion/brigade-level staff office(r) responsible for all matters concerning logistics, which includes supply, maintenance, transportation, and services.

SFC: Army abbreviation for sergeant first class (E7 grade).

SGT: Army abbreviation for sergeant (E5 grade), often referred to as buck sergeant.

Short: The progressively coveted status of one who is approaching the end of a tour (see DEROS) of combat duty.

shp: Shaft horsepower (the comparative horsepower rating for turbine engines).

Signal operating instructions (SOI): A booklet carried by aircrews, containing routinely changing SECRET radio frequencies and message encryption keys to keep enemy listeners from gaining access to real-time tactical information.

Slick: The term used to describe helicopters in *clean* configuration, which distinguishes them from helicopters with heavy, mounted weapons (gunships). In a combat environment, troop-carrying slicks generally have mounted door guns that are manned by the enlisted crewmembers.

Slit trench: Narrow earthen trench dug for defecation where improved toilet facilities are impractical or unavailable.

SOI: Signal operating instructions.

SOP: Standing operating procedure; an ad hoc document intended to interpret details how specific activities or operations are to be conducted in accordance with regulations and best practices. Alternatively, a normally accepted procedure.

SP4: Army abbreviation for specialist 4 (E4 grade).

SP5: Army abbreviation for specialist 5 (E5 grade).

SP6: Army abbreviation for specialist 6 (E6 grade).

SSG: Army abbreviation for staff sergeant (E6 grade).

Stack: The vertical advantage maintained by each ship toward the rear of the formation to stay in undisturbed (or clean) air, thereby maximizing available lift.

Straphanger: A term, generally derogatory, for passengers who contribute nothing to the success of a flight.

Synchronized elevator: A short, bilateral, inverted airfoil near the aft end of the Huey's tail boom. Its angle of attack changes with fore and aft movement of the cyclic control to keep the longitudinal axis of the aircraft as close to level as possible. This counteracts the tendency of the nose to "tuck" downward with increasing airspeed.

Tactical (tac) ticket: A very basic-level instrument qualification issued to many of the Army-trained Vietnam-era helicopter pilots. It was intended to give pilots just enough experience to allow them to safely retreat from inadvertent exposure to instrument meteorological conditions in a tactical environment.

Tail boom: The portion of a helicopter that supports the connecting drivetrain between the main transmission and the tail rotor. It is generally designed to include aerodynamic embellishments that help streamline the aircraft in forward flight.

Target fixation: The condition during a diving helicopter gun run when a pilot's preoccupation with putting ordnance on target overwhelms a higher priority to *fly the aircraft first*; the end result can be a controlled crash or worse.

Tet: The Vietnamese Lunar New Year, which occurs in January or February and lasts for seven days.

Tet Offensive: On January 31, 1968, a well-coordinated, major offensive operation, spearheaded by seventy thousand NVA soldiers, was unleashed in South Vietnam on the Lunar New Year. Major population centers and US military bases were targeted throughout South Vietnam.

TI: Technical inspector (aircraft). An individual appropriately qualified to identify, inspect, and evaluate maintenance required or performed on an aircraft.

Tip-path plane: The disk-shaped area through which the spinning main-rotor blades of a helicopter pass. The cyclic control can deflect the tip-path plane in any direction, which initiates a turn or a roll in a helicopter.

TJ Taxi: Tijuana Taxi; the vehicle nicknamed by SP4 Art Alvarez, which hauled ammo and equipment to the flight line as fast as needed and also served "other duties as assigned" in slack moments.

TOC: Tactical operations center.

TOE (or TO&E, when spoken): Table of organization and equipment; the organizational design and equipping document for Army units.

Trail: The last ship in a formation flight.

UHF: Ultra-high frequency. This is the frequency band utilized by the military.

UH-1: The generic designation for any of several models of the Bell "Huey" helicopter.

UH-1B: One of the earliest models of the Bell "Huey" helicopter that could seat nine troops. Its powerplants included the T53-L-5 engine capable of producing 960 shp, the T53-L-9A (1,100 shp), and the T53-L-11D (1,100 shp). The UH-1B had a cruising speed of about ninety knots and was generally used as a gunship.

UH-1C: Also one of the earlier models of the Bell "Huey" helicopter that could seat nine troops, but was distinguishable by the somewhat different 540 rotor system, wider main-rotor blades, and the left-side fuel filler port. It was powered by the Lycoming T53-L-11D (1,100 shp). It was best-suited to a gunship role.

UH-1D: A redesigned model of the Bell "Huey" helicopter capable of carrying eleven troops with a crew of four. It could be differentiated from earlier models by the two window panes in the cargo compartment door on each side. It was powered by the Lycoming T53-L-11 engine (1,100 shp).

UH-1H: An upgrade to the UH-1D. It was first fielded in 1967 and had the much more powerful Lycoming T53-L-13 engine that produced 1,400 shp.

UH-1M: An upgrade to the UH-1C, which included the more robust Lycoming T53-L-13B 1,400 shp engine. The first few were specially configured for use with the INFANT system.

Up report: Precoordinated signal from the "trail" ship that the formation is ready for takeoff.

USATMRB: US Army Tactical Mobility Requirements Board, also known as the Howze Board, after its chairman, LTG Hamilton Howze.

VC: Viet Cong. Locally recruited soldiers from among the South Vietnamese populace, persuaded to join the rebel cause by money, philosophy, or both.

VFR: Visual flight rules are those the pilot must follow when navigating an aircraft with primary reference to visual clues outside the cockpit, such as terrain features or a visible horizon (cf. IFR).

VNAF: The (South) Vietnamese Air Force who flew both fixed- and rotary-wing aircraft.

WIA: Wounded in action.

Willy (or Willie) Pete: Nickname for white phosphorous, generally used in grenades, artillery shells, or rockets as target markers due to the dense white smoke such rounds generate.

Wingnut: The maintenance platoon helicopter of the 191st AHC.

Wingover: Flight maneuver in which an aircraft is put into a climbing turn until nearly stalled, after which the nose is allowed to fall while the turn is continued until normal flight is attained in a direction opposite to that from when the maneuver was entered.

WP: Abbreviation for white phosphorous (see Willy or Willie Pete).

XO: Executive officer.

Yaw: A turn about a vertical axis of a helicopter controlled by changing the tail-rotor pitch (for those so equipped) with the pedals (also called a "pedal turn").

Index of Names